Useful Pleasures

The Shaping of Leisure in Alberta 1896-1945

Donald G. Wetherell with Irene Kmet

Alberta Culture and Multiculturalism/Canadian Plains Research Center
1990

P9-DWD-849

Canadian Plains Research Center
University of Regina
Regina, Saskatchewan S4S 0A2
Canada

Canadian Cataloguing in Publication Data

Wetherell, Donald Grant, 1949-
  Useful pleasures : the shaping of leisure in
Alberta, 1896-1945

  Co-published with: Alberta Culture and Multi-
culturalism.
  Includes bibliographical references.
  ISBM: 0-88977-058-1

1. Leisure - Alberta - History. 2. Recreation -
Alberta - History. I. Kmet, Irene, 1950-. II.
University of Regina. Canadian Plains Research
Center. III. Alberta. Alberta Culture and Multi-
culturalism. IV. Title.

GV56.A3W48 1989   790/.097123   C89-098152-3

Designed by NICHOLAS NEWBECK DESIGN
Typeset by LEADING TYPE

Printed and bound in Canada: John Deyell Company

For S. R. Wetherell

Contents

Illustrations

Picture Credits

The authors and publishers gratefully acknowledge permission to reproduce in this book photographs from a number of collections held by archives in Alberta.

The Glenbow-Alberta Institute, Calgary, kindly permitted the use of photographs from collections donated by Roy F. Anderson; Atterton Studios; Mrs. R. Barnecut; R.A. Bird; Brooks Museum/ Coultis Collection; Calgary Chamber of Commerce; CFCN Radio; Mrs. T. Carvell; W.J. Conrod; Gary de Leeuw; Donnenworth Collection; Mrs. Ruth Dowling; Eaton's Limited; Mrs. E. Erickson; Howard Fredeen; E.S. Gardiner; F.M. George; B. Giles; David Hargrave; James A. Hughes; Mrs. I.K. Kerr and Mrs. Jane Kerr Schofield; C. Kipling; Mrs. E. Kwiat; Mrs. Clayton MacMillan; Mrs. J.O. McIlhargey; Mrs. W.A. Mostyn-Brown; Mrs. J.W. Neilson; Miss Nancy Oliver; Palace Theatre; J.W. Palmer; Fred J.D. Patterson; Mrs. C. Patton; Jack Peace; Mrs. D. Pfeffer; C. Reach; Mrs. W.R. Shearer; United Church Archives, Toronto; Viking Historical Society; E.H. Waldram; Frank Wong; and Roy Woodley.

The Provincial Archives of Alberta granted permission to use photographs from the collections of the Archives; Anglican Church, Athabasca Diocese; Harry Bamber; Alfred Blyth; Ernest Brown; Robert Hoare; Kensit Studio; Harry Pollard; and the Ukrainian Cultural Heritage Village.

The Whyte Museum of the Canadian Rockies (Archives) granted permission for publication of "Boathouse and *Mountain Belle* on Bow River with Mount Rundle, Banff," photographed by John Woodruff, circa 1890; and "Boys ski race at Banff Winter Carnival, circa 1918," photographed by Byron Harmon.

The painting, *Skaters* (1935-36), by H.G. Glyde (oil on canvas, 60 cm. x 45 cm.), which appears on this book's cover, has been used with the kind permission of H.G. Glyde and Dr. D. Collinson.

Acknowledgements

This book is the product of research commissioned by the Historical Resources Division of Alberta Culture and Multiculturalism. The aim of the original study was to provide a thematic outline of the history of leisure in Alberta useful for the planning and interpretive needs of the Division.

For both the original and revised versions of this study, we owe thanks to many individuals at Alberta Culture and Multiculturalism who encouraged and supported the project, especially Frits Pannekoek, Ian Clarke and Les Hurt of Historic Sites Service, John Nicks, formerly with the Reynolds Alberta Museum, and staff of the Human History Section, Provincial Museum of Alberta. A very special thanks is owed to Carl Betke, Historic Sites Service, who wore numerous hats throughout the project as administrator, editor and counsel. Doug Cass and Georgina Klassen of the Glenbow-Alberta Institute, all of the staff, and especially Dave Leonard, of the Provincial Archives of Alberta, Trudy McClaren of the University of Alberta Archives, and the staff of the Bruce Peel Special Collections Library at the University of Alberta provided valuable guidance to the collections in their care. Helen Collinson's assistance and advice in selecting the H.G. Glyde painting for the cover illustration is also greatly appreciated. To the anonymous referees of the manuscript, a special thanks is due for precise, insightful and encouraging comments. Alvin Finkel, Paul Voisey and Bill Davies made useful comments at various points during the study, while Gillian Wadsworth Minifie's attention to the publication, press editing and design of the book is gratefully acknowledged. The staff of Historic Sites Service deserve special thanks, both for their direct assistance and for giving us the opportunity to pursue this study with complete freedom and in the manner that we chose. The corollary of such freedom is, of course, that any faults that the book possesses are ours alone.

This book has been published with the help of a grant from the Canadian Federation for the Humanities, using funds provided by the Social Sciences and Humanities Research Council of Canada.

Donald G. Wetherell
and Irene Kmet

Edmonton, 1988

Introduction

Work was, and still is, the central activity of most North American lives. This fact frames leisure, which is, Stanley Parker has argued, any activity "characterized by a feeling of (comparative) freedom" carried out during time "free from work and other obligations." Manifested in a wide range of individual and group activities and their related institutions,[1] leisure can be devised not only to amuse or entertain but also to serve such individual or group ambitions as personal promotion or the advancement of ethnic cohesion and interests.

While most people thought of leisure simply as pleasurable non-work activity, how it was practiced and how it was idealized varied over time and among different people. In this context, it is more relevant to understand the social settings that illuminate the changing place and meaning of leisure than to attempt a precise historical definition. "For the historian at any rate," Hugh Cunningham has observed, leisure "cannot be pinned down to a neat one-sentence definition" because the concept of what it was and what it meant changed over time.[2] This should not lead to the conclusion, however, that leisure was merely a series of disparate activities linked only by the type of time that they occupied. The statement that these activities took place during time free from work is more than a simple definition: free time was a social phenomenon which in itself created a relationship or, at the least, an interplay among activities and stimulated social responses and raised questions uniquely its own. As George Lewis perceived in a somewhat wider but applicable context, the notion that popular culture is simply a mirror of society is "too simplistic, too vulnerable," because it does not "point to a way to discover the social and psychological concerns culture reflects."[3]

This study covers the half century from 1896 to the start of the economic boom that followed World War II. The period bounded by a major upswing in the European settlement of Canada that began around 1896 and the opening of the Leduc oil fields in 1947 provides a meaningful framework for the historical analysis of leisure in Alberta. These are important points of departure in the modern history of Alberta, but they do not in some ways meet the traditional objectives of historical chronology by clarifying points of specific change. While social change in the past can rarely be pin-pointed specifically, significant shifts in society can be observed, and in Alberta World War II marked not only economic change, but also a number of changes in social attitude and in governments' and individuals' expectations about leisure. In the following pages, we advance particular chronologies for each of many leisure activities, but no attempt at precise overall chronology for "leisure" in Alberta could do justice to its complexity. For this reason, the treatment of some topics essentially ends in 1939, of others in 1945 or at the end of the forties. A rigid chronology would only obscure that leisure was ongoing, often informal, colloquial, and based upon routines and habits that were specific not only to individuals but also to cultures. Leisure was not uniform or discrete, but included a number of different activities that participants did not conscious-ly link in a single entity called "leisure." People in Alberta played baseball, watched movies, listened to the radio, and attended or acted in plays. For most people "leisure" was an abstraction, a con-cept applied only by those who observed it and stood aside from it.[4]

The settlement period in Alberta began with two related events: Canada's annexation of the region in 1870, and the arrival of the Canadian Pacific Railway (CPR) in Calgary in 1883. The CPR con-nected what was to become Alberta with central Canada and con-firmed Canada's control over the region. Subsequently, railways were gradually extended throughout the province: Edmonton was linked to the CPR main line in 1891 and almost all settled areas of the province were served by rail by World War I. At the beginning of the 1880s, the population was largely native and only about one thousand Europeans had settled in what was to become Alberta. By the mid-1880s, Protestant English-speaking settlers had established themselves as the elite and their culture as the domi-nant one in society, and this position was maintained for at least the next sixty-five years. By 1914, however, the population of the province had become increasingly mixed because of the settlement of a substantial number of non-English-speaking people.[5] Yet Alber-ta before 1945 was neither a cultural mosaic nor an egalitarian socie-ty: it was one in which the English-speaking group dominated by its numbers and by its control of cultural, political and economic life.

The relationship between the dominant group and the rest of the society has become an increasing concern of historical writing on prairie Canada. J.E. Rea has argued that the "most persistent social theme" in prairie history is "the struggle for cultural dominance,"[6] and Lewis G. Thomas has pointed out the shifts among the elites.

In Alberta, the dominant European group in the 1880s and 1890s comprised ranchers, adventurers, and some businessmen, but by 1905, when provincehood was achieved, the society was becoming a "more sedate and more settled community, more Canadian in the sense that it was more like Ontario."[7] This transition did not represent a fundamental change in the dominant culture or in the ethnic composition of its elites. According to Howard Palmer, although nativist sentiments varied in intensity between 1896 and 1940, by the beginning of World War II "people of British and Protestant background were still the dominant group" in Alberta.[8] These views have most recently been substantiated by R. Douglas Francis, who has traced the demographic and social implications of Ontario migration to Alberta and has demonstrated that Ontario immigrants were economically and politically most powerful and asserted the Ontario British tradition in Alberta.[9] Despite the significance of Ontarians in the province's elites, British settlers were also welcomed, and the cultural assumptions and attitudes of this Anglo-Canadian group, both conscious and unconscious, often provided the framework within which Alberta society operated. These settlers were disposed to see themselves, in Lewis G. Thomas's perceptive phrase, "as colonizers, not as colonials."[10] Their self-appointed task was the implanting of British Ontario culture rather than the making of a new culture.

This vision of the dominant group was given definition and meaning through the English language and through common cultural assumptions. Although Ontarian and British people had greatest authority in Alberta society and made up the provincial elites, the elites seem to have widened in later years to include other English-speaking settlers, notably those from the United States. Nevertheless, their acceptance was premised upon their concurrence with British standards and institutions. Thus, although the dominant culture was defined largely in linguistic terms, it was by no means upheld in an entirely unified front: the Ontario and British-born had suspicions about American settlers, and the Anglo-Canadian group was itself at times subject to tensions between English Canadians and British, especially English, settlers who were accused of arrogance, conceit, and laziness.[11] Nonetheless, these divisions within the dominant culture had become relatively meaningless by the time of World War II. Participants did not always agree, but all were conscious of their common culture which gave them status and overall social authority. While specific issues caused internal conflict, the dominant culture had sufficient dynamism to accommodate differences of opinion without endangering its cultural supremacy.

This expression of a common culture did not translate into equal partnership. There were class distinctions within the Anglo-Canadian group, although there appear to have been few real obstacles to movement between classes within the dominant culture. While access to the urban economic elite was probably limited, children of English-speaking farmers seem, for example, to have moved easily into the urban middle class, though the lack of studies on the history of social mobility in Alberta leaves most particulars unclear. Power and class in Alberta society were premised on ethnicity, yet the mythology of the society held that it was an open society in which social mobility was not hampered by tradition or pedigree. For the dominant culture, such a belief may have had some validity, but many non-English-speaking peoples must have found it less believable. For them, if anything was a barrier to mobility in provincial society, it was ethnicity, the major factor distinguishing those with influence from those without.

The first important analysis of class in Alberta yielded C.B. Macpherson's argument that the province had a "relatively homogeneous class composition" and that the dominance of independent commodity producers in the province meant that class tensions were mitigated and were directed outwards against external agencies and forces such as the national government.[12] This view has been challenged by John Richards and Larry Pratt, who have argued that such "single class analysis" is undermined by the recurring class tensions in prairie society.[13] Even so, class analysis alone is not sufficient for historical analysis of a general social phenomenon such as leisure. There were some notable instances of class consciousness in Alberta, particularly among miners, but as Gerald Friesen has concluded, despite clear class divisions in prairie society, the "power of the North American dream" of land and upward mobility "was an integral part of the prairie creed" and meant "that class identity was correspondingly weak."[14]

This dream of mobility and land was equally powerful for rural settlers and urban people. The importance of the urban English-speaking middle class within the dominant culture cannot be ignored since the professional and administrative groups of the urban middle class were often socially influential and powerful. However, the rural and farm elites, typified by the United Farmers of Alberta (UFA), established in 1913 as a farmers' lobby and later to form the provincial government from 1921 until 1935, and by the members of the Social Credit government that followed, also reflected the dominant culture. It is significant that the farm elite manifested and often spoke for the dominant culture, despite its objective economic differences with the urban middle class. The English-speaking organizations of farm life, such as the UFA locals, the Women's Institute, and the United Farm Women of Alberta (UFWA), all expressed the values of the dominant culture and spoke for it. English-speaking farmers may have disagreed with English-speaking urban people on many economic and political issues, but these differences did not negate the shared culture. While the dominant culture's viewpoint, with its devotion to the rights of property, its definitions of respectability and its assumptions about human behaviour, can be characterized as English-speaking middle class, it must be recognized that the term "middle class" has little objective meaning in the cultural history of Alberta. A better approach to the cultural history of the province lies in its analysis in terms of hegemony.

Hegemony has been defined as "an order in which a certain way of life and thought is dominant, and in which one concept of reality is diffused throughout the society in all its institutional manifestations, informing with its spirit all taste, morality, [and] customs."[15] In describing the operation of hegemony, historians often focus on the actions of a hegemonic culture's ruling class, which, through formal power and informal influence, imposes its "reality" on the society.[16] While such a formulation is useful, its application to leisure in Alberta is not wholly satisfactory. The dominant culture in Alberta was not the expression of a single class; it was sustained by various elite groups, intellectual, political, and economic. While these elites were not always discrete, neither were they monolithic, and leisure was not the product of one elite alone. Furthermore, for the dominant culture in Alberta, the ethos of the society clouded class lines and ethnicity added a significant dimension to the exercise of power.

The dominant culture in Alberta was promoted in more ways than just through its economic and political elites: it was also a broadly based process of cultural persuasion. Understanding the working of this hegemony requires a broad approach, such as that of E. P. Thompson's analysis of class in English society. Thompson argues that class is "a social and cultural formation arising from processes which can only be studied as they work themselves out over a considerable historical period." For Thompson, class is a conscious and subjective phenomenon, it is not a thing but a process and a social relationship.[17] By utilizing such an approach in analysing the cultural history of Alberta, the dominant culture can be seen as a historical phenomenon that gained its meaning through its developing context. Its influence was exercised both formally and informally, it gave rise to shifting concerns, it informed various elites and spokesmen, and the relationships among its participants changed in subtle and not so subtle ways. Yet for all that, the dominant culture remained hegemonic, championed by people conscious of its cultural terms and actively striving to promote its traditions, its institutions, its value system and its language.

The latter was crucial in defining commonality of purpose: language and the common traditions it expressed transcended other differences. This is not to argue a mere linguistic cabal promoted the dominant culture; the groups constituting the dominant culture existed in a fundamental social relationship that gained reality and purpose from their consciousness of themselves, their pursuit of power, and their assumption of legitimacy, superiority and mission. This viewpoint conditioned their ideology and, without suggesting a monolithic social structure, broadly affected all classes and groups adhering to the dominant culture: Anglo-Canadian farmers and urban working people (such as those in craft occupations) showed scarcely a different attitude than did the urban middle class or the economic elite. In a society pitting "us" against "them," the former commonly referred to the latter as "foreigners"—a term of opprobrium. Yet the dominant culture did not imply a caste system. Some "foreigners" were judged to be less "foreign" than others: those considered to be easily assimilable and willing to assimilate quickly, without fuss, were given conditional acceptance. It is true, of course, that those of non-European origin could expect no acceptance or access.[18]

Through the exercise of formal and informal power, the dominant culture's views were imposed upon the rest of society as the legitimate representation of the standards to which it should aspire. Such institutions as educational agencies and recreational facilities and clubs played an important role in serving the cultural needs of the English-speaking group: they enunciated and reinforced its views, and accommodated and sometimes stimulated social change. For the dominant culture, schools not only helped to extend and transmit its values to the next generation but also served to assimilate non-English-speaking people. Moreover, schools helped to accommodate the values of the dominant culture itself to social and technological change. Equally, adult educational and cultural programmes entrenched the dominant culture as the highest standard of society and provided participants with cultural opportunities, yet at the same time worked to assimilate non-English-speaking people. While the social institutions of groups outside the dominant culture often served many of the same purposes, they were handicapped by their diversity, lack of province-wide focus, minimal influence in government and their sense of nonconformity.

In such a framework, the place of leisure in the promotion of the dominant culture was not a simple matter of stimulus-response or dominance-submission. While the elites of the dominant culture cultivated their power to use the state and influence its policies, the realization of their wishes was not inevitable. The policies of the state with respect to leisure were not an automatic response to pressure from a particular elite, although the state always acted within the framework of the dominant culture.[19] While it is indisputable that the dominant culture's views were successfully imposed in Alberta, it needs to be appreciated that conflict occurred between English-Canadian culture and other cultures. Analysis of this process in terms of leisure is difficult, however, because the secondary literature is not substantial and historians' comprehension of this aspect of leisure is minimal.

A beginning has been made, however, and many of the contributors to *Peoples of Alberta*, edited by Howard and Tamara Palmer, have examined some of the issues involved in the relationship between ethnicity and social life.[20] In studies on particular ethnic groups, some groups have received more attention than others. The Ukrainian experience in Alberta, for example, has been ably synthesized by Orest Martynowych in *The Ukrainian Bloc Settlement in East Central Alberta, 1890-1930: A History*.[21] Such studies are often indirectly relevant to the history of leisure by demonstrating that the result of interaction between the dominant culture and non-English-speaking peoples was not simply passive acceptance of assimilation by the latter. It was a more dynamic process, and leisure pursuits were often at the fore. The range, cultural integrity, and evolution of leisure activities in the various non-English-speaking communities would fuel a separate study in itself. Nevertheless, it is clear that leisure represented an opportunity for ethnic groups outside of the dominant culture to control and sometimes resist the assimilative force of the hegemonic group. Because of their own institutions and the encouragement of their own traditions, non-English-speaking cultural identities did not simply disappear in a sea of Anglo-Canadian culture but, instead, were often transformed.[22]

At the same time, the dominant culture itself was not immune to change. Champions of the dominant culture often regarded communications and transportation technology as culturally neutral means by which to confirm and entrench their standards in Alberta. However, American commercial leisure was given force, and often credibility, through changes in communications and transportation technology. Film, radio, and the automobile each had significant implications for Alberta society. The dominant culture's response to the growing American presence in leisure activity was mixed: while those innovations perceived as serving its principles and its continued dominance were welcomed, those apparently threatening its hegemony met resistance. The increasing presence of American commercial leisure did not generate a straightforward contest for control between American and Canadian cultures, nor did it simply replace one set of cultural assumptions with another. Certain aspects of American leisure had become so important in Alberta by 1945 that they had been accepted and integrated into the dominant culture. Some American commercial leisure enterprises, such as touring stage shows, had been important in Alberta from the beginning of the century and American-dominated film and radio later confirmed the pattern. Yet, simultaneously, cultural leaders strove, through the state, to control the spread of some aspects of American commercial leisure by such techniques as public broadcasting and film censorship.

Leisure, both for the dominant culture and for those who stood outside it, thus posed a number of problems and opportunities, raised fears and optimism, and represented resistance and acceptance. Peter Bailey has shown that while the late nineteenth-century British middle class saw leisure as a social problem that challenged established social distinctions, the work ethic, social order, and morality, at the same time it increasingly took pleasure from new opportunities for leisure.[23] In Alberta, leisure created similar contradictions and an evolution in the particulars of the hegemonic culture. Although culture is constantly changing, as Hugh Cunningham shows in another study of English leisure, change does not mean that earlier practices are abandoned. They are transformed and remade, but seldom do they cease to exist suddenly, nor are they divorced from authority and power in a society.[24] For the history of leisure in Alberta, this premise has the flexibility to encourage an examination of changes in provincial life, such as those occasioned by technological developments, in terms of cultural persistence and continuity rather than abrupt change. Commercial leisure activities operated alongside noncommerical ones, "ethnic" activities alongside those of the dominant culture, each affecting at different levels the other.

This study is a preliminary exploration of themes and topics, with an emphasis on the institutional and structural components of leisure. The first three chapters, constituting Part I, set out some of the technological, social, and institutional components of leisure in Alberta history. They serve as an extended introduction to the chapters in Part II, which follow a topical approach by examining specific leisure activities. Often it is difficult to establish topical boundaries for the history of leisure because use of leisure time was complicated by psychological, ethnic, gender, age, economic, technological, class, and political factors, among others. Different people preferred different leisure activities. One person might read, another might listen to the radio, and yet another might play hockey. One individual or group might find a meeting for educational discussions far more recreational or entertaining than another. The disdain of the latter does not invalidate the enjoyment experienced by the former. Taking into account at least ethnic, class and locational factors, no intrinsic quality limits the range of leisure experiences. Accordingly, this study discusses general and typical activities, but does not attempt to be exhaustive or categorical.

As yet, the history of leisure in Canada and the social history of Alberta is largely uncharted. Maria Tippett recently argued for a "broad view" of cultural history and the study of how "changing patterns of leisure, technological innovation and economic activity have affected the production, distribution and reception of culture" in Canada.[25] Not only does leisure lie close to the heart of twentieth-century definitions of culture, its history is also one means of understanding authority and social change.

PART I

1. Infrastructures of Leisure

Leisure activity is not isolated or discrete; it is integral to daily life and responsive to social, economic and technological factors. This suggests that its operation in a society is not mechanistic or predetermined, but is in a continual process of change and modification in response to individual, economic and social needs and conditions. A number of cardinal factors define the limits within which an activity takes place over time. This framework is specific in its cultural and technological form and exhibits differences in its structure and in its working in different societies. Although the focus of this study is restricted to Alberta, it is obvious that Alberta shares many similarities with the other prairie provinces, with the rest of Canada, and with the western world.

In Alberta, the framework for leisure was determined by a number of interrelated factors: ethnicity and the views of the dominant culture; the rural basis of the population; transport and communications technology; the nature of work as well as the amount of time and money available for leisure activity. For the period of this study, these factors can be defined as social structures; as elements that may have changed over time in their particulars but which in their essence generally determined the nature of leisure.[1] These elements linked together at various levels to shape leisure. Ethnicity was most important because it defined, and then permitted, a dominant culture to take the leading role in determining what leisure was and how it could be manifested in public terms. Ethnicity was also important from a different perspective: it enriched the variety of leisure activities among the people of the province.

The dominant culture in Alberta was defined by linguistic and ethnic criteria. Most settlers during the 1880s and 1890s were of British extraction and had come to Alberta from Ontario, although some came directly from Britain. They shaped Alberta society and their dominant position remained secure well into the twentieth century. At the close of the nineteenth century, the ethnic profile in Alberta changed dramatically, and in the fifteen years before World War I a significant number of people from continental Europe and the United States settled in the province. Many of the American settlers were Canadians who had moved to the United States and then back to Canada when land in the West became accessible. While the ethnic composition of the province featured greater variety, the "British races," as they were officially called, largely continued to have a numerical advantage. Only at the turn of the century were they outnumbered: in 1901 they comprised not quite 48 percent of the population of the province. Within a decade, however, they again formed the majority, and by 1921 almost 60 percent of the population were "British." Not until the late 1940s did that proportion again drop below 50 percent.[2]

Although Germans, Scandinavians, and Ukrainians formed the largest non-English-speaking ethnic groups in the province, people from all the major European ethnic groups as well as people from Asia had settled in Alberta by 1914. Most of these ethnic groups had a local focus but little province-wide unity. The largest number of Scandinavians were Norwegians, followed by Swedes, Danes, and Icelanders. There was no "Scandinavian" unity as such, and little unity within each particular group. Scandinavians tended to assimilate quickly into English Canadian culture.[3] German settlers, because of "their high degree of religious sectarianism, their diverse origins, their geographical dispersion, and their preoccupation with pioneering . . . did not constitute a real German 'community' " before 1914 and World War I further limited the possibility of cultural unity among German settlers in Alberta.[4] Ukrainian settlers tended to be divided by sectarian and cultural factors created or confirmed, in part, by their immigration at different times before 1950. Most immigrants who arrived before 1914 were peasants; a greater number of those arriving after 1921 were educated and more nationalist.[5] Other non-English-speaking groups faced the same problems, although in some cases cohesion was a result of small numbers or discrimination or both. Japanese immigrants, for example, who were a very small minority in the province, experienced greater unity than did many other ethnic groups. The discrimination faced by most other groups paled in comparison with what the Japanese encountered and this drew the community together and levelled social and class differences that would have been divisive in other circumstances.[6]

Divisions within these non-English-speaking groups in the province did not destroy every vestige of cohesion. It was frequently expressed in community leisure activities centred in churches or ethnic clubs and associations. Nonetheless, province-wide organizations defined primarily by the ethnicity of these groups were rare before 1945. Thus, the heterogeneous and fragmented non-English-speaking population in the province made little impact upon the formidable advantages of the dominant culture: its political and economic power, a sense of unity and purpose,

4

and superior numbers throughout the province.

The dominant culture invested leisure with a number of key cultural perceptions. "Britishness" was crucial in this respect, but it was a highly flexible term. For some people, it was general and emotive as illustrated in the argument that "fair play" was a peculiarly British trait. For others, emotional rhetoric complemented a precisely defined adherence to British political concepts and organization. Britishness was defined in part as the social and political need for private property, the market economy, liberal individualism, self-initiative, and individual responsibility.

The emphasis on "Britishness" in Alberta's early days is apparent from the prominent display of Union Jacks at the Banff Winter Carnival Boys' Ski Race, in this photograph, circa 1918. Photograph by Byron Harmon. (Whyte Museum of the Canadian Rockies NA-71-3958)

Even for those Albertans who rejected traditional parliamentary forms of government, such as many farmers' groups, British traditions remained important. Ethnic arrogance and paternalism characterized the genuine and palpable belief that "British" culture was the best in the world. Yet this emphasis on Britishness was not a denial of Canadian national interest and identity: Canada was a "British" nation with its own political and social agenda, whose mission, in the minds of many, was to preserve (and implant in the West) an ordered and non-republican yet egalitarian society in North America. This narrow point of view was reinforced through political and economic power, and expressed in a particular social ideology. Especially important was the belief that character formation and behaviour were largely a result of environmental influences. In this connection, the home was crucial, but one's general surroundings and the prevalent ideas and images all influenced behaviour. This approach often linked behaviour not only to ethnicity and race but to environment as well. Alison Prentice has shown that such notions had been accepted by the dominant culture in English Canada since the mid-nineteenth century and had shaped much of the social policy of the country.[7] In the 1890s the application of environmental ideas in the debate over liquor revealed their pervasiveness in mainline Protestant thinking in Canada.[8]

Environmentalist thinking placed great emphasis on the home and other institutions within which individuals could be guided to act in an acceptable manner. E.A. Corbett, the director of the Department of Extension at the University of Alberta, expressed this notion precisely in a short story he wrote in 1925 about the Edmonton Boys' Band. Mr. Mike, the hero of the story and founder of the band, says:

> You take it from me, give a boy something that will interest him and occupy his spare time and he'll go straight. Boys ain't born crooked. Say, are you a Presbyterian?
> Yes.
> Well, listen to me, that stuff about original sin is the bunk see? Heredity goes a long way, and its me that knows it, but the biggest part of the difficulty is environment and nothing to do.[9]

The mention of heredity signalled an important debate about character, but notions about heredity rarely challenged environmental theories, rather they reinforced them. In 1931, a Dr. Stanley told the Calgary Council on Child and Family Welfare that "mental capacity is fixed by heredity and cannot be further developed throughout life, but the extent to which that capacity is utilized is decided solely by environment."[10] It was widely accepted that through a home-focussed system of discipline, training, and protection, a child's character would be formed in a proper mould for adulthood. This was expressed in terms of self-control: "our duty towards the child, in every case, is that of helping him to make a conquest of self."[11] If self-control and "right thinking" were not "installed into the individual at an early age," the deficit could manifest itself in various mental and social disturbances later in life.[12]

Adults could also be led to evil behaviour through bad example and idleness. Both were presumed to have greatest impact on people whose socialization had been incomplete or had become unstuck through negative stimuli, or the "disintegrating forces of life."[13] These forces and the mechanics of their operation were not precisely defined, but many people would have included sex, violence, liquor and drugs, and resistance to established authority in any list of forces that could lead to a breakdown of socialization. A large measure of social as well as political protection was therefore required to create and maintain a society worth living in. For leisure, this environmentalism and the belief in the malleability of human character led to a highly interventionist attitude on the part of the dominant culture; even if character and behaviour had been properly formed and subsequently reinforced through public standards of morality and taste, they could still be turned in the wrong direction, not just by bad example but also by idleness.

These environmentalist notions coincided neatly with an emphasis upon the importance of work to the society. According to Mr. Mike again, boys got into trouble if they had "nothing to do." For adults, it was said, "man has to work in order to live. Work is necessary to happiness." The proverb said, "he that labors is tempted by one devil and he that is idle by a thousand."[14] The belief that work was good for character and for the preservation of morality was tenaciously held in the dominant culture. The fact that it nicely coincided with the desire for a docile and hard working labour force made its theoretical appeal even stronger. The Anglo-American faith in the benefits, indeed, the virtues of work appealed to a community that had recently settled in a new land; a community that accepted the doctrine that individual success depended upon individual labour, for the land was rich and a man's failure was his own.

An emphasis on labour did not lead to a rejection of leisure but to an emphasis upon its integral place in a work-centred life. Although the importance of labour was clear, it remained a fact that many people in Alberta worked too hard and were too concerned with making money. In 1903, the Ontario Minister of Agriculture had visited the District of Alberta and observed that everyone was gripped by an "all absorbing desire" to make money. This was "typical of a new country," he believed, "but as time goes by the people must pay more attention to the aesthetic side of their nature or they will miss the real enjoyments of life."[15] Many Albertans agreed with this critique of their society, and by the 1920s it had become common for leisure to be described as a positive and necessary social force. The necessity for leisure did not lead to a questioning of the work ethic, however, because any potential conflict between leisure and work was neatly resolved by inextricably tying the one to the other. Leisure was seen in terms of recreation: the re-creation of the individual to enable him to work efficiently. Fun and play were necessary; people without a social life or diversions were "only cogs in a wheel, wearing themselves out before their time with hard labour." Recreation refreshed the individual who could then return to work and apply himself more "fervently" to his labour. "Amusements" that "send us back to toil with a glad heart and a vigorous mind are for our good."[16]

The definition of leisure as "amusement" contained a potential danger, however, and Albertans were warned in 1913 that "there is no amusement in existence which cannot be made a source of harm under certain conditions."[17] This difficulty was resolved by viewing leisure in terms of rewards. Mary Palmer, from Gopher Head, Alberta, wrote to the *Farm and Ranch Review* in 1913: "Of course, I don't want to have all play and no work, because I think pleasure is enjoyed more when we earn it."[18] Palmer's "of course" spoke eloquently about the place of work in the society, but the definition of leisure as reward and her assumption that human experience was given meaning through polarity did not address the basic concern that leisure could lead to dissipation. This danger was surmounted by recognizing the contribution that leisure could make to the intellectual and physical development of the individual. This was implicit in the argument that leisure should be re-creation to enhance one's ability to work, but "usefulness" also included a range of intellectual and social benefits. As *The UFA*, the official newspaper of the governing party, noted in 1932, "if leisure means laziness, if leisure means only pleasures, then the mind stagnates and leisure becomes a detriment not an advantage."[19] Fun had to be purposeful and numerous leisure activities were approved because they combined usefulness with fun. Physical activity should contribute to physical fitness and health. Fun should be attended by learning: thus, movies, for example, should be uplifting or socially redeeming or, best of all, educational. As one observer noted in 1927, "it is unhealthy, physically, to live on desserts and sweet-meats, so it is unhealthy, mentally, to take only the entertainment, ignoring the more nourishing, if less tempting, 'mind food'."[20]

Accordingly, the idealization of work entailed not rejection of leisure, but an emphasis of its usefulness in reinforcing the work ethic and the virtues of sincerity and purposefulness in daily life. These attitudes prevailed in the dominant culture in Alberta until after World War II. Mr. Ward Steckle, the supervisor of physical education for Calgary schools, observed in 1945 that "recreation should serve a dual purpose, that of filling in time suitably and well, and also leav[ing] the individual feeling well and improved, both mentally and physically."[21] This view represented a continued emphasis upon the utility of leisure, but it also suggested a new commitment to purely personal benefits. An important illustration of this change can be found in the report of the Alberta Post War Reconstruction Committee. It approvingly quoted the United States Natural Resources Planning Board's "New Bill of Rights," which posited that all people had the "right to rest, recreation, adventure [and] the opportunity to enjoy and take part in an advancing civilization."[22]

Thus, a number of assumptions about behaviour, social life, work, and the relative ranking of other cultures against the standards of "Britishness" conditioned the approach to leisure in the dominant culture. Many non-English-speaking groups in Alberta would not have quarrelled with some of these ideas. Japanese settlers, for instance, shared an emphasis on the work ethic and respect for authority.[23] Indeed, most people in the province, regardless of ethnicity, may have supported the view that work had important social benefits. Many would also have agreed with the dominant culture's emphasis on the importance of environment and its consequent effects on social organization. Nevertheless, agreement with certain ideals of the dominant culture did not lead to full cultural acceptance. The dominant culture's use of highly emotional criteria, such as "Britishness," excluded the meaningful participation of outsiders. While such emotive appeals helped to obscure objective differences within the culturally dominant group and projected a measure of unity that may not have been objectively justified, they also raised a fundamental obstacle to cultural pluralism and accorded with a policy of assimilation. At certain times, particularly during World War I, the emotive rhetoric of this Britishness became almost tribal.[24]

Leisure was framed and shaped not only by the dominant culture and the ethnic composition of the province but also by the fact that from 1906 until 1941 between 62 and 63 percent of the population lived in rural areas. This percentage began to decline only after World War II, a crucial watershed in the province's history. The role of farming in the provincial economy could not be ignored and the importance of agricultural interests in politics could never be forgotten. The rural character of life greatly influenced the nature of leisure in Alberta and determined the extent to which most people participated in the leisure activities available in the province. Rural people, especially those on farms, were often isolated and lacked formal opportunities for leisure. It is clear that before World War I there was a sharp difference between the leisure opportunities available to urban and rural people. Nonetheless, the two largest cities, Edmonton and Calgary, and many of the numerous smaller but locally important towns played a crucial role in defining and providing leisure opportunities for the whole society.

Between 1871 and 1901 the location of prairie urban centres was determined largely by railway lines or "the paths of projected lines."[25] In Alberta, towns and cities were located in three basic patterns: along a line running from Edmonton to Calgary, on the Lloydminster to Edmonton axis, and in a triangle in southern Alberta formed by Calgary, Lethbridge, and Medicine Hat. Size was an important determinant in the level of services provided, but all towns and cities were important recreational foci for their districts. Annual events such as fairs and sports days, and facilities such as poolrooms, bars, and theatres, provided recreational opportunities that were rudimentary or completely absent in the farming areas. Small towns became less important as retail centres in the interwar years because of improvements in transportation and such developments as the increase of mail-order retailing, but their role as service centres for leisure grew. Before 1920, many leisure opportunities were inaccessible to most rural Albertans. This did not mean that urban standards of leisure were unimportant for rural life. The pervasive boosterism of Alberta cities and towns bombarded rural dwellers with enthusiastic claims for the cultural and economic advantages of city folk.[26] Im-

Edmonton Ski Club members travelled to Banff by train in 1937. (PAA KS. 1/1)

portant too were developments in transportation and communications. Recognizing these transformations, it was observed in 1957 that "the modern city is the most persistent and effective propaganda for its own way of life. Through press, radio and television, it imbues the rural resident with a drive for urban standards of comfort and service." Most of the "social capital" of theatres and other recreational and sports facilities was concentrated in the urban centres and urban residents enjoyed a diversity of leisure opportunities not available in rural areas. Rural people could move or travel to the city to obtain the services or they could demand similar services for rural and small town areas.[27]

The view that leisure was a necessary part of productive life had obvious implications for rural people. By World War I, many observers contended that farmers' lack of cultural institutions like theatres, libraries, movie houses, and sports facilities meant that rural life was culturally impoverished and needed reform. Some argued for the provision of better facilities. Others, especially during the 1920s, assumed that the problem would simply go away because of increasingly efficient transportation and methods of communication. It was implicitly accepted that urban standards of leisure were necessary for rural people. In this sense, those who perceived a "rural problem" aimed to narrow the cultural differences between town and country and to remake rural Alberta in the image of the urban world. A topic of much debate in the United States before World War I,[28] the argument for better rural social and cultural opportunities was taken up by the Social Gospel spokesmen in the Protestant churches in Canada.[29] This drive was interrupted by the war, but by the early 1920s the idea had become common in Alberta.

The objective of this campaign was not simply to make rural life more pleasant. If leisure activities could make rural life more attractive, young people might stay on the farm. This was both a social and an economic necessity, for agricultural Alberta was "the industrial backbone of provincial prosperity" and "the breeding grounds of genius and character." Rural life, the *Edmonton Journal* argued, had been the source of English greatness throughout history and likewise would be the foundation of Alberta's future greatness.[30] Nevertheless, some observers held that rural society could not be rescued from cultural mediocrity. In 1930, A. L. Burt, a historian at the University of Alberta, contended that "our society has grown by continually returning to primitive conditions on the margin of settlement." When this frontier ended, the result would be cultural stagnation: Alberta's cosmopolitanism was neither inherent nor self-sustaining without immigration. Moreover, Burt doubted whether the province could develop a "leisured class and the culture that goes with it" because of its unfavourable climate. Thus, provincial culture would progressively become narrower and more parochial.[31] Despite Burt's pessimism, others suggested various agendas for rural regeneration through leisure. Some argued that farm people could lessen the dullness of their lives by studying nature,[32] but such notions had little appeal. In 1920, the *Farm and Ranch Review* called for an end to rural isolation and the lack of recreation. Alberta's "rather seriously inclined" farmers should be educated in the "doctrines of play, enjoyment, relaxation [and] recreation." These amusements needed to be "distinctly rural" and it was suggested that "old forms of rural amusement and entertainment" be revived "to suit modern conditions." For once, however, Britishness was abandoned. The traditional forms suggested were not the blood sports of pre-industrial

England or North America but merely spelling bees and the "modern idea of pageantry in its simpler forms [that] promises new opportunities for varied and popular expression of the social life in local rural communities."[33]

This perceived need to create a rural tradition in Alberta suggests that rural life was seen as existing in a cultural void. It has been observed that a rural tradition never developed in the United States because the distinctions between town and country could be levelled too easily through travel and migration.[34] In Alberta, urban British and Ontario homesteaders had no rural culture to transplant, and the same can be said of the Canadian settlers who came to the prairies after years in the United States. Many European settlers with rural antecedents came from cultures that were not acceptable to the dominant culture, and, in any case, rural traditions centred in a rural village with ethnic and religious unity were meaningless in a place where dispersed settlement was not only the practice but the law. The population in Alberta was too diverse for any rural traditions to be permanently transplanted. Hence, the "rural tradition" of prairie life, which saw agrarian life as resourceful, self-sustaining and independent, was largely an emotional commitment to the land that focussed on the individual or the family and not the broader community. In the face of twentieth-century mobility and commercialized leisure, even this commitment could not be sustained over two or three generations. For some, like A. E. Ottewell of the Department of Extension at the University of Alberta, the problem of rural life transcended its lack of tradition or cultural focus. Rather, that was but one element in the "most baffling social problem" of the age, "the profitable and safe use of leisure time made free by a machine served civilization."[35]

Generally, however, the machine was seen not as a problem but as a boon for rural life. The railway had been an important means of transportation in prairie life from the late nineteenth century and sometimes helped to blur the lines between town and country because rural people could travel, at least occasionally, to towns or even to a city. In a telling analogy, it was observed in 1907 that "railways are becoming arteries and veins leading to remotest sections and the city is the heart. The difference between city and country life is no longer a difference in kind but only in degree."[36] In the first half of the century, the gasoline engine was welcomed as a leveller of urban and rural distinctions and consequently as a means of preserving rural life. Not only did the gasoline engine make farm work easier, it also improved rural social life. As early as 1912 it was noted that the gasoline engine brought the farm boy "into closer contact with the social activities of his community," so that he "no longer fears and dreads the lonesomeness of farm life. . .[because] he can be continually in touch with the social diversions of the nearest town."[37] There was no expression of rural tradition here—only a drive to imitate urban life and standards of leisure.

Transportation in Alberta from 1896 to 1945 was dominated by rail and road travel, the latter becoming increasingly important after World War I. The railway had been a symbol of progress during the latter half of the nineteenth century, but by 1900 it was sufficiently integrated into peoples' lives that it no longer inspired rhetoric about progress. In the years before 1945, it was the most consistently practical means of long distance travel within the province,

The first Canadian Pacific Railway sleeper to cross the North Saskatchewan River at Edmonton, June 8, 1908, was carrying delegates to the Masonic Order Grand Lodge of Manitoba of AF and AM. (PAA B.6216)

although in 1905, a mere 1,060 miles of railroad served mainly the population located along the east-west CPR main line and the line north from Calgary to Edmonton.[38] In the following decade, however, the railway system expanded with the construction of two additional transcontinental lines and such provincial lines as the Edmonton, Dunvegan and B.C. Railway. After 1912, construction of branch lines throughout the settled parts of the province proceeded rapidly and by 1920 the province was served by a comprehensive rail system. Between 1910 and 1914, the total mileage more than doubled, and by 1927 there were 5,186 miles of railroad in Alberta.[39] Scheduled passenger service, which was the most practical way for most rural people to get to the city or to one of the larger towns, was available on almost all of these lines. This service was enhanced because trains regularly stopped at most villages and towns to provide mail and express parcel service. In southern Alberta, for instance, there was a "local from Medicine Hat to Lethbridge and return daily except Sunday; a local from Calgary to Lethbridge via Vulcan and return daily; and one from Fort Macleod to Calgary and return daily."[40] By the end of World War I, many of the most popular resorts in the province, such as Banff, Gull Lake near Lacombe, Sylvan Lake near Red Deer, and Lake Wabamum near Edmonton, were linked by railway to the large urban centres and scheduled service was sometimes arranged around holiday needs.[41]

The link between train travel and leisure activities was confirmed and expanded by the railroads' offers of reduced fares for travel to special events such as fairs, sporting events, and celebrations. Special fares were offered for travel along specified routes to the Calgary and Edmonton Exhibitions. For the 1909 Calgary Exhibition, the CPR offered reduced fares to people as far east as Winnipeg and as far west as Revelstoke, and to those along the Crowsnest Branch.[42] Such arrangements were even available for travel to small fairs, although the area to which the cheaper fare applied was usually much smaller.[43] Excursion rates for a return ticket were commonly set at the single fare plus one-quarter.[44] Reduced fares and special excursion trains continued to operate during the interwar years. The CPR offered reduced fares to the Calgary spring livestock show in 1922.[45] In 1939, special trains brought visitors to Calgary for the first visit of a reigning British monarch to Canada, and since an immense number of people wanted to see King George VI and Queen Elizabeth, reduced fares were available on scheduled services as well as on seven special charter trains. Each town could reserve one or more coaches, and the CPR anticipated that between nine thousand and twelve thousand people would come to Calgary by train from "as far south as the international boundary, north as far as Red Deer and east to

Bassano."[46] For major events such as the royal visit or the Calgary and Edmonton exhibitions, the railroads readily provided special fares because they recognized that there would be sufficient traffic to make the reduced rates profitable. In other cases, special fares were provided only for a minimum number of passengers or when the sponsors of an event put up a guarantee. As early as 1895, the town of Edmonton guaranteed the CPR $575 in fares to obtain a special $5 return fare from Calgary for the Edmonton sports day.[47]

The railway was important for leisure not only because people could travel quickly and easily to recreational events well beyond the confines of their communities but also because entertainers and shows could travel more readily throughout the province. Given the poor condition of roads, most of the midways, vaudeville shows and circuses travelled by rail before 1945. Within cities, people relied on streetcar service for urban transit, although bus service was temporarily established in the city of Calgary between 1907 and 1915. By the early 1930s both Calgary and Edmonton provided buses in areas not served by streetcars. The first interurban buses operated between Redcliff and Medicine Hat in 1914,[48] but major growth in such transportation occurred only after 1920. The first significant and continuing interurban bus line in the province (and, it was said, in Canada west of Toronto) began in 1926 when Brewsters inaugurated daily service between Banff and Calgary. It took three and one-half hours to cover the eighty-five-mile route.[49] In 1927, there were 11 bus routes in the province, most in southern Alberta with connections to Calgary and the mountains, although one route ran from Calgary to Edmonton. By 1931, there were 32 routes in southern and central Alberta, and just before World War II 94 buses were licensed to carry passengers in Alberta.[50] Many of these bus routes operated only in summer, although by 1930 Greyhound had undertaken to plough highways in order to maintain winter service.[51]

After 1914, motor vehicles became increasingly important. The first automobile in Alberta is reported to have been brought to High River in 1903.[52] The advent of the inexpensive model T Ford in 1908 marked the beginning of the great revolution in automobile accessibility. The novelty of automobiles led to a continual barrage of "auto etiquette" tips in newspapers, but it was soon obvious that more than etiquette was needed. One of the first tasks of the new Alberta Provincial Assembly in 1906 was passage of a law regulating the use of motor vehicles. It required drivers to be careful when approaching or passing a horse drawn vehicle, to observe maximum speeds of ten miles an hour in an urban area or twenty miles an hour on the highways, and racing and betting on car races were made illegal. Regulation and taxation of motor vehicles increasingly became a highly complex matter, but even so, it was not until 1929 that drivers were required to have a driver's licence, and testing was not instituted until much later.[53]

In 1906, Alberta officials licensed only forty-one motor vehicles, but in 1918 the number was 65,101, including trucks and taxis.[54] Judging by the case in Saskatchewan, the number of motor vehicles in Alberta probably declined slightly during the 1930s, but by 1941, 42.5 percent and 38.2 percent of households in Calgary and Edmonton respectively had motor vehicles.[55] However, it was among the farm population that the increase in ownership of autos and trucks was most spectacular. In 1921, 23.5 percent of farm families had a motor vehicle; by 1931 the figure stood at 42.1 percent, and by 1947 slightly more than 90 percent of farm families owned either a car or a truck.[56] On the farm, trucks could be used for cartage as well as for personal transportation, and the relative isolation of farms enhanced their appeal. In 1917, it was observed that automobile use was "removing the greatest evil of prairie life—isolation—and [by] promoting social intercourse, is making life on the farm less monotonous."[57] For urban people, ownership was not so crucial. Most urban areas had developed city transit systems by 1914, and residents could use railroads and buses for travel between communities and to the lake and countryside.

Despite their social and economic value, early motor vehicles were extremely troublesome machines. The journalist Miriam Green Ellis, who acquired her first car in 1914, recalled that driving was difficult because of the engineering of the car and road conditions:

> anyone who drove in those days will remember changing tires every few miles; we carried the extra tubes under the back seat together with a foot pump, and the tire was fastened to the wheel with three very firm steel rims. It was a major operation to remove those rims...and then more than likely the valve was leaking and it had to be done all over again. Everyone carried patches and a repair kit with him, spark plugs had to be cleaned every few miles...[58]

The frequent changing of tires was made even worse by mosquitoes and flies; Ellis observed in 1920 that she built a smudge to keep the mosquitoes at bay while she changed a tire.[59]

Before 1920, most roads in Alberta were dirt trails riddled with almost impassable ruts. This led to demands for control of the type of vehicles that could use the roads. In 1920 it was argued that sleighs should be made to "track with automobiles and other wheeled vehicles" so that the sleighs would keep the roads open by cutting a useable track.[60] Five years later, one UFA local argued that narrow wagon wheels cut up the roads and their use should be banned because "better roads to a large extent contribute toward making community life more agreeable and attractive."[61] Such concerns provide a significant measure of how rapidly motor vehicles had become a part of rural thinking, but their place in provincial life was most clearly shown by mounting demands in the interwar years for road improvement through grading, gravelling, and, later, through hard surfacing.

The government of Alberta spent large sums of money on road building and improvement: $12.6 million was spent between 1905 and 1920.[62] Even this satisfied neither the needs nor the wishes of automobile owners and lobbyists such as local boards of trade and the Automobile and Good Roads Associations. The petitioners often took the government's failure to respond immediately to their demands for road improvement as a deliberate slight and as an attack upon their social life and economic future. It was widely believed on the prairies that tourism should be encouraged and that road improvement was essential in this respect. In 1923, the *Western Municipal News* informed its readers that good roads brought tourists and that the tourist of "today" was not "some bloated plutocrat with [a] high priced car and trappings," but an ordinary person who was "travelling at the least expense and always viewing the country travelled with an eye to better opportunity. The town which furnishes the best conveniences, the country which furnishes the best and easiest roads. . .gets his trade."[63] It was an argument that had wide appeal in Alberta because people believed that tourists would be attracted to the mountains. The faith in tourism as a generator of wealth was strongest in southern Alberta, where local businessmen put forward strongly worded arguments on the importance of tourism for their communities.[64]

It is not surprising that road conditions were slow to improve throughout the large settled areas of the province. In 1929, aside from about one thousand miles of gravelled roads, the remainder were either "improved" dirt roads or ordinary dirt roads. The "improved" dirt roads were graded and levelled whereas the ordinary ones were often little better than passable tracks.[65] Primary roads were gravelled in subsequent years, but as late as 1946,

BREAKS ALL RECORDS

Edmonton to Calgary and Return
416 Miles of a Road Trip in
9 HOURS — 26 MINUTES — 55 SECONDS
Average Speed 43 ½ Miles per hour

This Wonderful Achievment was Performed by a

1923 McLaughlin Buick Master "Four"

Driven by PAUL WELCH, Service Manager at our Garage

The 1923 McLaughlin Master " Four " Model is the latest in car excellence. It is first for speed, endurance and reliability. Come and see these latest models.

McLaughlin Motor Car Co. Limited

Sales Rooms and Service Station, 104th Street, Edmonton

This automobile advertisement appeared in *Good Roads Magazine* in November 1922.

secondary roads were "poorly maintained" and were "impassable" at some times in the year.[66] Naturally, the condition of these roads directly limited the roles that cars and trucks could play in leisure. As the majority of Alberta roads were unsurfaced, they were useable only during the summer and on and off during the rest of the year. Most farm families, who had access only to secondary roads, were therefore still seasonally isolated. The urban population, however, could move relatively easily over primary roads between towns and cities year-round.

The impact of transportation on leisure also included the movement of goods and the communication of information. The prairies had effective telegraph service by the end of the 1880s, which served as an important counter to the isolation of the region. World, national, and regional news was accessible to prairie people through newspapers that received information and copy by telegraph.[67] Limited telephone service had been instituted in various parts of the province by the late 1880s, but private companies generally refused to provide service except to the most profitable markets. Accordingly, in 1907 the provincial government began constructing lines to ensure the extension of service throughout Alberta[68] and the telephone system expanded rapidly between 1908 and 1914. By the 1920s telephones were relatively common, and the public was routinely using long-distance service. By 1928 the average distance covered by a telephone call in Alberta was sixty-one miles.[69]

The telephone was especially important for rural people, who were specifically targeted in the advertising of telephone companies and suppliers. Advertising stressed that telephones were important tools for gathering information, getting help in times of emergency, and "strengthening the bonds of friendship" with neighbours.[70] Indeed, John Blackburn, who farmed at various places in the province, recalled that near Tofield telephones were used in 1911 "as much for visiting and gossip as for practical purposes."[71] In 1921, just over 21 percent of all farms had telephones, but by 1931, this percentage had dropped to 17 percent[72] because rental of a telephone cost thirty dollars per year, which in many cases represented a good percentage of a farm family's household expenditures during the Depression.[73] It was widely admitted during the 1930s that Alberta Government Telephones' service was poor. The government reacted to this criticism in 1936 by selling the rural telephone lines to mutual companies because it was believed that they could provide better service than Alberta Government Telephones.[74]

Because its presence is generally not intrusive, the significance of the telephone to life in North America has largely been ignored,[75] even though it created an unprecedented opportunity for people to communicate and socialize. Through telephones, and radio as well, Albertans kept themselves informed about community or personal events. Because of its immediacy, the telephone was probably as important for the planning and promotion of recreational events as were newspapers or magazines; and over time, it must have lessened the importance of the newspapers' role in notifying the public of events. In addition to telephones and newspapers, the postal system played an important part in people's lives, and despite perennial complaints of poor service,[76] it was central to the provincial communications network. The parcel post service, organized in 1914, permitted the shipment of small consumer goods, such as radios and sporting equipment, to all parts of the province. Air mail service, inaugurated in 1930 between Calgary and Edmonton, expedited communication by letter between the two cities and with others in the rest of the prairies.[77]

Improvements in transportation and communications permitted rapid publicity for special recreational events and attendance from some distance. But participation in leisure activities depended on the availability of time free from work. Sebastien de Grazia's observation that people in the United States in the late nineteenth century and early twentieth century had relatively little free time to devote to recreation seems equally applicable to Alberta during the same period. A farm family's hours of work were generally long and accounts of the numerous daily chores done on Alberta farms during the period under review are legendary. Hours of work on different types of farms varied. Grain farmers and ranchers, whose work was the most seasonal, were left with blocks of free or at least flexible time during the year. Mixed farming was more consistently labour intensive than straight grain farming, but even this pattern was affected by the number and type of livestock kept on a mixed farm. Farmers with more highly mechanized operations or those with a plentiful supply of labour may have had more free time; and certainly, a farmer who had electricity (although most did not before 1945) would have been in an enviable position. A farm family's free time was generally concentrated in midwinter, in the very early spring before seeding, and in midsummer after seeding and before harvest.[78]

For urban and industrial workers, work hours varied among occupational groups. During the 1920s, most urban white-collar workers worked nine hours on weekdays and from 9:00 A.M. until 1:00 P.M. on Saturdays, while tradesmen, mechanics and shift workers, among others, generally worked eight or nine hours per day for six days a week.[79] Work was highly regularized. Absence was treated by employers as a serious matter; regular and punctual attendance was demanded, although in some circumstances a leave of absence without pay was readily granted.[80] Some workers received paid vacations, especially after World War I. In 1922, permanent blue-collar employees in the Electric Light and Water Works Departments of the City of Edmonton received one week's paid vacation after one year's employment and two weeks after two or more years' employment.[81] However, most wage earners were not paid for public or personal holidays, and change on this front was slow. In 1945, the provincial Board of Industrial Relations enacted a Holiday-with-Pay Order, but the order was neither uniformly enforced nor universal, and it did not apply to casual labourers or construction and railroad workers.[82] Most urban and industrial workers in Alberta had relatively little time away from work, and what free time they had was concentrated in the evenings during the week, on Saturday afternoons and evenings, and on Sundays, when leisure came after personal maintenance, home chores, and family and community obligations.

For most people the only day of the week wholly free from work was Sunday. Its place in leisure had been important in prairie Canada since the late nineteenth century when most community recreational events were held on Sundays.[83] Although territorial and later provincial legislation restricting Sunday activity existed prior to 1907, Sunday activities began to change after 1907 because of the application of Sabbatarian legislation. The federal government passed the Lord's Day Act in response to pressure from a coalition of Protestant churches and labour groups. These lobbyists argued that "uninterrupted toil was brutalizing" and that leisure was necessary for an individual's spiritual and cultural growth. Leisure was not, however, seen as an end in itself. Sabbatarian forces interpreted leisure not in terms of rest but in terms of useful and uplifting activity; a life of "quality" rather than a life of labour or entertainment was the appropriate objective of man.[84] Thus, an individual's control of time away from work was restricted, ostensibly for his or her own good. While labour may have wanted Sunday observance laws as a means of restricting hours of work, the church groups had much wider social objectives and their influence shaped the restrictions placed on Sunday activity. During debate of the Lord's Day Bill in 1906, concern was expressed lest it be used to compel farmers not to work on Sunday or to restore conditions from the mid-nineteenth century.[85] The solution, according to the *Calgary Herald*, was to educate the individual "to take one day's rest in seven and to use that day in the manner best fitted to improve his spiritual, moral and physical condition; and strange as it may seem to some of the extremists, these three conditions are not by any means incompatible." Certain behaviour at Fort Macleod had been singled out by one Sabbatarian as an example of the need for Sabbath legislation, but the *Herald* disagreed: Sunday was already generally observed in Fort Macleod with "solemnity and decorum," and conversations were "carried on in subdued and almost reverent tones"; only the "cow punchers from the hills" were exceptions to this rule, but they no longer represented the public standards of Sunday behaviour in Fort Macleod.[86]

The July 1 Sports Day at Lesser Slave Lake, circa 1907. (PAA A.2331)

Sabbatarianism demonstrated the power of Anglo-Saxon Protestants in Canada, and in Alberta the dominant culture drew its inspiration from Ontario-based Protestantism. Adherents were able not only to have legislation passed that accorded with their views, but also had sufficient influence to ensure that the provincial government enforced the law. Most of the secular activities, such as rodeos and organized sports meets, which would have been held on a Sunday before 1907, were "gradually displaced by regular church services and . . . informal visiting." By 1930, the transformation was complete; Sunday had

> come to be marked by closed moving picture theatres, deserted athletic grounds, and absence of organized sport. In this as in many other phases of community development it is influences from Ontario and particularly of the large Protestant Churches in the province, which have become dominant in the prairie region.[87]

The late nineteenth century community focus of Sunday was lost; Sunday leisure turned inwards and became individualized.

The legislation was in several ways interpreted in a manner that created severe social restrictions and significantly curtailed Sunday activity. The sale of property and the "carrying on and transacting of any business" of one's "ordinary calling" on a Sunday was forbidden. Certain "works of necessity and mercy" were excepted, but the definition of necessity was murky at best. Selling cigars on a Sunday was not considered a "necessity,"[88] nor was selling gas, but the towing of a "disabled auto" was, because it was "unavoidable work to save property in cases of emergency."[89] Some businesses, such as restaurants, were allowed to remain open on Sundays, but this too created difficulties because storekeepers selling ice cream and soft drinks argued that they were restaurants and thus could stay open on Sunday.[90] Another thorny issue involved farmers. Threshing on Sunday was illegal and subject to prosecution, although this was an extremely sensitive matter in an agricultural province and was approached with great caution by the provincial government.[91] Sporting events held on Sunday were always contentious. The law permitted spontaneous sports to be played on Sunday but did not permit organized events where a prize was awarded or admission was charged. Among others, miners at Cadomin resented such restrictions because Sunday was the only day that they and their families could enjoy organized sports events or social gatherings.[92] Nonetheless, the Sabbatarian forces had their way, and by means of a network of informers and supporters, they demanded prosecutions whenever such sports were played on Sundays.[93] Even the Roman Catholic church was sometimes censored: bingos were commonly held in church basements on Sundays during the early 1940s, but because any game of chance or "contest for gain" on Sunday was prohibited, these bingos were subsequently ruled to be illegal.[94]

The restriction of Sunday activity certainly resulted in a loss of choice in leisure for those who had only Sunday free from work.

At the same time, Sunday closing laws meant that some people were no longer forced to work on Sunday, which for them must have meant an increase in leisure time. The extent to which these laws had an effect on the working habits of farmers, whose work was so greatly determined by seasonal and climatic factors, is unclear. It may be that they persuaded some farmers to apportion their time around a six-day work week. In the absence of detailed historical literature on late nineteenth century working conditions in Alberta, it is difficult to judge the full impact of Sabbatarianism and whether it represented a net loss or gain in leisure. Nevertheless, Sunday observance laws were a significant measure of control over people's lives. Farmers perhaps had flexibility of work time, but most urban and industrial workers, meeting demands of employers for rigid work weeks, were left only with Sunday as a day of free time. And even the use of this time was constrained by the Sunday closing laws. In this environment, public holidays and local celebrations were important opportunities for people to enjoy themselves away from work.

Public holidays were recognized and celebrated throughout the province from the beginning of settlement. By 1922, the statutory holidays were Christmas, Dominion Day, Victoria Day or May 24, Good Friday, Thanksgiving Day, Labour Day, and New Year's Day.[95] It was a calendar dominated by Christian and patriotic holidays. Other days, such as Boxing Day and Easter Monday, were observed as bank holidays. Although many businesses closed on bank holidays, not all workers received the day off. Garage mechanics, for example, received only statutory holidays in 1928.[96] Undoubtedly, the most universal statutory holiday was Christmas. Since Christmas had a family focus that set it apart from other statutory holidays, it deserves separate consideration later. Nonetheless, Dominion Day, Victoria Day, and Labour Day had comparable public dimensions.

Records of the celebration of Dominion Day in Alberta are plentiful from at least the 1880s and indicate that it was an important celebration early in the province's history. In the late nineteenth century, it was usually celebrated with team sports, horse and foot races, plenty of liquor, and a dance in the evening.[97] Horse racing and drinking were most popular with men. The 1884 Dominion Day celebrations in Edmonton were typical: "The usual amount of exhilarating liquid was partaken of by the pink-eye club, without causing the usual results, [and] with the exception of some 'wind fights' nothing of a pugilistic nature marred the day's proceedings."[98] By the early twentieth century, Dominion Day had become a more elaborate and patriotic celebration, which purposefully included the whole family. Although horse racing, sports, an evening dance, and plenty of liquor remained important, street parades and a patriotic programme at the fair grounds or some other public location were featured as well. In 1907, the Canadian Club, a nationalist voluntary club, organized the ceremonies in Calgary with an emphasis on patriotism. When the Union Jack was raised, its symbolism overwhelmed the *Calgary Herald* editor, who later wrote that the flag represented "the blood of a motherland and what she has done for freedom and liberty in a fight of centuries duration. It stands as the flag of law and order. It stands for the right of every man to earn his own bread and none shall make him afraid."[99] Although patriotism was important, sports, picnics, and outings to the lake were the heart of Dominion Day. By the 1920s, city parks were crowded with holidayers and, for those with vehicles, outings to a lake or a resort or simply a drive in the country had become a feature of the day.[100]

"Miss Canada" was the centre of attention at a pageant at Vegreville on Dominion Day 1927. (PAA B.2687)

In Leduc, the Diamond Jubilee of Confederation in 1927 was celebrated with a special parade featuring children representing the peoples of Canada's provinces. (PAA Ba.203)

The Diamond Jubilee of Confederation in 1927 called for special Dominion Day celebrations. During the 1920s there was an upswing in nationalism in Canada, and the fiftieth anniversary of Confederation was for many an occasion to move beyond simple patriotism and towards a more conscious nationalism. In Alberta, the debates that occurred during the extensive planning for the jubilee demonstrate the shift in contemporary attitudes towards Dominion Day and its function. The provincial government established a committee made up of political, civic, and other representatives to plan events in Alberta. Almost all committee members raised the issues of participation by non-British Canadians in the celebrations and the encouragement of nationalism. Some people argued that the day should be used to reinforce the greatness of Canada in the minds of the non-English-speaking groups in the province and that this could be done by military displays and multilingual pamphlets. Others suggested that sugar maple leaves be distributed to Alberta school children because most of them had never seen a "real" maple leaf. However, Dr. H.M. Tory of the University of Alberta seems to have touched a common chord when he stated: "I do not think it [Dominion Day] should be British or pro-British but distinctly Canadian." He opposed military displays and instead, along with the United Farm Women of Alberta, favoured community picnics to encourage "our foreign population to understand us."[101] It seems to have been assumed that to understand and observe English Canada was to love it and to yearn for assimilation into it. Despite attempts at centralized planning, the final format of the 1927 celebration was left largely in local hands, except for a cooperative national plan that involved all the provinces, the federal government, and various corporations and agencies in Canada's first transcontinental radio broadcast. It was an appropriate symbol for the ending of one era and the beginning of another.

The Union Jack was prominently displayed at the Athabasca Landing Empire Day parade in 1913. (PAA Aca.41)

Victoria Day, or May 24, was greeted with at least as much enthusiasm as Dominion Day. Schools and clubs organized patriotic drills, marches, and pageants with titles such as "Rule Britannia, a fancy flag drill for eight girls," and "The Making of Canada's flag, a patriotic play."[102] Even so, the popularity of the holiday went beyond patriotism; it marked the beginning of summer weather and the celebrations always featured picnics and sports. Not surprisingly, people's happiness at leaving winter behind was integrated into the celebrations and May 24 was associated with the time when one could finally greet the beginning of summer, plant the garden, forget winter for a time, and enjoy "a real outdoor holiday."[103]

Victoria Day was celebrated in Edmonton from the early 1880s and by 1910 it had become a major community celebration with bands, a picnic, and a great array of sports. May 24 shared with Labour Day the quality of marking and defining seasons. During World War II, the federal government, not recognizing the place of May 24 in prairie life, suspended its celebration in order to increase time available for war production. The Alberta government refused to allow such a diminution and countermanded the federal ruling by declaring May 24 a provincial holiday. While banks and federal government offices remained open on May 24 from 1943 until 1945, schools, stores, and provincial government offices were closed.[104] This policy was couched in terms of loyalty to tradition and the British connection, but it can be suggested that Alberta's defence of Victoria Day was as much a tribute to the final defeat of the prairie winter for another year as a display of patriotism and loyalty to a long-dead queen and a dying empire.

Labour Day, also widely celebrated in Alberta, was instituted by the federal government in 1894 in response to lobbying by labour organizations for recognition of their economic role and social objectives. Not everyone favoured the holiday, however, and one critic commented that there were already "more holidays on the statute books than the frugal workman desired." Moreover, "the wisdom and right of any particular class of the community to arrogate to themselves the title of 'workingmen' " was questionable because it would engender class consciousness and conflict between union and non-union workers.[105] Not all observers were so negative, and within a decade Labour Day was cited as an example of "the progress of the world" because it was an expression of the "growing sentiment in favor of mental diversion"[106] and a day for sports, parades, and picnics. In the late nineteenth century, it was largely celebrated in Calgary as the last holiday of the summer and had little association with labour unions.[107] In 1900, however, the organization of a Labour Day parade provided more focus. By 1904, the parade had become a major event including two bands, ten automobiles, four hundred trade unionists carrying union banners, two hundred children, three floats, and the city's fire engines. The parade was followed by speeches praising unions as the best means for working men to meet the high cost of living by gaining increased wages. Some speakers, however, included admonitions to workers, and the mayor of Calgary praised the "conservative" leadership of Calgary unions. When the speeches ended, sports took up the rest of the day.[108] In rural towns, Labour Day had little or no relevance in terms of unionism, but in the cities and mining towns it continued to have a unionist and often a political focus. Union parades remained a part of Labour Day celebrations in many communities until at least World War II, but by 1930 many Albertans simply used the holiday as an occasion for a last visit to a lake or park.[109]

Statutory holidays were for many years observed on the day on which they fell. By the late 1940s, however, business began lobbying to have these holidays on Mondays to make long weekends. In 1948, it was argued that both Victoria Day and Dominion Day, as well as any newly created holidays, should be observed on Mondays. This demand aimed "to avoid interruption to the working week by statutory holidays falling in mid week." This sentiment was supported by the Edmonton Chamber of Commerce, which hoped to avoid the "dislocation of industry and commerce" caused by midweek holidays.[110]

In addition to statutory holidays, events of national or provincial importance were also honoured with a holiday from work. Such holidays tended to support patriotic objectives with straightforward testaments to the importance of Britishness in Alberta life. The Queen's Diamond Jubilee in 1897 and Autonomy Day on September 1, 1905, were celebrated as public holidays, and special programmes were arranged to reinforce the symbolism of the events. In 1897, the Queen's Diamond Jubilee occasioned parades, sports, and community celebrations throughout the province. In Edmonton, floats carrying people dressed as Britannia and the colonies were dragged through the rutted streets. An attractively bound "souvenir" booklet of photos of the pageant was published to commemorate the day.[111] At the centre of the 1905 inauguration celebrations in Edmonton were the inaugural ceremonies, but the day featured a huge parade through decorated streets, sports, musical events, and a grand ball. In 1937, Coronation Day was declared a public holiday throughout the province. Similarly, the visit of King George VI and Queen Elizabeth to Canada in 1939 led to the production of a souvenir booklet of photos of the royal party on the Alberta portion of their tour in an appropriately regal format,[112] indicating the special nature of

Edmonton's streets were lined with crowds eager to greet King George VI and Queen Elizabeth when they visited the city in 1939. (PAA BL.473/4a)

these royal events and the public demand for a memento.

Other occasions and holidays were celebrated at the civic level. In the Territorial period, Arbor Day was celebrated as a public holiday with the objective of planting trees. Over time, it simply became a civic holiday in some communities, whereas in others it was not recognized at all. Perhaps the decline of Arbor Day was related to a recognition that it was futile to plant trees in some parts of Alberta, or perhaps it declined because it did not have the same national focus that prevailed in the United States. By the 1940s Arbor Day had become merely an occasion for cleaning school yards.[113] At the end of both wars most local governments sponsored festivities and parades. Special local occasions also provided the rationale for specific holidays. In 1909, Edmonton declared a civic holiday on the day when the governor-general laid the corner stone of the legislative buildings. In 1920, Edmonton's "historical pageant" emphasized the Hudson's Bay Company and the settlement of the West to honour the company on its 250th anniversary. Similarly, Fort Macleod held a celebration in 1924 to commemorate the arrival of the Northwest Mounted Police in Alberta,[114] and towns usually declared at least a one-half day civic holiday for their annual fairs.

The town of Vulcan celebrated the end of World War I with a parade. (GAI NA-748-60)

Businesses in Alberta also occasionally organized one-day staff holidays. In July 1910, the Hudson's Bay Company closed its Calgary store for a day and sent its employees on an excursion to Banff. It was a unique event in Calgary and was welcomed by the *Calgary Herald* as an antidote to the aggressive "get rich quick bug" that had so strongly infected Calgarians, who did nothing but work and refused to "hunt for pleasure as much as they might." Staff holidays were excellent for morale and thus, in the final analysis, were good for business.[115] Such holidays were not typical before World War I, but by the early 1920s towns began to declare civic half-day holidays each week during the summer. These holidays were justified not only on the grounds that people needed a break from work, but because they were good for business:

> business is based upon friendship, sociability and pleasure. Encourage these and you increase your business. Give a party and the host buys more groceries and the guests buy new clothes. Give a holiday and the whole population dress up in their best togs, buy

a lot of extra Knick-knacks; go out visiting and bring home friends. Money was made for holidays.[116]

Leisure in such cases did not challenge the centrality of work in people's lives; indeed, it served to reinforce this relationship by confirming the place of leisure in a cash-based and commercialized culture.

Selected groups had reason to celebrate specific events, frequently with outings that were at least partially recreational: St. Patrick's Day, Robert Burns's Birthday, St-Jean Baptiste Day, and Remembrance Day, among others. The level of celebration reflected ethnic or group influence. Events important to the British groups in the province always merited extensive press coverage, but holidays special to other groups rarely received much notice, in part because they lacked provincial scope and frequently were disunited. Moreover, only the English-speaking groups had sufficient population or political influence to have their holidays recognized at a provincial level. St-Jean Baptiste Day achieved recognition at the civic level and was celebrated annually before World War I in Edmonton and St. Albert with a parade, picnic, dance, and a Mass.[117] St-Jean Baptiste Day, however, had a national pedigree which gave it a measure of status, although reference to it (despite its continued celebration in French communities in Alberta) diminished in the English dailies in Alberta after World War I, perhaps as a result of the English-French polarization in wartime politics.

In the 1890s, St. Patrick's Day was celebrated by Roman Catholic Irish with a Mass in the morning and a programme of music, recitations, and plays in the evening which "united an immense audience in an atmosphere where good will and charity prevailed."[118] It is unclear if Irish nationalism played a role in this celebration, but by the early 1930s, St. Patrick's Day had been incorporated into the Protestant dominant culture where it lost its specific ethnic and religious context. It was subsequently used as an occasion for a theme party, for which the games and decorations were easy and straightforward because the relevant symbols and games "mostly wind themselves around the homely potato—so dear to the heart of the Irish! And potatoes are cheap and close at hand in most houses." There was a good deal of ethnic stereotyping in all of this: the games involved potato races, "gambling" (presumably an Irish propensity), a blindfold game involving the placing of potatoes into a jar, a "fortune-teller with 'vision' and humour" (supposedly two more Irish traits), Irish songs, and a dinner.[119]

Other non-Anglo-Saxon peoples of the province celebrated a number of other holidays, but these festivals were never appropriated by the dominant culture and scarcely attracted attention from Albertans of English-language cultures. Yet they were days that focussed religious and ethnic traditions. Among Ukrainian Orthodox settlers, the celebration of a "Patron Saint's Day" was an occasion for the individual whose saint's day was being celebrated to "invite his neighbours to his home to partake of his hospitality."[120] Although this celebration was highly individual, there were many others, such as national days and particular religious celebrations, which had a collective importance and even assumed civic status in some ethnically homogeneous communities. Icelandic Day, the national holiday of Iceland, was celebrated in Markerville, although the date on which it was celebrated was changed to suit Canadian conditions. Traditionally, it had been celebrated in June, but after World War I the date was moved to August when the weather was usually better and farmers were less busy.[121] This process of accommodation was typical. Until the late 1920s, schools in the Ukrainian school districts of east central Alberta closed for every religious holiday. This meant that schools were closed for as many as thirty days, or about 15 percent, of the school year. In the 1930s, following pressure from government and parents, schools closed only for Christmas and New Year on the Julian calendar.[122] In this case, the non-Anglo-Saxon group accommodated itself to the dominant culture, but at the same time, its members were unwilling to abandon all their traditions and continued to follow those of particular significance. The transformation was an important example of one aspect of cultural change in Alberta.

In addition to the variables of transportation, communication, free time, and special occasions, levels of income differentiated Albertans' responses to leisure. It is difficult, however, to establish income levels reliably in order to estimate the money people had available for leisure. No secondary literature has analyzed the incomes or cost of living of salaried workers in Alberta, although some fragmentary data exist for wage earners. Even from these sketchy data, it is nevertheless clear that substantial fluctuation characterized wages and cost of living in the half-century after 1896. These fluctuations often followed the boom and bust cycles of the prairie economy, but the impact on individuals varied greatly on the basis of cost of living, occupation, job security, location, and availability of benefits such as paid holidays or sick pay. Wages in

Participants in the school picnic at Pobeda School District in 1915 found it a solemn occasion. (PAA UV.597)

the construction trades were high in the late 1880s, but dropped by almost 50 percent within a decade. By 1914, a carpenter in Calgary would have been earning about 50 cents per hour and a labourer about 30 cents per hour. By 1920, these wages had increased by up to 75 percent, but the cost of living had increased even more than this during the war.[123] For a time in the 1920s, wages in most sectors increased substantially, but were rolled back in the 1930s. Calgary printers who had been earning $1.06 per hour in 1932 saw their wages drop to 85 cents per hour the next year.[124] By the mid-1940s, women working in small town hotels as chambermaids and waitresses earned only between $5.50 and $10 per week plus room and board, while men working in hotels earned between $10 and $20 per week plus room and board,[125] reflecting differences occasioned by economic cycle, location and gender. The income picture is thus extremely complex and difficult to detail comprehensively. It has been argued that "consistent statistics on income distribution in Canada are available only for the period following 1951" and that it is difficult to compare census data for the earlier periods because of "changes in concepts and classifications."[126] The average yearly incomes for an employed twenty-five to forty-nine-year-old male and an employed twenty-five to forty-nine-year-old female in 1920-21 were $1,278 and $792 respectively,[127] yet little more can be derived from this than the obvious disparity in the wages of men and women.

While it is difficult to estimate income variations, it is even more difficult to make a precise assessment of the cost of living and the amount of money available for expenditure on leisure. There have been no detailed historical studies of the cost of living or of expenditure patterns in Alberta. Clearly, these are intricate problems since one must account for inflation and deflation as well as changing standards of what was an essential expenditure and what was not. High rates of inflation during and after World War I were followed during the 1930s by considerable deflation as well as a decline in wages. Decreases in income did not always mean falling standards of living, although real income was seriously eroded for many during the 1930s. Similarly, wages rose during World War II, but so did the cost of living. In 1920, the mayor of Calgary argued that "a man who could keep a family on $4 per day was working a miracle,"[128] and clearly the cost of living in Calgary and Edmonton in the year preceding May 31, 1921, was substantially higher than four dollars per day. Utilizing the approach Michael Piva used for estimating cost of living in Toronto, total yearly expenditures for a family of five in Calgary averaged $1,896.75 while in Edmonton it was $1,814.48. This would roughly define the poverty level.[129] Income, of course, varied greatly by occupation, but as shown in Table 1, average annual earnings for males in Edmonton and Calgary were often below this poverty level. While figures for total family income are unavailable, it is obvious that both adult family members would often have had to work for wages. Although neither the cost of living estimates nor the earnings in Table 1 provide direct evidence on expenditures for leisure, they do provide a measure and underscore that for many people recreation costing fifty cents was a considerable expenditure indeed.

For farm people, the picture is complicated by different standards and needs. Most farmers seem to have accepted a lower standard of living than many urban people and their expenses were not as high because they had fewer services (no electricity, sewerage, and water), and they could produce more of their own food, especially protein. In 1931, the *Farm and Ranch Review* asked its readers to send in a balance sheet of home and farm expenses. The information supplied provides a glimpse of the spending patterns of some rural Albertans before the Depression. One respondent from a farm in the park belt stated that from 1928 until 1930 the family had spent an average of $640 per year for household and personal expenses.

Table 1

Selected Average Annual Earnings, Males, Calgary and Edmonton, 1921

	Calgary	Edmonton
Manufacturing		
—Machinists and Millwrights	1,179.56	1,331.61
—Bakers	1,167.96	1,659.02
Construction		
—Carpenters	1,092.98	1,093.93
—Labourers	755.89	951.38
Transportation, Steam Railways		
—Locomotive Engineers	2,235.92	2,319.26
—Switchmen, signalmen, yardmen	1,533.95	1,516.19
Trade		
—Mgrs. and Supts., Retail trade	2,062.95	2,164.52
—Salesmen, general & Dept. stores	1,470.17	1,196.37
Finance		
-Mgrs., Insptrs. & Supts., banks	2,965.69	2,493.46
Service		
—Garage repairmen	1,102.93	1,081.50
—Lawyers and notaries	3,027.86	2,061.43
—Clergymen	1,995.57	1,419.07
—Teachers	1,910.66	1,886.97
—Fed. and Prov. govt. clerks	1,398.56	1,398.31

Source: *Census of Canada, 1921,* Volume 3, Table 40. The figures are calculated from average weekly earnings and average weeks worked for each category.

Of this, they spent 7 percent on "recreation." Over the ten-year period from 1920 to 1930, another family had spent an average of 8 percent of a yearly average total home expenditure of $1,140 on "recreation/club fees," books, magazines and records, and upkeep of the radio.[130] These glimpses of income and cost of living for both urban and farm people are neither comprehensive nor clearly defined, but they provide some points of reference for ranking the cost of different activities and products. Neat correlations between leisure costs and income are especially difficult because leisure overlapped with so many other needs and priorities. Therefore, our notions of expenditures on leisure are murky at best. Precise analysis of the amount spent on leisure would have to include, for example, a percentage of the capital and operating costs of a car.

Disposable income became more important in leisure in the twentieth century as commercialization of leisure increased and became entrenched. This went beyond the spread of the cash nexus into all aspects of life; it also meant that leisure became a significant part of the economy and that the state increasingly saw leisure as a source of revenue. Through the Amusement Tax Act, the province taxed dances, movies, travelling shows, and concerts. These taxes were an important part of government revenues; $190,880 was collected through these taxes in 1927 alone. Better still, from a political perspective, most of these taxes were generated by the smallest percentage of the population: the urban residents of Calgary, Edmonton, Lethbridge, and Medicine Hat and their visitors paid 78 percent of all amusement taxes.[131] Amusement taxes were often bitterly assailed by interested groups, such as Alberta theatre owners, but the taxes remained firmly in place. In a society so passionately devoted to "usefulness," few seriously challenged the taxation of pleasure. Criticism of the amusement taxes was further mitigated because entertainment organized for charitable, religious, or community purposes was exempt from tax. As pleasure was best when combined with a higher motive, entertainments held to raise funds for worthy causes could hardly be faulted.

Provincial revenues were also raised through licence fees on commercial poolrooms, restaurants, bars, and movie theatres. Municipal governments too eagerly taxed and licensed, and when the taxing powers of all three levels of government were combined, numerous taxes and fees, many of which were related to entertainment and recreation, were levied. In 1923, a corner store in Edmonton paid $15 for selling cigars and cigarettes; $5 for selling 2 percent beer; $5 for selling ice cream and candy; $15 for a city restaurant licence (plus $10 for the provincial restaurant licence); a $2 federal tax on a soda fountain plus 1 cent on each soft drink sold from the fountain; a 5 percent luxury tax on candy; a 5 percent tax on pop; a $2 licence fee to sell fireworks; a $25 city licence fee for each slot machine, plus a general business tax.[132]

This ability to tax leisure suggests its importance to the business life of the province. In 1930, of 2,881 businesses in Alberta, 330 fell within the group categorized as "amusement and recreation." These businesses represented only 11.45 percent of the total number, but they took in 24.3 percent of the total business receipts in Alberta.[133] Leisure obviously supported lucrative business; but it was even more significant than these statistics suggest because the amusement and recreational category included only such enterprises as pool halls and cinemas. General stores which sold sporting goods, for instance, were not included but obviously benefitted from recreational activity. In 1941, the total number of businesses in Alberta had increased to 3,341, 397 of which fell within the amusement and recreation group. This represented about 12 percent of total businesses, only a marginal increase over 1930. While total receipts of all businesses had declined since 1930, the amusement and recreation group accounted for 25.3 percent of the total, a slight increase since 1930,[134] which may suggest that leisure was becoming viewed as a necessary expenditure in daily life. Although more research on the place of leisure in the economy of Alberta is obviously needed, it can be suggested that definable economic interest groups were well developed around leisure activities before World War II. The economic dimension of leisure, then, operated at a number of levels. Leisure increasingly provided a source of revenue for governments and played a greater role in business, and interest groups evolved from leisure related activity. In personal terms, income not only affected leisure choices by determining the sort of entertainment to which an individual could afford admission, but also dictated the range of leisure activities one could experience by determining such things as accessibility to transportation.

Access to leisure was certainly affected by the amount of time that people had free from work. Despite changes in technology after World War I, the time people had available for leisure seems not to have changed markedly. Hours of work for wage earners remained in the range of eight to nine hours per day for five and one-half or six days per week. The number of statutory holidays did not increase between 1896 and 1945. But technology, especially in transportation, did affect the use of free time. The increase in ownership of private motor vehicles broadened leisure opportunities from the 1920s on. Automobiles gave people greater flexibility and choice in their activities within the same time constraints.

Leisure was also shaped by social conditions rooted in the ideology of the dominant culture and its origins in Ontario and British traditions. Leisure was legitimate if it was useful, and this concept of utility encompassed a number of possibilities. Above all, leisure was useful if it did not detract from work and improved, or re-created, the individual for labour. At the crudest level of understanding, leisure was seen as a reward for work, but this reward had to be exercised in such a way as not to make one unfit for work. Leisure which improved one's physical and mental agility was therefore useful, and, in this sense, simple outings for pleasure were legitimate as long as they did not lead to dissipation. More abstract definitions of useful leisure emphasized instruction contributing to intellectual and spiritual development.

The ideology of the dominant culture, and its accompanying power to grant legitimacy to certain leisure activity, was important in informal terms because it provided the highest standards for leisure in the society. In many cases, as will be shown in later chapters, this ideology justified the regulation and control of leisure. The dominant culture set the standards for the activities and programmes of major institutions. These standards applied to all citizens in the province, whether they subscribed to the ideals of the dominant culture or not. For those who did, these standards fixed boundaries for acceptable behaviour on the part of English-speaking and non-English-speaking people alike. Non-English-speaking groups were often fragmented and unable to resist the dominant culture, or had little desire to resist and assimilated readily. In either case, the dominant culture defined public standards of leisure on its own terms, which helped to sustain its hegemony.

This hegemony was reinforced by linking work, usefulness, and leisure in complementary terms which became the basis for the legal and socially accepted standards for leisure and work. It helped to determine the purpose of public holidays, and it gave authority to Sabbatarian beliefs. Although the dominant culture had the power to influence what leisure time people would have available in the form of province-wide public holidays, it did not have the power to force individuals to celebrate in the fashion that it thought best, only the authority to exert influence against what it thought wrong. It posited no sweeping objection to leisure, but it did insist that leisure activities be framed and justified by utilitarian considerations, and, at root, this was integral to the ideology of the dominant culture.

2. The Structure of Everyday Life: Home and Family

The home was a central institution in the social theory of the dominant culture in Alberta. The home was perceived as the essential force in the socialization of children and in the control and training of adolescents. It provided adults with purpose in life and with a set of responsibilities and personalized structures that ensured social order and cohesion. But it was also a place of relaxation, informality, and retreat from the stresses of life and society. Consequently, leisure activities that took place away from home were often seen as a challenge to its place in the social order. Yet, paradoxically, the home could not meet the demands that were placed upon it without aid from external agencies. The home was described as an institution that was separate and apart from the society in which it existed, but home activities increasingly depended upon community facilities, and institutions such as libraries were welcomed as reinforcements for home based leisure activities. Despite this contradiction, the home truly was central in leisure because so many everyday leisure activities such as reading, music, games, hobbies, gardening and crafts took place there. Moreover, many family celebrations were focussed on the home. The most important of these was Christmas, which expressed both faith and cultural continuity.

Leisure in the home was seen as a means of encouraging family cohesion and discipline. Given the environmentalist assumptions about behaviour, a good home was linked to social order. In 1915, 90 percent of juvenile delinquents in Alberta were said to be children who had neither discipline nor any "suitable form of occupation or amusement" at home. They were led into crime because they were allowed to wander about in the evenings looking for entertainment.[1] Such an analysis helped to confirm the importance of leisure in preserving the home. As one 1907 prescription had it, "let there be plenty of light by day and in the evening plenty of good pictures, music and. . .good books. . .cultivate hospitality, be sociable."[2] This was an idealized image that fit the needs of a literate class, conscious of aesthetics and the ranking of merit in art. It elevated the home to the primary focus for the social life of the family and its circle of friends and relatives. The home lay at the heart of social relations, yet it was separate from society. At the same time, there was a commonly held belief that the home's autonomy was endangered by new forms of entertainment and by community organized leisure that drew family members away from family and friends. All of these forces were characterized as "modern civilization" which challenged the autonomy of the home and threatened to destroy it as a social institution. This view formed the basis of a government report by Gerald Pelton, a Calgary lawyer who was commissioned in 1927 to report on the causes of juvenile delinquency. Pelton contended that

> the home as a social centre has almost ceased to exist. Most of the entertainment is outside—large houses are not feasible under present economic conditions and the divisions and sub-divisions of parents and children into countless leagues, clubs and organizations, have reduced the home to a rendezvous where the family sleeps and eats at regular or irregular hours.[3]

Pelton's mistrust of leisure in the form of "countless leagues, clubs and organizations" was at root a denial of community life. Yet the majority of these agencies attempted to reinforce the virtues of a home centred life. Moreover, many of the home activities that Pelton would have admired and supported, such as reading, often relied upon community organizations, such as libraries.

The idealization of the home as the primary location for socialization and its connection with environmental notions about behaviour were premised on certain assumptions about the place of women in society. In each household, the mother was the formative influence, and housekeeping and motherhood had an important link with leisure because home duties included not only housework but the creation of a perfect environment where family life could flourish and children could be protected and guided in their activities.[4] Such ideals created contradictions for some women, both within and outside the dominant culture. Many farm women did far more on the farm than housework, and among Slavic farm women, this practice was culturally based.[5] Moreover, for many people, there was no family life at all. Because of restrictive immigration policies, the Chinese population in Alberta was largely male: in 1921, of the thirty-five hundred Chinese people in Alberta, only two hundred were women.[6]

Although women were perceived as the keepers of home life and the home was seen as somehow set apart from society, many publicly supported institutions served home leisure activities. One important example was libraries. Almost all cultural groups in Alberta would have seen reading as a valuable activity. In the dominant culture, reading was consciously linked with self-improvement and individualism and, as such, was related directly to the political, economic and social ideology of the dominant culture.[7] In contrast to other groups in the society, the dominant culture was able to receive public support for libraries that stocked English-language books. This support was so accepted as a natural state of affairs that nobody questioned that it could be otherwise.

Nor was the belief in a linkage between reading and behaviour questioned in the dominant culture. It was firmly believed that books, through suggestion, could shape character and could affect the moral and intellectual standards of the society. Just as "good" books could elevate the individual, so "bad" books could corrupt. Indeed, the corruption engendered by "bad" books was particularly insidious because reading could be concealed. Winter was the time for reading, but as E.A. Corbett of the University of Alberta Department of Extension warned, "the long winter evenings in Alberta and the isolation in many places make it doubly important not only that books should be available, but that some guidance should be given as to what is worth reading and what is not."[8] Potentially negative influences were countered in several ways. Books deemed to have truly depraved or seditious characteristics were censored through import restrictions, enforcement of relevant chapters in the Criminal Code, or both. During World War I, books were censored simply because they were printed in an "enemy alien" language. The great majority of books, however, were dealt with through moral suasion. According to one commentator in 1929, "generally speaking, our reading is either an opiate or a stimulant, something that soothes or produces a drowsy mental state, or something that is a spur to action." Nevertheless, it was recognized that everyone needed diversion, which reading could provide: "a certain amount keeps our minds brighter, our sympathies broader," but caution was essential to prevent such a diversion from becoming a "drug habit." Everyone had to be wary: it was piously observed that in reading, "as in all other things in life, we reap what we sow, so that it is up to us to sow wisely and help our children to do the same."[9]

Advocacy of parental guidance and self-control reached its most fervid pitch in the late 1930s in the National Crusade for Good Reading. This crusade aimed to sweep from Canada publications that were supposedly wrecking the social fabric. It was led by the Roman Catholic church through the aegis of the Canadian Catholic Youth Union. The crusade attempted to meet its objectives through mass rallies and the encouragement of individual commitment through pledge cards deposited in diocesan offices. The church hoped to lead an interdenominational attack on such publications, but the movement remained sectarian and the Protestant groups in the province never actively participated. What the crusade was opposing, other than salacious literature, however defined, was never clear. The movement was unequivocal in its campaign against "bad reading matter" that "undermines the best spiritual and religious values of the nation; and in itself provokes some of the worst forms of physical disease; it fosters crime, and strikes at the very roots of the family." The publications in question were not named: "we have no desire to contribute to their publicity," but all were "rotten," many "like 'whited sepulchres', attractive enough and almost decent at first glance, but corrupt and insidious in their spirit."[10]

Circular and pledge, National Crusade for Good Reading. (PAA, Premier's Papers, File 69.289/1234)

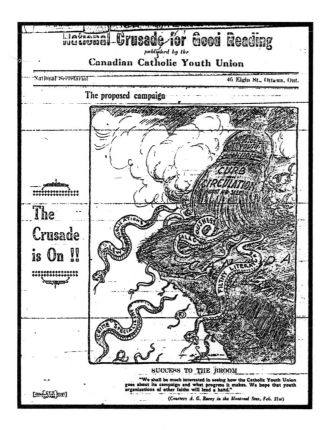

Books could be borrowed either from a local library or from various travelling libraries. At the turn of the century, there were no public lending libraries in Alberta and one could borrow books only from literary societies, clubs, and commercial lending libraries. By 1903 Calgary had a commercial lending library and employees of the Canadian Pacific Railway formed a lending library for their own use.[11] In many small towns, drugstores operated commercial lending libraries and the borrower paid a fee for each book borrowed.[12] Literary societies were the commonest sources of books. Although literary societies were often designed for people who enjoyed music or debating, they also functioned as lending libraries for their members. A literary society operated intermittently in Edmonton from 1882 and maintained a reading room stocked with donated magazines and books. Its list of publications was surprisingly broad and included British, Ontario, and western Canadian newspapers and magazines.[13] Many non-English-speaking groups also formed literary clubs and these societies stocked books in their own languages and sometimes in English as well. A literary society was established at Markerville in 1892 and built up a small library of mainly Icelandic books. Despite the society's collapse soon after its creation, the library functioned as a lending institution until the early 1930s, growing through additional purchases funded by annual dues.[14] Similarly, one of the objectives of an Estonian cultural group established in 1910 in Medicine Valley was to keep a library of Estonian books, while in the Crowsnest Pass the Polish Youth Progress Club maintained a library of about three thousand Polish books and pamphlets that could be borrowed for a small fee. In 1928 the library had between thirty and forty borrowers each week.[15]

The provision of books through voluntary and essentially private literary societies and clubs met the needs of neither the reading public nor social reformers who saw libraries as a means of improving society. It has been argued that in the United States the establishment of public libraries after the mid-nineteenth century became a cause for authoritarian and elitist social reformers who saw the public control of reading as a means of directing the behaviour of the poor, especially immigrants. Similarly, Egerton Ryerson's library policies in Ontario stressed "useful knowledge" to improve and elevate public taste and morality. In both cases, the intended audiences found the books too serious and boring and boycotted the public libraries.[16] In part, the reform point of view was reflected in the concerns expressed in Alberta about the type of books that public libraries should hold. When libraries were being established, demands were made that each library maintain the highest standards of literary taste lest it "degenerate into a place where cheap up-to-date novels can be gotten easily." Such concerns continued to be expressed in the years after World War I, and librarians were always pleased to note the excellence (and tradition) of the works they stocked and the service that the public libraries were providing in their communities. There was, perhaps surprisingly, little public debate over what was good taste in literature and what was not, although suspicions about the novel as a literary form were continually voiced. In 1907, it was suggested that it would be best to shun modern novels altogether in favour of poetry, plays, or essays. The public's demand for novels should be met through emphasis on the works of the great eighteenth and nineteenth-century British novelists: Richardson, Fielding, Thackeray, Dickens, and Scott.[17] In 1923, books of these authors, as well as those of Stevenson, were defined by a librarian at the Edmonton Public Library as the "standard works"; they were, he

proudly said, "the best read books in the library." Indeed, he claimed that the "taste of the regular fellows—the plumber and the doctor, the lawyer and the auto-mechanic. . .is inherently and absolutely" correct and was "just the same as it was down in old Ontario, way back when I was in library work there."[18]

The supposed "correctness" of public taste was not accidental.
The public libraries served the aspirations of the dominant culture
and met its view of good literary taste and the utility of reading.
Reading was not, in this view, a mere diversion but a useful expenditure of leisure time. While libraries partly reflected a social
reform effort, more importantly they served, through public funding, the literary needs and tastes of an influential sector of the
dominant culture. Accordingly, it was not by chance that public
libraries as well as travelling libraries stocked books mainly written in English and defined their "standard" authors as traditional
British ones. The Edmonton Public Library did, however, hold a
few books in French and these volumes received "considerable
patronage." As well, they held some books in German, Italian, and
other languages,[19] but no information has been located on the
number of people who borrowed these books. The provision of
books in languages other than English was never an issue,
presumably because when such books were stocked at all, their
numbers were few.[20] Similarly, modern light literature was never
really an issue for libraries: they simply did not stock such books
and people were forced to purchase "best sellers" from bookshops.
Even so, people clearly enjoyed light fiction; they liked stories by
Zane Grey, H.B. Wright, James Curwood, "or any one of a dozen
of the like caliber who possess trained type-writing machines."[21]
These books were usually written to a standard theme and format. Zane Grey wrote "Western" novels and Curwood wrote about
"northern" themes. E.A. Corbett thought that the popularity of
such writers was "a serious reflection upon our civilization."[22]
Nevertheless, such preferences persisted during the 1930s. If one
wished to purchase a book in High River in 1934, all that was
available was the "usual. . .light fiction."[23] E.A. Corbett's rejection
of Zane Grey and similar writers was a telling reaction in light of
Leslie Fiedler's assessment that the "Western" novel was "a
challenge to notions of high culture" and was scorned by western
Canadian intellectuals because of their "cultural insecurity."[24]
However, it can be argued that this rejection came not from cultural
insecurity, but from the belief that one's standards could be imposed upon society at large because they were inherently superior.

In 1908, the province passed legislation permitting the incorporation of public libraries. In the following decade a number of
libraries opened in the largest Alberta cities and towns: in Calgary
and Strathcona in 1912 and in Edmonton in 1913. The Calgary and
Strathcona libraries were built with the aid of grants from the
Carnegie Foundation, and when Edmonton constructed a new
library in 1922-23, it also tapped the same source for funds. These
were good libraries with extensive holdings and varied programmes, such as children's story hours and exhibitions. Libraries
were established in other centres as well, and by 1935 there were
two large public libraries in Calgary and Edmonton, and smaller
libraries could be found in Lethbridge, Medicine Hat, Red Deer
and Wetaskiwin. A large number of small libraries had also been
organized in towns and villages throughout the province.[25] Of the
latter, it was observed that:

> a few get a grant of money from the municipal council in addition
> to voluntary contributions. All are examples of willing co-operation
> on the part of individuals and of groups. Such organizations as the
> Women's Institutes, the I.O.D.E. [Imperial Order of the Daughters
> of the Empire], the U.F.A. and the U.F.W.A., the Knights of Pythias,
> the Catholic Women's League and others have done splendid work
> in establishing and maintaining small local libraries.

By this point, however, it was clear that the establishment of small
libraries in every town in the province was financially impossible,
and it was argued that regional library systems were the best means
of sharing resources over a large area.[26] Despite the value of such
regionalized systems, they were not adopted to any great extent,
and the number of small libraries continued to increase. After 1922,
public libraries received an annual operating grant from the
government. These grants were small, but they did signal an official commitment to public libraries. In 1945 the province established the Alberta Library Board to advise on libraries and to encourage improvement in the province's library system.[27] By 1949,
there were seventy-five public libraries in Alberta, of which twenty-
five had been formed between 1946 and 1949. Even so, 68 percent
of Albertans still had no public library service and again it was
argued, as it had been for a decade and a half, that a regional
system was the only practical solution.[28] The Edmonton library
system attempted to alleviate this problem in late 1947 when it
began to use a city bus converted into a "bookmobile" to reach its
"outlying districts."[29]

One alternative to public libraries was the University of Alberta Department of Extension travelling libraries and open shelf library. The travelling libraries held books covering a wide range of topics. The "library" was shipped to a community organization, such as a service club, which was responsible for lending the books to the public and for returning the whole collection to the university at the end of the loan period. Extensive use was made of this system. Travelling libraries reached 241 groups in 1924 and 240 groups in 1938-39. By World War II, however, the travelling libraries were "out of date except as a subsidiary to a more mobile type of service. The need for a reorganization of the whole library policy for rural districts is a crying one."[30] The service provided by the travelling libraries was supplemented by the more flexible "open shelf" library. The Department of Extension published a catalogue of books and anyone could borrow these books upon payment of the necessary postage. The range of books was wide and sophisticated, running from Tagore through Tolstoi to Aldous Huxley. The library contained a good selection of contemporary fiction, including Ralph Connor and H.G. Wells (but no Zane Grey).[31] Its total holdings probably exceeded the range of books available in most public libraries in the province.

By 1931, the demand for service from the university's open shelf library and travelling libraries had increased. This was a result of "the hard times" that had forced people all over North America to turn to cheap leisure activities such as reading.[32] The increased demand was not matched by increased funding for repair or purchase of new books, and by 1934 the books were getting "shabby and unattractive." Moreover, "quite a number of borrowers did not have money to pay for postage on books" and on occasion apologized for lateness in returning books because "they had no money to buy stamps."[33] Notwithstanding these problems, the number of books in circulation increased. Despite the long waits experienced by borrowers because of the increased demand, and despite the decline in the number of books in fit state to circulate, nearly twenty thousand books circulated in 1934-35.[34]

Public libraries in Alberta concentrated on lending books, but all had subscriptions to some newspapers and magazines. Nevertheless, newspaper and magazine circulation was mainly through home subscription. Many magazines and some newspapers carried serialized fiction, poems, and stories. The *Farm and Ranch Review*, a magazine published in Calgary, commonly carried serialized stories.[35] In 1908, the *Red Deer Advocate* ran a fifteen-week serialization of Arthur Conan Doyle's *The Hound of the Baskervilles*. By 1918, newspapers had generally dropped literary features but provided cartoons and comics, usually from American syndicated services. The newspapers probably found that they could not compete in fiction and stories with magazines such as *Maclean's, Saturday Night,* and the highly popular American mass circulation magazines such as the *Saturday Evening Post* and the *Ladies Home Journal,* all of which had wide circulation in Canada by the 1920s. The *Ladies Home Journal* had a national circulation of nearly 140,000 copies per issue in 1924 while the *Saturday Evening Post* was selling about 90,000 copies of each issue.[36] The only Canadian magazine in English that was equally popular was *Maclean's,* which had a circulation of about 90,000 in 1925.[37] American magazines were therefore dominant in Canada, a fact that created worry among many Canadians about the fate of the nation's culture.[38] Magazine content was largely recreational, either in the form of nonfiction articles, fiction, or "how-to" articles. *Maclean's* ran one hundred short stories in 1925 plus eight "novels or novelettes" by popular fiction writers.[39] All of these magazines, whether Canadian or American, used the same sort of format in which the text was staggered or broken frequently with pictures, cartoons, jokes, and aphorisms.

It is difficult to determine readership of English-language newspapers and magazines in Alberta. In 1925, there were 8,651 subscribers to *Maclean's* scattered through almost every part of the province, although the greatest concentration was in urban areas.[40] During the 1920s, the rural areas were served by both Canadian English-language and foreign magazines and by local and regional newspapers. The large urban dailies published in Edmonton, Calgary, Lethbridge, and Medicine Hat had almost no circulation in the rural areas. On the other hand, the *Farm and Ranch Review* had thirty-two thousand rural subscribers in Alberta in 1926, the highest circulation of any Alberta-produced publication in the province, including the urban daily press.[41] Because readership of a single issue of a magazine would have been higher than that of a single issue of a newspaper, the *Farm and Ranch Review* represented an important force in the Alberta magazine market.

It is even more difficult to determine readership and distribution in Alberta of non-English-language newspapers and magazines published in Alberta or elsewhere. Among those published in Alberta, the most successful were French-language weeklies. In 1898, *L'Ouest canadien,* which had a provincial focus, began publication in Edmonton and was succeeded by other papers such as *La Survivance*, which was published in Edmonton from 1928 to 1967. As its name suggests, the latter was a vehicle for preserving French language and culture in the province. The Edmonton French community, which was the second largest linguistic group in the city before 1916, was served by two weekly papers at the time: *Le Courrier de l'Ouest* (1905-16) and *Le Progrès* (1909-13).[42] Several Ukrainian newspapers were published in Alberta. *Novyny*, the first semi-weekly Ukrainian newspaper in Canada was established in Edmonton in 1913.[43] Other non-English-language newspapers circulating in Alberta during this period included two Icelandic-Canadian papers from Winnipeg, an Estonian paper from New York, and several Ukrainian ones, often of a religious nature, published in Winnipeg. Two German-language papers, one partially funded by the Liberals, the other by the Conservatives, were published in Alberta between 1900 and 1914. It is not clear whether these newspapers delivered votes, provided satisfaction to their readers, or both, but the papers ceased publication because of the war. The federal wartime proscription of newspapers published in "enemy alien" languages eliminated not only German-language newspapers, but also papers published in languages from the Austro-Hungarian Empire, such as Ukrainian. Many of these papers resumed publication after World War I, and new ones, such as a Canadian Hungarian newspaper, were started.[44]

Reading at home was often combined with other activities, especially musical ones. While music had much wider application for leisure than mere home entertainment, an evening made up of reading and music was idealized as the perfect family event. The ambition of creating a family social life that would be didactic and would at the same time reinforce the family as the focus of life was sometimes phrased in terms of applying Ontario standards to the prairies. One homesteader from Ontario argued in 1913 that such an ideal of home life would duplicate in Alberta the "profitable" entertainments said to be enjoyed by rural families in Ontario. With an evening's leisure on the farm made up of reading, music, and other useful intellectual pursuits, "what an inspiration might be given to our young people whose lot, like my own, is on the monotonous prairie, if we amused as well as improved ourselves in this way." Moreover, young women would gain social skills important to marriage, as a man looked for a wife who could do her part in "good conversation and music etc."[45] An increasing amount of this music came via the radio or phonograph during the interwar years, but there often were musical instruments in the home as well. It was claimed that music could provide cheap and satisfying home recreation, especially during prairie winters. Piano sellers claimed that "your wife, children and friends" would, by playing the piano, turn the "dreariness" of winter "into times of great joy."[46] Music in the home also had other benefits. One letter writer to the *Farm and Ranch Review* argued in 1927 that music "should have its place in every home" because there was "no cheaper form of amusement and certainly none so inspiring." If one's children were taught music and were encouraged "to form an orchestra," they would be "popular wherever they go." Music could create family unity and counter the children's instincts to wander: a musical environment would keep the family together at home.[47]

Among the great variety of musical instruments in Alberta homes, pianos, violins, banjos, and accordions were especially popular. People learned to play these instruments by trial and error, or they took formal lessons through personal instruction or by mail. The Edmonton Violin School urged people in 1933 to learn to play the violin the "real way, by mail."[48] Of all instruments, pianos received most public attention, although organs were popular before the 1920s. Among popular pianos were those made by the Heintzman Company, which had a showroom in Calgary by the end of World War I and later established another in Edmonton. Heintzman had targeted the Alberta market as early as 1905 with the claim that their pianos withstood "the climate of Alberta better than other makes."[49] Pianos were expensive to purchase, they had to be maintained professionally, and learning to play classical music well was a long, difficult and expensive process for most people. It would seem that in a pioneer society pianos were important marks of distinction and were perceived as dignified and conventional instruments, and for those whose ethnicity placed them outside the dominant culture, piano lessons and training in classical music in general were sometimes interpreted as a sign of accord with the standards of the dominant culture.[50] For those people who came from cultures with much richer classical musical traditions than the British, music lessons could serve, at one and the same time, as an affirmation of their own cultural standards and an accord with the standards of the dominant culture in Alberta.

Between the world wars, many Albertans had pianos in their

homes. In 1928 one manufacturer alone claimed to have sold more than six thousand pianos in the province.[51] Although demand for pianos in Canada, and doubtless in Alberta, declined in the late 1920s and early 1930s, it picked up by the end of the decade. By 1947 for instance, 40 percent of farm families in the Wetaskiwin area owned pianos.[52] The annual Alberta Music Festivals, modelled on British precedents, encouraged musical training, whether for piano or other instruments. The first was staged in Edmonton in 1908 under the patronage of the lieutenant-governor. It was similar to the festivals the organizers "had known in Scotland and England" and was the first competitive festival in Canada.[53] These annual competitive festivals always concluded with a public concert by the winners, and as the location of the festival changed each year, people throughout the province could attend the concerts at one time or another.[54] The 1927 festival in Calgary was described as "the heart of the musical life of the city." It raised standards, brought out "a wealth of unsuspected talent," and stimulated activity in all musical fields. Moreover, "it . . . taught thousands among the general lay public to take an interest in music, to appreciate good music and to further the spread of its cultural value as a substitute or corrective for some undesirable tendencies in modern civilization."[55] By the mid-1920s, certain conventions had developed at these music festivals. One observer from England noted that at the prize winner's concert, Albertans followed a practice also seen in Australia: "the encore is inevitable, and if the performer is a girl, no matter how youthful, a bouquet is inevitably presented. The custom has become a harmless convention, merely indicative that friends of the performer are present."[56]

Appreciation of music expanded with technological change. Phonographs, invented in 1878, were available, although not common, in Alberta by the mid-1890s. By 1917, electric phonographs could be purchased but were expensive: the Columbia "Grafonola" cost $270 but was "the very height of convenience."[57] Cabinet, table, and portable models were all available, and portable phonographs were advertised as "just the thing for the summer camp."[58] It is not clear, however, whether many people routinely took the "record player" along with them to the lake or on a picnic. Before 1915, records came in either cylinder or disc types. The discs became dominant by 1915 and cylinder types were obsolete by 1920. Before 1910, most disc records were single-sided, but by 1909 Victor was marketing records at 90 cents apiece which had "a different selection on either side of the disc."[59] Albertans did not even have to purchase recordings after 1929 when the University of Alberta Department of Extension began to operate a lending library of recordings of lectures, readings, and some classical music.[60] As phonographs became increasingly popular in Alberta, observers voiced only minor concern about their impact. By "merely turning a handle and starting a tune," one critic protested, one could replace the "home made music which if not so mechanically perfect is after all the most vital to happiness."[61] The phonograph, however, was generally seen as a positive development for the appreciation of music in Alberta, and doubtless it was. It, like the radio, exposed people to very high standards of music, which likely increased general appreciation and, perhaps, musicians' skills.[62]

Just as music and reading were deemed suitable leisure activities for children, and for the whole family, the same was often true about games. The play-spirit in man is perhaps most clearly illustrated in children's random play, with its flexibility, seeming innocence, and inventiveness. Although these qualities have escaped precise historical description, in Alberta, as everywhere else, they were valued as a vital quality of childhood. This did not mean, however, that such play was devoid of social relevance or meaning. Play, it was noted in 1928, was "as legitimate and lovely as any of the finer instincts in life, and that instinct should never be divorced from religion and handed over entirely to the forces of the world."[63] Moreover, a childhood spent in happy play would attach the child to the scene of such happiness, and in the case of farm children, it would keep them at home in later life.[64]

The swing in Earnest Reeves's farm yard in 1927. (PAA B.628)

Stilts gave children a new and exciting view of the world. (PAA A.5917)

Dressing up has been a favourite pastime for years, as shown by this 1917 photograph of the McCalla children at the family farm on Old Man Creek, near Bremner.

More structured play included yard games such as hide 'n seek, red-rover red-rover, various sorts of tag, marbles, skipping, and dressing up as "Indians" and "grown-ups." Many yards also had a swing or other play equipment. Yard games were largely seasonal because of the climate, but children had a greater opportunity to play such games during school summer holidays, which had been extended in 1889 from one month to two.[65] Indoor games for children, such as board games, were relatively limited at the turn of the century, although crokinole and chequers were very popular. Often, a crokinole board had a chequers board on the back. Chequers and crokinole continued to be popular, but the variety of board games had increased by the 1920s. Games such as parcheesi and snakes and ladders were gaining in popularity, and other games such as Monopoly and Scrabble were invented in the next decade. There were also numerous other games; dominoes, for example, were played throughout the period under review, as were a number of card games like snap and old maid.[66] Although these games were most frequently played by children, adults often played crokinole, Scrabble, and chequers as well.

Mr. and Mrs. C.W. Mathers (foreground) enjoyed playing crokinole with their guests. (PAA A.6238)

The great adult passion was for card games like cribbage, bridge, whist, and canasta. Whist was the most popular game and had many devoted players, especially during the 1920s and 1930s.[67] Changes evolved in these card games, and their popularity ebbed and flowed. In 1909, the *Calgary Herald* advised its readers that "a card game which has no bidding is not up to date. They are playing nothing but auction bridge in Great Britain now."[68] To keep up with these fashions, whist was evolving into a bidding game that did away with "the insuperable objection to straight whist, which was that the distribution of the cards settled the score; because no amount of skill would beat aces and kings."[69]

Adults also played outdoor formal games such as croquet and horseshoes, but the yard was more important for those whose hobby was gardening. Gardens were often kept for utilitarian purposes, but gardening was a passion in its own right. As most Albertans lived on farms or in urban detached houses with yards, almost anyone who wished to garden could do so. Gardening was unrestricted by gender and was a pastime beyond reproach because it involved outdoor physical labour. It took much time and attention, especially in Alberta's climate, but this was sometimes seen as only further reason to garden. As was observed in 1933, the difficulty of gardening in Alberta was "one of the reasons we get so much pleasure from it."[70] This attitude perhaps reflected a conscious effort to overcome an unfamiliar and often hostile environment, and was perhaps a throwback to mid-nineteenth century expansionist assumptions that successful cultivation was one proof of the "civilization" of the West and the quality of its land and climate.[71] Further, gardens created beauty and reinforced the place of the home in family life and leisure. A lawn, trees and flowers, as Professor Harcourt of the University of Alberta contended in 1923, made a good environment in which children could play and grow up securely. For Harcourt, a home without a garden was not a "real home—it is only a stopping place."[72] Gardening fulfilled spiritual, moral, and physical needs and enhanced the social objectives of the home and home based leisure, while the rhetoric on gardening was a distant echo of the virtues of farming and all its attributes.[73] Gardening therefore had many public defenders; it was one of only a few leisure activities that escaped concern about its potential for social harm.

Card players at the home of Matt Olson, Calmar, circa 1912. (GAI NA-4171-14)

Alberta gardens displayed a great variety of flower beds by the 1920s. It has been suggested that landscape design in the prairies was determined by a desire to replicate the landscape of eastern Canada or Britain.[74] Many people in Alberta grew, or at least tried to grow, the by then fashionable English perennial border. However, contradicting the notion that all gardeners aimed to recreate "Old England" in their gardens, some interest was expressed in growing and domesticating native plants.[75] Nonetheless, it is apparent that by the 1920s the greatest interest was in dahlias, sweet peas, gladioli, and roses, although other annuals and perennials were widely grown. These plants represented cultural continuity and an effort to remake the prairie landscape in the image of another place. Annora Brown, the Fort Macleod painter, recalled a great yearning for roses among "people from the Old Country."[76] Rose growers in Alberta soon found that the climate was unsympathetic to their passion, but many bush roses were hardy and new varieties were bred in the late 1930s and 1940s, especially in Manitoba. In Alberta, George Bugnet made a significant contribution to rose growing in the prairies through his work with bush roses on his plantation north of Edmonton.[77]

The popularity of gardening was evident from the formation of gardening clubs throughout the province. Edmonton gardeners formed the Edmonton Horticultural and Vacant Lots Garden Association; other towns, such as Camrose and Claresholm, had active horticultural societies during the 1920s and 1930s. In Calgary, a dahlia society was sponsoring an annual show by 1926.[78] Garden fanciers always exhibited their prize flowers, plants, and vegetables at agricultural fairs. Alberta gardeners could obtain seeds from various local and national seed houses. In the late 1920s, Steele Briggs stocked a truly impressive array of seeds, tubers, and bulbs in Edmonton, and in 1938, R. Pike & Company of Edmonton advertised "the finest seeds in the world for this climate."[79]

As a hobby, gardening was somewhat atypical because it was seasonal. Most other hobbies, especially those that can be described as handicrafts, were pursued year-round. It is difficult to define "handicrafts" precisely, especially because of the tendency in the European world to divide such activity into exclusive categories of "art" and "crafts." This was also the case in Alberta in the years before 1945, and sometimes resulted in amusing anomalies. Although nobody could precisely define either "art" or "crafts," everyone knew that quilting was a craft whereas painting, no matter how poorly done, was an art. Annora Brown, who

Mrs. Blyth's carefully planned and colourful garden in Edmonton, 1937. (PAA BL.214.1)

taught painting in Calgary in the early 1920s, observed that the work of amateurs in Calgary consisted of "painting on china and watercolour copies of post cards and of other people's paintings, all carefully paled and deadened to match their fear of colour, form, or any indication of life."[80] Before World War I, even the *Calgary Herald*, despite its usual blanket defence of the West, admitted that Alberta had "very little" in the visual arts.[81] During the 1920s and 1930s, however, various programmes were developed to teach painting and to provide facilities for exhibitions of art: in 1924, the Edmonton Museum of Art (later the Edmonton Art Gallery) was established, by 1927 the Provincial Institute of Technology and Art (now the Alberta College of Art) in Calgary was offering evening painting classes, and in 1931 the Alberta Society of Artists was incorporated. In the late 1930s, H.G. Glyde of the University of Alberta Department of Extension began offering painting classes throughout the province as well as at the Banff School of Fine Arts.[82]

Handicrafts were much more popular than painting, perhaps because they were considered to be utilitarian. Zella Spencer, a regular columnist in *The UFA*, wrote in 1929 that any hobby could preserve mental and physical health and that many people with mental illness "might have a happier interest in life in the form of some hobby, however trivial it might seem to the outsider."[83] Such hobbies as collecting stamps or coins were therefore excellent, but crafts which "quicken the spirit and spur creative activities" were even better.[84] There were demands that crafts be taught in schools and that school fairs be held for the exhibition of such crafts.[85] The crafts movement in Canada gained momentum during the interwar years because handicrafts were also seen as an antidote to industrialization and machine-made goods. But here too, the notion of productive activity was involved: in 1940, the town planner Humphrey Carver claimed that "unless we are to become sickened and decadent from too much entertainment, the new leisure hours must be employed in a creative way." The best way to accomplish this, he argued, was through handicrafts which stimulated creativity and individuality.[86]

In the first quarter of the twentieth century, handicrafts were produced informally to meet needs for clothing, linens, decorative objects, bedding, and rugs, among other things. These were frequently described as "fancy work" and fair prize lists provide good examples of what crafts were practiced. Most handicrafts shared certain characteristics in that they were almost always needlework, were integral to household needs, were utilitarian, and were undertaken by women. The only major exception was woodcarving by men. It must however be noted that while these products were useful, they were often crafted to a much higher standard than was necessary for simple utility. Handmade lace, finely tatted pillows, and embroidered linen would have been used only for special occasions, if at all, or would have been presented as a gift.

After the mid-1920s, other crafts, such as leatherwork, weaving, and basket making gained in popularity. By the early 1930s, new directions in handicrafts were confirmed or stimulated by the activities of organizations such as the Women's Institute, the Department of Extension, and the Canadian Handicrafts Guild. In 1933, the provincial boards of the Canadian Handicrafts Guild and the Alberta Women's Institute sponsored a handicraft exhibition at the University of Alberta. The 250 entries presented strong indication of the great interest in handicrafts in the province. The show included needlework, basketry, leatherwork, and a few pieces of iron work.[87] By this time, there were branches of the Canadian Handicrafts Guild operating in Medicine Hat, Calgary, and Edmonton. These clubs had little contact with each other; George Hoadley, Alberta's minister of agriculture, unfairly characterized them as social clubs that were "just...a meeting and tea drinking proposition."[88] In 1935, with money provided by the Carnegie Foundation, the Alberta Guild of Handicrafts circulated an exhibition of Alberta crafts to twenty-eight communities in Alberta. The exhibition travelled by truck, which set out at the end of January. It included "samples of weaving in wool and rags, a display of raw materials and another on how silk, cotton and wool were manufactured." In terms of the handicrafts themselves, "lace, embroidery, tie and dye pieces, batik, petit point, [and] crochet were represented, earthenware, from local clay, china hand-decorated, pierced and hammered brass and copper, tooled leather, forging, machine articles, woodwork, reeds and raffia, hand made tools, wood carvings etc. were included." All of the pieces had been made in Alberta by Alberta craftspeople, primarily those located in Calgary, Edmonton, and Fort Macleod.[89]

The 1935 tour was important because it stimulated new interest in crafts. Moreover, many people already working in crafts gained confidence in their work and their commitment deepened. Craft programmes sponsored by the University of Alberta and the Handicrafts Guild subsequently fostered this development. The crafts movement was somewhat curtailed by the war, but it was back in full swing by 1946. In the immediate postwar period, the most popular handicrafts were various needlework crafts, weaving, and ceramics. Most were home-based activities and they increasingly gained public attention through exhibitions, which legitimized them as an activity and provided comparative samples and ideas for further developments in the field. The crafts movement was in many respects a reaction to the uniformity and commonness of mass-produced goods, but it must also have been an affirmation of many traditions and folk arts. Crafts provided continuity and connected the individual artisan, who worked at home, with the broader society.

The linkage among home, society, and cultural tradition was particularly clear in the celebration of special events such as holidays. Of these, Christmas was among the most important. It not only had strong private and family orientations, but its celebration was also public in that it was a statutory holiday, was observed by a majority of Albertans, and included a variety of public events and activities. The Christmas concert was a standard feature of Christmas celebrations. In the early years of the century, these con-

At one Santa Claus parade, Santa Claus and his helpers greeted Calgarians from a covered wagon decorated with toys. (GAI NA-3992-51)

certs were often called "Christmas Trees" and were put on by children associated with schools, churches, and community groups. The concerts were similar to amateur variety shows in format and included skits, plays, songs, dances, and recitations on Christmas themes. The concert also always included an appearance by Santa Claus. Santa was reported in one case to "be in an affectionate mood, as he wished to kiss the young ladies,"[90] but his usual function was to distribute gifts to the children. At most concerts during the twentieth century, all children received gifts. In the late nineteenth century, however, gift-giving had not been so automatic: at the Edmonton Methodist Sunday School Christmas concert in 1888, gifts were not given randomly but as part of a rewards system. Santa tried "to award the presents as far as possible according to regularity of attendance, attention and progress."[91] These concerts were usually held in churches or schools. In the typical school, a raised teaching platform at the front of the room was converted into a stage. The room was decorated with seasonal pictures and, of course, a Christmas tree. Concerts were commonly followed by dances.[92]

Concerts were significant in the public celebration of Christmas, but the private, home events were more important. These involved visiting with family and friends, house parties, family outings to church, sports meets, and games. By the late 1930s, listening to special Christmas radio broadcasts had become part of the festivities. Social aspects of the season also included the exchange of Christmas cards, which had come into wide use by the late nineteenth century. Many of these cards depicted Christmas scenes, others illustrated local landmarks or places. In 1896, C.W. Mathers, the Edmonton photographer, produced a series of Christmas cards with "views of the old time modes of travel, dog trains, Red River carts and birch bark canoes. . .views of Edmonton, South Edmonton, Fort Saskatchewan and St. Albert. . .[and] a selection of views of farms." At between twenty-five and fifty cents each, however, these cards were too expensive for most people.[93]

One enduring focus of Christmas was the Christmas dinner, deeply influenced by tradition and religion. Many Ukrainians who celebrated Christmas according to the Julian calendar preserved their tradition of a meatless meal of twelve dishes on Christmas Eve. Norwegians also had a Christmas Eve celebration in which the children held hands and circled the Christmas tree singing carols. The evening often ended with coffee, fruit, and lefse (an unleavened flour and potato bread). As one further example, one

A Lutheran Church Christmas play, circa 1910. (PAA B.9995)

aspect of Polish celebration of the Christmas season in the Crowsnest Pass was the mounting of traditional Christmas plays.[94] The traditional holiday fare of English-speaking people was chicken, goose, or turkey, and mince pie and plum pudding.[95] Over time, these different traditions often mixed into a unique blend intrinsic to the season. One new tradition, eating Japanese oranges, engendered public hostility during World War II when boycotting Japanese oranges became associated with the war effort.[96]

The most important part of Christmas, however, centred on the Christmas tree and the exchange of gifts. A tree was commonly put up in the home and decorated. Trees were often cut on public land, and in urban areas the cutting of trees in parks and in the river valleys was a continual problem. In 1924, it was noted that trees around the country club in Calgary were cut down and left on the ground "because the vandal saw or thought he saw a better tree still standing."[97] Trees were decorated with traditional ornaments and ribbons and, by the 1920s, with electric tree lights. Presents were often hung in the tree, an indication of the modesty of the gifts. In 1908 people in Red Deer were urged to consider books, handkerchiefs, collars, belts, scarves, combs, and ribbons as Christmas gifts.[98] Handicrafts were also acceptable and desirable gifts. Children received toys, candy, skates, and dolls, as, for once, utilitarianism was eschewed. In 1911, H.G. Wells had argued that children's toys should be more educational and oriented to the realities of industrial life. This suggestion was roundly condemned by the *Calgary Herald*, which contended that children wanted "flights of imagination. . .they do not want to discuss gravity water systems."[99] Such a denial of utility was a significant measure of the specialness and uniqueness of Christmas.

The role of the home and family in leisure was shaped by a number of different and sometimes conflicting factors. It was logical and even inevitable that the home would be the centre of the family's leisure activities. Many farm people, because of isolation due to impassable roads or remoteness from neighbours or family, were forced to rely upon themselves and their home environment for leisure. The home was an important focus for leisure for all people simply because very few could afford commercial recreation all of the time; nor, it would seem, did they want it— they needed time and activities that were private and theirs alone. On the other hand, people were subjected to immense pressure to conform to certain ideals of home life, in which the home serv-

Paper chains and a decorated tree brought Christmas cheer to the William Wigg home in Lewisville, circa 1900. (GAI NA-2449-14)

Christmas was a family affair for the Bergers in 1944. (PAA BL.846)

ed as the centre for positive reinforcement of socially acceptable behaviour. In this vein, the idealization of leisure in terms of social utility and work became integrated into the home and the activities that took place there. Handicrafts and gardening were utilitarian activities that satisfied a work-defined leisure and also responded to the individual's innate aesthetic sense and need for beauty. Music also responded to aesthetic needs, although arguments about recreation as re-creation incorporated aesthetics into their schema. Respectability was a part of the picture as well: music in certain forms was a respectable activity for the middle class.

Leisure in the home was integrated with concerns about childhood and the formation of character. As the home was thought to be a primary force in character formation, and because it was an important focus for childhood, children's leisure was always an important element in home life and was often sharply differentiated from adult leisure. Children's games were different from adult games, but as they were played at home, they were commonly a part of family life which, to some extent, led to an integration of generations. Above all, the home was a highly personal structure in which people could entertain themselves and each other in an easy, unaffected manner. People read, played games, played musical instruments, and listened to the radio and phonograph. A great number of special events not discussed here were also important. Weddings, family reunions, and funerals were occasions for the gathering of family, friends, and neighbours and were often characterized by visiting, eating, dancing, and drinking. The family was an important institution in the ordering of daily life, but its importance extended beyond the mere disciplining of its members and the enforcement of certain standards of behaviour. While the home was a focus for leisure and socialization, in the case of non-English-speaking people, it was also a place of resistance to the dominant culture. It was the mainstay for language retention and a place where traditions could be preserved or modified to suit new cultural and personal needs. This aspect of home life is nearly impossible to deal with historically since studies of ethnicity in Alberta have tended, quite naturally, to focus upon the community rather than the home. It is clear, however, that agents of the dominant culture recognized the home as a source of resistance and attempted to break down this resistance through public institutions such as the school.

Overall, the home increasingly lost autonomy and relied more and more upon public agencies and the mass media for inspiration. In many ways, the home had always acted as a bridge between public and private culture and had cushioned and transformed many of the public forces that operated in leisure. This tendency was confirmed during the interwar years by the increased use of private transportation and by movies, both of which further eroded the isolation of the home. The view that the home was under attack was bolstered by these encroachments upon its isolation and authority over the individual. This not only created an ongoing crisis for those who saw this as a sign of the collapse of the home as a social institution, but it also confirmed attempts to restrict and control public forms of leisure in order to protect an institution that, in reality, was not entirely isolated in the first place.

3. Leisure and the Community

Churches, schools, fraternal clubs, and other community institutions were important agencies in leisure because their wide range of activities and formats met a broad range of recreational needs. Some people were concerned that these institutions threatened the home as the primary social focus of individual lives. However, it is evident that such organizations represented not a challenge to the values of the home but a reinforcement of home and family life. These external recreational agencies can be grouped in five broad categories: religious institutions; organizations for children and adolescents such as the Canadian Girls in Training and the Boy Scouts; community-oriented organizations such as the Young Men's Christian Association, Young Women's Christian Association, community leagues, and playgrounds; public bodies such as educational institutions; and private agencies such as fraternal organizations and clubs. Many of these agencies were interrelated, and many sported overlapping objectives and memberships. Some had more far-reaching objectives than others, with interests varying from the purely local to provincial, regional, or national affiliations.

All of these institutions provided leisure opportunities for their members and sometimes for others as well. They operated within a frame of reference that brought like-minded people or people of similar background or class together. This was especially significant in Alberta where society was often deeply divided by ethnic, religious, locational, occupational, and other forces. Most institutions that had a provincial focus and province-wide organization represented or were controlled by the dominant culture. This played an important part in defining the dominant culture as the legitimate spokesman for provincial interests. This hegemony was countered, to a degree, by institutions, including some churches, which lay outside the dominant culture. To see the problem merely in terms of dominance and resistance, however, is to miss the process of change that took place, both in the institutions of the dominant culture and the rest of the society. The cultures of the province were modified through these institutions and the social realities that they represented. Certain institutions provided a focus for resistance and cultural preservation, but they also provided a mechanism through which change could be filtered and accommodated in response to particular needs. This process in many cases operated through leisure and entertainment activities.

Among the primary institutions in the province were the churches. They provided leisure time indirectly as some church holidays freed people from work. More directly, many churches provided facilities and organized recreational events for their members, often through church clubs, such as reading clubs in the Greek rite churches, and the women's clubs associated with every church. At the same time, churches were not overtly recreational agencies. Theoretically, they did not exist to entertain their members or to serve their social needs. For English-speaking Protestants, this seems to have been an especially pointed issue, perhaps because the preservation of their culture, in ethnic terms, was never as closely linked to the church as it was for others. Edmonton Presbyterians were told in 1884 that "a church was for the purpose of cultivating piety. It was not a literary, or metaphysical, or scientific society, but was a society instituted for the purpose of leading men to Jesus Christ."[1]

This was the hard line in an old debate which had sometimes been bitterly contested in the Protestant churches of nineteenth century Britain. The British nonconformist churches had often rejected all pleasures except for those in service to the soul. By the late nineteenth century this stance had crumbled and they began to employ secular leisure activities in order to hold their congregations, win new converts, and raise funds. Consequently, they accepted leisure, but in doing so they attempted to "elevate its objectives" to improve character and morality.[2] Protestant churchmen in Britain, who also accepted the proposition that physical activity, especially sports, could instill moral qualities, had by the late nineteenth century incorporated team sports into a conception of life that made the wise use of physical strength and intelligence a religious expression.[3]

These ideas influenced the English-speaking Protestant churches in Alberta where Methodists, Presbyterians, and Anglicans in particular used leisure to reinforce congregational unity, raise money for the church, and prevent people from being drawn into leisure pastimes that threatened their morality. Various churches in Edmonton operated sports leagues in the 1920s and such leisure was indirectly used to support these churches; participation in church league games, theoretically, was allowed only for those who had attended church service or Sunday School.[4] Similarly, Methodists attending a missionary convention in Calgary in 1903 were told that "spiritual life" could be promoted through recreation and the integration of the church with the community and its standards. In the tradition of "muscular Christianity," ministers were advised to be "men among men, getting into close touch with the life of the community and showing themselves manly at all times, [and] avoiding namby-pamby notions." Leisure was central in this social integration, for "social means too, should be used to counteract evil. In this connection it was best to pursue a policy of substitution rather than prohibition."[5] It seems, however, that this approach was more common on the prairies than in some other parts of Canada. In 1903, the "Calgary correspondent" of the *St. John Globe*, reporting on customs in the "wild and wooly west," humourously asked, "are you horrified beyond all recovery, my dear St. John people, at the idea of a dance as a finish to a church supper? It is quite the custom in the west, they tell me." And a good thing it was, he argued, for the young loved to dance and it made the old feel young again to hear the music and watch the dancing.[6]

Even so, the place of entertainment in the church, especially as a means of raising funds, was a contentious issue. The Roman Catholic church routinely used bingo games to raise money, but this seems to have occasioned little comment within the church. In the Protestant churches, fund raising and entertainment sometimes occasioned debate. The Anglican church seems to have harboured strong reservations, and in 1909 Bishop Newham told the Saskatchewan Diocese that he deplored such practices because they raised money by "exciting rivalry which was not the proper spirit in which a gift should be made." These practices, and the surrounding debate, did not disappear; in 1922 Bishop Pinkham observed in Calgary that the churches were resorting more and more frequently to "questionable or irregular methods of raising money for church purposes. Constantly we hear of whist drives, socials, raffles, guessing contests, dancing and other forms of amusement. . . for the express purpose of obtaining funds." But, as Archdeacon Hayes reminded the bishop, the objective of these entertainments was not only to raise money but also "to create a wholesome supervised atmosphere of sociability for the young" that would be "safe from questionable pleasures."[7] It was a frank admission that entertainment had become one of the primary means of combatting perceived social evils and of ministering to young people.

This justification of entertainment also resulted from a fundamental problem faced by almost all churches in the province: there were too many of them competing for adherents and there was, in some areas, a high measure of apathy towards the church. Churches in the Vulcan area, for example, continually complained of a population that was generally uninterested in attending church.[8] Yet because all churches in Alberta had always been voluntary, insufficient financial support was a continuing problem. Because of ethnic and sectarian divisions, an overabundance of churches served some communities. In 1921, Calgary had a population of about sixty-three thousand that supported 134 churches, representing fifty-seven different denominations and sects. Financing these institutions through local or external contributions was not easy and many churches continually faced penury.[9] This further reinforced the use of entertainment to raise funds and hold adherents.

Children and adults alike enjoyed the Sunday School picnic at Three Hills in 1916. (PAA A.4324)

The debate over the place of recreation in the church was probably shared by all Protestant churches serving the dominant culture. However, for many of the churches standing outside the dominant culture, a more powerful stimulus for the incorporation of leisure activities into church functions arose from the desire to retain ethnic values. The Dutch Reformed church played an important role in cultural retention among Dutch settlers in Alberta, and although the Dutch tended to assimilate quickly, the church provided a cultural focus to preserve Dutch cultural identity.[10] The Lutheran churches did likewise. By 1902, Swedish Lutherans in Calgary had their own church and received services from an itinerant Swedish minister based in Wetaskiwin. They raised funds by putting on a social featuring music, speeches, and recitations. Although Swedes had no objection to learning English, "they liked to worship their God in Swedish, the most beautiful language in the world."[11] The Lutheran church played a similar role in the Danish community at Dixon.[12] Schismatic tendencies often weakened this role in other non-English-speaking Protestant churches. The Lutheran Icelandic community at Markerville was deeply divided by philosophical differences, and the church played a lesser part in preserving Icelandic traditions than did secular agencies. As the latter too were riven with dissension, the retention of the Icelandic language and traditions in the area seems to have been more a matter of isolation than of institutional intervention.[13]

The Roman Catholic church's role in cultural life varied because of the range of ethnic groups represented among its adherents. It played an important role in the preservation of French Canadian values in some communities and in the early French-language press.[14] Polish priests were crucial to maintaining Polish cultural life in Alberta although their influence was often complemented by the work of lay cultural organizations.[15] In more general terms, a Catholic cultural focus combined with leisure through organizations such as the Knights of Columbus, a men's club. The Knights of Columbus were incorporated in 1882 in the United States and in 1913 in Alberta; by 1932 they had two thousand members in Alberta.[16] The Knights of Columbus acted as a lay religious organization and raised funds for the church by sponsoring events such as bingos and socials, but they were also a fraternal club for Roman Catholics. By 1924 they had a clubhouse in Edmonton,[17] and in 1939 the Calgary Knights of Columbus opened a clubhouse for servicemen in the parish hall. Servicemen could attend movies, concerts, and dances; between 1939 and 1946 over 250,000 members of the armed forces attended these functions.[18]

The churches of the Greek rite also played an important cultural role in their communities. One notable organization in Ukrainian communities was the reading club, which had been widespread in the Ukraine in the late nineteenth century as a forum for teaching literacy and national culture.[19] In the Ukraine it had been a quasi-secular agency, but in Canada it often had strong church connections. A visiting Greek Catholic priest established a reading club at Edna-Star in 1898, and in subsequent years many more reading clubs were established in east central Alberta by both

Greek Catholic and Orthodox communities. However, because of a shortage of priests in the area, many of the clubs were established by lay people. In the earliest years of settlement, the reading clubs often included people of all shades of political opinion, but by about 1905 many of these organizations began to be specifically identified in political terms.[20] The fundamental religious divisions in the Ukrainian community were accentuated in 1918 when the Ukrainian Greek Orthodox Church of Canada was established. The development of clubs specifically oriented in religious or, increasingly, in political terms was a result of the complexity of Ukrainian society in Alberta, and suggests one reason for the lack of unity in the Ukrainian community.

Of all the church-related clubs in the province, the commonest were women's clubs. Women's clubs were associated with nearly all churches in the province and played an important role in their members' leisure activities, although they were often officially justified and legitimized by their fund-raising function or as a focus for volunteer labour for the church. In the Roman Catholic church, organizations such as the Catholic Women's League carried out charity work, operated a summer camp for children, and raised money for the church.[21] Women's clubs were prominent in Protestant churches; indeed, it appears that few clubs were organized for adult males. At club meetings, women got together to "have a social time and sew or knit, or make quilts" which were sold or auctioned at a church event.[22] The format of the meetings of the United Church Ladies' Aid in Clover Bar from 1935-45 seems to have been typical. The women met once a month and their meetings involved a few hymns, prayers, and a discussion of business. The latter usually concerned planning the next fund-raising event and deciding how to spend club money on the church or on people in need. Tea and visiting followed. When an organization put on a "chicken supper" as the annual fund-raiser, leisure and utility were again served by the same event.[23] Another popular event often sponsored by women's church groups was an annual picnic. A 1937 description of such a picnic indicates its importance as a community event:

> During the summer, the Ladies' Aid holds its annual picnic... with baseball, races and games. There is a refreshment booth on the grounds where candy, gum, oranges, lemonade and ice cream are sold. The picnickers bring their suppers, which are spread out on

big white tablecloths on the grass, and there is always food...to spare for the bachelors.[24]

Women's organizations were also common among non-Christian groups. By 1914, Jewish women had organized the Lady Zionists Club of Edmonton. At the beginning, the club seems to have been a social and benevolent organization. It had regular meetings at which members drank tea, played whist, sewed, and listened to readings. Money was raised through membership dues, teas, and occasional social evenings for members and their husbands. During the early 1920s, religious and cultural objectives became more important. Meetings now opened with the playing or singing of Hatikvah, and the club became affiliated with the national Hadassah movement. Political concerns had become central, and the club was frequently addressed by visiting Zionists, such as Rabbi Eisen who spoke to the club in 1937 about conditions in Palestine.[25]

Leisure was most often integrated with church activities through affiliated clubs, which were used to reinforce both congregational and ethnic unity. Churches also provided leisure opportunities more directly; indeed, it has been said that in Calgary during the 1880s, "attendance at church was a relief for many people because there was little to break the monotony of pioneer life."[26] The church provided additional leisure opportunities in the form of lectures, demonstrations, and talks by visiting personalities. Many lectures were held in churches during and following the 1890s, although their popularity declined by World War II. They often involved descriptions and recollections of missionary work or travels to foreign lands. In 1925, for example, Dr. Somerfel of the Overseas League of Norway toured western Canada. While investigating Canada as a field for Norwegian immigration, he also gave lectures and showed lantern slides of Norway. These lectures were sponsored by Lutheran churches, which charged admission to help meet his expenses.[27]

Events and organizations that held the church together and entertained its members were frequently required simply to raise money. The problem of funding was one reason for the growth of cooperation between the Methodists and Presbyterians in the West. It was the West that produced the driving force in the movement that culminated in church union in 1925 and the establishment of the United Church of Canada. The early cooperation often involved leisure activities where denominational differences could be resolved and minimized. As early as 1896, Presbyterian, Methodist, and Baptist Young People's Societies in Edmonton were holding "union socials."[28] These opportunities were largely for young people, and although denominational clubs for youths were a common feature of many churches, several clubs were interdenominational. One of the most important of these was the Canadian Girls in Training, or CGIT.

The CGIT evolved from a growing belief among North American Protestants that the religious training of youths needed reform to reflect "modern educational principles and a more liberal theology." This aim was directed by the idea that adolescence was a particularly impressionable and turbulent time of life.[29] These perceptions led to the formation of youth clubs in which adolescents could receive Christian teaching through a young peoples' programme that stressed a mixture of didacticism and entertainment. The CGIT became active in Alberta in about 1919 through the combined efforts of the Young Women's Christian Association and the Anglican, Baptist, Congregationalist, Methodist, and Presbyterian churches. Some interdenominational Protestant church girls' organizations had existed prior to 1920, but the CGIT marked the true beginning of a directed and consistent effort to provide a "church centered programme for teen-age girls."[30] From the beginning, each CGIT girl received an official costume consisting of a "white middy, dark skirt and black tie," which "remained basically the same except for fluctuations in skirt levels and middy styles." Age distinctions were recognized by the creation of different groups within the organization, such as "Chevron" groups for older girls. The purpose of the CGIT programme was to provide "four fold development of the girl—physical, mental, spiritual and social."[31] Time was spent on Bible study, but recreational activities were also important. This approach endorsed the view that leisure, as a necessary element in life, should be given purpose and social utility through reference to wider objectives. The members met on a regular basis to study and hold discussions, play games, mount plays, or work at crafts. The CGIT also ran a highly successful summer camp programme.

All of these activities were coordinated by a central office known initially as The Girls' Work Board and later as the Alberta CGIT Association. This office distributed materials to CGIT groups, organized camps, published a newsletter, and helped local groups to plan programmes, organize events, and maintain the vigour of the association. It was financially supported by the churches, by periodic government grants and, later, by Community Chest funds. The CGIT itself, however, was largely self-supporting. Accordingly, local CGIT groups were required to raise their own funds. Fund raising was not, however, just crude solicitation of money from the public; "money raising activities" combined fun with lessons in self-reliance, usefulness, and play. CGIT groups put on pancake suppers and theme teas, such as a "Chinese or any other nationality tea," operated hot dog stands at the rink, and put on bazaars at which handicrafts and baking were sold.[32]

CGIT was a large organization, continuing after 1920 to play an important social and recreational role in the lives of Protestant girls in Alberta. CGIT drew its members mainly from girls aged between twelve and eighteen. In 1921, CGIT groups in Alberta boasted a total enrollment of 4,000 across 60 centres outside Calgary and Edmonton. By 1933, the membership had grown to 4,222 and groups could be found in 126 different towns and cities in Alberta. While membership declined after World War II, CGIT remained significant; more than 10 percent of all urban and non-farm rural girls, aged twelve to eighteen, belonged to the organization in 1947.[33] However, CGIT was beginning to lose its appeal for some. By 1954, it had

> become increasingly difficult to hold the interest of senior girls due, in part, to the tremendous upsurge of secular club activities for the teen-ager(s). New program approaches. . .have helped, but the problem of how best to reach and hold the Senior girl within the church remains a challenge.[34]

While CGIT was linked directly to the church and various social agencies, other organizations for children and adolescents were more independent, notably the Boy Scouts. The Boy Scout movement was established by Robert Baden-Powell in England in 1908, and within two years it had spread to North America. The Boy Scouts represented a confirmation of masculinity, physical and moral development, and respect for the law, and through emphasis on these qualities, it attempted to shape boys into productive citizens. In the United States, the movement was justified on the grounds that it emphasized wilderness and outdoor activity and served to counter the limits of urban life. Further, it was a response to the immigration of non-Anglo-Saxons, juvenile delinquency, a lack of exercise and wholesome adventure for urban boys, and the view that masculinity was threatened by prolonged schooling which left boys under maternal control for too long. The solution lay in the creation of boys' clubs, where boys could belong to a "gang" that was not morally debilitating and provided exercise and challenge within an environment devoid of women and their influences.[35]

Wilderness and outdoor activity were emphasized by the Boy Scout movement. Here a Cub Scout enjoys the surroundings at the Winterburn Camp in 1932. (PAA A.9536)

These objectives were well received in Alberta. An editorial in the *Calgary Herald* in 1912 held that boys were "gregarious animals" who formed gangs, and "the good gang of Boy Scouts more than offsets the bad gangs that gather on street corners." Idleness led to delinquency because boys were by nature adventurous and full of energy. "The Scout movement directs that activity, enlists the loyalty of the individual to the gang, [and] controls and directs it all into proper channels," said Boy Scout supporters, yet it preserved a boy's "inborn love of adventure." In sum, the "best there is in the boy is appealed to and enlisted in wholesome, elevating activities."[36] The Boy Scouts sought to channel this energy through highly structured activities such as hobbies and crafts, camping, and community work. A core component of many of these activities was the awarding of badges for passing tests. A scout was tested in such activities or tasks as athletic exercises, knot tying, learning to cut his nails, clean his teeth and "breathe through his nose," and knowing the composition of the Union Jack. Ideally, all of this took place in "nature," in a scout "hut" (preferably built of logs), and was surrounded with ritual and symbolic acts, some of which were apparently invented by local Scoutmasters.[37] The outdoor location was important: "nature" was teacher, healer, and inspiration, and according to Baden-Powell, it would prepare Canadian boys "physically and mentally to defend their empire in time of peril."[38] The aim was to instill in each boy a range of platitudinous virtues including thrift, courteousness, cheerfulness, health, and loyalty "to his King, his officers, his parents, his country and his employers."[39]

The Boy Scouts promoted an image of boyhood and nascent masculine character redolent of late nineteenth century juvenile adventure stories. Many Albertans confirmed, indeed even applauded and entrenched, such views. It was still part of the collective memory in Red Deer a decade after the local Boy Scout troop had "won fame for itself in June, 1911, for its detection of Kelly, who had shot Chief of Police Bell."[40] If it was a step at all, it was a small one to the trenches of Europe where true adventure, and very real death, awaited. Yet the horror of the war and the patriotism shown by former Boy Scouts in volunteering for the front became a justification for the organization because, while the Boy Scout movement did not aim to make "the youth of the land into soldiers," it did teach them that "a citizen must 'be prepared' to take his fair share among his fellows in the defence of the homeland against aggression." It was easy and inflammatory rhetoric, reinforced with promises of social and economic success, for "one of the greatest tributes" of the Boy Scout movement was "the continual demand of public and private institutions, business men and others for the services of boys who are and were scouts."[41]

Boy Scout troops had been formed in Alberta in the years before 1914, but World War I decimated the movement's leadership. The postwar years presented a challenge to rebuild the organization.

Although some criticism was expressed by labour groups and the UFA of the Boy Scout movement and its quasi-military ethos and the "false national and imperialistic patriotism" it fostered,[42] the movement met little real opposition, let alone from the UFA government in Edmonton. The Kiwanis Club of Calgary provided some money and support for the movement, and during the 1920s the Scout leadership expended a good deal of effort in attempts to obtain government grants. They were singularly successful in this endeavour, and received $1,200 in 1923-24 and $1,000 in each of 1928-29 and 1929-30 to organize new troops.[43] As a consequence of aggressive recruitment, there were 6,200 scouts and cubs in Alberta by 1927.[44] While membership dropped during World War II, it had regained its prewar levels by 1947.[45]

A majority of Boy Scouts were Anglo-Saxon and Protestant, although the Boy Scout leadership often spoke about the movement as a multi-ethnic and interdenominational organization. Committees organized to support the movement certainly did not indicate an ethnic mix: in Calgary, the committee included R. B. Bennett, and in Edmonton it was made up of the leaders of the local business community.[46] On a designated Sunday of each year in many small towns, the Boy Scouts paraded to church, usually the Anglican or United Church of Canada. Nevertheless, the Boy Scouts did see part of their task as the recruitment of the "foreign born element" in order to "try and imbue them with the ideals of British citizenship"; and it was this argument that convinced Premier Herbert Greenfield to approve a grant for the organization in 1923.[47] The Boy Scouts, as could be expected, were true to their word. In 1924, the executive officer of the provincial organization travelled throughout rural Alberta giving talks on "Honour and Loyalty." He held thirty meetings in "foreign settlements and ten troops were established in these districts with an average of thirty boys enrolled in each."[48] Such recruitment of targeted groups continued through the 1920s. In 1929, the social objectives of scouting were expanded when the UFA resolved that all UFA locals "take up Boy Scout work as a means of keeping boys on the farm."[49]

The Boy Scouts and CGIT, among other groups, were established in Alberta because of a perceived need for special organizations in which children and youths could participate in age-specific activities in a group setting and through which the values of the dominant culture could be reinforced. Their purposes were closely related to wider social concerns about childhood, order, and the use of leisure to reinforce the status quo, not incidentally but consciously, in both rhetoric and programmes. Their objectives were publicly recognized and applauded; in 1941, the Calgary Council on Child and Family Welfare praised CGIT, Boy Scouts, and Girl Guides as agencies that "help to encourage tolerance and good sportsmanship and Christian ideals," and it urged all adults to encourage the boys and girls entrusted to their care to join one of these groups.[50]

Many of the same objectives were pursued by the Young Men's Christian Association (YMCA) and the Young Women's Christian Association (YWCA). The YMCA had developed in the United States in the 1850s, and by 1900 it had become a large and sophisticated agency that aimed to provide a Christian framework for boys and young men. Many of the assumptions about youthful character that underpinned the Boy Scout and CGIT movements were also part of the rationale for the YMCA, which attempted to provide youths with an antidote to the drawbacks of an urban industrial life. The YMCA was an urban phenomenon; in Alberta, it operated in the largest urban centres, where it served as a focus of leisure activity for boys and young men by providing facilities and training in sports, crafts, and camping.

The YMCA was closely associated with other young men's Christian clubs. The YMCA in Edmonton grew out of a boys' club, the Edmonton Young Men's Institute, which had strong Protestant connections and had been established in 1899 under the patronage of the Edmonton elite, including J.A. McDougall. The institute was located in a downtown building and had a gymnasium as well as a games and reading room. Essentially, it was a private club to which new members were admitted by the vote of the membership committee. The institute provided a range of sports, lectures, and debates, and a place for members to socialize. It closed in 1904, but the feasibility of establishing a YMCA in Edmonton was already under consideration. By 1907, funds had been subscribed, land had been purchased, and a secretary had been hired. The building was formally opened early in 1908.[51] The development of the YMCA that opened in Calgary in 1909 was similar to the pattern seen in Edmonton.[52] A YMCA was also in operation in Lethbridge before World War I.

The relationship with the English-speaking Protestant churches continued to play an important part in the operation of the YMCA in Alberta. Various agencies, especially in the English-speaking

Protestant churches or church associated clubs, worked with urban boys as part of a broadly conceived social work programme after 1914. When the Boys' Work Board of Alberta was established in 1920, it joined forces with the YMCA in its work with boys.[53] The Boys' Work Board provided assistance to local groups and associations in their activities and directly promoted some of its own objectives. In 1927, for example, the board sponsored "the Boys' Parliament, leadership and district summer camps, athletic contests, boys' conference, the elections for the Boys' Parliament, Bible Study examinations. . . [and] Father and Son activities." The board also worked with Trail Rangers and Tuxis, which participated in the Boys' Parliament and operated summer camps. These boys' organizations were often directly affiliated with various Protestant congregations, usually those of the United Church or its predecessors, and served as the male counterpart of CGIT. In 1927, there were 3,400 Tuxis Boys and Trail Rangers in Alberta, all operating under the general umbrella of the Alberta Boys' Work Board.[54] By 1935, the YMCA was providing volunteer help and secretarial services for these groups. This united approach resulted in coordination among various churches, social agencies, and the YMCA in the operation of summer camps and often in the mounting of special events. The YMCA became an important part of city life in Edmonton, Calgary and Lethbridge. It provided training, encouragement, and facilities for many sports, and it was one of the formative and central institutions in amateur sports in the city. It taught crafts, established hobby clubs, ran summer camps for boys, conducted a wide range of social work, and later supported the youth hostel movement in Alberta.[55]

The "Y" was built on a belief in the need for a special and meaningful personalized environment in the face of an urban society that seemed indifferent and uncaring. The YMCA promised sociability, structure, and the development of skills through hobbies, pastimes, and sports. In the minds of the YMCA leaders, it was crucial that all of this activity be "permeated with the spirit of good sportsmanship, [and] fair play," so that the boys and young men would be inspired "to a higher realization of the values to be found in the study of Art, Music, Nature and Poetry." In this way, boys and young men could be "brought into a further realization of the Life Abundant." All of this rested on the premise that formal, institutional structures effectively promoted sociability and good character. "Give a boy the chance of meeting in some club, no matter how unpretentious, and he is happy," wrote one observer in 1937. "Add to this a balanced direction of his energies in hobbies and sports which he delights in and much of the problem of juvenile delinquency is solved." The "Y" attempted to direct leisure into channels that built strength of character, for "health, friendship, recreation and purposeful living are necessary for the building of Christian personality and a Christian society."[56] In keeping with these social obligations, the YMCA was also active during the 1930s in assisting the victims of the Depression. The Edmonton YMCA gave unemployed young men special attention,[57] and the Calgary YMCA provided them with vocational guidance and physical education, with an emphasis on "profitable study in preparation for the time when they may be able to find work."[58] Five hundred men had made use of these free programmes by 1937.[59]

For a number of years before World War II, the "Y" had responded to particular needs through organizations such as the Hi-Y, a club that drew its members from students at city high schools. The Hi-Y put on films, dances, and concerts with the objective of promoting "high standards of Christian character."[60] It was significant that the Hi-Y drew its social context from the existing social framework of the high school. The old city-centred "Y" was still the primary unit in the YMCA, but it was becoming clear that the YMCA had to compete with the high schools and their internal social network. The "Y" saw the Hi-Y as a means of penetrating this new social environment. As a consequence of the social upheaval following the war, the YMCA established additional branches throughout Edmonton and Calgary and expanded its services by establishing new clubs such as "So-Ed," a coeducational entertainment club, the Edmon-Teen Club, and the Phalanx Fellowship. The two latter clubs were intended to promote "an improved social order and. . .the establishment of a just and durable peace."[61] In 1944 it was noted that:

> It is common knowledge that the war and its accompanying social changes have rendered the juvenile problem infinitely more complex and acute than it is in normal times. There are more opportunities for a young person to establish himself or herself upon an improper basis in the social structure.
> The Edmon-Teen Clubs do not aim to correct this tendency by overdoses of moral precepts, but simply by providing healthy and interesting and useful things for young people to do.[62]

The war and the changes it brought were clearly a challenge to the YMCA.

The YWCA operated for the benefit of girls and young women in much the same manner as the YMCA did for boys and young men. A YWCA established in Edmonton in 1907 provided its members with sporting facilities and organized sports, and with occasions for sociability in a Christian context. The YWCA operated only in Calgary and Edmonton, although women could use the swimming pool and gymnasium at the Lethbridge YMCA.[63] The prevention of juvenile delinquency was not as strongly emphasized in the YWCA as in the YMCA; rather, the YWCA saw itself as a protective organization for women and girls who travelled alone and for single women who worked in the city.[64] Such "prevention aspects" of the YWCA's work were thought to be important because "by meeting strangers and giving information and advice when they first arrive many a problem is averted."[65] In pursuit of this goal, however, the sports programmes and facilities provided a valuable opportunity for women in Edmonton and Calgary to learn and play various sports, to take dancing lessons, or to join in a wide range of recreational activities from drama to bridge nights. Like the YMCA, the YWCA promoted skills or hobbies that would make leisure time productive, and the YWCA and church organizations, such as CGIT, also sometimes overlapped in personnel, objectives, and programming. The YWCA, for example, drew many of its volunteer leaders from "CGIT Graduates" and the existence of a special club made up of former CGIT members within the YWCA testified to the importance of this link.[66] The legitimacy of play was clearly recognized in the programmes of both the YMCA and the YWCA, but both institutions used highly structured systems to make play useful, to socialize children and youths, and to promote the "humanization" of life.

The goal of making the popular culture of the province more dynamic and sophisticated or, in other words, of "humanizing" it, was also reflected in the work of publicly funded educational institutions. It was especially clear in the work of the Department (later Faculty) of Extension at the University of Alberta. E.A. Corbett, one of the most important figures in the history of university extension work in Alberta, saw the university's programmes as "missionary" work in which spiritual and cultural concerns were united. In 1922, Corbett described a visit to a "very poor pioneer" community in the Peace River country for its "harvest festival." He had lectured, preached on Sunday, and baptized six children. Such events were typical for him, and Corbett stated that he knew "of no finer missionary enterprise than that of bringing some life into the monotony" of winter life in remote communities.[67] This missionary impulse, albeit in a more secular fashion, had been part of extension work from 1912 when the Department of Extension was created. At that time, the objective of the department was to "take the University to the country,"[68] an ambition which was given further stimulus in the 1920s by concerns about the standards of rural life. A.E. Ottewell of the Department of Extension saw the "rural problem" as a dual one. "First, we have the so-called foreign problem, how can we best enable our large population of non-Canadian birth to become adapted to a strange environment." Second, how could "the limited horizons of the people of our own stock who feel to an intense degree 'cribbed, cabin'd and confined' by the conditions of rural life" be expanded.[69] Consequently, while the department was deeply concerned about adult education, it also aimed to provide high culture as a leisure activity. From 1912, the department encouraged the production of drama, and lent books, classical music recordings, slides, and films to individuals and groups. It also sponsored handicrafts, public debates, and reading and literary circles.

These activities served educational needs and the view that leisure should be useful and uplifting. They undoubtedly provided enjoyment, stimulation, and recreation for many people throughout the province. In this way, the department tried to meet the ideals of the dominant culture and its changing needs by endeavouring to elevate the quality of popular leisure. Early extension work, as Corbett suggested in 1922, was highly seasonal and was concentrated during the winter months. As winter isolation became less trying during the late 1920s because of better transportation and new communications systems, the university moved smoothly with the new technology. Its establishment of radio station CKUA in 1927 was a striking example of the adaptability that characterized extension work in Alberta. CKUA carried educational and "cultural" programmes and provided a focus for extension activities. While even CKUA did not operate during the summer for most of its history, the department established a summer drama programme at Banff in 1933. This programme expanded rapidly and became the School of Fine Arts at Banff,[70] which had evolved by the late 1940s into one of the finest schools in Canada for the performing and visual arts.

The magnitude of the university's extension work is shown by the fact that 800,000 people "received service of some kind from the department" during the period from 1912 to 1947.[71] These services were most important for rural and farm people who had only limited access to books, music, and expertise in drama, debating, and music. By giving people the opportunity to study and enjoy various activities well beyond the resources of their local communities, the Department of Extension fulfilled an important need for "higher" leisure opportunities. It also provided Edmontonians with leisure opportunities in the form of debates, lectures, and films, and local people freely used the Department of Extension library, record, and film services. CKUA counted many urban people among its most avid supporters, and the university also provided Edmontonians with opportunities to watch organized sports played by university teams. Important as these contributions were, the university nonetheless was most important for rural people because it provided them with a window on a wider world of ideas and leisure. Yet, although the Department of Extension provided sophisticated opportunities, its services were delivered without

The University of Alberta radio station, CKUA, aired "cultural" programmes, including concerts given by its own orchestra, seen here in 1926. (PAA A.3535)

condescension and with a level of respect and seriousness that made the university's extension work among the most imaginative, important, and respected in the country. Because of the nature of these services, participation was a highly individualized experience. There were important exceptions, such as the Banff School and the various drama and art workshops, but on the whole, the university's extension services stimulated individual rather than group endeavour.

The wheelbarrow race at Lubeck School picnic in 1932. (PAA A.5780)

In contrast, public and high schools fostered local and community life by providing school facilities for meetings, dances, and other collective events. The early community leagues in Edmonton initially used schools in this way, but urban areas soon developed a sufficient number of alternate facilities. The YMCA, YWCA, fraternal order halls, commercial halls, and theatres served community purposes, and, as a result, the role of the urban school as a meeting place declined. For rural people, facilities for public gatherings were few, so the rural schools continued to be used regularly for community dances, meetings, receptions, and other gatherings. The schools themselves staged events that were of importance to the local community: annual Christmas, spring, and autumn concerts, the drama festivals that became common during the 1930s, and the school picnics, sports days, team meets, competitions, and special events for public holidays like Victoria Day.

Especially during the 1920s, some people considered public schools to be the front line in the war against rural social decline and isolation. Ideally, the teacher was not just an instructor but also a social worker who would teach the community to adopt "wholesome recreation" that would shape a better society.[72] Because "one of the patent needs of the country is the education and direction of the play spirit," the rural school should teach people how to play.[73] A. E. Ottewell contended that the school was the only unifying force in the society because "nearly every other social agency we have, whether economic, cultural or religious, is in its very nature divisive in effect." The school would unify and cultivate the society.[74] Such ambitions were tempered, however, by the utilitarianism that characterized Alberta thinking. Although the UFA believed that drama and music were excellent pursuits, useful subjects such as "home economics and manual training" deserved equal attention in the schools.[75]

Under the general regulations of the Alberta Department of Education, the boards of trustees of each school district could permit use of the school and school grounds "for any lawful purpose—social, education, or religious. . . but no advertisements other than the statutory notices and notices of public meetings shall be posted on the school." In fact, the Department of Education "always advised" the board "to be generous in allowing the use of the buildings" for community events.[76] In 1930 the department went further and stipulated that the design of schools and school grounds must accommodate such community needs, in line with the "modern attitude" that the school was "public property" and should be available for community activities. Accordingly, "the grounds should be large enough to allow for games for those above school age out of hours." Here was a recognition that most rural communities had no public parks or "only weed patches" of limited recreational use.[77] The 1930 decree specified that school grounds should be beautified (which basically meant that trees should be planted) and that they should be large enough for community recreational needs. The typical three-acre rural school yard was to be increased to at least four to five acres.[78]

While the province encouraged community use of schools, it also exerted pressure on trustees to exercise their authority judiciously. To Premier William Aberhart, a school board was obligated "to see that the social affairs" held in a school met the

> highest standards of conduct recognized by the people of the community, and certainly no intoxicating liquor or containers for the same are allowed within the school building or grounds at any time.

> The school in a rural community is very commonly the centre of the child's social life and it would appear that only the finest type of associations in regard to the school should be allowed to grow up in the mind of the child.[79]

Community use of school facilities raised a number of social and moral issues. Rural society was monolithic in neither philosophy nor class, and disagreement sometimes arose. A Mrs. Wirsch wrote Aberhart in 1936 stating that as "a child in Christ," she did not approve of the "dancing and parties in the school and the Children Books always get lost and Torn and Thinks get Broken" because the people using the school were "such a ruf Bunch."[80] In another case, a local school board refused a local Social Credit group permission to use the school for meetings and dances. This was a setback to the group because there was no other building in the community for such purposes.[81]

School regulations and local rivalries and sensibilities complicated the use of schools for public purposes, and communities began to build their own community halls or meeting centres. This trend was given impetus by the closure of schools. School consolidation was almost continuous after 1913,[82] and a large number of small rural schools were closed and consolidated into larger institutions during the mid-1930s. An outburst of protest from rural Alberta followed the closure of schools, many of which had been important community institutions for decades. As one group of protesters in Altmore, near Lac la Biche, informed Premier Aberhart,

> we will never forget the loss of our school, where our children were baptized, where we held our meetings and reunions, where we attended Church once a month and which building we were so satisfied with we learned to regard the same as our own home.[83]

In other cases, however, rural society was split by the issue of school consolidation. Some individuals at Nose Creek, near Calgary, petitioned the government to close the local school to reduce local taxes while others saw the school as a "community centre" and demanded that it be kept open. The crisis highlighted divisions within local society. The one group, who wanted the school closed,

> appear to be people who have no interest in the local community affairs either through being non-residents, or being sufficiently

well-to-do to use Calgary for their pleasures. Last Christmas eve...250 children and adults assembled in the school for their annual Christmas festivities. They have Young People's Dramatic group and many other activities.[84]

Thus, the lessening of rural isolation that occurred because of developments in transportation was counterbalanced by the closing of institutions that had often provided a focus for rural communities.

Despite the collective memories of the old school house, neither rural nor urban schools were wholly satisfactory as leisure facilities. Schools could not be used for all leisure purposes and even limited use sometimes conflicted, or was perceived to conflict, with the school's primary responsibility to educate and socialize children. As they became less effective as dual purpose facilities, more specific leisure-oriented facilities were required in both urban and rural communes. As one observer noted in 1920:

> The gym, the public library and reading room and rooms equipped for games are almost unheard of in the open country and small towns. Consequently, the rural barber shop, the livery stable, the grocery store...get in their full quota of influence with the rural youth in the form of obscene pictures, questionable gossip, vulgar stories, bad literature, card games and the like.

Accordingly, rural areas and small towns needed public parks, sports fields, playgrounds, and community halls, all under "the supervision of a properly constituted authority."[85]

The need for such facilities had been recognized from the beginning of settlement, but they began to develop only during World War I. Among the earliest were community halls. In the Ukrainian settlement area of east central Alberta, *narodni domy*, or community halls, were frequently built by reading clubs that had initially met in private homes. As the reading clubs' activities broadened and people could afford more leisure activities, these halls often provided facilities for dances, sports, and picnics. Nonetheless, they supported a conscious cultural role in the community by providing a facility where Ukrainian cultural consciousness could be developed. In many cases, these halls also reflected political divisions in the community. They have been described in three categories: as independent halls, Catholic halls, and pro-communist halls. There were at least 110 of these halls built in east central Alberta between 1914 and 1940, the "golden age" of the *narodni domy*.[86]

The need for community halls, such as this one at Moose Mountain, near Bowden, photographed in 1931, had been recognized since the beginning of settlement. (GAI NA-3976-33)

During the same period, community halls were also constructed elsewhere in the province. The UFA locals were often instrumental in constructing community halls[87] although, in Ukrainian communities, the *narodni domy* that preceded them prevented as firm a UFA foothold as could be found in many other rural communities. As the UFA was frequently unsympathetic to Ukrainian needs and sensibilities, it never played an important role in the social life of Ukrainian communities.[88] In other cases, agricultural societies and community leagues built halls and, in still other situations, fraternal organizations and clubs made their halls available in a relatively unrestricted manner.

Most community halls in both towns and farm communities were simple structures with a stage, kitchen, and large meeting room. The Rycroft Community Hall, which was built in 1934 on the fair grounds, seems to have been typical. It measured thirty-two feet by seventy feet with a sixteen by thirty-two-foot stage, "dressing rooms," a partial basement, and a kitchen. Although it was built by volunteers, mainly with donated materials, the hall still cost about nineteen hundred dollars and the Rycroft Agricultural Society took out a mortgage to build it.[89] The typical hall contained few furnishings: a stove, cupboards, benches, tables and usually a piano. Not all community halls were newly constructed: existing structures were sometimes fitted to serve the new purpose. In 1937, one southern Alberta community purchased a vacant store in a neighbouring town and towed it fifteen miles. After making relatively simple renovations, the residents had economically managed to acquire a community facility.[90]

The 1920s and 1930s were the golden age not only of the *narodni domy* but of community halls in general. Community events such as dances, box socials, whist drives, concerts, and movie shows raised the money needed for upkeep of halls and mortgage payments. Over the years, members produced and raffled literally thousands of quilts throughout Alberta in support of community associations. Dances typically cost twenty-five cents with lunch included, and if a woman brought lunch, she got in free. In other cases, the hall was rented at a flat rate for meetings, private receptions, dances, and fund-raising events held by local clubs and organizations. In the summer, sports days, ball games, rodeos, and races took place on the grounds adjacent to the hall. Hockey games and community skating occupied a rink beside the hall in winter.[91]

The use of community halls in farm areas declined steadily during the 1940s in the face of competition from small town facilities. By then, roads had improved so that people could easily travel year-round to the surrounding towns for entertainment. At Spirit Valley in the Peace River area, the rural hall was no longer regularly used: from 1948 to 1950 it was used only once for a private wedding reception. This decline was the result not of changing interests but of changing standards: people now went to dances at the village of Spirit River that attracted "better orchestra[s]."[92] This process had, however, begun long before 1950. As early as 1930 in the Peace River country, it was apparently becoming common for rural groups like the UFA "to meet in the village centres" with the result that "the older neighbourhood groups" were replaced with wider farm-village alliances.[93]

World War II was highly disruptive to the continued use of some community halls. In 1940, the "Custodian of Enemy Property in Alberta" made a "somewhat curious but interesting proposal" to the University of Alberta. The custodian was holding "a large number of community halls, most of which were built apparently by funds collected by alien organizations which have been suppressed by the dominion government." He asked the University of Alberta if it wanted the halls to set up educational and recreational programmes in these communities. With no information on the number, location, or condition of these halls, the university still agreed to take them all and to set up programmes of "community education" for the "Canadianization [of] an alien element in the community at a time when the effort would be most valuable."[94] Although the university never did obtain the properties in question, the incident illustrates the impact of the war on facilities identified with cultures labelled as "enemy alien."

Wartime tensions reflected that politics, among other factors, had often played an important role in community facilities. The UFA halls had an implicit political orientation and the construction of more than one hall in many a Ukrainian community reflected political divisions. Accordingly, it would be naïve to see in rural community halls simply an expression of abstract community that was created through a need for leisure facilities. They were the result of a more complicated process, originating in wider and often political and religious issues. Similarly, community halls in urban areas often reflected a broader agenda than simply the preservation or extension of a sense of community. Many, like Edmonton's Robertson Hall at the turn of the century, were commercial ventures and made their facilities available at charge. In small towns, these halls were often grandiloquently called "Opera Halls," but no opera was ever sung in them.[95] As well, many club and fraternal order halls were rented to outsiders.

Community leagues provided additional urban facilities, not simply as a community focus for leisure but to serve a wider range of objectives. The first community league in Alberta was established in 1917 in Jasper Place, a small bedroom community on the outskirts of Edmonton. In the face of a low standard of living, its aim was to deal collectively with the lack of urban services and recreational facilities. This response to the combination of recreational objectives and the need for local improvement of urban standards became a model followed by other communities in and around Edmonton. By 1924, twenty leagues operated in all parts of the city. Membership in some leagues was high—the Alberta Avenue League had a membership of seven hundred—but most leagues were much smaller. Many grew out of existing organizations, such as taxpayers associations and parent teacher associations, and maintained an abiding concern with civic improvement: utilities, drainage, tree planting, and construction of sidewalks.[96] In the beginning, the community leagues used local schools as meeting places, but many soon built their own halls, community recreational grounds, and skating rinks. The provision of such facilities was a significant part of league work and a means of "creating an esprit de corps among the members."[97]

The league movement in Edmonton was institutionalized in 1921 with the creation of the Federation of Community Leagues, which aimed to give permanency and stability to the league movement with an overall objective of creating "recreation, education, entertainment and a better type of citizenship." The federation purchased a movie projector for use by member leagues and borrowed films from the University of Alberta Department of Extension. It also organized sports meets and worked with the local horticultural society in tree planting and garden improvement. The federation worked closely with the Edmonton Public School Board and the city, even using the city council chambers for its meetings. It also worked with such service clubs as the Gyro Club in playground and park improvement.[98] The relationship between community leagues and service clubs demonstrated shared effort to provide local services in the interwar years.

An Edmonton public park, date unknown. (PAA BL.2602/1)

Another manifestation of this phenomenon appeared in the growth of urban public parks and supervised playgrounds. By 1900, urban playgrounds had become an issue for the National Council of Women, which demanded that all urban children have easy access to playgrounds. By 1910, such demands were being made in Alberta, mostly by urban people, although there were occasional attempts to bring the playground movement to small towns and even rural areas.[99] The playground movement followed contemporary understanding not only of the needs of children, but of the relationship between childhood and character formation and between childhood exercise and health. Before World War I, the playground movement in Canada was inspired by the call of American social reformers for playgrounds in American cities.[100]

Playgrounds, such as the East End Park, Edmonton, were expected to aid in building a better society. (PAA BL.2602)

Arguments for playgrounds in Alberta were accordingly linked with local economic growth, crime prevention, health and physical development of children, and general social betterment.[101] The belief that playgrounds showed civic pride, which would then translate into economic growth and investment, was particularly important in Alberta. Nonetheless, playgrounds were primarily expected to build a better society. The Calgary Superintendent of Parks observed in 1917 that there was no justification for public provision of playgrounds "as mere hilarious centres to excite the nervous system of children." Rather, playgrounds should serve as a "means of building up the morals, health, strength and physique of the rising generation and thus making better citizens of them."[102] Playgrounds were a matter of public health and education. As the Edmonton Supervisor of Playgrounds saw it in 1913, they were a "natural sequence to the pure milk and pure food movement" and a means of creating a nation of "healthy, virile people who will have the power to make full use of their mental talents."[103] A criticism of intellectualism was also a part of the argument; it was claimed that long school hours led to intellectual development at the "sacrifice of physical welfare." Through playgrounds, however, the society could have both: mental development in schools and physical development through exercise.[104]

With these ambitions, playgrounds became more than just open space for play. Ideally, they provided a separate set of swings, teeter-totters, sand boxes, slides, and horizontal ladders for small children of each sex, and facilities such as courts for net games and jumping pits for older children. Play in such playgrounds would provide exercise for body and mind within a group setting. Although they were more often in public parks than in playgrounds, wading and swimming pools were also important facilities for children. In Calgary, St. George's Island Park, Elbow Park, and Riley Park all had wading and swimming pools by 1922. These pools had sand and gravel bottoms that became churned into the water when the children were swimming.[105] They provided an activity that children loved and helped to keep them from swimming in the river, a common practice among adults that was characterized by the *Edmonton Journal* as a "form of insanity."[106] For children it was frequently fatal, and early demands for swimming pools always accompanied reports of more drownings.[107]

Expectations for physical and mental development were accompanied by strong social objectives. Playgrounds would encourage patriotism by promoting "one community" through play[108] and, specifically, a community based upon English Canadian ideals. In part, this view assumed that the school, although important, was not as effective a tool for assimilation as play. As G. R. Jackson, the supervisor of playgrounds in Edmonton, observed in 1913: "the little foreigner who plays with his Canadian fellows will learn their ideas and ideals a great deal quicker and better than he can do in any other way, and if we are to build up a great and united nation, we must use every possible method to preserve our Canadian ideals and inculcate them in the strangers within our gates."[109]

Even though the little English Canadian child might serve as the instrument of assimilation, presuming an ethnic superiority by birth, it was believed that all children needed supervision. Establishing an unsupervised playground was simply creating a school for juvenile delinquency. Playgrounds needed adult supervisors who would see that "the boys and girls are taught the true spirit of sportsmanship and manliness, and that by the conduct of their games they learn true ethical standards."[110] The playground agenda thus included not only ethnic assimilation but sexual streaming as well. This was in part based on the same "gang theory" that informed the Boy Scouts: gang proclivities and restlessness in boys could be directed into useful channels. Male supervisors who were of "high character and well developed physically" were considered to be best for establishing authority and providing an appropriate role model for little children.[111] Nevertheless, supervision was not always provided. In 1917, Calgary had twelve playgrounds, but apparently none was supervised. It was not until 1940 that a full-time supervisor was appointed for Calgary playgrounds.[112] Edmonton had fewer playgrounds but a better record of supervision. There were only three formal playgrounds in the city in 1924, but all were supervised.[113]

Urban parks parallelled playgrounds in their objectives, but they were intended as a facility for the whole family and not only for children. From the turn of the century, notions about civic pride, beauty, and planning played a great part in the growing demand for urban park development, but parks were linked to the idea that the society could be made better and more orderly through leisure. This was further tied to the idea that outdoor recreation in itself was beneficial. "Amusement is the spice of life," it was said in 1922, and "without some form of recreation, people take to backbiting, slandering and all manner of uncharitableness." Parks corrected these tendencies, for "the very best of amusements are those that are found in the open."[114] Moreover, parks were important for the poor, and it was observed in 1910 that although many people from Calgary could afford to go to Banff or to British Columbia in the summer, a great many more could not. Urban parks levelled these differences because they could be a "home summer resort" for those who could not afford to travel.[115]

Parks were established in both Calgary and Edmonton shortly before World War I. In the beginning, they were rudimentary; Central Park in Calgary was described in 1910 as "poor, neglected, [and] dried up."[116] It was sometimes difficult to obtain land for public parks because of the high levels of land speculation common in prairie cities,[117] but park space in both cities expanded. By 1932, Calgary's Bowness Park was more like a summer resort than a traditional urban park. It had cottages for rent, a dance pavilion, boating, concession stands, and miniature golf among its many attractions. The park was operated by the city and was truly a summer resort for those unable to travel.[118] No other city or town in the province operated anything like it, and only the intermediate-sized centres such as Red Deer and Lethbridge had even developed small public parks by the 1920s.[119]

Calgary's Bowness Park shown here in 1920, boasted a tea room and a dance pavilion, among other facilities. (GAI NA-2885-2)

Public parks and playgrounds were partially supported by urban governments, which often owned the lands.[120] Some service clubs also became involved during the 1920s. The Rotary Club was prominent in this activity; in Red Deer, it held "carnivals" to raise money to equip the public playground. The 1924 carnival was a "big holiday event" that on the first day attracted four hundred people to games, skits, prizes, food concessions, and a car raffle. The Rotarians raised one thousand dollars for the purchase of swings, rings, slides, an "ocean wave," and seating for parents and spectators at the Red Deer Civic Park.[121] The Imperial Order of the Daughters of the Empire (IODE) was also involved in this project and contributed three hundred dollars for a rest house from which the mothers could "watch the juniors."[122] Similarly, the Calgary Rotary Club established a large playground in Mount Pleasant Park in 1931. The playground, called the Rotary Recreation Park, cost the Calgary Rotarians $8,500. It had a wading pool, track, bowling green, a putting green, and baseball, tennis, and basketball areas. The "Boys' Section" and "Girls' Section" each included such equipment as swings, slides, and horizontal bars.[123] By 1943 the Rotary Club had equipped seven different playgrounds in parks throughout the city. Once the club had provided the equipment, the playground was turned over to the city for operation and supervision. The city was always delighted to have its parks improved at no cost to itself, but it was clear by 1938 that adequate supervision was not being provided. Much to the consternation of the Rotary Club, the equipment was being wrecked by vandals. Nevertheless, Rotarians continued to provide equipment; in 1949 they were still working closely with the city in equipping playgrounds in parks in new parts of Calgary.[124]

The Calgary pattern was repeated in Edmonton. The main player in Edmonton was a service club called the Gyro Club, which had been established in 1921. Its objective was to support playgrounds in the city. Like the Rotary Club, it used a highly successful carnival to raise money. The annual Gyro Club Carnival became an institution in Edmonton life, and was "as much a source of recreation for the citizens of Edmonton as were the playgrounds."[125] By 1924, the Gyro Club was involved with three playgrounds in the city, and it split the cost of supervising the playgrounds with the city. The Gyros also asked community leagues to take responsibility for maintenance, supervision and improvement.[126] These facilities were more than playgrounds because they were also extensively used by adults for athletics and various team sports, especially soft ball. The Gyro Club continued its work with playgrounds into the early 1950s, when responsibility for such facilities was largely assumed by the city.[127]

The Gyro and Rotary Clubs and the IODE and other fraternal and benevolent organizations were active in many other community projects involving leisure. The IODE established and funded a number of libraries throughout the province, and the Elks and Kiwanis clubs encouraged and supported the Boy Scout movement. In other cases, these organizations provided support for institutions such as the YMCA and YWCA. On a different but equally important level, these service clubs and benevolent and fraternal organizations included leisure activities in their own affairs.

Building on a long tradition, the popularity and number of service clubs and fraternal and benevolent orders in Alberta grew rapidly in the interwar period. During the late nineteenth century, Alberta had many active fraternal orders, such as the Masons, the Foresters, the Orange Lodge, and the Oddfellows. In some cases, they, along with their women's auxiliaries, were set up almost immediately upon settlement. The first Masonic order in Calgary was established in 1883, and by 1905 there were eighteen Masonic lodges in the province. By 1888, Oddfellows meetings in Calgary could draw seventy-five members, and in mid-1893, the Foresters were established in South Edmonton.[128] During the interwar years, American organizations, describing themselves significantly with the socially leveling term of "service clubs," became increasingly popular in Canada. It was another example of the incursion of American ways in Canada, for "their administrative structures linked clubs in Canadian provinces with those in the adjoining American states." The Rotary Club, which established a branch in Calgary in 1914, advertised itself as the "first service club in Alberta,"[129] and groups such as the Rotarians, the Gyros, the Kinsmen, and the Elks expanded rapidly during the interwar years. They were largely urban, middle class, and Anglo-Saxon, much like the older fraternal clubs. Many, like the Rotary Club, emphasized the recruitment of businessmen,[130] but others were also welcomed which sustained club claims to serve the collective needs of the community. Like the older ones, these organizations placed great stress upon the centrality of fraternal spirit among members, on the grounds that greater cohesion increased the social usefulness of the group through a collective dedication to community needs.

All of these organizations were male clubs, and women were accommodated in auxiliaries which had distinctive names and rituals. The women's auxiliary of the Oddfellows was the Rebekahs, and the first such lodge in Alberta was formed in Calgary in 1907. By 1914 there were thirteen other Rebekah lodges in the province. The Rebekahs provided social opportunities for women and a forum for their social concerns such as women's suffrage. The Rebekahs often supported their male counterparts in the Oddfellows with domestic services like lunch at meetings. They were clearly a subservient organization—while women were barred from Oddfellows meetings, men could attend those of the Rebekahs. The relationship between the Rebekahs and the Oddfellows thus reflected wider social realities, and similarly, most of these organizations in Alberta were more or less exclusive in ethnic, class, or religious terms. These factors of course evolved and changed over the years; the Oddfellows in the 1880s in Calgary seem to have been a relatively open organization, but by 1911 the annual dues had risen to eight dollars per year; a prohibitive amount for most working people. Yet from the beginning, certain occupations were barred from membership, such as bartenders, saloonkeepers and gamblers, and membership was restricted to "white males of not less than 21 years of age," and "of good moral character." Membership was gained through sponsorship by a member and a vote by the lodge.[131]

In general, even without an analysis of the membership of these organizations, it is apparent that, among the fraternal clubs, the Masons were generally seen as the elite organization, whereas the Knights of Pythias and Oddfellows were of somewhat lower rank. Business interests, personal needs, and tradition undoubtedly played a part in attracting members to these organizations. Most were linked to national and international organizations that provided a social framework transcending the local chapters. Nonetheless, it is clear that the local chapters played an important social role in the everyday lives of their members. The regular meetings,

E.A. Braithwaite in his Masonic regalia, date unknown. (PAA B.7121)

The Masonic Hall at Trochu. (PAA A.2159)

with their ritual, regalia, emphasis upon secrecy, and claims to origins in antiquity created a socially secure environment in which one could meet friends and acquaintances.[132] Most of these groups had their own meeting halls or buildings and many of them mounted several annual events. For instance, the Masonic ball and banquet was one of the social highlights of the year in some communities, the Orange Lodge paraded each year and held a picnic in celebration of the Battle of the Boyne, and members of the Calgary Oddfellows formed an orchestra and played for lodge meetings, dances and the order's annual New Year's Eve party.[133]

Most nineteenth century fraternal and benevolent organizations contended that their primary goals were the creation of fraternal feelings among their members and the extension of benevolence to needy members and their families, although assistance was sometimes given to outsiders. The Masons proudly held that trifling temporal matters such as partisan political loyalties and the geographical location of members were transcended by the "brotherhood" of the Masonic Lodge. In 1894, a group of visiting

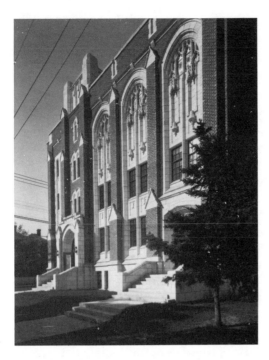

The Masonic Hall in Edmonton in 1931. (PAA BL.93)

Liberal Masons were feted by their Edmonton brothers. Despite political differences, they met "as brethren" and exchanged the "fraternal greetings that bind masons of all nationalities and differences into one brotherhood as an oasis in the desert."[134] At the same time, the new rhetoric of "service" was having an impact. Immediately before World War I, and to a greater extent during the 1920s, these nineteenth century benevolent and fraternal organizations began to shift towards a broader social base. The Orange Lodge began to speak more frequently about social service work. The Knights of Pythias, founded in 1864 as a "secret society and a fraternal society—secret in its inner workings, fraternal in its ramifications," established a lodge in Red Deer in 1922. Despite public ignorance about the order, the Knights were able to attract one hundred people to their "first social dance" in the city. The Knights stressed their commitment to the modern world and, perhaps in the face of new competitors who spoke about "service," they mixed their commitment to democracy with allusions to prominent members: notably the Honourable Arthur Meighen and United States President Warren G. Harding.[135] No one asked if these individuals were especially good examples of social levelling, or if secret organizations could by definition be democratic, but the articulation of the issue in itself illustrated changing ideals.

Nineteenth century fraternal and benevolent organizations continued to be important in Alberta to 1945. In the Peace River area during the early 1930s the Orange Lodge, Masons, and Oddfellows, along with their women's organizations, could be found in nearly every town. On the other hand, the newer clubs, such as the Elks, were only beginning to take hold in the larger rural centres such as Grande Prairie.[136] Nonetheless, the variety of clubs and associations operating in the province by 1914 had increased dramatically and had expanded in new and more specialized directions. By 1930, no city or town in Alberta would have been without a fraternal, service, or other club. In 1930, it was observed that social organizations in the relatively new town of Grande Prairie displayed "an almost urban complexity." In addition to schools and churches, there were at least thirty-four organizations, "including a Board of Trade and Women's Institute, eight agricultural associations, eight lodges, ten athletic clubs and six organizations exclusively devoted to the interests of boys, girls and young people." These organizations contributed more than immediate benefits to their members. By sponsoring such events as sports days and fairs, which brought people into the town, they helped to consolidate Grande Prairie's commercial and political power. According to a contemporary analysis, these events in conjunction with the local clubs' "institutional and administrative function. . .demonstrate how Grande Prairie plays a leading role in extending and integrating the economic and social structure of the region."[137]

Other organizations operating in Alberta after 1900 are far too numerous to permit discussion of each in turn. An idea of their impact on patterns of leisure may, however, be gained by giving some attention to four representative types: the various veterans' clubs, such as the Canadian Legion, representing a narrowly defined but large group of people united by historical events and often in the forefront of patriotic endeavours; the United Farm Women of Alberta (UFWA) and Women's Institutes, representing rural political and social clubs; the Elks, one of the urban service clubs that became popular during the 1920s; and certain clubs whose membership was consciously defined by ethnic criteria.

At various times, there were a large number of postwar veterans' clubs and associations in Alberta. Among these were the Imperial Veterans in Canada, the Great War Veterans Association (GWVA), the Red Chevron Club, the Army and Navy Veterans in Canada

Members of The Loyal Orange Lodge No. 1908, Bowden, in an undated group portrait. (PAA H.820)

The July 12, 1937, celebrations of the Orange Lodge at Wetaskiwin. (PAA A.4877)

Club, and the Canadian Legion. Over the years, many of these clubs amalgamated; for example, the Army and Navy Veterans in Canada was made up of the United Services Clubs, the South African Veterans Association, and, among others, Her Majesty's Army and Navy Veterans.[138] In addition, the Canadian Legion was founded in 1925 as part of an imperial solidarity movement among ex-British empire and dominion veterans. The Legion grew extremely quickly, and by 1935 it had 160,000 members in Canada. In Alberta, there were 129 branches and 20 women's auxiliaries.[139]

While "patriotic" objectives were sometimes expressed by the numerous returned soldier associations and clubs in Alberta, the stated purpose of these organizations was to protect and to articulate veterans' rights and needs, at both a local and national level, and to extend assistance to needy veterans and their families. But the common experience of military service was also the basis on which these organizations met social needs of ex-servicemen. Almost every veterans' organization maintained a club room or a hall for social events and as a permanent meeting place. After World War I, the province provided grants of up to 25 percent of the construction costs for "soldiers' clubs." To be eligible for this grant, the building had to be built of brick or stone, had to be located in a city, and had to contain sleeping accommodation. The latter was intended to assist veterans from the country who had to visit doctors or do other business in the city.[140] Under this programme, the GWVA built facilities in Edmonton, Lethbridge, and Calgary with a total grant support of $67,500.[141] During the 1920s and 1930s, various veterans' organizations, especially the Canadian Legion, built halls throughout the province, and most cities and medium-sized to large towns in the province had a Legion hall by the mid-1930s. These halls were important social centres for veterans, and in some communities they were also used for community events. During the 1920s and 1930s, the Legion Hall and the Oddfellows Hall were the only meeting halls in Cochrane. In 1941, a government inspection revealed that the wiring in both halls was dangerous and they were closed. In the ensuing uproar, the protesters claimed that the halls had served the community well for twenty years and were important community institutions. Their closure during wartime, for so paltry a reason as faulty wiring, was labelled disloyal because they were being used for Red Cross meetings, war service campaigns, and other patriotic work.[142]

Beyond the evident role of Legion halls in community life,

veterans' clubs and halls served primarily the social needs of returned men. According to a 1923 report, the Army and Navy Clubs were "maintained for the benefit of the returned men and there are a great many men belonging to these Clubs who are unmarried men and have no where to go in the evenings if they do not go to the club."[143] While these clubs increasingly were licensed to sell beer, which enhanced both the clubs' social attractiveness and their revenue, they were funded primarily through members' dues and special fund-raising events. In 1936 the Edmonton branch of the Legion held a three-day "Monster Carnival" at the Memorial Hall and promised "all the fun of the fair," including bingo and games of chance.[144] The Legion played a significant role in the lives of many people and membership crossed most class lines. Legion clubs were nearly always located in cities, towns, or villages, but were accessible to farm people as well.

Early in the twentieth century, rural communities had begun to develop their own associations, among which were a number of significant women's organizations. Whereas the United Farm Women of Alberta (UFWA) were associated with the increasingly political United Farmers of Alberta (UFA), branches of the Women's Institute remained nonpartisan. The Women's Institute was formed by Adelaide Hoodless in Ontario in 1897 as an expression of "maternal feminism" which linked women's work outside the home with their concerns about home and family.[145] The first unit of the Women's Institute in Alberta was established in 1909. In 1915, many units merged into the UFWA, in which membership was restricted to women who were farmers, farmers' wives, or farmers' daughters. This forced the Women's Institute to broaden its membership beyond farm women. Nevertheless, the two organizations remained closely allied and they became the two dominant women's organizations in rural Alberta. By 1918, the Women's Institute had 212 units in Alberta, with eight thousand members from farms and towns throughout the province.[146] The UFWA continued to represent only farm women, while the Women's Institute continued to broaden its membership by drawing members from the whole spectrum of rural society. Another of its strengths lay in its nonsectarian nature for the Women's Institute avoided denominational questions that occupied some women's church organizations. The Women's Institute styled itself as a progressive institution that represented a new age: "only as we are civilized can we co-operate. If we cannot work as a unit we have not gone very far along the road of civilization."[147] This was an interesting use of UFA rhetoric by a nonpartisan group.

The Women's Institute, like the UFWA, sponsored fund-raising community events such as dinners and picnics, but the monthly meetings were in themselves a time for socializing and a time away from husbands and homes. UFWA and Women's Institute meetings alike skillfully blended socializing and education into attractive leisure events.[148] The objective of the Walsh Women's Institute was "first — social, a place to meet your friends once a month and every country woman knows what a boon that is," and second — educational. At each meeting three members presented papers: "one a culture subject like literature or travel; one a house-hold subject like butter making, preserving; and one on current events."[149] Many UFWA and Women's Institute meetings were highly structured. The Women's Institute in Barons publicized the forthcoming year's schedule with a typeset calendar. And despite the fact that the programme was mimeographed by 1939, doubtless a reflection of hard times, the events were largely the same.[150] Like many women's groups, the Women's Institute met in different members' homes throughout the year. The women:

> claim their afternoon off and flock to the Women's Institute meeting. The hostess for the day has put her best foot forward, and brought out her choicest pieces of linen and china and prepared the most delicious lunch her stores will permit, for this is really her yearly reception.[151]

Entertainment was important and was deliberately used to attract and hold members. At UFWA meetings, various games made even the business part of the meeting fun, and this was followed by the entertainment programme. As UFWA locals were advised in 1927, "if you have musicians, elocutionists, singers, dancers, get on their tail and make them work for the Local!" At the same time, however, locals were cautioned to "have at least one educational item on every program."[152]

Because of the prevailing attitudes in the communities within which it operated, the Women's Institute, like the UFA and UFWA, blended educational and social functions. One woman observed in 1937 that she enjoyed "the companionship" the institute fostered because the members had "so many interests that their minds are not allowed to stagnate."[153] It was therefore not surprising that the provincial government encouraged the Women's Institute movement. In 1912, it began providing locals with small grants and organizational assistance and services. This public subsidy lasted until the early 1930s, and it has been argued that this financial support was crucial in the early years but that the movement was strong enough by the 1920s to survive the withdrawal of government support easily.[154]

The service club, which grew in popularity during the 1920s and 1930s, also blended service to the community with the traditional objective of fraternity. The Benevolent and Protective Order of Elks, a good example of this type of organization, was established nationally in 1912 and a provincial association was formed in Alberta in 1928. The earliest lodges in the province seem to have been in Lethbridge and Calgary where they were active by 1921. The Elks canvassed aggressively for members, and lodges competed to show the greatest annual increase in membership in the province. The Elks claimed to provide people with an "opportunity to fraternize and make new friends" and to carry out socially beneficial projects. These objectives were understood to be mutually reinforcing: "friendship, like happiness, frequently comes to men unsought while they are working together in some worthwhile cause." In 1936, according to spokesmen like Grand Exalted Ruler Alex McIntyre of Calgary, the result was sure to be cooperative benefits for the nation and its communities:

> I see in the future of Elkdom a golden link in a great chain stretching from...Newfoundland across the Canada of tomorrow, spreading the spirit of good-will and mutual helpfulness, and building on a solid foundation that will make us better men, our lodges better lodges, our communities better communities and Canada a greater and more glorious nation because of our lives as individuals and our work as Elks.[155]

The Elks held regular local meetings, often twice a month. As well, annual provincial and national conventions held in different cities in Alberta and Canada respectively linked all lodges on both a provincial and national level. Elks spoke unabashedly about social obligations and the Alberta Elks Association took on the sponsorship and encouragement of Boy Scout troops. By 1936, it was sponsoring and assisting more "Scout and Cub Troops and packs than any other organization in Alberta, with the exception of the churches."[156] Most lodges had local projects as well. The Calgary lodge established the Calgary Elks Band in 1912; and it soon became an institution in Calgary life and was regularly featured in the Stampede parade and at concerts, horse shows, and various charity events.[157] Fund-raising events supported local projects. The Red Deer lodge held a "carnival" in 1925 to raise money for a new covered skating rink for the town. In the previous year, they and the local Rotary club had given money to the town to support its programme for indigents.[158] In 1946, the Drumheller Elks brought in Victory Shows for a four-day carnival to raise funds for the Children's Aid fund.[159] The combination of community entertainment with benevolent fund raising was clearly a feature of Alberta urban life.

The Elks Club, Calgary, 1947. (PAA P.5493)

Most of the organizations already surveyed claimed to represent the interests of all citizens, but it is clear that many people felt the need for associations that were strictly and formally defined along ethnic and religious lines, or both. Many of these clubs were purely local in nature, but some local groups were linked to national clubs or political groups. The names, objectives, and membership of an immense number of clubs based on ethnic or linguistic criteria changed over time. As John Norris has demonstrated, this type of club usually performed three functions: provision of mutual aid in coping with economic and social difficulties, organization of social fellowship, and preservation and transmission of culture. He notes that mutual benefit often characterized club activities early in the life cycle of the immigrant community, as did social fellowship through the staging of recreational activities that were "familiar in the land of origin: the dances, music, songs, games, food and drink of the ethnic past." The importance of the latter diminished somewhat as assimilation took place and the links to the place of origin became clouded with time. The provision of economic and social aid also declined in importance as people became more established and a social safety net was put into place in Canada. In later years, the preservation of culture often gained prominence, and social fellowship, perhaps in an altered form, continued to play a significant part in the club's function, often as a tool for the transmission of the culture to the upcoming generation.[160]

One of Alberta's German Clubs celebrated the coming of 1914 with a masquerade dance. (PAA B.7254)

There were many such clubs in Alberta, some of which promoted the dominant culture. For the Scots, the Burns Club, the Scottish Society, and the St. Andrew's Society all put on annual banquets in celebration of Robert Burns's birthday.[161] Annual events as well as regular meetings served to reinforce unity among members. During the 1890s the St. Andrew's Society typically followed its business meetings with programmes of songs, readings, and skits, all of which emphasized in one way or another how great and wonderful was Scotland and how fine it was to be a Scot.[162] Such assertions of ethnic or religious solidarity promoted social cohesion within the group.

Groups outside the dominant culture also had such organizations, but they were often deeply influenced by unique events and circumstances. Italian organizations in Alberta underwent various transformations during the 1920s and 1930s, often in response to political developments and changes in Italy.[163] Polish clubs and organizations had generally been local in nature in the years before 1920, but during the 1920s and 1930s "many mergers of local organizations" initiated a process of consolidation that increased after World War II. Polish clubs served a wide range of religious, political, cultural, and social needs through "fraternal associations, professional and business organizations, mutual aid societies, social, cultural, sport and hobby clubs and their numerous auxiliaries." Like the Italian clubs, Polish clubs in Canada were highly responsive to political developments in Europe, which gave Polish club life a complexity all its own.[164]

Clubs such as those organized by Polish and Italian groups were a response to a number of factors in Canadian life. In part, they were a logical reaction to the exclusion that many non-English-speaking immigrants experienced at the hands of the English-speaking majority.[165] Ethnically and increasingly politically homogeneous organizations could help immigrants fight back or at least preserve their self-respect. In this sense, they were clearly within the tradition of fraternal organizations. The frequent unwillingness of many English-speaking Canadians to accept non-English-speaking people on equal terms no doubt increased the readiness of these Canadians to maintain a commitment to political developments in their home lands. Such a commitment was a logical combination of interest in one's place of origin and the ease one felt with the language and culture of one's childhood and youth. Many clubs had clearly articulated cultural objectives. The Medicine Valley Estonian Society, a purely local club established in 1910 near Eckville, defined its objectives as both economic and cultural, and in pursuit of the latter, its

> social activities included dramatic productions, a mixed choir and a string ensemble which performed at concerts and dances. Choirs and singing festivals were an important part of life in Estonia and the settlers in Alberta continued this musical tradition.[166]

The preservation of cultural traditions and the maintenance of a connection with the politics of the homeland, by means of clubs

116

or other organizations, often created conflict within the ethnic community or between it and the rest of Canadian society. This issue was especially intense during the 1930s. In 1936, for example, the German-Canadian Society of Edmonton became involved in a protracted quarrel with the city which had prohibited the club from flying the swastika flag at its annual picnic. The province overruled this order, but the Canadian Legion then became involved because its hall had been rented for part of the festivities. Once the hall had been decorated with Nazi flags and a picture of Hitler, the Legion refused to allow the events to go ahead unless the decorations were removed.[167] While not all German Canadians were in tune with the Edmonton German-Canadian Society, or much involved in debates about Europe, special problems arose during the war years. German Baptists at Carbon wrote to Premier Aberhart in 1940 asking about the advisability of holding their annual religious and social convention. As they rightly noted:

> We are of the opinion that since most of our People Have lived here for 28 years and in the year 1915 became British subjects, others have been born here, and None of our People ever seen Germany, We are as loyal to the British Crown as another Canadian, And just the fact that we are German should not interfere with our rights as British Subjects.

In reply, Aberhart suggested that given "the present inflamed condition of the public mind," it would be best if the convention was "postponed indefinitely."[168] Similarly, Italian organizations, political in nature or not, came under a general proscription during World War II.[169]

The activities of ethnic clubs, fraternal orders, and service clubs were an additional element in the institutional parameters of leisure in Alberta. They provided a focus for leisure, just as the church and the school did. Like some churches, they also played a role in the retention of culture and language. Most important, these organizations were most effective at a local level, with widespread impact on daily experience.

Indeed, the susceptibility of so broad an experience as leisure to formal organization created excellent opportunities for government regulation and taxation. The province regulated public facilities and collected revenue from leisure pursuits through amusement taxes. Yet government put relatively little back into leisure, in financial terms, in the years before 1945. And when it did, it did so only in respect to activities that served the leisure ideals of the dominant culture. By the end of the 1930s, however, many people were unhappy with the level and nature of government support. Although the Alberta Youth Congress of 1937 admitted that institutions such as the YWCA, YMCA, and the University of Alberta could be "used more effectively by the youth of the province," it maintained that a comprehensive programme should provide "additional facilities along the line of physical activity, cultural pursuits and post-school education" for young people and adults.[170]

Such demands for government to provide leisure facilities were encouraged during the late 1930s by the development of social programmes to deal with the effects of the Depression. The Youth Training Programme of 1938 that aimed to "fit" the unemployed for "gainful employment" had an important recreational dimension. In the early years of the war, the National Physical Fitness Act expanded government involvement in recreation by encouraging both cultural and physical fitness programmes at a local level.[171] It was through postwar reconstruction programmes, however, that governments became willing partners in efforts to provide facilities and programmes for leisure. In 1946 Mayor Ainlay of Edmonton noted that most towns and cities in Alberta had "taken some steps towards raising local funds to assist in various projects, including community halls, gymnasia, swimming pools, libraries, playgrounds, handicraft centres, etc." Although between 40 and 60 percent of the costs could be raised locally, additional funding was needed from the federal and provincial governments. In the postwar years, government willingness to meet these demands stemmed in part from a desire to avoid unemployment and its attendant social unrest. Community centres for recreational and cultural programmes could raise the physical fitness and "moral" character of Canadians.[172] The longstanding appeal of useful leisure also gained support from the idea that community centres could serve as "living war memorials" in honour of Canadian soldiers who had died in the war. The federal government provided architectural plans, and government and public agencies, such as the university, encouraged communities to build community centres.[173]

This postwar government involvement was crucial in providing new facilities. It had been clear for some time that private agencies could no longer serve the public demand. Moreover, the reliance on private or local initiatives created an inequality, favouring urban over rural districts, which had been recognized since

World War I. Despite the introduction of motor vehicles and new communications technology, the inequity became worse in some respects: hence the increased pressure on senior governments to provide at least partial funding. Some urban programmes received funding in the 1940s from such local charity drives as the Community Chest campaigns, but these funds were limited and were very rarely applied to programmes that were province-wide. For instance, the Community Chest would not fund the Girl Guides because they had too many members and carried on too many of their activities outside the city. The Girl Guides then turned to the province for an increased grant, which they received.[174]

In this and other ways, the community level at which different groups operated had consequences for the organization of leisure activities. Many fraternal organizations were initiated through local chapters, yet took their reference from provincial, national and even international organizations, integrating local practice with broad leisure patterns. The fraternal bonds of Masons and the collective sense of Elks, Legion members, and Polish clubs, among others, regardless of their location, transcended geographical definitions of community. These networks were most important for the dominant culture, because it had the support of large numbers and because such organizations were already in place in more established parts of the country, especially in Ontario. Only the dominant culture had the wealth, confidence, and power to make extended organizations a reality. Because they could raise sufficient money locally and expressed a commonality based upon religion and ideology, purely local Protestant men's clubs were able to integrate themselves into a national and international organization through the YMCA. Interlocked local groups of institutions, like the combination of some Protestant churches, church clubs, and social work boards, also contributed to provincial and national networks sharing similar objectives and ambitions. It is logical to assume that some members realized individual benefits from such common pursuits. Certainly, the Boy Scouts advertised this kind of objective, but proof of benefit would require extensive biographical analysis of members. Nevertheless, the existence of institutions with provincial, regional, and national connections provided participants from the dominant culture with an advantage that could not be as easily realized by people who were outside the dominant culture and its institutions. Non-Protestants, for example, would have found themselves uncomfortable within the YMCA.

The operation of leisure within other institutions introduced a different complexity. Many churches used leisure to attract and hold members, and many justified the provision of entertainment in terms of fund raising. This was often sharply differentiated by gender; while women served the church through their labour and their abilities to raise funds through local events, the hierarchy of all the major churches remained firmly in male control. While the use of leisure to raise funds created a certain moral ambiguity for some churchmen, pure entertainment seems to have raised even more questions: a revealing indication of the challenge that leisure presented. But whatever the implications, churches used leisure in varying degrees to support their objectives and functions. These objectives sometimes reflected a broader community responsibility, as evidenced by church involvement in leisure aimed at the preservation of language and ethnic traditions.

Secular agencies such as the University of Alberta Department of Extension, public schools, community halls, playgrounds, and community leagues represented yet another level of leisure organization with broader objectives. Community leagues reinforced community objectives with recreation. The extension programmes at the University of Alberta clearly reflected the dominant cultural view that leisure time should be usefully and, in this case, intellectually employed. The university's work was often innovative, challenging, and sophisticated, but its success was also due to its possession of necessary facilities and equipment that were frequently unavailable to other institutions, especially before World War I. The gradual introduction of rural community halls and urban halls, parks, and playgrounds represented a shift away from reliance upon schools and churches for the staging of community recreational events. This significant trend gave the community some independence from sectarian or state priorities, although community facilities could, for example, display the political dimensions of the *narodni domy* and UFA halls.

Despite the development of community facilities, it is seemingly paradoxical that the direct involvement of the state in leisure organization increased. Local governments of the early twentieth century made only limited contributions to leisure activity through the construction of parks and the encouragement of playgrounds and, in Edmonton, of community leagues. After World War II they were more active and willing partners in providing leisure facilities on the grounds of local boosterism and social stability, but prior to that many local organizations operated with little or no government financial assistance. Provincial government grants for leisure were uncommon, and were impossible to secure purely for entertainment; the government supported only those agencies that could be seen to serve precise social objectives or that agreed with the notion of useful leisure. During the 1920s, organizations that received grants, such as the Canadian Legion, Girl Guides, Boy Scouts, Alberta Girls' Work Board and Boys' Work Board, all promoted useful leisure and took their reference from the dominant culture.

The increased involvement of all levels of government in leisure and cultural programmes in the postwar period marked the end of an era in which the leisure and cultural needs of the population were met through voluntary collective initiatives often involving a particular concept of social reform. The services provided through these means were sometimes adequate, and sometimes even excellent, but they were not consistently offered at either the local or provincial level. Coupled with the demands for social change and cultural enrichment that arose in the immediate postwar period, the effort to overcome the earlier unevenness prompted new approaches to leisure facilities and programmes.

PART II

4. To Be a Gentleman: Sports in Alberta

Many organizations in Alberta attempted to hold and attract members through the enjoyment of sports. Sports meant more, however, than mere collective or individual exercise—they were also a focus for concerns about health, gender distinction, class, and social development. Thus, sports took their reference not only from the qualities inherent in each sporting activity, but also from the social structure within which they operated. While the great number of sports played in Alberta prohibits discussion of each individually, certain sports held particular importance: golf and baseball were extremely popular in the summer, and hockey and curling were dominant during the winter.

Although sports for most people simply meant enjoying the outdoors and fellowship with friends and neighbours, this apparently straightforward character disguised complex underlying assumptions. According to Morris Mott, English-speaking Manitobans of the late nineteenth century saw sports, in part, as a means of transplanting British institutions to the West. This group, which increasingly constituted the dominant culture in Manitoba, judged sports within the criteria of "manliness" and "usefulness." Incorporating courage, physical vitality, discipline, and fair play, manliness characterized all physically strenuous, military, and team sports. The manly requirements of team sports were not only strength and endurance, but also discipline and mental agility, attributes all assumed to be peculiarly male and British. The establishment of such sports in Manitoba thus helped to make Manitoba a British society.[1] Mott's analysis suggests that sports were tightly bound up with social and political issues in the dominant culture of early Manitoba.

This attitude was also apparent in Alberta. The Alberta Football Association claimed in 1932 to be "strictly an amateur body" that was "endeavouring to foster a British sport in our Province."[2] Moreover, from the turn of the century, those with power in Alberta society accepted the outlook that manliness, fair play, and team sports were characteristically British. Indeed, fair play had sufficient merit to be invoked in almost every discussion of sports. Although it was rarely defined, it was based upon a range of assumptions about equity, justice, honesty, decency, and courtesy. Fair play was not only a manly but also a gentlemanly quality. This vague but potent concept was applied to team sports in a number of ways. Because team sports were essentially a male activity, the team resembled the boyhood "gang," which could as easily become an expression of disruption as of order. Like a boys' gang, the team needed control in order to make it into a positive force, but boys could be treated with a directness in these matters that could not be applied to adults. For adults, the same end could be achieved through an emphasis on concepts such as sportsmanship and fair play. These attributes would make the team efficient and purposeful, excellent practice for "the more serious game of life."[3] The "game" itself was elevated to a position of sanctity and moral autonomy and it was said that one could do a disservice to the game, just as one could harm a fellow citizen. The game was therefore given definite form through rules codifying its traditions and its transcendent character.

Team sports were characterized as a force for social levelling and understanding among classes because "cliques and classes are broken up in team play." Wealth and social status meant nothing on the playing field, where all sportsmen were equal. This did not, however, mean political individualism, but some form of Christian moral democracy; "when a person had learned the art of sinking his prejudices and ambitions for the good of the team he had learned something of real moral worth. A common loyalty trained in games is of value in godliness." Thus, team playing became a force for religious expression and training. Moreover, team sports, if "well conducted," would "develop restraints in life." The good sportsman had to "learn to restrain temper. He must conserve his strength to expend it in the most effective way for the success of the team." Further, one had to face "hazards" in sports that, if faced squarely, taught the individual an important virtue.[4] And an integral part of facing these hazards, and of developing restraint or discipline, was learning fair play.

Fair play was also useful in controlling the emotions caused by winning and losing. Although competition was frequently cited as a positive economic and social force, it also had a destructive potential that could not be ignored, and might be particularly damaging in the context of a community event. In 1913, one observer argued for limits on the competitive character of team sports events because only "the slightest flavor of rivalry to lend vim to the contestants" was necessary.[5] Some concluded that competitive sports were altogether bad for children, since they often ended in "wrangling and unpleasantness."[6] Between the wars, physiological arguments reinforced the tendency to restrict childhood sports. In one view, girls would derive the greatest benefit from folk dancing and all adolescents who did not have a "rugged" physique should avoid strenuous exercise. This was not a denial of the benefits of exercise, for some form of exercise, scientifically and systematically devised, was necessary to counter the stress of long school hours.[7]

Such concerns about sports and the effect of competition on children reinforced the importance of fair play — of winning and losing with grace and decency. While winning was always important, often many advocates of fair play were more concerned with how to lose. A well-conducted and honourable life involved losing gracefully to one's superiors. One could admittedly win with "dirty tactics," but this was unfair, unsportsmanlike, and a disservice to the game. A sportsman had to learn to take defeat with grace and without fuss, to take it "smilingly and with his hand extended to his victorious opponent, appreciating the skill and endurance of the victory." Although such virtues were taught by the church and the school, they were put "into action [and]...developed...in the arena of wholesome play."[8] For some, fair play was not merely the antidote to the dangers of competitive sports to children, but a positive benefit of properly conducted competition. A Mount Royal School teacher in Calgary asserted in 1920 that athletic competitions should be made compulsory in all schools and that no student should be allowed to "escape" them because "there is no experience which enters into the formation of character of greater value to the boy and girl than that which trains him or her to be a good loser." Such training was part of the school's social responsibility and no school had fulfilled its social duty until it had "made" every student into "a clean, big-spirited, sporting Canadian."[9] The ambition of the Canadian to be a good loser has rarely been stated more clearly.

The rhetoric about team sports and fair play tied nicely into the belief that failure in life was largely the fault of the individual. In the context of a belief that the playing field was a social leveller, it was easy to assume that sportsmen who had not achieved social or economic success in life could experience a more important moral victory in well-conducted sports that demonstrated true worth and dignity, not mere transient material success. Such an attitude was a significant reinforcement of views about social order.

The view that team sports and fair play would serve social order elevated sports well above the realm of mere play. Moreover, sports incorporated physical exercise, accepted by World War I as a method of preserving health and easing the effects of old age.[10] A healthy population meant a more successful and wealthy nation: a society could only be as good as the physical health of its citizens.

By the 1920s, it had become common to argue that "athletics, properly supervised and regulated, may be regarded as a national vitalizing force."[11] This led in turn to the necessity for imbuing the young with an appreciation for exercise.[12] In this light, it was asserted that the state should subsidize sports and athletics. In 1920, the federal Commission of Conservation reduced this idea to its crudest level, arguing that the expenditure of public money to develop physical fitness among Canadians "would be as beneficial as the money spent on improving farm stock."[13]

Military needs were said to strengthen the case in favour of physical exercise. In the early 1920s, some Canadian sport advocates argued that the glory won by Canadian soldiers resulted from their physical fitness. Even so, wartime recruitment had shown that 30 percent of the men were physically unfit for service, a condition requiring correction for Canadian military preparedness. Thus, physical training should be provided in the schools and the play instinct should be directed toward physical fitness to stimulate "national life."[14] Similarly, although more directly, the Alberta Provincial Rifle Association demanded a government grant because the popular sport of rifle shooting promoted patriotic military preparedness since rifle club members assisted the militia, which was "always willing and ready to back up the laws of our province."[15]

The post-1918 arguments connecting sports with military needs were essentially hollow. Before World War I, Canadians did have a form of military training in schools provided by the Strathcona Trust, which aimed to prepare Canadian school boys for military service with training in military drill, rifle practice, and physical fitness. However, the programme implemented in Alberta schools in 1912 included little more than gymnastics. After 1921 the UFA government revised the curriculum to emphasize physical fitness over military drill, which was confined to the higher grades. Military objectives were downplayed in favour of social benefits, and sports were used to create health and to teach obedience, courtesy, and personal discipline.[16]

On a different level, organized sports advertised and promoted urban areas. The number and quality of sports played in a town were often cited as proof of its great future and the vitality of its population.[17] Representation at provincial and national competitions was seen as good advertising for a town, exactly the reason advanced in Fort Macleod in support of setting up a hockey team in 1911.[18] And when a local team played in an international competition, so much the better. The Commercial Graduates Basketball Club, a women's team from Edmonton, provided a focus for local pride and boosterism: the team's uniforms loudly proclaimed "Edmonton," "Alberta," and "Canada." When the team won the world championship at the 1924 Olympics, it was said that its players had "brought to many thousands of people the fact that Alberta, and particularly the Edmonton district, produces the finest type of Canadian womanhood."[19]

In another sense, the Grads were an anomaly. Ordinarily, women were simply ignored in sports rhetoric, their role and place in society made subservient, even irrelevant, through a form of symbolic annihilation. Women's recognition of this fact was demonstrated by their increasing efforts to participate in sports, although only those women with sufficient wealth, status, and time were active in sports before 1914.[20] The continuing debate over the danger of many sports, especially contact sports, to femininity and reproductive health, no doubt also had its effect.[21] When women did participate in sports before World War I, they usually did so through sexually segregated teams. Sexual segregation remained the context even when participation became more extensive in the 1920s, as was evidenced by the formation in 1926 of the women's amateur athletic federation in affiliation with the Amateur Athletic Union of Canada (AAUC).[22] In the absence of detailed and specific research about the history of women and sports in Alberta, the question of the extent of their participation remains unclear. It is nevertheless evident that sports perpetuated and reinforced gender distinctions in the society.

Far more prominent than gender in sports rhetoric in Alberta was the ambition to make sports a force for the reconciliation of urban and rural communities. Stanford Espedal, the physical education instructor at the Olds Agricultural School, contended that athletics and team sports should be promoted to expand the physical culture of rural Alberta. While everyone loved to play baseball, it was often difficult to get the required number of players together. Soccer was popular only in English-speaking districts, and skating and hockey, which were popular everywhere, were too seasonal. Regular, planned athletic activity in both school and home would give farm boys "suppleness, agility, and gracefulness of movement." He rejected the early twentieth century view that farm life was healthy simply because it involved hard outdoor work. While farm work might build strength, Espedal felt that it had a "tendency to make one awkward and slow" and "the big husky" from the farm proved "not so husky when it comes to doing some gymnastic feat or playing in an organized game." Thus, the popular characterization of the farm boy as strong but clumsy could be overcome through organized sports and athletic training in gymnastics, wrestling, boxing, and track and field. Moreover, participation in team sports created social skills, and while the farm boy was developing an athlete's body, he was also improving his self-image. No longer ridiculed and full of self-confidence, he would be more likely to remain on the farm, much to the benefit of rural society and the province.[23]

Many advanced another, related idea: that sports and physical exercise could be used to combat or prevent juvenile delinquency. The Calgary City Council was confidently informed in 1928 that, if Calgary had more playing fields, "there would be less need for juvenile courts."[24] This idea was loosely based upon the notion that sports built character and kept children and adolescents busy and out of trouble. Stanford Espedal summarized all of these notions:

> Sport is one of the best means of building good character. A boy learns to take pride in himself and does his best to keep in good condition. He "cuts out" tobacco, keeps more reasonable hours; he holds himself erect and walks lightly. He learns "to play the game" fair and square and be a good loser as well as a good winner.[25]

The YMCA and YWCA saw their major investment in sports programmes and in athletic training as a means of combatting urban listlessness and the Calgary YWCA argued that its physical training programme provided "the opportunity for recreation which youth and health naturally craves and which is denied the girl during the working day." A workout in the gym or a swim would provide the girl with "a hopeful outlook."[26] Physical exercise and sports were promoted as antidotes to the stresses of life, and in 1935 gymnastic classes for civil servants were organized in Edmonton, with the idea that physical training would create and develop "human beings best fitted to cope with the conditions of modern civilization." [27]

This reasoning was reflected in a number of arguments made during the 1930s about the social role of sports and exercise. In 1934, an Ontario correspondent told Premier Brownlee that sports were "the logical and safest means of occupying the greatly increased leisure of the masses brought about by shorter working hours."[28] To the more common problem of unemployment, sports and physical exercise also could be part of the answer, for "there are many who have been unemployed for so long that a return to their old jobs would prove a physical difficulty while a new job might be an impossibility."[29] In a similar vein, the Youth Training Programme established by the federal government in 1937 emphasized both physical and job training to reverse "the loss of morale among the young unemployed."[30] On another front, physical training would help correct the laziness and consequent ill health caused by people who used "their automobiles so much that necessary exercise has become a task too tiring for them."[31]

The prevalent theories of exercise, sports and fair play all supported the dominant culture's ambition to see a British society in Alberta. British and British North American sports were promoted in schools and by the interwar years acceptable games such as baseball were being played by children and adolescents of most ethnic groups. Given the dominant culture's behavioural theories and its assumption that there was a causal link between sports and assimilation, the mere playing of a game was sufficient reason to see such participation as a cultural victory. Further, sports presented no challenge to the centrality of work. By the time major settlement began in Alberta, rules had been modified and games had been shortened to fit them into definable periods of time. Sports thus presented no challenge to regularization of time around work for either spectators or players.[32] Technological change also enhanced the effect. Changes in transportation permitted greater participation and spectatorship without increasing the amount of time required for such activity. Further, many skating, hockey, and curling rinks in Alberta were lit with electricity by the 1890s, permitting evening skating and hockey, and in 1939 floodlighting was installed in both Calgary and Edmonton stadiums for evening football games.[33] These developments were simple but powerful means of confining sports to non-work time and of maintaining the supremacy of regular work hours.

To a large extent, sports were localized before 1945. While better transportation broadened the scope, the focus remained local because of a dispersed population and poor communications, except between the largest cities and towns. Sports were prominently featured at fairs, community picnics and public holidays, and sports days were held in most communities every summer. Sport was a highly flexible term and included competitions involving man or beast. Before World War I, horse racing was unequivocally defined as a sport, probably the most popular in the province. Many early sports days were occupied by little more than horse races; the Wetaskiwin sports day in 1895, for example, complemented the horse racing programme with some foot races.[34] Within fifteen years, the range of sport activities had widened considerably; the Camrose sports day in 1909 included horse racing, baseball, tennis, track and field and tug of war.[35] This broadening was especially evident for children and adolescents, and in 1921 typical sports events for children included potato races, sack races, jumping, and running.[36]

This local or community orientation frequently fit into a provincial or even a regional context. From the mid-1890s, "provincial" championship games were played in the area that was to become Alberta. Such contests were concentrated in urban areas, no doubt because of their transportation and commercial advantages.[37] Calgary and Edmonton Rugby teams competed against each other after 1891, when the two towns were linked by railway. Teams from Fort Saskatchewan, Edmonton, and Calgary contested challenge hockey games by 1895. Other competitions in the nineteenth century were subregional and took in only one portion of the province or the prairies. Cricket games after 1890 involved teams from Medicine Hat, Swift Current, Maple Creek, and Calgary,[38] though most of these were challenge games leading to no regular play-off schedule. Such intercommunity sports networks presupposed a common sports experience and the development of facilities and clubs to accommodate competition. Accordingly, in the infrastructure that grew steadily in the late nineteenth and early twentieth centuries, the establishment of leagues was central. Their number increased dramatically and spread from Calgary and Edmonton to the smaller towns of the province in the first years of the twentieth century. By the outbreak of World War I, the main team sports of hockey, baseball, and football were organized on the basis of provincial leagues.

At this level, sports became highly regulated and organized. To a certain extent, systematic organization was essential to the very nature of team sports. Competition among dispersed teams depended upon commonly accepted rules. The formation of clubs permitted the organization of regularly scheduled games and maintained team unity. While many sports were played in an informal and impromptu manner, there was a strong tendency before 1920 to institutionalize recreational play within clubs encouraging participation rather than spectatorship.[39] Clubs organized on the basis of ethnicity, occupation, or church affiliation provided an opportunity for teams to play in existing leagues or gave rise to new leagues based on these same criteria. In 1910 various church teams in Calgary were playing other teams in city wide leagues, but by 1914 an interdenominational league had been established for church teams only.[40] Some leagues had little stability, and disappeared altogether or changed over time. Church leagues in Edmonton declined in the 1920s in the face of competition from the sports leagues created by the Federation of Community Leagues.[41] Further, through the organization of provincial leagues by amateur associations such as the Alberta Amateur Hockey Association, the framework of occupational or other social criteria declined. Clubs and leagues not only expedited the organization of sports but often sponsored development of facilities. Private clubs built tennis courts, curling rinks, and golf courses for their members.

The Thistle Rink, Edmonton, opened in 1902 (PAA B.6528)

Facilities were also operated as private businesses, especially skating rinks. Of course, rinks were not always essential; it was common practice to clear a pond or river for recreational skating, but the commercial rinks soon built in most towns and cities served the scheduled needs of organized hockey. Calgary had a number of commercial rinks after 1884, the most important of which was the Auditorium Rink (later known as the Sherman Rink), which opened in 1904. It was said to be the best building of its type in western Canada, with an ice surface measuring 77-by-170 feet and a seating capacity of about five thousand. Spectators had an unimpeded view of the ice because the roof was supported with wooden circle trusses,[42] rather than with the pillars that had hindered most spectators' view of the ice in earlier rinks. Although smaller, the Thistle Rink in Edmonton, opened in 1902 by the Edmonton businessman Richard Secord, also provided a clear view of the ice.[43] The design of these rinks is one indication that paying spectators were becoming an important part of hockey, just as they were for other attractions booked into the arena. Yet the commercial nature of these facilities also meant restricted access because they charged admission. Before 1914, a typical single admission for skating in an urban rink cost 25 cents. Season tickets were also available, and around 1910 a season pass at a Calgary rink cost $4 for men and $3 for women or children.[44]

When they were established in Alberta centres just before World War I, the YMCA and YWCA provided an alternative to commercial and club sports. Among other things, they offered facilities for sports such as basketball and swimming and did much to promote both sports in the province. During the same period, some schools made their sports facilities freely available to students and sometimes to the community at large. These were among the few facilities in the province before 1920 that could be characterized as being public. Playing fields were also important, but were not available everywhere as might be expected. According to one 1920 report, in rural areas, where "land is plenty and cheap," there were almost no parks and playing fields. "Even the rural baseball team must pay rent for the use of some pasture field."[45] Nevertheless, school, fair, and community hall grounds were commonly used for community team sports, and by the 1930s, many of these had dugouts, backstops, and bleachers.

As for the urban areas, Calgary had few playing fields in 1909 and city sportsmen mainly used the fields in Mewata Park. The city's playing fields were used almost to capacity, and it was said that there would soon be insufficient space with the result that only the "stars" would get the field and weaker players would become mere spectators.[46] In 1913, in the midst of such apprehen-

sions, the city gave four acres of Mewata Park to the federal government for an armoury. In the ensuing uproar, the *Calgary Herald*
claimed that young men and boys would be deprived of fitness
and health acquired by playing football, baseball, lacrosse, and
"other good manly games." The manliness of city council was
called into question, for "few real live men, who have, or ever had,
any red blood in their veins" would ever surrender a playing field.[47]
While limited space for team sports continued to be a problem in
Calgary well into the 1920s, Edmonton was somewhat better off
because the university's playing fields were open to the public until
1935, when they were restricted to people affiliated with the
university. By this point, however, Edmonton had developed an
additional twenty-three acres of playing fields on the old peniten-
tiary grounds.[48]

By World War I it was obvious that more public facilities were
necessary if participatory sports were to be widely available. Substantial expansion followed, especially in skating and hockey
facilities, during the interwar years. The Edmonton Community
Leagues constructed rinks, and the City and the Public School
Board helped fund this construction on the understanding that
children could use the rinks each afternoon after school and on
Saturday mornings. The rinks were uncovered but were enclosed
with a high board fence and had indoor dressing rooms. Similarly, rinks were installed on Calgary public school grounds, to a total
of sixty-nine by 1944.[49] In 1924, pressure by residents in Red Deer
for a rink as a "public necessity" failed to get the local government
to act, but led the local Elks Club to raise funds for a covered rink.[50]
The YMCA and YWCA, continuing expansion of their facilities
and services, became an important force in organized sport in
Calgary and Edmonton in the interwar years. By 1934-35, the
YMCA in Edmonton was training sixty to seventy boys in wrestling
and twenty to thirty men in boxing, was sponsoring seventeen
basketball teams and thirty softball teams, and had organized its
own softball league.[51] The schools also expanded their efforts in
sports and in the 1920s became important promoters of track and
field.

In the organization and regularization of sport, no issue assumed
greater importance than that of amateurs being overshadowed and
demoralized by competition from professional players. The support of amateurism was important for those who wished to institutionalize fair play and saw play as an idealized activity that built
character through purity of purpose. This objective was threatened

by commercialization and materialism, and the struggle against professionalism was expressed as an assertion of personal discipline, fair play, and the interests of true sportsmen. In theory, the problem of distinguishing an amateur from a professional had been solved by the early twentieth century, but the question continually resurfaced. By the turn of the century, an amateur was defined as a person who had never competed for a money prize or practiced athletic exercise as a livelihood.[52] This definition remained the basis of discussion for the balance of the period under review, but there was ongoing debate because of the increasing commercialization of sports. The betting that was endemic at some sports events sometimes led to corruption. Moreover, as Calgary Methodists were told in 1907, gambling defiled the noble potential of sports and demeaned sportsmanship, fair play, and the integrity of the game.[53] One way to "clean up" sports was to promote amateurism, often expressed in terms of "sports for sports' sake," which was in many minds a British notion.

All professional players fell under the opprobrium attached to playing for money. Professionals were not regarded as gentlemen, although some were worse than others. The greatest invective was reserved for professional boxers, who were very popular in the province after 1900. In 1909, the *Calgary Herald* argued that professional boxing matches took place too frequently in the city and recommended a limit of one every three months. This view arose from two related and commonly held beliefs. According to the first, professional boxing was inherently corrupt and once it became organized and established in a community, "the faking and crookedness inseparable from such sport" rose to the surface.[54] According to the second, professional boxing was a vicious and brutal activity totally lacking the moral qualities of sport. Indeed, some felt that "the bull fights of Mexico and Spain are pardonable compared with the human sort, whose bloody frays" received more public attention than did "the triumphs of art and learning."[55] Oddly, only professional boxing was seen in this light: amateur boxing, perhaps because of its military and manly applications, was rarely viewed with disdain.

The most important sports played by amateurs in Alberta were governed by sports associations like the Alberta Amateur Hockey Association, the Alberta Golf Association, and the Alberta Amateur Baseball Association. They organized the play, settled disputes about players and games, and arranged play-offs. Those established shortly after the turn of the century were early examples of the regulation of amateur sport in the province. Of these, the Alberta Branch, Amateur Athletic Union of Canada (AAAU) was the most powerful. It was the provincial branch of the Canadian Amateur Athletic Union (renamed the Amateur Athletic Union of Canada in 1909) which had been established in 1884.[56] In 1908 at a meeting in Calgary, people "interested in clean amateur sport" formed the AAAU "to govern, promote and protect all amateur sport in the province."[57] The association issued amateur cards to athletes and sanctioned athletic contests. Its establishment marked the true beginning of comprehensive sports regulation in Alberta.

The AAAU's main objectives were to curtail professional sports and enhance amateur sports. Thus, it existed primarily "to keep a watchful eye over those who take part," though it did organize championship events for sports such as track and field, swimming, and boxing, which had no provincial organizing bodies.[58] The AAAU was able to entrench itself through the affiliation of specific sports organizations like the Alberta Rugby Football Union and through its close connection with institutions like the YMCA. But its regulatory power was based upon its authority to issue amateur cards to its members that established an athlete's status as an amateur and his right to play in amateur competitions. In 1920, the association issued nearly eight hundred such cards. To receive and keep a card, an amateur could not play with or against professionals, a requirement that implicitly extended the AAAU's influence to sports lacking regulatory affiliation with the AAAU. Their participants were "often forced to adopt amateur standing, since many of the athletes who participated in these 'non affiliated' sports were AAA[U] members in other sports."[59]

The authority to organize and regulate also sustained the commitment to manliness by officially asserting gender distinctions in sports. In 1914, the AAUC, the parent body of the AAAU, ruled that women could neither belong to the AAUC nor be registered in any sports or competitions controlled by the AAUC. Women could compete, but only against each other. These rules would also have applied to the AAAU because of its affiliated status, but whether this ruling occasioned debate in Alberta is unclear. In any event, the coming of World War I ended for a time any debate about women in sports; sportswomen tended to be wealthy and leisured and they turned their efforts towards war work.[60]

The power of the AAAU was clearly demonstrated during the war. In 1916, under the increasing pressure for military recruitment fanned by mounting war hysteria, the AAAU banned all senior league and then all intermediate league civilian sports in Alberta. Applied to all sports where an admission was charged, the ban remained in force until conscription was implemented late in 1917. No other provincial amateur athletics organization in Canada followed Alberta's extraordinary lead in this respect, an action said to demonstrate Alberta's commitment to the war "ahead of all other matters."[61] To the AAAU in 1916, "it looked as though athletics must be totally forgotten because of the greater game that was being decided upon the battlefields of France." Thus, athletics, "other than those in military leagues for patriotic purposes," had become irrelevant for directing the energy of the people to war objectives. Moreover, the introduction of the ban in 1916, just at the time when conscription was becoming a public issue, may have been an attempt by the AAAU to promote conscription by granting legitimacy only to enlisted sportsmen. The enlistment of sportsmen was publicized as a matter of provincial pride. Though many of them were killed, "they showed the world that [they] could play the game of life as they had played their athletic games, in the true British Sporting Spirit."[62]

Another war-related issue involved the status of returned men, who had played with, against, or as professionals while in service but had been amateurs prior to enlisting. The AAUC ruled in 1919 that it would not reinstate such individuals as amateurs. The AAAU refused to accept this ruling and "whitewashed" all Alberta athletes as of 17 May 1919. At the same time, it redefined the term "amateur" in a more moderate fashion to permit some games between professional and amateur teams and also allowed an athlete to be "professionalized" in one sport but remain an amateur in another.[63] The general restrictions against amateurs playing or even practicing with professionals were otherwise maintained. This postwar relaxation in rules for amateurs created a more flexible approach and allowed such events as exhibition games between touring professional British Rugby teams and Alberta amateur teams. Between 1921 and 1932, seven British teams toured Alberta promoting Rugby football and providing Canadian and Alberta amateur players with top rank opponents to help improve their game.[64] As it was observed in 1919, "the west wants to put amateur sport on a good basis and to help good clean professional sport," hopefully by putting all sports "on such a basis that there will be no bootlegging tactics."[65]

The AAAU rules on amateurs raised only occasional debate in

Alberta, and this usually centred around baseball because sports day and fair organizers were willing to pay for good players to draw a crowd. It was clear in 1920 that many towns commonly offered cash prizes for ball games and then scoured the cities for good players.[66] Despite the opposition of the AAAU, this remained a problem throughout the 1920s. In 1928 the AAAU finally asked the provincial government to prohibit cash prizes for sports at agricultural fairs.[67] Even so, the attitude of the AAAU towards professionals was more lenient than that of its parent body, no doubt because Alberta's smaller population and its distance from central Canadian national amateur championships necessitated an approach that would put as many good players as possible into Alberta games.[68] Nonetheless, the AAAU distinction between amateur and professional came increasingly into question by the early 1930s. With general public support, some amateur sports associations began to challenge the total separation of amateur and professional. In 1931, there were "those who still feel that a player who has turned 'pro' has placed himself beyond the pale," but the majority of people no longer equated the ideal sportsman with amateur status because "a professional in sport may still be a gentleman; and the more he is treated like one, the more likely he is able to live up to expectations."[69] This significant shift accepted that a professional was capable of fair play.

While the AAAU was one of the most powerful forces in the regularization of sport in Alberta, newspaper and radio reports played a major part in standardizing many sports by making rules of play the same across the country or the continent. More importantly, such coverage greatly increased sports' popularity. By the time major settlement began in Alberta at the turn of the century, the extent and sophistication of the presentation of information about sports was well advanced elsewhere in Canada. In 1908, a play-by-play telegram report of the Stanley Cup hockey game between Edmonton and Montreal teams was transmitted from Montreal to fans in Alberta.[70] In 1910 the same technique was used for the Johnson-Jeffries championship boxing match, and fans in Camrose followed the telegram report at the Windsor Hotel.[71] Alberta newspapers gave particular attention to professional matches which probably increased the popularity of commercial spectator sports. It has been suggested that in Edmonton before World War I the frequent newspaper reports of national and international professional sporting news did more to promote professional sports than did local sports entrepreneurs.[72] By the 1920s provincial, national, and international professional sports received regular and comprehensive coverage. By 1924 the world series was front page news, not only in large urban dailies but also in small town papers like the *Red Deer Advocate*.

Newspaper and telegraph communications were important in Alberta for creating an audience for professional sports and in commercializing public interest. Radio and film intensified this process, but even before radio broadcasting, some sports, especially hockey, baseball, and boxing, were highly commercialized and created a demand for highly skilled players to attract spectators and increase the profits of game sponsors. But with radio and film, the commercial possibilities of sport were increased. It may be that some sports were better suited to radio than others, but the overall effect was to advance the mass appeal of sports. In the 1920s, Alberta cinemas screened films of famous boxing matches and by 1926 they included items on sports events and personalities in the news reels presented before feature films.[73] Radio was even more important: local or provincial games were sometimes broadcast in the late 1920s and regular national broadcasts of games had become common by the 1930s. The quality of local sports broadcasts was frequently uneven. Gord Williamson, an Alberta broadcaster, recalled that, without a broadcast booth, the equipment was set up on the sidelines and the broadcaster ran up and down the field dragging his microphone and cord. Crowds could present problems; one of the worst, Williamson recalled, occurred at the Drumheller Minor Hockey club when the Bentley boys (the standard bearers of a famous Saskatchewan hockey family) were playing:

> I was broadcasting from the seats. Behind me I had the whole Bentley family. I guess there'd be 15 or 20 of them. And their language was not always the best. And they never shut up. They kept yelling all the time and it made it a little difficult. [74]

Such pioneer problems were soon overcome, even in local sports coverage. By the end of World War II, broadcasting was firmly in place, integrating commercialized sports into popular culture in an unprecedented manner. While much is made of the fact that spectator sports are passive and non-thinking activities,[75] it can be suggested that intensified public interest may also have increased individual participation in amateur sports.

The range of sports played in Alberta has always been extensive, with varying levels and periods of popularity. Golf and baseball dominated summer sports, although other games were important. In most rural areas, baseball and softball were the only summer team sports, often played in conjunction with fairs, community picnics, and special celebrations. Polo was popular among English ranching settlers in southern Alberta at the turn of the century, but never attracted province-wide participation. In cities and towns, the range of sports was much greater. Lawn tennis was popular in the late nineteenth century, but the great boom in its popularity came during the 1920s. In Edmonton there were two tennis clubs before 1914, but both disbanded during the war. Following a revival in the early 1920s, Edmonton had ninety tennis courts by 1924 and the largest number of members in the Canadian Lawn Tennis Association of any prairie Canadian city outside of Winnipeg. Largely a middle-class sport, most tennis clubs were private, but non-club members could play on courts maintained by the city's community leagues.[76] While tennis ebbed and flowed in popularity, it continued to be played in Alberta throughout the period under review.

Cricket experienced swings in popularity before 1914 but virtually disappeared by the 1920s. Lacrosse shared a similar fate: perhaps the most popular team sport in Alberta by 1906, it was on the way out by 1914.[77] One sport that showed a steady increase in popularity was football, a confusing term used at the turn of the century for several games in which a ball was kicked. By the early 1890s, a number of football clubs operated in the province, and in 1921 Edmonton represented the west in the first east-west Grey Cup challenge championship match. Football in Winnipeg was deeply influenced by American rules of play because local teams played against nearby American teams. This American influence spread to other western teams, especially as they began importing American players by the 1930s; a move that created conflict with the Canadian Rugby Football Union and the AAUC.[78]

Track and field "athletics" were common summer events throughout the years, and running was especially popular. Before World War I, a number of talented native runners of Alberta achieved fame. Moosewa was a star at many Edmonton and prairie races in the 1890s,[79] and Alex Decoteau was judged the "champion runner of Alberta" in 1910.[80] Prior to 1920, the term athletics was loosely used to describe everything from tug of war to running. In the 1920s, in the absence of any provincial athletics association, the AAAU oversaw athletics which it defined in the restricted sense of track and field and gymnastic events. Later, local amateur athletic associations adopted the AAAU definition.[81]

Despite the great variety of summer sports, golf and baseball were the most consistently popular. Golf had become common in Ontario and Quebec during the 1870s.[82] The first game in Alberta was played at Fort Macleod in 1890 and by 1900 people were golfing at Edmonton, Calgary, Medicine Hat, and Banff.[83] In 1896, the Edmonton Golf Club (later the Edmonton Golf and Country Club) laid out Edmonton's first golf course. By 1914 the club had 400 members, though the negative impact of the war reduced membership to 125 members by 1918.[84] Provincial tournaments, held annually since 1908, were suspended from 1915 to 1918 but resumed in 1919. Although golfing increased steadily before 1914 with the influx of population, it was a game enjoyed mainly by city and town elites in exclusive private clubs.[85] At the beginning of the century, golf was believed to be a peculiarly Scottish game that few people (other than the English) were psychologically equipped to play. It was argued that the "Scottish temperament was exactly suited to bear with philosophical calm and self-control the hard and distressing buffets encountered in the course of play." This notion had been discredited by 1910 by American and especially French golfing victories in world championship matches.[86]

The private clubs that dominated Alberta golf were often licensed to sell liquor and were open seven days a week. As private institutions, clubs could avoid censure for Sunday sports, but Sunday golfing was never allowed to become an issue. The St. Andrew's Golf Club in Calgary (later the Renfrew Club) recognized the sensitivity of the matter and purposely arranged its interclub matches on days other than Sundays, a significant indication that its membership had incomes and occupations that permitted flexible use of time. In addition, a motion at one of its business meetings apparently ensured that "reports of Sunday golf played by this club" should not be "printed in the newspapers."[87] Over time, some social levelling did take place in the sport, and more middle-class people took up golfing during and after the 1920s. The appearance in newspapers of illustrated teach-yourself advice on golf[88] gave further evidence of its increasing popularity and accessibility. This trend became possible only when the cost of golfing was reduced through the construction of municipal golf courses. In 1913, Edmonton's purchase of land for a municipal golf course[89] made it the first city in Canada to establish such a course, and by the late 1930s, Calgary, Medicine Hat, Lethbridge, and other towns operated municipal courses. Because they charged a fee instead of requiring a membership, they permitted greater accessibility that resulted in a major boom in golf in the early 1920s. In 1924, seventeen thousand golfers played the Calgary municipal golf course.[90] Municipal golf courses were not, however, acts of philanthropy by urban governments. Such courses served the needs of middle-class civic voters and the profit of approximately $4,100 made by the City of Edmonton from its municipal golf course between 1916 and 1921 provided a solid justification for its operation.[91]

Messrs. Goddard, Alexander and Sommerville at the golf course, circa 1914. (PAA A.5618)

Even with municipal courses, the game remained expensive. In the late 1920s golfers were still recognized to be "of the well-to-do class,"[92] and in 1928 it was observed that golf not only had an addictive quality but also cost an "ungodly sum."[93] The elaborate and expensive equipment included special clothing, balls, bags, and clubs. Green fees were high, partly because golf courses, with their large acreage, were expensive to develop and maintain. Although most courses had grass greens, some, including the Bowness Club in Calgary and the club in Grande Prairie, installed "sand and oil greens" because of a chronic shortage of water.[94] Regardless of the nature of the course, membership fees were often beyond the means of most people. In 1922, the membership fee at the Edmonton Mayfair Golf and Country Club was thirty dollars per year,[95] and when the fees rose to forty dollars per year in 1924, one observer commented that the "present Governors [of the club] have altogether lost sight of the hope that was cherished that Mayfair would always remain a club for a man of moderate income."[96] Most golf clubs and courses tended to be on the outskirts of a town or city, which made access difficult for those without cars. In some cases, this problem was alleviated by the clubs themselves and the Mayfair Club in Edmonton provided members with a round trip shuttle service for fifty cents.[97]

The Alberta Provincial Golf Meet took place at the Mayfair Golf and Country Club, Edmonton, in 1943. (PAA B.632/1)

From the beginning of the century, golf was a highly organized sport. This was perhaps a reflection of the small size of the largely urban golfing fraternity in those years and of a certain unity in terms of class; both were reinforced by the nature of the game, with its expensive facilities that could be used for no other purpose. As well, perhaps because they tended to be wealthier, golfers travelled more and played golf away from home. The Alberta Golf

Association (AGA), formed in 1908, primarily organized tournaments for Edmonton and Calgary golfers[98] until the early 1930s. Golfers in other areas had little contact with the AGA, and it was not surprising that some of the "country" golfers found the AGA irrelevant. As the president of the Wainwright Golf Club noted in 1936, "we in the country towns have felt at times that we were being neglected and that the Association existed only for the benefit of the golfers in the cities."[99] Despite this situation, Alberta golfers followed relatively standard rules, which although modified by local practices, were based upon those of The Royal and Ancient Golf Club of St. Andrews, Scotland.

Although golf expanded in Canada as a whole during the 1930s,[100] there was little change in Alberta. There were fifty-two golf clubs in Alberta in 1926-27 and about the same number ten years later. Since only about one-half of them belonged to the AGA,[101] the association was obviously not meeting the needs of all Alberta golfers. In the late 1930s, the AGA shook off its lethargy and began an active programme of reorganization and promotion. The association negotiated special privileges at the large urban clubs for small town club members, organized tours of leading amateurs and professionals to the country districts, made the effort to include country golfers in the provincial tournaments, and provided various educational and technical services.[102] Of course, these programmes could not totally eliminate the differences between country and city clubs. The latter had better facilities and services because their memberships were larger and wealthier: unlike most other clubs in the province, almost all of the Edmonton and Calgary clubs had resident professionals by 1948.[103] The mobilization of the AGA was matched by new national initiatives after World War II. The Royal Canadian Golf Association (RCGA) began to play a larger role, establishing a national handicapping system and coordinating national tournaments by 1949. These activities were financed by a "Dollar a Year Dues Plan" for all male golfers, with one-half of the fee going to the provincial golf association and the other half to the RCGA.[104] These programmes represented a watershed in the history of Canadian and Alberta golf.

While golf grew in popularity, baseball remained the dominant summer sport in twentieth century Alberta. Baseball was widely played in southwestern Ontario by the 1860s and in Manitoba by the 1870s. In Ontario, it was played by all social classes.[105] This tradition was brought to Alberta by Canadian emigrants and later was entrenched by American immigration. Thus, baseball was part of the leisure of the dominant culture in Alberta from an early date, and it was always a feature at summer events like the 1884 Dominion Day celebrations in Edmonton.[106] The enthusiasm for baseball was reflected in the establishment of both amateur and professional leagues. The Alberta amateur leagues were organized geographically, by 1914 including the Southern Alberta League, the Crowsnest Pass League, the Bow Valley League, and the Canadian Northern Railroad League.[107] This enthusiasm also expressed intercommunity rivalry, and the competition between Lethbridge and Cardston, for example, was legendary.[108] As the success of the team was always a matter for celebration, it is apparent that the teams represented both local pride and ambition. Indeed, it would not be surprising to discover that rivalry between teams mirrored economic and political competition, and that its absence indicated a lack of this underlying motivation. Baseball and hockey seemed to have been the only sports to engender such intense spectator identification.

Competition between towns was also expressed through the development of professional ball teams. Professional ball started in Alberta before World War I with teams in Calgary, Edmonton, and Wetaskiwin. These teams played each other as well as touring professional teams like the Winnipeg Maroons and the Seattle Anacortes. The Western Canadian Baseball League, which scheduled games and policed the clubs, was recognized as a class 'D' League by the U. S. National Association of Baseball Leagues. The fortunes of Alberta professional ball teams were uneven; between 1907 and 1914 teams were formed and others collapsed. By 1912, only teams from Bassano, Red Deer, Edmonton, and Calgary were playing, and in 1915 the league was disbanded because of the war.[109] During the 1920s, there was little interest in Canadian professional baseball because, it has been suggested, corruption discredited professional baseball and good players deserted the Canadian clubs to play for higher wages with American professional teams. Of greatest significance was the appeal of American professional baseball. In the 1920s in Canada the World Series was the country's "greatest 'national' sporting event," made possible by wire service transmission of live games. In comparison, home-grown professional teams had little appeal.[110]

The decline of local professional baseball was not matched in amateur baseball, which remained popular at sports days, picnics, special celebrations, and summer holidays such as Victoria Day and Dominion Day. The Cardston celebrations for the coronation in 1911 featured a ball game drawing between three thousand and five thousand spectators.[111] In many rural and small town communities, ball was the only summer team sport played in the interwar years. Team sponsorship came from a variety of organizations, but many games were played solely for fun and, as Paul Voisey notes about the Vulcan area, "special games often pitted half of a town's streets against the other half, or its fat residents against the lean."[112] In large part, amateur baseball retained its popularity in Alberta because it had important and powerful sponsors, could be played at differing levels of skill and interest, required only simple facilities, and was cheap to play.

A ball game at Vegreville fair grounds in 1931. (PAA, UV.582)

Between 1900 and 1918, amateur baseball in Alberta had broad support in the public schools, the churches, and the community leagues. Edmonton had a five-team church league plus a five-team Sunday School Baseball League and Calgary had four teams in each of two similar leagues. During the same period, Calgary had a thirty-three team public school baseball league. An extensive league system was also organized under the Alberta Amateur Baseball Association. Although the YMCA never established a baseball league or teams, it provided extensive training, expertise, and promotion for the game.[113]

Baseball was a highly flexible game. One variation, softball, was "developed by Canadians early in this century and was played extensively, especially by girls and women throughout the twenties and thirties."[114] It was promoted by the public schools, the YMCA/YWCA, and various organizations such as the Gyro Club. In the beginning, softball was a slower game than baseball, and was considered to be more suitable for girls and women. The rules of softball varied and could be set by local leagues, but underhand pitching and a larger ball were always used.[115] The bases were closer together than in baseball, and this reduced size was important in communities which only had small playing fields.

The Eastwood Community League Girls' Baseball Team, champions of the City League in 1925. (PAA A.9962)

Softball could be played on almost any open, relatively smooth area and the equipment needed was relatively straightforward. In the twentieth century, most baseball league teams had uniforms often displaying the names of the sponsors; a popular form of advertising for local merchants and towns. The use of gloves became widespread in the twentieth century; in the late nineteenth century, most fielders had been "bare-handed artists, only the catcher having a glove of any kind."[116] Before 1945, all bats were made of wood. They were frequently marketed under the names of the greats of U.S. baseball, such as Ty Cobb, Babe Ruth, and Eddie Collins, which illustrates both the influence in Alberta of American baseball heroes and the commercial opportunities presented by mass-audience sports for both game and equipment endorsements.

Although baseball and softball were extremely popular in Alberta, play was restricted by Sunday closing legislation. Whereas golfers at private clubs were better able to circumvent complaint, organized ball games requiring public facilities were curtailed by the Lord's Day Act. The problem was that Saturday was not a free day for many young farm people. In 1920, it was observed that farm children had only Sunday as a day free from school or from work on the farm and "more Sunday baseball in rural communities is due to this cause than any other." Because his "religious conservatism" induced the farmer not to work on Sunday, he demanded that his children work around the farm on Saturday instead, taking the risk that Sunday games "may permit his children to be damned."[117] Damnation or not, by 1930 most interested parties agreed that public grounds, such as those in provincial parks, could be used only for "individual recreation and voluntary play such as would develop spontaneously amongst people who might happen to be there on any particular Sunday." Even so, violation of this understanding was common. In 1930 the government received a complaint that Lacombe and Aspen Beach teams were playing prearranged "fast" ball games at Aspen Beach on Sundays. Advertisements for the games claimed that "visitors to the lake will be glad to know that some kind of entertainment is being provided for them." Since the game was being played on private and not public land, the province refused to become involved, but Premier Brownlee contended that had the game been played on public land, the province would have had it stopped.[118]

Before 1945, Albertans played far more summer sports than winter sports. Tobogganing and snowshoeing were two popular, unorganized outdoor winter activities and some people also skied, although skiing was limited before the 1920s. Except at Banff, skiing was generally restricted to Scandinavian settlers and to children and adolescents. It was organized locally: Scandinavians at Camrose set up the first ski club in the prairies in 1911. Competitive ski jumping and touring predominated until participation began to broaden in terms of both ethnicity and age when the

Canadian Amateur Ski Association was established in 1920. Although the association had no national unity and limited influence in western Canada before 1935, it gradually introduced national organization into Canadian skiing.[119] By 1923, western Canadian regional ski championships included skiers from Alberta,[120] although downhill skiing did not become popular until the 1930s. A ski resort opened near Banff in 1930 and by 1938 the Jasper Ski Club was operating a two-mile run on The Whistlers Mountain. A scheduled "ski-train" to Jasper operating from Edmonton after 1937 was important in promoting downhill skiing to a limited extent before World War II.[121]

By the interwar period, a number of indoor sports were also gaining winter popularity. In Calgary, Edmonton, and other places, boxing, wrestling, and court games were carried on year-round in the schools or at the YMCA and YWCA. Just before World War I, basketball became an important winter activity in southern Alberta towns that had school gymnasiums. The popularity of basketball in southern Alberta grew out of the American origins of the Mormon settlers and some of the school teachers. It no doubt helped that it was frequently impossible to skate and play hockey during southwestern Alberta winters when chinooks caused ice to disappear in mid-winter.[122] As a result, the Raymond Union Jacks, a prominent men's team of the 1920s, was one of the notable basketball teams in Alberta. Despite this southern tradition, the most famous of all Alberta teams was the Edmonton Commercial Graduates Basketball Club coached by Percy Page. The Grads had already held the provincial women's basketball championship for eight years when they won the national championship in 1923. They then won the world championship for Canada in a demonstration tournament at the 1924 Olympic Games in Paris and their domination of women's basketball continued until 1940. The Grads gained national prominence, partly through skillful promotion, but fundamentally by consistently excellent play: from 1915 to 1940 they played a total of 522 games and won 502; an outstanding record that bolstered Edmonton's civic pride.[123]

Without doubt, however, the most popular winter sports in Alberta were skating, hockey, and curling; indeed, ice hockey came to overshadow even baseball in overall popularity. During the late nineteenth century, the ice was dominated by recreational skaters and not hockey players. Beyond Sunday afternoon skating parties, skating clubs put on fancy dress skating carnivals, skating parties, dances, and dinners.[124] At the turn of the century, owners of large,

That skating was a popular winter pastime is shown in this photograph of skaters at McKernan's Lake, Edmonton, in 1913. (PAA B.6361)

In Crowsnest Pass, a skating rink was built in an old smelter, circa 1913-15. (PAA A.1760)

improved rinks encouraged hockey by sponsoring teams and by selling season tickets to their games,[125] and because it was more profitable, hockey had eclipsed recreational skating at the large commercial rinks in Alberta by about 1910. In 1913, the YMCA built a recreational skating rink in Calgary,[126] but this was an exception before 1920, even though recreational skating continued to be highly popular on ponds, lakes and rivers. After the war the needs of recreational skaters justified construction of municipal or community rinks so hockey would not be allowed to "dominate everything and shut. . .[the] young folks out of their share of skating."[127] Indeed, recreational and speed skating enjoyed something of a renaissance during the 1930s, and in 1936 the Alberta Amateur Skating Association was established.[128]

In the late nineteenth century, hockey was played mainly by gentlemen members of clubs modelled on the English pattern.[129] Growing interest in hockey soon spawned a number of leagues. A senior league organized four Calgary teams in 1901, and two years later the Central Alberta Hockey League brought together teams located on the CPR line between Calgary and Edmonton. There was little early agreement about the conduct of the game, causing much wrangling over rules. The Alberta Amateur Hockey Association (AAHA) was established in 1907, the first such association for amateur hockey in western Canada, and after the formation of the AAAU in the following year, the AAHA became an affiliated association. In 1910, the AAHA included sixteen senior teams, divided into four districts. In the years leading up to World War I, the AAHA expanded to an intermediate league in 1913 and a junior league in 1914. Up to this time, organized hockey had generally been a game for adults, but with the formation of a junior league, younger players were brought into provincial league play. The age limit for players was continually lowered over the next twenty years, and in 1935 the Pee Wee National League in Calgary was established for boys aged twelve to thirteen.[130]

After the dampening effect of World War I, hockey became progressively more popular. The victory of the Winnipeg Falcons at the 1920 Winter Olympics created enthusiasm for hockey across western Canada, and in the interwar years, the University of Alberta hockey club participated in interuniversity games of the Intercollegiate Athletic Union, which had been established in 1920 to organize prairie university teams. [131] Schools, churches and businesses sponsored an immense number of leagues and teams with the Edmonton Community leagues mounting ninety games in

1925 alone.[132] Although men's teams dominated,[133] some important women's hockey teams played in both Edmonton and Calgary during the 1920s,[134] only to disappear after World War II. Senior men's hockey was the main attraction for spectators from 1907 until after World War II and in 1946 and 1948 Alberta teams won the Allan Cup, representing the senior amateur hockey championship in Canada. Hockey also remained a major participatory sport, and its popularity in the west increased each year until by 1940 the province was blanketed with hockey teams.[135]

Before World War II, professional hockey teams periodically stimulated spectator interest. In the Western Canada Professional Hockey League formed in 1921, Calgary and Edmonton were represented by the Tigers and the Eskimos respectively. After its collapse after the 1925-26 season, the Western League was followed briefly by the Prairie Hockey League. Professional hockey revived for a short time in the early 1930s, but then not again until the 1950s. Ice conditions and financing posed the main problems for professional hockey. Ice conditions were often erratic, especially in Calgary chinooks, and artificial ice was only first installed in Alberta in a Calgary rink in 1935-36.[136] It was also said that facilities were inadequate and that Alberta cities were incapable of supporting teams that could compete with the National Hockey League (NHL) teams based in much larger cities.[137] Indeed, in the 1920s the NHL became continentalized through American capitalization of teams and the franchising of NHL teams in the United States. Poorly capitalized western clubs could not afford the cost of travel to eastern Canada for games, let alone the cost of buying the best players or providing appropriate facilities. After the 1926 season, the NHL bought the entire Western League, including the Calgary and Edmonton teams, and allocated the players to its other clubs.[138]

The rapid evolution of regulations and equipment before 1920 significantly changed the game and its appeal. By 1913, six instead of seven players were on the ice, and most hockey teams in Alberta used the regulations of the Manitoba and Northwest Territories Hockey Association. Some of the rule changes before 1920 produced a faster and more publicly attractive game: more substitutions and "the three zones, with forward passing in each,. . . developed as the result of a drive to speed up and improve the game."[139] Improved equipment also increased the game's speed. In the nineteenth century, skate blades were sold separately from the boot. Hockey boots with a fixed blade, which became available in the 1890s, soon replaced the separate boot and skate, at least in professional and senior hockey. Their greater rigidity and soundness permitted faster skating.[140] On the "spoon blade" hockey stick introduced about 1909, the blade had a double wedging that gave the toe of the blade equal strength at both the top and the bottom to prevent splitting at the top of the blade.[141] This greater strength and resiliency permitted a player to hit the puck harder than could be managed with the old "wedge" stick. These and other improvements in equipment, ice conditions, and facilities all contributed to the increasing popularity of hockey for both spectators and players in Alberta.

Curling, the other great winter sport in Alberta, demonstrated Alberta's British and Ontario inheritance. Clubs organizing the play were common in Alberta towns by the 1890s. By 1900, curling was "second only to hockey as the most popular winter participant sport" in Alberta.[142] It was inexpensive and accessible, and by the interwar years it had come to symbolize prairie rural social life like no other game. In her 1946 study of the Hanna area, Jean Burnet observed that of all the sports played, curling was most popular:

> No farmers play golf but almost all curl. Curling is in the winter a major village-country link, drawing the country men from distances as great as fifteen and twenty miles. Hockey teams and baseball teams are less effective. They are singularly inactive and would in any case draw boys and young men only.[143]

It has been suggested that curling had numerous virtues in prairie communities: it gave people a perfect opportunity for socializing, it could accommodate an "unlimited number of teams," it could be played equally well by men, women, young and old, and it took place in mid-winter when there was more leisure time in farming communities.[144]

Most people curled on the traditional open ice in the early years, but abandoned it as soon as possible. Although Edmontonians may still have been curling on the river during the early 1890s, Edmonton's first curling rink opened in 1889. At Fort Saskatchewan people used the river and a nearby slough until a covered rink was built in 1908. By 1902, Edmonton had one indoor curling rink with three sheets of ice, but by 1922 five such rinks offered a total of twenty-nine sheets.[145] Calgary curling facilities experienced even faster growth; by 1911, they included the Victoria Curling Club, the largest curling rink in North America, with seventeen sheets of ice.[146] Although curling rinks were highly specialized structures, it was not unusual for sheets of curling ice to be laid out in skating rinks for bonspiels. Rural and small town curling rinks frequently consisted of only one or two sheets of ice and were often built and operated by volunteers, in much the same manner as community halls. The curling rink in Debolt was constructed with volunteer labour and materials in 1919, shortly after the settlement of the area. For several days each year, volunteers flooded the rink with water from local lakes and sloughs hauled in water tanks pulled by teams. This chore ended in 1946 when a well was dug beside the rink. It also "fulfilled a very great need of the people of the community; that of supplying water for household use." Other improvements came equally gradually. The gas lanterns installed at the beginning were subsequently replaced by a small light plant and later by line electricity. A ladies church group ran a lunch counter added in 1946, from which the curling club received 15 percent of the profits.[147]

Open air rinks were common in the early years. The men shown here are playing on the first curling rink in Peace River. (PAA A.2549)

The Scottish connection of Alberta curling was maintained formally by acknowledging the Royal Caledonian Curling Club of Scotland (RCCC) as final arbiter of curling matters in Canada. Curlers from Scotland occasionally visited Alberta and a 1938 tour was described as the "greatest boost curling ever received in Alberta." The representatives of the RCCC were greeted at the train station in Calgary by the mayor, other civic officials, an honour guard of police, military officials, and Indians from the Sarcee Reserve. They played match games (and lost) and attended frequent official receptions celebrating the Scottish flavour of the game.[148]

A two-sheet curling rink in the Drumheller area, in 1930. (PAA A.7994)

One did not, however, have to be a Scot to curl and curling appealed to a broad spectrum of people. Women were apparently curling in the 1890s in Alberta, but the first women's bonspiel was not held until just before World War I. Nevertheless, women's curling rapidly gained in popularity and women's curling clubs, women's bonspiels, mixed teams, and women's teams soon became familiar and accepted. Further, curling's appeal to young and old alike led to a great deal of competition on an intraclub, interclub, and bonspiel basis.[149] Interclub and bonspiel competition benefitted from improvements in the provincial and regional transportation system. Even in the early years, some people were willing to travel considerable distances to curl. Edmonton curlers went to Winnipeg to compete in bonspiels in 1893 and in 1903.[150] However, most curling competitions were provincially based. The interclub matches played from the turn of the century between Edmonton and Calgary clubs on Christmas or New Year's Day of each year were among the best known.[151]

The popularity of curling justified centralized regularization. In 1904, enthusiasts founded the Alberta branch of the RCCC in Calgary and adopted the rules of the Manitoba branch. The Alberta organization aimed to provide standard rules and to encourage the formation of new clubs. The Alberta branch of the RCCC soon faced discontent from some of its northern members, especially those in Edmonton, who charged that Calgarians ran the Alberta organization to the detriment of the northern rinks. The typical rivalry between Calgary and Edmonton led in 1917 to the formation for northern curlers of the Alberta Curling Association in Edmonton, although both associations apparently continued to play under the same rules.[152] In 1948, the Alberta Curling Association alone counted eleven thousand affiliated curlers.[153] Complementing these local organizations, the Dominion Curling Association governed curling as a "national" sport after 1935.[154]

Curling appealed to many people, including the members of this Ladies' Curling Club, photographed in 1900. (PAA B.6538)

Provincial and national aspects of organization could not detract from the local appeal of curling. For many curlers, the bonspiel was the highlight of the curling season and the winter social calendar. The first bonspiel in Calgary took place in 1894 and by 1912 the Calgary bonspiel attracted fifty-three rinks, more than half of them from outside Calgary.[155] The most important prizes were the trophies donated by individuals or businesses. Liquor was a common prize in the late nineteenth century, but sweaters, silver spoons, and car rugs had become typical by the interwar years.[156] A bonspiel invariably concluded with a banquet and dance in a hall usually decorated to express a curling theme. In 1922 the decorations for the banquet and dance at Red Deer included "flags and bunting" which, along with the "lavish use of brooms" and "the solid granite stones in their place," provided an appropriate setting. The dance programme also reflected the organizers' obvious zest for curling: the "9 o'clock draw" and a "12:30 Draw" included dances labelled "The Roaring Game" waltz, the "Chip the Winner" fox trot, a "Draw Up to 'er" quadrille, and the "Let 'er Curl" fox trot.[157] Each bonspiel was a major event, occupying several days and attracting enthusiastic spectators. By 1943, the bonspiel of the Alberta Branch of the RCCC lasted for a week after it was officially opened by the Mayor of Calgary, who threw the first rock.[158] The Canadian curling classic, the Macdonald's Brier Tankard, brought Calgary an even bigger event in 1948. It lasted four days and the final match between British Columbia and Quebec drew 5,900 people to the stands.[159] Calgary boosters took the opportunity to promote the Stampede City, decorating store windows and staging a parade featuring officials of the Brier, various politicians, the curlers, and "the required bands, Indians, outriders, conveyances of early days, etc." [160]

From the example of curling alone, not to mention the variety and ubiquity of sports in Alberta, it is clear that the centrality of sports to leisure was not simply a straightforward matter of play. It has been argued that sports promoted fundamental needs for community cohesion, gender distinctions, social mobility, and social control.[161] There is evidence that sports promoted cohesion in Edmonton society,[162] although it can also be argued that institutionalized sports reinforced class and religious distinctions in church and occupational leagues. Nevertheless, community league teams and amateur leagues drew on community identities. Some, like those organized by the AAHA, were based purely on geographical criteria. It would be useful to have a comparative analysis of the participating teams in religious, ethnic, or occupational terms to enrich our understanding of the place of sports in everyday life. In another area, whether sports built character and encouraged a sense of responsibility, as its proponents were fond of arguing, remains an open question. Certainly, the emphasis upon manliness contributed nothing to women's self-esteem or confidence and clearly prevented them from fully realizing their potential. Male exclusivity was further exercised in the gender segregation of teams for basketball, hockey, softball, and baseball. On the other hand, the mixed play of golf and curling, and apparently tennis as well, begs further investigation of both the terms and meaning of such integration.

The Calgary Braves played the Edmonton Eskimos in this first night game under lights, August 15, 1947. (PAA A.7284)

Sports must have promoted social control to some extent simply by dissipating energy, but any greater understanding of their operation in this manner in Alberta is beyond the current state of knowledge. No matter how logical it may seem to engage in sports as escapism in the face of everyday problems, we know neither the extent of class and ethnic participation and spectatorship, nor anything about individual perceptions of the sports system. In a related vein, the role of sports in creating social mobility for professional players did not figure prominently in Alberta before 1945. Professional sports in the province were too limited to present a meaningful opportunity for many Alberta players to acquire wealth and social mobility. Moreover, Alberta professional teams, especially in baseball and hockey, often imported some players. More information on the class and ethnic composition of amateur teams would be required to determine whether amateur sports fostered social mobility through friendships that could contribute social and material advantages.

It is clear, however, that sport was a means of implanting the views of the dominant culture in Alberta. The doctrine of usefulness was applied to sports, and some hoped that sports would integrate rural and urban society, promote social stability, and assist in creating a British society in Alberta. The most popular sports, hockey, golf, curling, and baseball, were part of the British-Ontarian cultural tradition. Yet their wholesale adoption was achieved more through a process of patterning than by direct imposition; a telling example of the working of hegemony. Even so, the regulation of sports to instill a respect for the ideals of British fair play led the AAAU to make strenuous and ultimately futile efforts to sustain amateurism. Amateurism faced a growing challenge from local, national, and even continental commercialized and professional sports, and the general population seems to have increasingly rejected the idea that professionalism was incompatible with being a "gentleman." Yet this acceptance of professionalism represented not a loosening of the hegemony of the dominant culture but an adjustment within that culture itself; being a gentleman continued to matter, but it was admitted that these qualities were possible in changed circumstances. The acceptance of commercialized sports was a long process, but it did coincide with increased exposure to professional sport (often American) through newspapers and radio. Moreover, the opportunities to participate in sports increased during the interwar years with the construction of more and better community facilities where imitation of professional techniques and practices could find personal expression.

The popularity of British-Ontarian sports in Alberta is *prima facie* evidence of the dominant culture's success in implanting another tradition. The process often operated from the top down: hockey was an elite sport in the late nineteenth century but was rapidly adopted by the whole society. Another elite sport, golf, also gained middle-class participants. Curling and especially baseball were more egalitarian from the beginning, but both were extended during the twentieth century to all levels of Alberta society. Moreover, basic concepts of the dominant culture were furthered by using its language of sport in everyday life. "Fair play," for one, had meaning for behaviour well beyond that of the playing field. From this it is evident that sports were one important means of creating a British-Canadian society in Alberta. While there were increasing American overtones, many of the dominant culture's assumptions conditioned the sports experience in the province. In this sense at least, the development of sports represented a triumph for the hegemony of the dominant culture.

5. A Sense
   of Sportsmanship:
      Hunting and Fishing

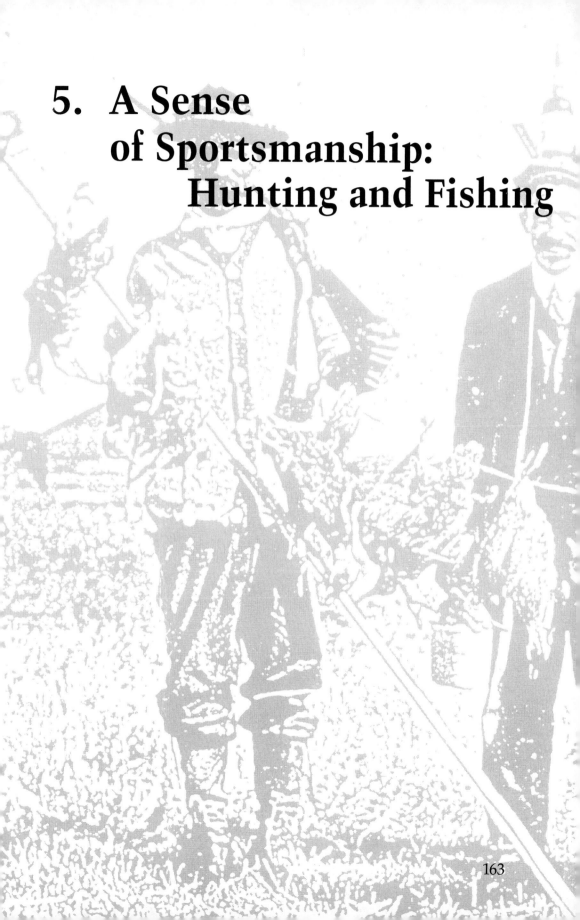

The formalization of activity through rules, organizations, and concepts about appropriate behaviour, such as fair play, was not restricted to conventional competitive sports. It also applied to hunting and, to a lesser extent, fishing, both of which were typically included in the common understanding of sports. Because the abundance of wildlife in the province and the traditions of the country encouraged these activities, hunting and fishing were probably the most consistently and avidly pursued male recreational activities in Alberta. During the twentieth century, government regulation of hunting and fishing intensified because of game depletion, the needs of hunters, and the status of hunting and fishing as sport. Wildlife conservation in Alberta was made up of many elements, one of which was wildlife's contribution to leisure activities.

In Alberta's early years of settlement, hunting was as much an economic as a leisure activity. Although market hunting was not as common in Canada as in the United States, in 1909 the Royal North West Mounted Police (RNWMP) sergeant at Wetaskiwin noted the practice and reported that P. Burns and Company bought wild ducks for meat processing.[1] The use of wildlife for food and income persisted in many areas of the province and, as late as 1939, the justification of hunting for food for personal use, and not for recreation, was made.[2] Many Métis and Indians and some white settlers relied upon hunting for food throughout the first half of the twentieth century, and the Depression of the 1930s reinforced this tradition. In 1933, a number of settlers in the Hoadley and Rimbey areas, pleading poverty, petitioned the provincial government to waive the fees for hunting licences. The government rejected their petition because such a precedent in a time of general distress would mean free licences "issued to practically all the farmers and homesteaders" west of the CPR line between Calgary and Edmonton as well as north of the North Saskatchewan River. Moreover, such a policy would deprive the government of its revenue from hunting licences and create conservation problems.[3]

Although people hunted for food, hunting still had a strong recreational element derived from a long European tradition. Hunting in England was directly linked to upper-class ownership of land,[4] but in North America the abundance of wildlife and the nature of settlement made hunting available to all. In early Alberta, good hunting could be found on public land close to most areas of settlement. The rapid development of a transportation network made most hunting areas accessible to everyone. The rich could hunt in style and in remote locations with the aid of pack trains and outfits like those operated from Mountain Parks in the Coal Branch area during the 1920s; in 1922, one man from Chicago reportedly spent thirty thousand dollars to kill a mountain sheep. Although this amount may have been exaggerated, excursions lasting between one and three weeks, and generally three weeks "to get a full bag,"[5] were beyond the reach of almost all Albertans. Nevertheless, hunting trips of a few days' duration were relatively common. The distance travelled depended on the prey—while the ubiquity of waterfowl made it unnecessary for many hunters to travel far, upland game birds presented another problem: depletion had become apparent early in the century. By 1903, Calgarians had to travel north of the city by train to hunt prairie chickens which could no longer be found near Calgary.[6] Big game hunters had in most cases to travel some distance to hunt, even in the late nineteenth century. Distances increased during the twentieth century as settlement and depletion of game pushed big game habitats into remoter areas. In 1912, residents of Camrose could hunt fifteen varieties of ducks, three of geese, and various kinds of snipe, plover, prairie chicken, grouse and partridge close to town, but they had to travel "a hundred miles or so" north for big game.[7]

Three hunters pose with their bag after a successful trip, circa 1900-1902. (GAI NA-2831-6)

In addition to bison, depletion of game generally had become noticeable within a short time of settlement. In 1884, the North West Territories Council passed an ordinance designed to protect birds and big game animals, in part by prohibiting Sunday hunting, and closing the big game hunting season from February 1 to September 1 and the waterfowl season between May 15 and August 15. Fines were instituted and game wardens were given wide powers of search and seizure. Only Indians were exempt from the provisions of the law, and then only "for the purpose of supplying their immediate wants."[8] In 1893, certain hunting practices and equipment were made illegal. "Swivel guns, batteries, sunken punts or night lights" were outlawed, as was the use of grain soaked in opium or other narcotics "for the purpose of stupefying and capturing" birds.[9] The Territorial laws were adopted by Alberta after 1905 and remained the basis for game legislation there for the next half century.[10]

Enforcement of hunting laws was largely ineffectual during the Territorial period, and the main function of game officers appears to have been issuing hunting licences. Neither the police nor public vigilance provided effective enforcement. Although the Game Ordinance of 1893 authorized rewards to those reporting infractions of the hunting regulations, paying the informer half the fine levied against those convicted,[11] the result was uneven at best. In 1893, a resident of Sturgeon River complained of "a number of gentlemen(?) from Edmonton" who regularly travelled to Sturgeon River to hunt on Sunday, and "Last Sabbath a number of these fellows had the boldness to come within a few rods of the church, where service was being held, and commence their shooting." A similar offence had led to prosecution the year before, yet the complainant stressed the need for more policing and enforcement.[12] By the 1920s, hunters and their associations were demanding abolition of the law against Sunday hunting, but public pressure for the preservation of the Sabbath defeated them.[13]

By World War II, the enforcement system had become more elaborate and game officials were posted throughout the province. The thirty provincial game officers on staff in 1939 compared with six to nine officers in earlier years.[14] Despite this increase in staff, inducements for obeying the game laws depended heavily on moral suasion and the occasional salutary conviction. Newspaper advertisements and posters threatened lawbreakers with punishment and directed hunters to be "sportsmanlike" and obey the law. Given the wide distribution of this official rhetoric, at least no one had the right to plead ignorance of the law.

Game conservation could not, however, be attained solely through provincial legislation. In the case of migratory birds, national and international legislation was necessary and in 1910 Great Britain and the United States negotiated a convention to protect migratory birds. In the United States, the agreement was "a direct product" of lobbying on behalf of "American wilderness societies, naturalist clubs, zoological societies...sportsmen's organizations, and arms and ammunition manufacturers."[15] Canada immediately implemented the provisions of the British-American convention, and Alberta amended its game laws to accord with the federal legislation[16] "to shield these remnants" of the North American bird population, "no matter how easily their breeding or migratory feeding grounds may be reached by sportsmen."[17] Eventually, a complicated series of regulations sought to protect migratory birds by creating various continental hunting seasons according to type of bird, region, province, and subdivisions within a province.[18]

Government involvement in the regulation of hunting followed from a number of issues. Some Canadians were deeply influenced by the arguments of wildlife conservationists in the United States where a strong conservation movement had emerged by the turn of the century. American thinking on conservation was complex and its evolution in the nineteenth century represented a number of motivations and objectives. The dominant themes divided unevenly between those who argued for conservation and those who demanded preservation. Conservation, the view that nature is a resource that requires protection to ensure its continued availability for food, sport, agricultural production, tourism and, among others, social regeneration, was dominant. Preservation, the view that nature be preserved unspoiled, was less common. In general, there seems to have been little concern in principle about hunting, although its control and regulation were clearly necessary.[19]

In Canada, ideas about conservation were slower to develop. A number of natural history societies, which included among their pursuits the study of wildlife, existed across Canada and some were active in Alberta. Nonetheless, the general public and the government were apathetic about conservation at the turn of the century, although as Janet Foster has argued, there had been a dramatic reversal by 1919 and wildlife conservation had become an established part of federal government policy. This shift resulted from the influence of American precedents and the growing awareness in Canada of the need for federal involvement in wildlife conservation.[20]

In the prairies, the near extermination of the bison had become part of prairie folklore and few could rationally justify the repetition of such excess. In addition, the economic needs of settlers and Indians had provided early justification for game laws, a tradition that was extended after 1905 through provincial wildlife legislation. In 1915 Alberta created a travelling exhibition of natural history specimens to stimulate public interest in the province's wildlife resources. Along with the display, copies of the Game Act were distributed. Such techniques remained popular; in 1928 the province illustrated the last page of the Game Act with a picture of a lone bison standing head down in a forest clearing over the caption: "Don't treat the FOREST as you treated ME."[21] This warning arose from the tradition of conservation, not preservation, and killing animals and birds for pleasure was rarely criticized. Given the popular bias against vegetarianism and similar exotic ideas, few Albertans would have disagreed with an American zoologist who argued at the meeting of the Canadian Commission of Conservation in 1920 that "the Western world contains few fanatics of the oriental type to whom all killing is abhorrent and wicked. The white races. . . believe in the legitimate doctrine of sport and sensible utilization" of nature. Indeed, the extermination of the fauna of the continent could sometimes be cited as a measure of progress. In 1907, several members of the Alberta Legislative Assembly opposed game regulation on the grounds that "the protection of large game. . .was inconsistent with the advance of civilization" and that it was "the right of every man" to kill big game.[22]

And kill they did. The destruction of wildlife in the province, as in the rest of the region, was phenomenal. Depletion of game had of course been a fact in prairie Canada since the time of the fur trade, but it grew in magnitude after the mid-1890s. Although bison were not hunted during the period under review (they had nearly disappeared by 1880, and less importantly, a totally closed season had been implemented in 1894),[23] other animals and birds were hunted, and they too soon became scarce. By 1913, the government of Alberta had imposed a totally closed season on the hunting of antelope; a prohibition that was not lifted until 1934. A similar situation existed in the case of prairie chickens. An 1894 report spoke of their "wholesale slaughter" each year, resulting in part because the hunting season opened too early, and the young birds were "so tame that you might almost knock them over with your hat."[24] By 1917, prairie chickens had become so scarce because of changes in land use and overhunting that a closed season was imposed until the autumn of 1918.[25]

The same pattern was true for ducks. When the Alberta legislature debated game regulations in 1907, it deliberately chose August 23 as the opening date of the duck season. This was a full week earlier than in other prairie provinces but was justified on the grounds that people needed ducks for food. Yet the legislators knew that young ducks could not be kept long enough after being killed to be practical for this purpose, and the main reason for the early season was its popularity with the sporting public. Indeed, many towns and cities declared a "holiday on the twenty-third of August of each year in order that the so-called sportsmen may go out and destroy the innocent flapper."[26] Many of these birds were too young to fly, and the reports of the slaughter are chilling examples of the destruction of North American fauna. At Medicine Hat, young ducks were "simply butchered in the sloughs and were so young that they were not worth picking up"; and "in one case a rope had been stretched across a slough, in which there were a number of broods, and the whole lot were forced to one end and then killed with sticks." Similar practices were reported from around the province.[27] Recognizing that the slaughter could be limited at least in its duration and by giving ducks another week of growth, in 1911 the province amended its regulations to open the duck season on September 1.[28]

Even so, from a population in prairie Canada estimated at 180 million in 1900, the duck population in 1938 had dropped to 50 million.[29] Much depletion was caused by the drying up, drainage, and cultivation of prairie sloughs and lakes, but much followed from excessive hunting in Canada and the United States. According to a 1932 estimate, of "every 100 ducks that cross the boundary [into the United States] in the fall not more than five and certainly not more than ten return in the spring."[30] From an early date, this led some people to argue that hunting regulations in Alberta were pointless and that Albertans should be allowed to kill as many ducks as they wanted: "why should we do all the work of protection while there is an indiscriminate slaughter to the south of us."[31] Natural replacement of the bird population could not keep pace with high levels of hunting and the simultaneous destruction of natural habitat.

Recreational hunting also killed off big game animals, such as pronghorns, especially in areas close to major settlement. By 1902, mountain sheep, moose, and deer had been seriously depleted through hunting in the mountain areas near Calgary.[32] In the more remote big game areas of the province, fewer people killed less game. Yet, even there, reports indicated excessive hunting. In the mid-1930s, the premier was informed that hunting practices in what was vaguely defined as the "big game country" were shocking. Local inhabitants told of animals

> killed and left to rot because the bag limit had been exceeded or a prohibited animal shot. Deer and moose...deliberately slaughtered from a lust to make living targets of them or because the "head" which it yielded did not come up to the hunters' expectations. Of carcasses from which only the choicer joints had been cut, leaving the rest to spoil as not being worth the effort of packing out.[33]

Although such practices were said to be unusual, they were serious enough to require that the premier be informed of them in graphic detail. Furthermore, the steady expansion of transportation systems enhanced hunting. Forays on horseback of several days' duration in the late nineteenth century had necessarily covered only a short distance, but by the end of World War I, trains made many areas accessible to an expanded population. As Professor Rowan of the University of Alberta noted in 1921, the spread of farming, lumbering, and mining "followed by the inevitable railroads are making all parts of the Province accessible to gunners."[34] Automobiles were even more important. During the 1920s, most issues of automobile magazines like *Good Roads*, published in Edmonton, highlighted hunting and fishing as major recreational opportunities presented by automobiles. Initially, the automobile provided hunters with easier access to game birds such as prairie chickens and waterfowl, since their habitat was frequently accessible by motor vehicles even if roads were poor. The extension and improvement of roads soon allowed hunting of all animals and birds, regardless of their location.

Improvement in gun technology also compounded game depletion. The invention of breechloading rifles in the nineteenth century, and the subsequent development of automatic shotguns and pump guns, meant that more birds and animals could be shot in a single day. In 1898, muzzleloading guns could still be purchased from Eaton's, but they had generally been replaced by breechloading rifles[35] such as Winchester rifles, which were widely advertised in the prairies as "the easiest rifle to shoot, any duffer can hit with them."[36] By 1910, National brand six-shot pump-action shotguns were sold in Alberta under the caption "there is no lost time reloading, no long delay, no uncertainties," and the gun was guaranteed "to put more than 325 pellets in a 30 inch circle at 40 yards, using 1¼ ounce of No. 8 chilled shot." This fire power could be purchased for $25,[37] but in subsequent years, guns became even cheaper in real terms, and by 1949 a rifle sold at Macleod's for between $11 and $17.50.[38] Increasing efficiency and availability of guns in Alberta could not help but contribute to significant game depletion within a relatively short time after settlement.

Automobiles provided hunters with easier access to game. This hunting camp was in southern Alberta and the photograph was taken in 1932. (GAI NA-1918-15)

As game became scarcer because of greater travel and technological efficiency, so greater travel and technological efficiency were ever more necessary to hunt successfully. This depletion cycle helped to frame beliefs about the need for the conservation of wildlife and to strengthen the arguments of conservationists. The levels of hunting were leading to depletion, with all its attendant economic implications. According to a 1938 argument, birds had high energy needs and consumed great quantities of weed seeds and insects. This "destruction of tons of weed seeds and millions of insects must necessarily have a great influence upon human welfare," notably agriculture.[39] As well, game conservation was considered essential to the realization of Alberta's tourism potential. W.H. Wallace, the Alberta Fish and Game Commissioner, observed in 1939 that the government received only five thousand dollars per year from the sale of nonresident hunting licences and he felt that this figure could be increased substantially. "With proper advertising in the United States," he wrote, and provided that "we have the game for them to shoot in sufficient numbers when they come here," government revenues from hunting could increase to about $10,000 or $15,000 per year.[40] The protection of game from Alberta hunters so foreigners could come and kill it to enhance government revenues was a common case made on behalf of Alberta tourism.[41]

A hunter relaxes by his automobile after a successful day in the fall sunshine. (GAI NA-3174-2)

Yet conservation was not simply about economic objectives. It also met leisure needs for, obviously, if game was exterminated, there would be no more hunting. As time went on, since fewer people undertook hunting for food and game became scarcer, hunting's justification was commonly expressed in terms of sport. Concepts of sportsmanlike behaviour, taking their reference from the notion of fair play, had been commonly applied to hunting since the early years of settlement in Alberta, and they soon became part of the argument in support of conservation programmes.[42] In 1909, the *Calgary Herald* interviewed a number of hunters about the slaughter of ducks in the province, and all argued in favour of conservation and further state regulation of hunting by reducing bag limits, extending the closed season, and enforcing the game laws. As R.L. Gaetz of Red Deer observed, "it is no use leaving the protection of young ducks to the sense of sportsmanship supposed to be inherent in those who carry guns, because in many cases it is not there." One hunter argued that the law should prohibit the shooting of any duck not in flight, and another observed that if a duck couldn't fly, it was "no work for a sportsman." Hunting represented a challenge that was meaningful only if the prey had some chance of escape. Indeed, George Scott of Okotoks said that existing rules (which were in any event equivalent to no rules at all in the case of ducks) would be fine "if only sportsmen were hunting," but the presence of nonsportsmen in the field necessitated tighter regulation.[43]

This display of geese was photographed for an ammunition advertisement. (GAI NA-3884-24)

Thus, if nonsportsmen were controlled through hunting regulations, game would be preserved for sportsmen. Government regulation was seen as a means of enshrining hunting as a sport; rules would test skill and preserve the raw material for the sport. From that perspective, the greatest invective was reserved for those who stood, even in part, outside the laws or the idealization of hunting as sport—namely, market hunters and treaty Indians. The partial exemption of Indians from hunting regulations created much bitterness among white hunters and their supporters. "The white man usually hunts for sport, the Indians to gratify a love of slaughter, and incidentally for food," asserted the editor of the *Calgary Herald* in 1902.[44] Such complaints were continual, although nobody was able to offer statistical proof that depredation by some Indians was typical.[45]

Those who saw hunting as a sport often argued that certain animals and especially certain birds, such as hawks and crows, should be killed because they were predators of game birds. In 1909 one commentator observed that "some sportsmen made it a rule to shoot these birds [hawks and crows] whenever occasion presents itself," and recommended that a bounty be paid for killing crows because they ate the eggs of game birds.[46] In 1921, the Alberta Fish and Game Association sponsored a "crow shoot" and the "valiant crow shooters" (who were compared to allied soldiers) killed sixty-three crows and thereby "saved the lives of precisely 300 game birds, as yet unborn, from death in the egg stage."[47] The preeminence of hunting as sport justified the probable outcome of this act; not only were the "saved" game birds, once grown, likely to be shot by hunters, the crows were killed as well.

Hunting as sport became formalized and even bureaucratized in the 1920s. Various fish and game associations published advice for hunters and the 1928 Office Consolidation of the Game Act included a hunters' code of ethics. Its aphorisms included "love nature and its denizens"; "study and record the natural history of wild life in the interests of science"; "obey the laws, work for better laws and uphold the law enforcing authorities"; "discourage in every way the taking of game for commercial purposes"; and above all, "BE A GENTLEMAN."[48] Inclusion of the dominant culture's virtues of sincerity and respect for property and the law would surprise only by their absence. The concern about market hunting was legitimate in view of market hunters' depredations in the nineteenth century in North America, but the last dictum was significant evidence of the transformation of hunting from need to sport. The warning to "be a gentleman" mimicked aristocratic snobbery towards those who were not sportsmen—a notion that indicated, at least in the official mind, the final transformation of hunting from a means of survival into a leisure activity that took its reference and justification from the language of sport.

Sporting organizations representing hunters made their appearance in Alberta at an early date. Serving a need for fellowship, these clubs were significant male social institutions. There was a well-established Rod and Gun Club in Edmonton by at least 1894,[49] and similar organizations, usually called fish and game associations, followed elsewhere. In 1928, the Calgary Fish and Game Association spearheaded the provincial organization of all game associations in the province by coordinating the formation of the Alberta Fish and Game Association. It met for the first time in Calgary in 1929 and by 1935 had three thousand members in fifty-six branches.[50] Each local association, regardless of size, was entitled to send two delegates to the annual meeting "in order," said the president, "that the Association may be thoroughly provincial in its legislation and administration."[51]

The Alberta Fish and Game Association acted to defend hunting as a sport and to enhance the hunting and fishing opportunities of its members. Consequently, it advocated conservation of wildlife and the provision of an adequate game and fish supply through stocking and breeding programmes. As well, it attempted to prevent what it believed to be excessive government regulation. Even so, the association and the government worked closely together. The province approached wildlife purely from a conservation viewpoint and had encouraged the creation of the Alberta Fish and Game Association so that it would have only a single hunting lobby to deal with, instead of numerous uncoordinated local organizations.[52] The government and the game associations cooperated to restore or increase the number and type of game birds. Between 1908 and 1929 at least four types of upland game birds, including Gray (Hungarian) Partridge, were introduced in Alberta. The birds were usually imported from the United States, and most adapted successfully to Alberta. The province cooperated by imposing a closed season to allow the bird population to increase,[53] and the programme was so successful that by the early 1920s Gray (Hungarian) Partridge were being transferred from areas where they were plentiful to areas where they were scarce. In 1923, the provincial government captured one hundred birds in the Calgary district and transferred them to the Edmonton area, then reversed the move in 1927 when partridge became scarce around Calgary.[54] These manipulations artificially provided hunters with stocks of game, much of which was not even indigenous in the province.

Conservation of birds was also the aim of Ducks Unlimited, an American organization established in 1937, which began work in Alberta in 1938. Its primary goal was to serve its American clients, and since 80 percent of the ducks shot by American hunters came from the Canadian prairies, restoration of the North American duck population had to begin in Canada. Accordingly, Ducks Unlimited became involved in breeding, water and land management, magpie control, and other programmes to increase the duck population on the prairies.[55] The programmes were highly successful and Alberta hunters benefitted incidentally from them. Ducks Unlimited did have its critics in Alberta, however, especially among the many farmers who hated waterfowl that ate grain in the fields. Indeed, it seems that many farmers would not have minded if ducks had followed bison into near extinction, and some of their antagonism focussed on Ducks Unlimited. In 1946 the UFA Annual Convention passed a resolution demanding an increase in the number of duck hunting licences and the allocation of licence revenues to farmers in compensation for the "unlimited production of ducks as encouraged by Ducks Unlimited."[56]

Intimately related to these stocking efforts was the development of bird sanctuaries which performed a range of conservation and hunting-related functions in providing breeding stock, giving birds refuge from hunters, and serving as public attractions. The most important of them, the Inglewood Bird Sanctuary in Calgary, was established about 1929 and attracted over ten thousand visitors a year by 1940.[57] Its natural warm water springs provided a winter refuge for a great many ducks and, since they no longer migrated, saved them from American hunters.[58] Inglewood bred and released Ring-necked Pheasants and partridge, and in 1934 its research programme on the control of bird diseases produced an important breakthrough in the treatment of diseases in wild ducks.[59] The national parks, where hunting was prohibited, also served as wildlife refuges, although poaching was sometimes a problem.[60] One observer thought in 1910 that national parks would soon be "the last resort of the wild creatures of the west," making the parks even more attractive to tourists.[61] The importance of national parks in Alberta in preserving birds should not, however, be overstated since few were "located in the nesting grounds or along the flights of our migratory waterfowl."[62]

Increased regulation during the twentieth century represents only one facet of hunting, which had important psychological and personal dimensions. Some people have argued that hunting is merely a socially acceptable outlet for human aggressiveness and destructiveness; the hunter does little more than indulge a primitive urge to kill.[63] The indiscriminate slaughter of birds and animals that has taken place gives this interpretation some credibility, but as Eric Fromm has argued, hunting is a social activity in which the hunter applies his skill and knowledge about wildlife and the environment. The exercise of this skill is, in itself, a reason for hunting.[64] This notion was important in Alberta and accounted, in part, for the categorization of hunting as a sport, the increased regulation of hunting, and the implementation of conservation programmes. The "knowledge of a hunting district," went one piece of advice in 1922, "means a full bag instead of an empty handed hunt which often falls to the lot of many who travel before they assure themselves that they are travelling to game instead of away from it."[65] For hunters who could afford guides, however, the necessary level of skill was naturally much lower, and hunting could be a pleasant jaunt rather than an exercise of skill.

As a social phenomenon, hunting also reflected gender divisions in the society. The male domination of hunting in Alberta was often assumed to reflect an inherent difference between men and women. Even so, a number of women defied the conventions of society and were successful hunters. Byrde McCarthy of Cardston recalled in 1927, after killing a bighorn ram, that "no one can ever know what the great outdoors means to me, the great open world with its store of tonics offered by good, old mother Nature to just such 'weak sisters' like I was when I determined to live and live abundantly."[66] Despite such examples, hunting remained essentially, in practice and in image, a male activity. The slaughter of birds and mammals seems to have been understood to express male aggressiveness, physical strength, resourcefulness, and need for power and authority. Conversely, an abhorrence of hunting was expected to arise from female domesticity, frailty, love of peace, and maternal empathy with all living things. Although one can question the accuracy of such an attribution of qualities, there is no better illustration of men's assumptions about their place in the hierarchy of human society, or of their dominance over the earth, than the ubiquitous photographs of hunters displaying animals killed in the chase. These photographs are an invitation to accept the hunter's power; a power which, through the image of the photograph, has transcended its prey and become purely symbolic of his triumph over nature. In the 1920s, when the automobile was firmly integrated into hunting, these images became even more potent: the car carefully decorated with the bagged animals or birds, and the hunter posing with his gun, demonstrated the unequivocal marriage of two of the great modern symbols of power.

In these photographs, the men often posed in groups, frequently with liquor in full view, leading to the suggestion that hunting fulfilled a desire in men for sociability away from women. Hunting, at least symbolically, provided men with an escape from home, wife, family, and all the artifices of established society. "Oh! The luxury of pitching your tent by a secluded lake where the ducks are plenty, with two or three jovial friends, plenty of ammunition and someone with you who can play the banjo or the guitar."[67] And it is clear from the context that the "jovial friends" were male. Hunting was also a part of the myth of the frontier, and in the late nineteenth century this was often reflected in hunting clothing which suggested that the hunter was a woodsman and a refugee from civilization. The apparently common phenomenon of the urban hunter outfitted as a woodsman sometimes generated mirth and as the *Edmonton Bulletin* joked about a local hunting party in 1893,

> A little bird whispers to us that one of the party is a terror to behold well calculated to paralyze the first bear that sets eyes upon him. Arrayed in a buckskin suit of irreproachable fit, bedecked with pennons that gaily stream behind in the wind, and armed with a gigantic six shooter that resembles a small field piece, he is indeed worthy of mention in Fenimore's Last of the Mohicans.[68]

Such sartorial elegance did not survive into the twentieth century. Hunting clothes became more functionally specialized by 1900, although heavy fabrics, plaids, and tough footwear reflected the continued appeal of the "woodsman" tradition. Hunting clothes were officially controlled as early as 1926 and by 1938 big game hunters were required to wear a "flaming scarlet" cap and coat, although even then, as a wag pointed out, where a hunter had mistaken "an automobile for a moose, and his own car at that," a man would hardly be protected by a "Joseph's coat of many colors." [69]

The photograph, the hunting story, and the trophy became the primary means of communicating and establishing a permanent record of the gender exclusivity and male bonding characteristic of hunting. While exercised in the wilds, male authority was presented forcibly and consistently at home through photography, taxidermy, and stories in which neither home nor family figured. Of infinite variation and nuance, the stories generally stressed fun in the company of other men and the possibilities of male valour. The seasonal nature of recreational hunting restricted this male escapism mainly to the fall, which added to the season's unique quality. The *Edmonton Bulletin* did not have to elaborate in September 1893: "the season of shooting is here, and the smell of powder and shot."[70]

The results of a goose hunt at Sullivan Lake in 1921. (PAA A.4833)

While fishing had as long a tradition in Alberta as did hunting, it had a much different image. The crucial distinction appeared to be that killing fish was a different experience, in conceptual terms at least, from killing feathered or furred animals. Fishing seemed less aggressive, more contemplative, and crossed all social lines: "all ages, all sexes, all philosophies, all professions and all trades have their representatives among those who fish." It could be undertaken with simple equipment and little training.[71] By the early twentieth century fishing was known as a "family" activity, far different in that respect from hunting. Fishing, along with camping, thus joined the new found opportunities for family leisure made possible by automobiles.[72]

While fishing was an immensely popular activity, it was regionally confined because the best fishing waters were found only in the foothills and in the northern part of the province. Pickerel, pike, and perch were most commonly taken in northern waters, along with whitefish in the far north. The foothills' streams and rivers were known for trout. While people from Camrose fished at Dried Meat Lake for pike and pickerel, those in the southwestern part of the province angled for trout.[73] Regardless of location, considerable quantities of fish were caught at the turn of the century: Lee's Creek, at Cardston, was "literally teeming with cut-throat trout," while it was possible to catch more than sixty perch a day at Sylvan Lake.[74] Nonetheless, as early as 1890, trout numbers in the Calgary area were greatly reduced,[75] and by the 1920s the sport fish population was in serious decline, affected by the spread of predatory fish, drought, pollution of rivers and lakes, and over-fishing. Depletion reached serious levels by 1930, and trout numbers declined by 1940 to the point where lost recreational and tourist opportunities became noticeable.[76]

Ice fishing at Burnt Stick Lake in 1912. (GAI NA-1914-19)

Before 1931, the Canadian government exercised jurisdiction over all waters in Alberta and therefore regulated fishing. By 1913, federal regulations requiring permits, defining closed seasons, prohibiting certain fishing practices, and setting maximum catches and size requirements for different species of fish were in place, although it is unclear how effectively these regulations were enforced.[77] On the transfer of natural resources to the prairie provinces in 1930, the provincial governments became responsible for regulating and conserving fish resources. Alberta's regulations were similar to those previously set by the federal government,[78] but in either case, regulations regarding fishing were always far less comprehensive and contentious than those concerning hunting.[79]

Depleting fish stocks led to stocking programmes to increase both the number and variety of game fish. The federal Department of Mines, Marine and Fisheries unsuccessfully stocked some Alberta lakes by 1904, introducing black bass (which were not indigenous to Alberta) at Sylvan Lake, Gull Lake, Cooking Lake, and Buffalo Lake.[80] It also cooperated with local groups and, in response to pressure from the Sylvan Lake Board of Trade in 1925, supplied pickerel eggs for a "floating fish hatchery." The board of trade maintained the hatchery and built a dam at the "creek outlet" in order to prevent the fish from escaping. The board hoped that "in three or four years from now a good supply of pickerel"[81] would reverse the depletion that had taken place since the time, not twenty years earlier, when one fisherman had been able in a day to take more than sixty perch from the lake.

In an arrangement similar to that at Sylvan Lake, the Calgary Fish and Game Association became involved in stocking rivers and lakes in 1930. The association recognized, however, that a successful stocking programme required the use of fingerlings of four to six inches in length, instead of fry. A mortality rate of about 85 to 100 percent for fry demonstrated the futility of the Sylvan Lake effort. Fingerlings required more work and money, but the Calgary group built eight rearing ponds at a cost of two thousand dollars and secured thirty thousand rainbow and cut-throat trout fry free from the Dominion Fish Hatchery at Banff.[82] In the next year, they also began plans for a deep wintering pond to which the fish could be transferred from the rearing ponds.[83]

By the late 1930s, the provincial government had supplanted most of these private initiatives by establishing and managing stocking programmes. In 1939, the government bought a "fish wagon," a truck with an oxygenated water tank, to transport fingerlings to various parts of the province. The government bought its fish stocks from the Waterton Fish Hatcheries and raised fry to the fingerling stage in twenty-three privately operated rearing ponds.[84] Following a 1943 recommendation that the province's fish programme be placed on a more solid and continuing basis, the province had established and was operating one trout hatchery and four trout rearing stations within a decade.[85] These efforts by government and private groups illustrated not only the important role that fishing played in Alberta recreation, but also the attention given to enhancing the tourist attractions of the province. As was the case for hunting, conservation undertook to promote recreational use of wildlife for residents and visitors alike.

Fishing techniques in Alberta changed somewhat during the twentieth century. Trout fishing, by its very nature, was more active than lake fishing because it involved casting with a fly. Lake fishing, on the other hand, traditionally involved the use of bait while trolling. By 1938, however, such techniques were changing and it was observed that "the more active sport of casting. . .is rapidly gaining favor."[86] Although the reason for this change is unclear, it is possible that trout fisherman, who preferred casting, may have transferred their techniques to the traditionally more sedate lake fishing because of the depletion of trout in the province. This change may also have been related to the expense of trolling, since the additional costs involved in owning or renting a boat may have increased the number of fishermen who fished from the lake shore.

Fishing was identified as a family sport, as is shown in this photograph of fishermen with their gear and catch, circa 1930. (GAI ND-27-33)

The identification of fishing as a family sport or activity was crucial for many people because it was felt that it would confirm and sustain the ideals of family life. Hunting could not be so easily accommodated into domestic life, nor, it can be suggested, was there any attempt to do so. Rather, the ideas of manliness and of escape associated with hunting were the significant elements that determined participation. Hunting, in this sense, transcended recreation: it was an exclusive seasonal rite for many male Albertans which, through its character and its exclusivity, was both a confirmation and a denial of their role in the society. Yet this temporary abandonment of the restraints of society was publicly sanctioned, encouraged, and given social standing through the trophies of the hunt and a political presence through the organizations that promoted and protected the activity.

Hunting not only had implications in gender terms but impacted on broader aspects of cultural attitudes as well. The rhetoric that surrounded hunting utilized notions about British sportsmanlike behaviour and "good breeding," and in this framework, hunting was regulated and channelled to accord with the values of the dominant culture. In this case, however, these values were expressed more in racial than in ethnic terms, and sportsmanship was oftentimes used in an attempt to limit any hunting by native peoples outside of the restraints imposed on others. Since the dominant culture's notions behind hunting lay so close to the heart of their social relationships, and since the mythic qualities of hunting so precisely served to reinforce these relationships, the Indians' place apart was viewed as a challenge, and as one that could be met, at least partially, through elimination of their exclusive hunting position. To this end, notions about "sportsmanship," which implicitly confirmed the view of the Indian as "savage," were utilized because "few, if any, Indians hunted for 'sport.'"[87]

This conceptualization of hunting as a sport was significant not only in terms of how a "sportsmanlike" hunter should behave. It was also integrated into early wildlife conservation efforts. By the beginning of the century, it was clear that if hunting was not curbed, there would soon be no wildlife left to hunt, and hunters quickly recognized that conservation served their needs. This in itself was sufficient justification for regulation, but when combined with a slowly emerging view that extermination of the region's wildlife was in itself undesirable, an acceptable framework for hunting could be developed. The general transformation of hunting into a leisure activity did not, of course, affect all people equally.

By the interwar years, it is likely that urban hunters were mainly drawn from those who could afford the transportation costs. Farmers seem to have had little sympathy for wildlife if it interfered with farming, and they clearly recognized that cultivation and wildlife were not always compatible. Farmers, however, had relatively little influence on the issue of conservation, and, in any event, few conservation efforts (with the exception of Ducks Unlimited) were successful enough to lead to complaints by farmers. As well, the transformation of hunting into a seasonal leisure activity, restricted to certain times in the year, sometimes had a profound impact on both treaty and non-treaty Native peoples, many of whom saw their position in the society made even more vulnerable and marginal when hunting and fishing regulations were increasingly enforced against them.[88]

Accordingly, the precepts governing hunting and, to a lesser extent, fishing had an impact well beyond those who enjoyed these specific activities. The view that wildlife was simply a resource like any other lay at the heart of hunting and fishing. A highly interventionist attitude towards nature and a belief that man could control nature through scientific management meant that wildlife, theoretically, could be managed through conservation, stocking programmes, and regulation. This view posited that nature could be infinitely manipulated and directed, and this attitude was integral in conservation programmes, in the introduction of nonindigenous birds and fish for sporting purposes, and in the regulation of hunting and fishing which had become purely leisure activities for most people. Such management of the natural resources of the province for leisure purposes was not restricted to wildlife conservation; it also had implications for park development and the provision of services for camping and touring, which by the interwar years had become significant outdoor leisure activities in Alberta.

6. 'In God's Great Glorious Outdoors'

Hunting and fishing as leisure activities made one use of the natural resources of the province. Other and increasingly popular uses were camping, touring, and visiting mountain and lake resorts. While hunters and fishermen frequently camped, the focus of recreational camping was entirely different. It provided a family vacation which was believed to rejuvenate one for work. Yearly or seasonal holidays became institutionalized, and changes in private means of transportation facilitated the evolution of personal holidays and weekend and daily outings.

Vacations, especially at resorts, had become an accepted aspiration for all classes in England by the late nineteenth century.[1] In Alberta, they were justified as a necessary part of life, but the use of the outdoors for leisure raised complicated views about nature. In the early nineteenth century, many Americans were said to have a strong dislike and fear of wilderness, although such attitudes had weakened appreciably by the turn of the century. Similarly, George Altmeyer has noted that Canadians were commonly said to have had a negative attitude towards nature and feared the wilderness, but he presents evidence of more complex thought. Whereas many Canadians in the late nineteenth century had indeed seen nature as a resource to be exploited at will, by 1900 more were expressing the view that nature was not inexhaustible, that natural resources had to be husbanded, and that nature was a "healing mother," a corrective for urban ills and a source of religious expression and experience. As illustrated in attitudes towards hunting, the conviction that nature existed for man's benefit and pleasure prevailed, but with greater commitment to conservation.[2] The value of nature to man was widely publicized in Alberta by World War I and was integrated with views about holidays. The *Farm and Ranch Review* advised women that, because their work was "so continuous and so apt to be monotonous," vacations were essential to allow them to "forget there is such a thing as a dishcloth or a dust pan" and "just live and laugh and grow young and carefree in God's great glorious outdoors." Holidays were also necessary during the short prairie summer because winter would soon enough return with its "cold fingers to shut our doors and windows and us behind them."[3]

The imagery of winter, with its implication of death, added a condition of prairie Canada to the typical North American belief that a vacation was a time to restore one's vigour.[4] Holidays provided re-creation for work, and it was argued that a vacation "to be enjoyed, must be well earned. It should not be granted mechanically and accepted as a mere matter of custom. It is after months of faithful service in which the best of life has been given out that one will know something of the sweetness of vacation days."[5] This attitude placed the individual's obligation to work and employer unequivocally at the centre of life, and made the vacation essential for mental and physical health. A holiday was a chance for "a period away from the restrictive forces of a complex civilization."[6] Because work had become "so exacting and so highly specialized," taking holidays was the only way to maintain health and productive work. The ideal holiday was not mere diversion, but a time of "spiritual as well as physical renewal."[7] While its expression varied from the "arduous rest of youth with its strenuous sports" to the "quieter open-air activities of maturity,"[8] every holiday had to be carefully planned to provide orderly and wholesome rest rather than a "mentally and morally ruinous" occasion, as so many holidays allegedly did.[9]

In keeping with these notions, the best holiday was expected outdoors where the balm of nature could soothe away the cares of the world and enrich one for the coming year. Sleeping outdoors led to "deep, quiet, restful sleep—dreamless and nerve restoring sleep; the kind that puts new red blood in the veins, [and] new vigor into the frame."[10] Fresh air and sunlight were commonly held to be efficacious for maintaining health and strengthening the body against germs. In this respect, Canadians were especially fortunate, for while Canadian summers were said to be too hot for travel, they were perfect for a summer holiday because "nature's tonics of forest and prairie, of mountain, river and ocean are at our doors wherever we happen to live."[11] At the turn of the century, however, concerns about summer heat showed a certain ambivalence about the outdoors for it was believed that the "white races" were not genetically equipped to withstand much heat and sunlight.[12] People fearing sunstroke and "prickly heat" were advised to avoid acid fruits before breakfast, to avoid washing one's face when hot, to wear loose fitting clothing in cool colours such as white, grey, yellow, and light green, and even to put damp cloths or damp leaves in their hats. Freckles and excessive tanning—the marks of people who worked outdoors—could be avoided by using freckle cream, which could be purchased or made at home from ammonium chloride diluted in water.[13] Fears about sunlight had begun to disappear by the early 1930s when arguments about the value of fresh air and sunlight became dominant and were reflected in a new emphasis upon "abbreviated bathing garb as a preventative of diseases, especially in the case of children."[14]

The extent to which people responded to such rhetoric about the benefits of vacations, and outdoor holidays in particular, is unclear. For many farmers at least, regular vacations simply were not a part of their lives before the 1940s. During the 1920s, according to one view, farmers did not mind "not having a holiday each year, because ordinary farmers of that day never thought of taking a vacation."[15] By the 1940s, however, private means of transportation and road conditions had improved and the number of farm people who took holidays increased. In 1943 only about 20 percent of farm families in the Red Deer-Wetaskiwin areas took vacations but this increased dramatically to 60 percent by 1947. These farm families spent an average of ninety dollars per family on a vacation, or slightly over 6 percent of their total yearly cash income.[16] Although the increase may not have been so great in more recently settled areas of the province, it nonetheless represented a major change in the lifestyle of many Alberta farm families.

It had always been possible for Albertans to travel widely if they had sufficient means. During the 1890s, the CPR office in Edmonton could book trips not only to various parts of Canada, Europe and the United States, but also to Australia, China, Japan, and Hawaii.[17] During the interwar years, Alberta newspapers contained many advertisements for Christmas excursions to Europe under the slogan "Xmas in the Old Country,"[18] but such experiences were rare enough to make noteworthy reading. In 1895, the *Edmonton Bulletin* carried a detailed description of the sights Edmonton businessman John A. McDougall saw on vacation in the southern United States and at the Pacific Coast.[19] In 1924, the editor of the *Red Deer Advocate* serialized an account of his trip to England and Europe in the newspaper.[20] Similarly, after a Canadian Girls in Training member went to England in 1935, the CGIT paper carried an extensive description of the trip.[21] Reports of exotic vacations persisted until the end of World War II, and while egoism cannot be discounted, the travellers' tales underlined the unusualness of their trips.

Because travel took considerable time and money, it is not surprising that few could indulge in trips to faraway places. In 1912, the return train trip from Edmonton to Toronto took a week and cost about eighty dollars,[22] excluding hotel and other vacation costs. A few more could manage excursions to nearby lakes or resorts like Banff, but only the increased use of autos, the improvement of roads, and the development of resort facilities throughout the province in the interwar years finally encouraged widespread vacationing, particularly among urban middle-class residents. One account describes a vacation trip from High River to Edmonton in 1926 that took two full days of driving. The vacationers packed along their own food, as well as car blankets to keep out the dust. When they arrived in Edmonton, they took a tour of the Arts Buildings at the University and "travelled practically all over Edmonton and the surrounding country and were very sorry when it was time to leave."[23] Such trips involved no small effort on roads that were dusty, rutted, and so rough that cars often broke down because of the severe jolting.[24] Nevertheless, by the mid-1920s, touring had become highly popular and was easily justified by its educational and informative value.

The Calgary Auto Club was always interested in discovering "sights" which people could visit. In 1925 the club identified one in the "large pile or bed of bones" of "prehistoric animals" near Carbon, but it feared that the site would soon be vandalized by visitors taking bones as souvenirs. Accordingly, they urged the province to acquire the site to control public access and to pass legislation to protect the resource.[25] By 1930, enabling legislation in the form of the Provincial Parks and Protected Areas Act was in place, but there is no record of any heritage site being designated under the act. Under its separate programme, the federal government marked fourteen sites for public information by 1937.[26] Local groups also used historical resources to enrich the holidays of visitors. Promoters of Sylvan Lake advised visitors to drive out to historic Rocky Mountain House,[27] and the value of historic sites for tourism was further recognized in 1943 when, as part of planning for postwar development, it was recommended that small museums with curators, tearooms, flower beds, and souvenir shops be developed throughout Alberta to "hold the tourist for a longer period of time in the Province."[28]

Vacation travel therefore promoted not only self-improvement but the economic life of the community. Tourists would publicize community attractions, stimulating further visitation and perhaps even outside investment. Tourism promoters recommended that serviced "auto camps" be situated close to the business section of town to draw tourists' dollars into local hands.[29] One of the first in Alberta was opened in Red Deer in 1923 and others soon followed. In 1924, various Edmonton business groups, the Edmonton Automobile and Good Roads Association, and city authorities sponsored construction of an auto camp in Edmonton. It accommodated fifty cars and had hot and cold running water, electricity, a sewage system, and shower, laundry, and cooking facilities.[30] The majority of visitors came from Alberta and Saskatchewan, although a significant number from other parts of Canada and the United States also used the camp.[31] While facilities varied from rudimentary to sophisticated, camps were operating by 1929 at Calgary, Banff, Waterton, Lethbridge, Medicine Hat, High River, Red Deer, Peace River, Edson, Wainwright and other places.[32]

This advertisement for Banff appeared in *Farm and Ranch Review* in June 1922. (PAA A. 17913)

Most vacation travel was destined for local lakes or resorts. The most famous resort was Banff National Park. Established in 1885, primarily because of the hot springs located there, it gradually expanded in the following years. Although the park was established to promote tourism, national parks soon figured in the belief about the value of nature and conservation. In 1921, a typical view stressed their moral value for teaching a love of nature and the "privilege of living in this great Dominion."[33] Served only by the CPR transcontinental line, Banff catered largely to affluent international and Canadian tourists in the early years.[34] After the turn of the century, many people from Calgary and nearby points visited Banff,[35] and weekend excursions from Calgary had become so common by 1911 that summer accommodation was difficult to find in the town site.[36] Day trips were equally common: on the Carstairs Methodist Sunday School's "fifth annual excursion" to Banff in 1916, the children left on the early morning train and returned the same day.[37]

These cars photographed at Fort Macleod, circa 1918, were loaded for a camping trip. (GAI NA-1432-27)

Automobile travel further extended use of the park. After construction of a road from Calgary to Banff about 1909, cars were allowed inside the park boundary in 1911.[38] This helped to transform Banff into a mass resort for people from Calgary during the 1920s.

The eighty-five-mile journey was not an impossible drive for a weekend outing, and vehicle traffic to the park steadily increased. The number of cars annually entering Banff park rose from 24,529 with 50,900 passengers in 1925-26 to 74,246 with 142,337 passengers in 1929-30.[39] The majority was from Alberta and one limited count in 1928 revealed that only about 10 percent of the cars entering and leaving the park through Kananaskis Gate were from outside Alberta.[40] Banff became even more accessible in 1926 when Brewsters started a regularly scheduled bus service from Calgary. By 1940, their operation was capable of handling fifteen hundred passengers per day. Over the protests of some Banff residents, that same year the American-based Greyhound busline was also granted the right to service the park.[41]

Camping became more sophisticated as the years passed, as this photograph taken in the 1920s demonstrates. (PAA A.7612)

Many people went to Banff to take the baths or just to rest in the mountains. When the bath complex at the Upper Hot Springs opened in 1903, many had already been using the resort for therapeutic purposes. By this point, however, medical theory discounted such therapy, a change which, it has been suggested, led to the near complete closure of health spas in Ontario by 1900. Even so, the popularity of the Banff waters increased, and by the 1930s, they were the best known in Canada for their medicinal value.[42] In 1905, 5,802 people bathed at the Cave and Basin Sulphur Springs; in 1929-30 the number of bathers at the Upper Hot Springs and the Cave and Basin reached 126,591.[43] It is unknown if these bathers accepted contemporary North American medical hostility to spa therapy and took the waters only as a pleasant leisure pursuit or combined pleasure with hope of therapeutic benefit. Many visitors did, however, combine other recreation with taking the waters. During the 1920s, Banff commonly advertised the baths along with various recreational opportunities such as fishing, hiking, trail-riding, and mountain climbing. Although hunting was prohibited in national parks, Banff did serve as the headquarters for big game hunters who hunted in the area north of the park until 1927 when the area lying between Banff and Jasper was annexed to Jasper Park.[44] By the late 1940s, Banff was becoming increasingly popular with Calgarians for an entirely different reason. Banff, unlike Calgary, allowed men and women to drink together in public establishments, and many Calgarians began to "take part of their summer holidays at Banff" for this reason. One Banff merchant demanded that the province force Calgary to change its drinking laws so that "Banff will not be continually polluted with a common quality of Calgarians who could otherwise be kept in their own city if mixed drinking prevailed there."[45]

The first Banff Springs Hotel opened in 1888, and by the 1920s Banff had numerous hotels with medium-priced hotels costing from two to four dollars per day including meals.[46] Public camp grounds near the Banff Springs Hotel were free. The facility established at Banff during World War I by the Calgary YWCA accommodated 335 guests in 1917, either in the club house or, "for the girls who preferred out-of-door life," in tents.[47] The park offered a variety of summer activities with its baths, hiking trails and a fine golf course. The Alpine Club established in 1909 encouraged mountain climbing and the CPR brought in Swiss guides to teach the skills, but the cost of both guides and highly specialized equipment ruled out participation by the average person.[48]

Among the annual events staged to attract tourists, the Banff Indian Days began in 1894 and the annual Banff to Calgary canoe race sponsored by the Calgary Canoe Club became a regular feature during the 1920s.[49] The Banff Winter Carnival instituted in 1917 was designed specifically to change the popular view of Banff as only a summer resort.[50] The CPR offered excursion fares to the carnival of winter sports, with its two-storey ice palace and fancy dress ball. Despite such efforts, Banff remained a summer resort before 1945, with its premier hotel, the Banff Springs Hotel, open only during the summer months.

Jasper and Waterton, Alberta's other national mountain parks, attracted mainly people who lived close by, although some other Albertans and out of province tourists visited intermittently. Of the two parks, Waterton was probably the most important before World War II. It became a national park in 1910 and was connected by highway to southern Alberta by 1914. Only twelve hundred people, most from the Calgary, Lethbridge, and Fort Macleod areas, visited the park in 1915, but after highways into the park were extended and improved, more than fifteen thousand arrived in 1920. Only a few came from the United States,[51] but Americans dominated the resort within the decade. Further road construction connected the park to British Columbia and the United States, and an American railway company built the major hotel, the Prince of Wales, and oriented it chiefly to the United States tourist trade.[52]

The Banff golf course and the Banff Springs Hotel, circa 1930. (PAA P.6775)

Although Jasper had been set aside as a park in 1907, it did not develop rapidly as a tourist attraction and the first hotel opened only in 1915. Although the Jasper Park Lodge was built in 1922, the park remained accessible only by train for most of the period under review.[53] The road from Edmonton that was in place by 1946 was nearly impassable in spots. It was widely expected that the Banff-Jasper Highway that opened in 1940 would attract tourists to the magnificent natural scenery along its route[54] and would make Jasper into a mass resort on the Banff model. By 1943, these hopes had not yet been realized; most tourists visited the Banff townsite, drove out to Lake Louise and Moraine Lake, and after about two days left "by way of Radium if they do not care to take the long trip to Jasper." Advocates of Jasper called for more and better roads, airports in the park, and more skiing facilities and other attractions.[55]

Calgary tourism promoters had always viewed Banff as their hinterland and Edmontonians who increasingly viewed Jasper in the same way were especially bitter about the lack of development there. They railed against the provincial and federal governments in the 1920s because there was no highway connection, and later complained that the road eventually built was not hard-surfaced. Increasingly, they also accused Banff residents of spreading anti-Jasper propaganda. To right these wrongs, an Edmonton group established the Jasper Park Development Committee in 1941 to force the federal government to improve conditions at Jasper and build better roads to attract greater numbers of tourists.[56] Despite such complaints, the mountain parks were by World War II becoming firmly integrated into the holiday driving patterns of many Albertans, who were drawn by an increasing supply of commercial accommodation and serviced camp sites.[57]

The increased use of national parks in the interwar years was not an isolated recreational phenomenon. People with cars could also travel easily to a nearby lake for a day, a weekend, or longer, without requiring an increase in leisure time. In 1926, it was observed that the best camping trips were those close to home, "where one may drive from work without feeling too tired" and from which one could return "to the daily grind with a new sense of peace."[58] Changes in camping equipment matched the new means of transportation. Prior to the 1920s, camping equipment was relatively expensive and difficult to transport. Tents were commonly wedge or wall types made from duck cotton, primarily intended for military use and designed without reference to weight, easy packing, assembly, or cartage. Stoves, metal frame cots, and sleeping bags were equally difficult to transport. Sleeping bags, that first appeared about 1900, were covered with heavy waterproof duck and usually were lined with sheepskin and wool cloth. Some even sported a fur lining. The recommended clothing added yet more weight: women were advised to wear a flannel or towelling robe with a hood which would leave "only the face exposed" while lying in a sleeping bag.[59]

This bungalow, or umbrella, tent was advertised with other camping equipment in the May 1926 issue of *Good Roads Magazine*.

Before widespread use of cars, it was necessary to transport such equipment on the train and then by wagon to the camp site. For most, this ruled out camping in favour of day trips to developed resorts, such as Banff, or to nearby lakes. Before 1914, camping was popularly seen as expensive, inconvenient, dirty, and dangerous,[60] except by those with sufficient means to hire assistance with cartage. Although wall and wedge tents continued to be commonly available in the 1920s, the introduction of umbrella or bungalow tents and tents that could be erected on the side of a car promised travellers independence and flexibility.[61] Camp stoves, a variety of folding camp furniture, and carrier boxes that fit onto the running board of a car all enhanced the appeal of camping.[62] Further, the popularity of camping by the 1920s stimulated the promotion and retail sale of all sorts of associated items: cameras, deodorants, depilatories, mosquito repellants, flashlights, thermos bottles, and even portable phonographs.[63] Of course, many campers improvised and used old quilts for bedding and tarpaulins for tents,[64] but in the dominant view, manufactured equipment was essential to maintain the comforts of home at the campsite. "Too much paraphernalia" was better than not enough so one needn't " 'rough it' too roughly";[65] a revealing comment about the attitude of many towards outdoor leisure.

Boathouse and *Mountain Belle* on Bow River with Mount Rundle, Banff. Photograph by John Woodruff (Whyte Museum of the Canadian Rockies, NA-66-1344)

The resort of Gull Lake is shown in this undated postcard view, taken at some time in the second decade of the twentieth century. (GAI NA-1644-71)

The increasing demand for camping facilities in the 1920s led to great expansion in the number and extent of lake resorts. Resorts like Aspen Beach on Gull Lake near Lacombe, Ma-Me-O Beach on Pigeon Lake, Seba Beach on Lake Wabamum, and Sylvan Lake near Red Deer, which were popular before World War I because they were on rail lines, expanded greatly during the 1920s. The Village Act was amended in 1918 to allow for the incorporation of summer villages, with powers similar to those of ordinary villages except that they could not issue debentures. To serve the leisure needs of seasonal populations, elections and annual ratepayers' meetings could be held in the summer and members of Councils did not have to reside in their village.[66] Even so, the number of people who visited a lake on a daily or weekly basis greatly outnumbered the cottage owners. Cottages were relatively rare in Alberta before World War II, although a number of people lived in tents at a lake all summer. Cottages (popularly and affectionately called "shacks") were often rather informal buildings of "the slenderest construction" built by the owners according to their own plans. In Jasper and Banff, more elaborate log or stuccoed frame cottages had many of the comforts of town life.[67]

Increasing private access to automobiles extended the area from which visitors came. Before World War I, Rochon Sands on Buffalo Lake was a small resort used mainly by people from the nearby towns of Stettler and Erskine. After the war, the resort began to grow and by 1929, when it was incorporated as a summer village, it had sixty cottages, a wharf, and a dance hall, all developed by individual enterprise or through "subscriptions amongst the cottage owners." By the time of incorporation, pressure on the facilities was excessive because the resort was drawing people from such a large area. As it was the only lake resort between the Saskatchewan border and Red Deer, it served Stettler, Drumheller, Hanna, and the area north to Camrose.[68] This resulted in a "large influx of campers, or parties which simply put up tents and stay for a few days or a week." Because Rochon Sands did not have the sanitary, campground, or commercial facilities to handle the crowds, the provincial government received demands to take charge of conditions at the resort.[69]

MacGregor Lake summer resort, near Vulcan, early in the 1920s. (GAI NA-2163-9)

Development was faster paced at Sylvan Lake, which by the early 1930s had become a "garish mecca for pleasure-seekers in the summer."[70] It had an ideal location close to Red Deer and midway between both Calgary and Edmonton. In the 1920s, tourists came to the lake by train and by automobile. By 1929 the road to the resort was gravelled and the increased number of vehicles entering the resort required additional parking lots.[71] This was a far cry from the thrice weekly "stage line" service that had taken visitors to the lake in 1907.[72] In 1932, Sylvan Lake had a winter population of 350 and there were four hundred cottages at the village and around the lake. The summer population ranged between 3,000 and 5,000, except on public holidays when it peaked at up to 10,000.[73] A highly developed modern commercial resort, it had electricity twenty-four hours a day, hotels and boarding houses, cabins, camp grounds, shops, a dance pavilion that featured "the West's well known orchestras," movie theatres, commercial amusement booths, boat rentals, slides, rafts and diving platforms, three shale tennis courts, a golf course, and lawn bowling greens. Giving evidence of the new obsession with sanitation, Sylvan Lake proudly advertised that its water and food supply were regularly tested and kept up to standards by experienced professionals. Because buses ran three times a day from Calgary and Edmonton during the summer, Sylvan Lake was accessible to the whole province through those centres.[74]

In recognition of the demand for parks and lakeside recreational facilities, the provincial government announced in 1929 that it would establish small parks "scattered throughout the province as playgrounds for the people and dedicated to their social enjoyments."[75] A survey selected sites "as permanent reserves" for public use and in 1929 the new Town Planning Act included provisions for Crown purchase of land for provincial parks. The Alberta government projected eight parks in 1930 and purchased property at Ghost Lake near Morley, Sylvan Lake, Gull Lake and Gooseberry Lake for park purposes.[76] Under the Provincial Parks and Protected Areas Act of 1930, provincial parks were administered by a parks board. Although park development was slowed during the 1930s, the government had proclaimed eleven provincial parks and assembled the land for five more by 1943; less than a decade later, there were thirty-five parks in the province, most of them picnic grounds and recreational areas designed for "people who cannot get away for more than a day or two at a time."[77]

In its task, the government encountered two basic problems. First, resources worth developing were scarce in some locations. Many Alberta lakes proved to be "virtually large sloughs whose water breed fungi" making the water unfit for swimming. "Their beaches, such as at South Cooking Lake, are often muddy and for long stretches, the shores are covered with reeds and other water growths."[78] Nonetheless, descriptions of popular bathing locations in 1929 indicate that people often used lakes that were little better than sloughs. Birch Lake near Innisfree, with alkaline water, a poor beach, and black sandy mud, had a dancing pavilion, a refreshment booth, a few boats, and about six cottages. Gooseberry Lake, near Consort, sported a large dancing pavilion, one cottage, a booth and a baseball diamond. While stock would not drink the alkaline water, it was "apparently quite safe for bathing purposes." And at Elk Water Lake, near the Cypress Hills, the water was described as "not entirely suitable for bathing purposes, [but] there is nothing else available."[79] Yet there were some suitable lakes, and people from the Red Deer, Edmonton and Peace River areas, who had easy access to good lakes close by, could become quite lyrical in their appreciation.[80] The promoters of Sylvan Lake described it in classical pastoral terms, while Camrosians were "enthusiastic" about the charms of Miquelon Lake. "They may not be surrounded," said the *Camrose Canadian*,

> by the rich coloring and hazy atmosphere that has inspired the poets of the English lakes. They may not have the music and gaiety or the beautiful summer homes of the Thousand Islands. But they are able to get closer to nature's heart—all the closer because of the absence of these other things.[81]

The government's second problem was financial. In 1929, when Premier Brownlee announced that parks would be established, the province anticipated shouldering the costs involved but the financial pressures of the Depression crushed that optimism. In 1932, as part of government retrenchment, the town planning commission responsible for provincial park development was abolished and its director fired.[82] Accordingly, park development slowed, although it did not stop altogether, and in one case at least a local community attempted to fill the void. The people of Coalhurst wanted a park developed at Park Lake. The province provided administrative assistance while local volunteers handled all the work at the site, planting some fifteen acres of land with forty-five hundred trees and shrubs gathered from nearby places. The park was an immediate success, drawing people from fifty miles away by 1937.[83] The provincial government obviously liked such a method of developing public facilities, but because the operation and maintenance of a park on a purely volunteer basis proved impossible to sustain, it was soon forced to provide annual subsidies.

The sandcastle contest at Sylvan Lake in 1918. (GAI NA-2139-1)

At the essential camp fire by the lake, stories, songs, and conversation were the main forms of entertainment. Food was also important, and it is apparent that people went to considerable effort to bring the right kinds of food. In 1907, a local store in Red Deer offered "intending campers" various sorts of canned fish and meat, cakes, biscuits, cocoa, chutney pickles, jams, and "corn on the cob, put up in tins—a most delicious treat at this season of the year."[84] In one description of an outing to Sylvan Lake, raisin pies, hams, lemons, and French liqueur (for sea sickness it was said), plus the ingredients and equipment for making fudge over the camp fire were all part of the camp outfit.[85] The *Camrose Canadian* graphically described eating as a ritual at lake outings: "How they do eat! The eyes become 'great rolling eyes of prey' and the cheek does 'bulge with the unswallowed chunk'. . .Maxim's. . .could not provide a better morsel."[86]

Canoe in tow, Calgary, 1913. (GAI NA-2332-36)

The most important lake resort activities, of course, centred around the water. In a period when lifeguards and lifesaving equipment were not generally used, the tragedy of several drownings at Rochon Sands in 1928 was not unusual.[87] In 1935, the Alberta Federation of Labour demanded that the provincial government require lifesaving equipment and lifeguards at all public bathing areas and that laws be passed to prevent the rental of unsafe boats.[88] While swimming and playing in the water remained immensely popular, boating was more limited. At the end of June in 1910, there were four motorboats at Miquelon Lake, although "there is every indication that the number of lesser craft will be greatly increased from week to week."[89] Private motorboats remained relatively rare before World War II and were owned only by the elite who had the money and time to own and use a cabin and boat house at a lake.[90] Most boat owners had "lesser craft," that is, canoes or rowboats. These could also be rented at many lakes and resorts, whereas motorboat rentals were rare before 1930.[91] A more popular alternative was to take rides on commercial excursion boats. *The Australia* began in 1907 to carry about forty-five passengers at a time around Sylvan Lake and this attraction continued to be popular until at least World War II.[92] At Banff in 1911 an eight-mile ride on the river cost seventy-five cents.[93]

By 1914, boating regattas were able to draw large crowds at a number of places including Banff, Sylvan Lake, Gull Lake, and Wabamum.[94] The popular Sylvan Lake regatta originated in conjunction with the local UFA annual picnic. In 1916, the large crowd included two hundred people from Red Deer who came on a special train. A picnic, sports day and evening dance augmented the event in the absence of sufficient boats for a day-long regatta.[95] By 1924, however, the regatta focussed on water sports which took place between a parade in the morning and a dance in the evening. The presence of only canoes and rowboats in the boating competitions indicates the limited use of motorboats for recreational purposes at the time. Among the swimming events and "fancy diving," the latter proved "the most attractive and enjoyable event of the sports."[96]

The Silvertone Seven, who played at dances at Sylvan Lake, are shown broadcasting from CKXL, Calgary. (GAI ND-10-121)

To accommodate the popular lakeside activity of dancing, by 1929 dancing "pavilions" were located at many lakes and resorts, even small ones like Shorncliffe Lake near Czar and Birch Lake near Innisfree. The Sylvan Lake dance hall always booked good bands, including the Silvertone Seven in the 1930s. They "had a unique style," recalled one fan, and "when they played 'Stormy Weather', as I've never heard it played before or since, everyone stopped dancing to listen."[97] The dances at Sylvan Lake were organized as "jitney" dances. The dance floor was enclosed by a railing with "several places of entry and exit." One could stand outside the rail and watch the dancers without paying admission. Jitney was slang for five cents, the amount paid to get onto the floor. This arrangement accommodated the great number of people attending simply to watch. Fearing that amusement taxes might not be collected from every dancer, the provincial government disliked this system and dropped its opposition only when convinced that no one was trying "to defraud the Amusement Tax Branch."[98]

Dancing, at Sylvan Lake at least, also caused other worries. In 1933, the local Presbyterian minister became convinced that the morality of young people was endangered by the activities at the resort. During the early 1930s, Sunday night movies were followed by a midnight "frolic"—an occasion he believed to be "fraught with much danger." Indeed, "people coming here for the summer from Calgary and Edmonton are shocked to find that such dissipation is allowed."[99] The province acted with remarkable speed; within nine days it had amended the appropriate regulations to prohibit dancing on Sundays, on Saturday nights after midnight and on other nights after 1:00 A.M. Further, nobody under the age of eighteen was allowed at a dance unless accompanied by a parent or guardian.[100] Moreover, the Department of the Provincial Secretary, which was responsible for cinemas, insisted that the Sunday night movies be stopped. The mayor and council of Sylvan Lake pointed out that this entertainment was an important part of the summer leisure activities of people living nearby and that Sunday was the most popular day at the resort. A day at the lake followed by a movie in the evening provided inexpensive entertainment for farmers who had little money and who came to the lake "to make a day of it." Though the deputy provincial secretary might say that people should "go to Church," there were "thousands of people at Sylvan Lake on Sunday evenings in the summer and therefore the movie fulfills a real need."[101] These protests were futile and the prohibition stood.

Summer camps, on the other hand, were considered valuable for children and adolescents. The most active sponsors of these camps were the Girl Guides and the Boy Scouts, who were organizing camps in Alberta by about 1910.[102] The Edmonton Catholic

Women's League established a summer camp at Lac Ste Anne in 1917 with 209 "guests."[103] Other churches and quasi-religious bodies, such as the YMCA, the YWCA, the CGIT, and Tuxis, also organized camps. All camps were sexually segregated and had similar activities, although Tuxis boys' camps involved more competitive activities and events than did CGIT girls' camps.[104] The following observations about CGIT camps therefore apply in good measure to Tuxis boys' camps as well.

After the YWCA organized the first girls' camp in Canada at Lake Couchiching in 1910,[105] such camps became common throughout the country. In 1919, shortly after its establishment in Alberta, the CGIT organized three summer camps: one at Sylvan Lake and two at Lake Wabamum (one at Fallis and another at Kasota Beach). The Kasota Beach camp had cabins and "pavilions," and the campers and camp leaders at Fallis were housed together in a "clubhouse"—an arrangement that was reported to have developed "a particularly fine camp spirit."[106] Over the following years, the CGIT established additional camps throughout the province: in 1928 there were eight and in 1945 there were twenty-one with a total of 1,018 campers.[107]

The campers were kept busy with hiking, swimming, canoeing, Bible and nature study, handicrafts, and camp fire singsongs, all intended to create fellowship and friendship, provide exercise, and train campers in religion and handicrafts. The camps did not merely provide a week's summer entertainment; they reinforced and sustained moral values and combined education with pleasure. The highly regimented lifestyle and educational focus of these camps no doubt revealed belief in the power of one's environment to mould behaviour and establish good character. The provision of religious training in a highly structured format, in conjunction with clean air and plenty of exercise, reflected a number of turn of the century assumptions. If nature could be seen as the handiwork of God, the appreciation of nature could become a form of recognition and worship of God's omniscience. The alternative argument in the wake of Darwin's theories on evolution, that man had to recognize his place in nature "as a part of an evolutionary process,"[108] seems not to have been of any importance for campers. The view that nature showed God's power was typical of camping rhetoric in the interwar years. Yet, at times, the rhetoric about "nature" seemed to arise more from some vague pantheism and nature worship than from Christian doctrines. The use of the campfire as the focus for the camping experience was also peculiar in terms of Christian ideals: the fire was identified as a symbol for everything from "nature" to "fellowship" to "His Holy Name." The CGIT ceremony at the campfire was "conducted in Indian fashion" and closed with an Indian war whoop.[109] In addition, aphorisms, such as "the Spirit is within our hearts, we will hand it on," were attributed to the Indian ceremonies and the campfire.[110] Such language and symbolism must have confused if not bewildered many adolescents, especially those reared in the austerities of the Methodist, Presbyterian, and Baptist churches. Nevertheless, in keeping with the didactic purposes of camping, great emphasis was placed on the role of camp leaders as figures of authority. In 1928, the CGIT instituted training for camp leaders, including courses on "Organization and Administration in Girls' Work" and "Dramatics and Pageantry."[111]

Opportunities for summertime outdoor activity for young people expanded further during the 1930s through the establishment of youth hostels. The first hostel in Canada was located in a tent at Bragg Creek in 1933, but the hostel movement in Alberta was not formally established until 1937 when the Canadian Youth Hostels Association was admitted to the International Youth Hostels Association. This opened the doors of Alberta hostels to non-Canadian travellers and allowed Canadian youths to use the forty-five hundred youth hostels throughout the world.[112] By 1938, there were eight active hostels in Alberta which could accommodate 167 hostelers. A yearly membership in the Canadian Youth Hostels Association cost two dollars, and a member could use the facilities for twenty-five cents per night and per meal. By 1940, the number of hostels had grown to twelve and they were all located "a good day's hike from each other." World War II reduced the number to seven in 1944.[113]

The youth hostel movement was backed by the YMCA and YWCA and hostelers were able to use the YMCA and YWCA facilities while passing through Edmonton, Calgary, and Lethbridge.[114] Such sponsorship was important for the success of the movement, but its greatest source of strength was the perseverance and hard work of the four pioneers who organized and administered the Alberta hostels: Catherine and Mary Barclay, Dorothy Allen, and Ivy Devereux. Except for those at Bragg Creek and Spray River, the hostels were owned by hostel wardens who collected the daily fee and maintained the hostels from the proceeds, often on a shoestring budget. The hostels had wood stoves and screens on windows, were equipped with cooking and eating utensils, dishes, blankets, and straw ticks,[115] and provided the bases for hiking and a limited range of other activities. The youth hostels movement in Alberta aimed to provide healthy outdoor exercise for youths who had little money but wanted to holiday in the mountains. In broader terms, however, it stood for much more: it was a part of a general movement which aimed to counter nationalism and militarism and create world peace by giving people the opportunity to meet each other in friendship at little cost.[116]

Unlike this group at Drumheller, who are admiring the hoo-doos in the 1930s, few people appreciated undisturbed nature. (PAA A.7988)

The youth hostel movement, like the development of provincial parks in the 1920s and 1930s, grew partly from tradition and partly from a new interest in outdoor activities. The belief that the outdoors held particular charm for people had been part of Canadian thinking well before the settlement of Alberta, but it was transformed during the interwar years. Private motorized transportation not only reduced the time required for activities such as camping but also expanded the geographic scope of outdoor recreation for an increasing proportion of the populace. The automobile served at the same time to integrate such activity into regularized hours of work and the family ideals of the dominant culture. Free time and vacations were a reward for labour, entrenched in annual holidays and outings on specific days. Since holidays did not challenge work and even regenerated workers, the state could legitimately encourage outdoor recreation by providing provincial parks and camping facilities. In this framework began the development of the weekend as the primary focus for leisure, and by 1930 Edmonton's urban planners took into account the weekend and Sunday exodus in developing the city's street plans.[117]

The development of provincial parks was thus shaped primarily by economic and recreational needs and not by the need for conservation or preservation of nature. At some provincial parks and resorts, especially large ones like Sylvan Lake, the dance halls, sporting facilities, cinemas, and other commercial outlets could not be characterized as getting "close to nature." Perhaps this was an inevitable outgrowth of the utilitarian approach that informed so much of the Canadian view of nature: nature had visual charm, but had no integrity outside of direct human needs or human perception,[118] and few were willing to sacrifice their comforts in order to appreciate an undisturbed nature. Exceptions like Annora Brown, the Fort Macleod painter, encountered few like-minded people in her wilderness treks during the 1930s.[119] The outdoors became attractive to most people only when it no longer seemed dirty, dangerous, and inconvenient.[120] In part, developments in equipment and transportation that mitigated the rigours of outdoor life helped to increase people's willingness to go camping.

Preservation, in its modern sense, did begin to emerge in Alberta during the interwar years. The flashpoint in this change occurred in 1924 with the outcry over the destruction of the Spray River basin through hydroelectric development. The organization of the Canadian National Parks Association to fight this development on environmental grounds was probably one of the earliest expressions of a preservation ideal in Alberta.[121] Nonetheless, even the Canadian National Parks Association always closely allied its environmental campaign to outdoor leisure activities such as camping and wilderness hiking, sustaining the utilitarian tradition within an environmental sympathy. Perhaps this was a pragmatic recognition of how best to appeal to the majority of the population and politicians alike, but, generally, one test of prevalent attitudes to nature, and its supposed moral and social benefits for the correction of modern tendencies, appeared in the standards that people wanted in their outdoor leisure. If "modernism" did indeed represent a social threat, few showed a willingness to abandon modern material standards in their quest for the restoration of their souls through nature. Such rhetoric may have inspired camping and outdoor activities, but it did little to divorce such leisure from the technical and material standards and assumptions of the society.

7. Theatre and Music: The Performing Arts as Leisure

Theatrical and musical performances were significant and regular leisure events in Alberta. They exhibited great variety through community concerts, touring shows, Chautauqua, vaudeville, drama, concerts, operas, recitals, symphonies, and dances. Vaudeville alone presented drama, comedy, music, acrobats, and even movies. So great a range of performances involved both amateurs and professionals; for amateurs, stage and musical events expressed local talent and creativity, while professionals earned their living travelling from stage to stage. The standards and models presented by these commercial professional performers affected the selection and style of amateur performance, which gave them an impact beyond the simple provision of entertainment.

Amateur variety shows had become traditional events in Alberta communities by 1890, and they continued to provide a focus for community life and an outlet for local talent. They had a consistency only in the discrete and unrelated character of their performances. At one rural concert in 1929, after an impersonation of the vaudeville star, Harry Lauder,

> recitations and songs followed one after another and were well received. 'Blaydon Races', 'A Farmer's Boy' and 'The Keys of Heaven' illustrate the simplicity of the material used throughout that made the concert such a success. At no time was there any pretense of great talent. The musical fraternity, who had sung these songs time and again in each other's homes, were now including the community in the fun. That was all. And it was evidently enough.

The one-act comedy that followed was so good that the audience forgot "the meagre stage, the faded turkey-red chintz curtains, the gas lantern shaded with a cookie pan," and, for a while, they "glimpsed real life." The programme ended with conjuring tricks and a magic show, and the evening concluded with a supper and dance.[1]

Although such random selections were typical, some amateur variety shows had at least a thematic rationale. One was the Christmas concert and another was the minstrel show, which was popular into the 1920s. Minstrel shows featured sets evocative of the "old south," and actors and singers performed in a blackface act and imitated the idiom of American blacks, mainly in clog dances, "negro sketches," and songs. Typical songs included those by Stephen Foster or racist ditties such as "Mary's Gone Widda

Coon."[2] Many of these minstrel shows were extemporaneous, like most amateur variety shows, but others were mounted by amateur troupes that performed regularly for several years. In the late 1890s, the "Komical Koons" troupe was a group of local "boys" from Edmonton. Another troupe from Medicine Hat travelled through the province in 1896 putting on a "clean, comical and generally up-to-date performance" to raise funds for the Medicine Hat hospital.[3]

Minstrel shows offered an outlet for the theatrical and musical talent of all sectors of the community. In 1882, the Fort Saskatchewan NWMP mounted a minstrel show of "songs, recitations, farces and dances." After the show, the crowd, said to number about three hundred, ate a midnight supper, danced "with vigor until daylight," had breakfast, and then went home.[4] In 1924, the minstrel skit at the Red Deer Rotary Club Carnival featured "Uncle Josh," "Aunt Jemima," and "Jiggs."[5] Reports of the performances always stressed their hilarity, but their cultural implications are puzzling. American in origin, with little reference to the traditions of culturally dominant British groups in Alberta, minstrel shows were a fad in most of North America, including Canada, from 1840 to 1880.[6] Their persistence in the prairies until the mid-1920s represents an interesting cultural atavism and repeated American infusions. If minstrel shows presented an opportunity for white people in the United States to enjoy Black music while simultaneously denigrating its creators,[7] they might have found the same appreciation in a Canadian society that was undoubtedly racist, although never to the extent evident in the United States. Even so, the context of the minstrel show had little direct relevance to people in Alberta, with the possible exception of some American settlers. One can only assume that Albertans found minstrel shows to be good entertainment. Aside from confirming negative attitudes towards Black people,[8] they provided culturally alienated entertainment, a phenomenon reinforced by the productions of many other professional touring shows. Yet by the time William Sherrah's Colored Minstrel Duo travelled through the province in 1929, the minstrel show was in serious decline and Sherrah received a poor reception. In part, he blamed competition from movies, but he also noted that "just two people and colored" had only "a poor chance" to book many shows.[9]

Sherrah's was a relatively minor example of a diverse system of professional touring shows well-known in the province for nearly half a century. By the late 1880s, they had begun to appear

216

occasionally in such frontier villages of southern Alberta as Calgary and Medicine Hat.[10] These touring shows rarely appeared in Edmonton and the northern communities until after 1891, when South Edmonton was linked by rail to Calgary and the CPR main line. Facilities were also as crucial as transportation, and before 1906, Edmonton could boast few facilities of merit. Edmonton's sheriff, John Robertson, built Robertson Hall on the second floor of a downtown commercial building erected in 1892, and in 1902 Richard Secord built the Thistle Rink, the first facility capable of housing large shows. When Edmonton businessman Alexander Cameron opened the Edmonton Opera House in 1906, it was "destined to become one of the city's major cultural institutions."[11] Of the theatres that followed, the grandest was the third Empire theatre, opened in 1920 by a consortium made up of Calgary's Senator Lougheed and a number of Edmonton businessmen. In the early years, Calgary was much better off. Hull's Opera House, built in 1893 by William Roper Hull, was the best theatre on the prairies at the time, and quite a number of theatres, including the Grand, owned by Senator Lougheed, were operating by 1912.[12] While some of these theatres were plain, others were lavishly decorated with plaster, gold paint, murals and velvet upholstery to create palaces of entertainment.[13]

By 1906, good facilities were available in both Edmonton and Calgary, a transportation network was in place, and a metro population of about fourteen thousand in each city could support commercial stage presentations. In their heyday, touring variety shows displayed a great number of forms and inconsistent quality. While some included the greats of the theatre world, others essentially presented a standard format of variety entertainment. Mounted by an individual, a small group of performers, or by large troupes, they often resembled in their variety the vaudeville of the Pantages, Orpheum and Webster circuits. The variety shows of the 1890s and the first part of the twentieth century usually included a skit or two, instrumental music, songs illustrated by a lantern show, trained animal shows, perhaps a gymnastic performance, hypnotist or magician, and often a star performer.[14] Admission prices in the larger urban centres like Edmonton were about fifty cents.[15] Even as late as the 1930s, acts such as Ken-Mage Mysteries, a "Deluxe Magic Show" including the act "Sawing a Dog in Halves," and Peter Michkota's Magic Show, a varied programme of "Magical tricks—Supernatural Act—and—wonderful escapes," travelled through the small towns of Alberta.[16]

Before 1930, dramatic companies and stock companies also commonly toured the province. Dramatic companies usually visited a city for only a few days, while stock companies generally set up in a city or town for several months or for as long as they could attract a full house. Both types of companies produced a wide repertoire, sometimes with highly talented and famous performers, especially before World War I. In 1912, one of the great actors of the age, Sir Johnston Forbes-Robertson, performed at the Empire Theatre in Edmonton and lectured the University Dramatic Society on "the merits of Ibsen and naturalism in acting."[17] In 1914, Sir Frank Benson brought his Stratford-on-Avon Players to Alberta, and it was said to be an "exceptional privilege to see an organization which has had so much to do with keeping alive the best Shakespearian traditions in the old Land."[18]

Few others brought such credentials, but many of these shows were competently acted and directed, although often the actors received little challenge or inspiration from the light drama and comedies the public demanded. In the years before World War I, "comedies, farces and romantic dramas. . .were the staples of the age,"[19] but the quality of the scripts often took second place to elaborate sets and special effects. As these became more complex and astonishing, local audiences saw portrayals of the eruption of Vesuvius and the crucifixion of Christ. Moreover, the intermissions necessary for set changes were used to present acrobats, cyclists, or movies; a format verging upon touring variety shows.[20] With larger repertoires than the dramatic companies, stock companies mounted series of plays in one location, often with little rehearsal. A different play could be mounted each night and most sets and costumes served in a number of plays.[21] Prices for dramatic and stock company shows generally ranged from fifty cents to two dollars, although the highest admission price to Forbes-Robertson's performance in 1912 was three dollars.[22]

Touring companies did not always follow regular circuits. Calgary was consistently a bigger and better market for circuit drama than Edmonton,[23] from the 1890s when only a handful of companies appeared in either place[24] to the halcyon days of touring companies just before World War I. Some of the companies specializing in commercial plays would play in smaller towns near the cities if a sufficient audience would justify a run of even a few days. In 1908, the Allen Players played in Edmonton and then went on to Camrose and other towns.[25] A few groups, such as the Tom Marks Company, specialized in playing small towns before World

War I and had loyal followings.[26] However, most rural areas did not receive dramatic or stock shows. None visited the Peace River country until 1932 although there had been "plenty of jip shows but not real dramatic shows."[27] By the early 1930s, the stock companies that worked the small towns began to face major problems because of the Depression. Like touring groups in other rural areas of Alberta, the Richard Kent Stock Company found business very poor in the Peace River district in 1932.[28]

Touring companies had encountered problems long before the 1930s. While Edmonton still welcomed more dramatic stock companies than any other similarly sized city in North America in 1916,[29] British companies virtually ceased to tour the prairies during the war. This decline continued in the 1920s and, as Alberta playwright Gwen Pharis Ringwood recalled, there were times in the early 1920s when the professional theatre was no longer a part of Alberta life and "you and the theatre were strangers. Not that you wished it so, but there were no plays to go to." During the late 1920s, she acknowledged, there was a revival of sorts in touring drama, and urban theatre goers were able to see the Stratford-on-Avon Players with their "understandable, warm, living" approach to Shakespeare, the Barry Jackson Players with productions of *Dear Brutus*, and the Colbourne Players, among other groups.[30] On the other hand, no stock company played the city in 1928 "except for one of those 'tabloid outfits' which divide the program with a 'movie'." In Calgary, the reduction was not as serious because touring companies stopped over during their travels across the country.[31]

Vaudeville was among the famous touring shows of the first quarter of the century. It began to have a major impact in Alberta in 1909 when Senator Lougheed, who then owned the Lyric Theatre in Calgary and the Empire Theatre in Edmonton, arranged joint bookings of the Pantages circuit for both theatres. The Pantages was a relatively new troupe in 1909, but it was large enough to mount acts for a "thirty weeks' continuous booking on a route covering much of the northwestern USA and western Canada."[32] These circuits were hectic, and one prairie schedule planned by "the vaudeville kings" in 1912 had the artists travelling from Minneapolis to Winnipeg for a week's engagement, then to Moose Jaw and Regina for a split week of three days in each city, then to Calgary for a week, on to Edmonton and Saskatoon for a split week of three days each, and then from Saskatoon to Spokane.[33] Vaudeville in Alberta thus was part of a complex continental system of commercial entertainment.

Pantages did not perform regularly in Edmonton before 1913 because of booking problems. However, it opened its own theatre there in 1913[34] and then dominated vaudeville in the city. The Edmonton Pantages Theatre was an opulent building with two balconies, plenty of gold trim, a gold satin stage curtain, and a seventy-foot scenic backdrop. In Calgary, Pantages competed with the Orpheum circuit's shows which were mounted at the Sherman Grand. While the Orpheum circuit saw itself as more sophisticated than the brash Pantages, there was little difference between the two. Each theatre aimed to present an eclectic new bill every week, with the Pantages stressing high energy presentations.[35]

The cast of Pantages Theatre, Edmonton, circa 1915. (PAA A.3239)

Vaudeville provided a "direct sensory experience" through effective use of colour, gesture and sound, in "a fluid form which could mold and shift in considerations of the current tastes and mores of the audience."[36] It raised the variety of the earlier touring shows to new heights, including gymnasts, trained animals, short plays and films, comedians, pantomimists, musicians, singers, and minstrel performers. Some Pantages vaudeville performers seen in Alberta went on to become movie stars: the Marx

Brothers, Jimmy Durante, and Stan Laurel, among others.[37] But not all vaudeville was comedy. Nineteen thirteen, the year the Orpheum circuit in western Canada featured Sarah Bernhardt, was considered the "annus mirabilis" in provincial theatre history. Bernhardt appeared in four performances in Calgary in two days and in two performances in one day in Edmonton.[38] Tickets cost up to three dollars, but as A. B. Watt of the *Edmonton Journal* recalled, "the privilege of even so brief a glimpse of so commanding a figure was one to be prized during the length of one's life."[39] Most vaudeville performances before World War I were less expensive, however, and in Edmonton usually cost about fifty cents while gallery seats could be had for as little as twenty-five cents.[40]

Vaudeville troupes continued to perform throughout World War I but in the 1920s experienced difficulties that grew to crisis proportions in the 1930s. The Edmonton Pantages Theatre closed for a time in the early 1920s, but then reopened. Finally, all of the Pantages theatres were sold in 1929, many of them to Warner Brothers and the Orpheum circuit, and in 1931 the Edmonton Pantages Theatre was fitted out as a cinema.[41] Film had been an early feature of vaudeville, and silent movies were on the programme at the opening of the Edmonton Pantages Theatre in 1913. Short films lasting only a few minutes fit the vaudeville format, but feature length movies soon proved more popular than vaudeville.

Vaudeville may have provided great entertainment but its moral impact consistently came into question. Vaudeville companies often stressed that their shows were "clean" and they made some attempts to keep them above criticism. The provincial government occasionally instructed all touring shows about what they could and could not perform, and in 1919 circularized all theatres that "no performer would be permitted to use the name of any person in making laughter at their expense."[42] This was not regularized censorship, however, and despite pressure, the government refused to become involved in formal censorship of vaudeville. The Calgary Local Council of Women claimed in 1929 that vaudeville shows at the Grand were "vulgar in the extreme" and were "not even clever, just vulgar and coarse,"[43] while in the previous year, the Calgary Council on Child and Family Welfare had demanded censorship of the Pantages and Orpheum vaudeville because "there was hardly a bill that didn't contain at least one act at which something coarse or vulgar or suggestive was either spoken or acted or both." Censorship was needed, the council argued, because such models of behaviour "tended to create in the youth of today wrong ideals." As Premier Brownlee noted, however, there were "practical difficulties" that prevented government censorship of vaudeville programmes.[44]

Since the provincial government had no hesitation in censoring movies which it saw as socially and morally dangerous, the official reluctance to censor vaudeville may also have indicated an official perception of less depravity in vaudeville or the influence of its effective integration into the provincial economy. With the exception of the Pantages in Edmonton, companies rented facilities from local entrepreneurs, some of whom, such as Senator Lougheed, were at the pinnacle of the local elite. While there is no evidence that these people defended the vaudeville companies from censorship, their connection with vaudeville may have given it a degree of respectability in provincial society. While most vaudeville and other touring shows created a capital drain in the form of departing profits and wages, they also left money behind in the form of rent, travel fees and meal payments.

In cultural terms, most touring shows ignored the local context. Stock companies often featured American productions and scripts. Even before 1914, the allure of the New York and London stages allowed stock companies to make a living on the prairies rehashing current Broadway or London hits. [45] By the 1920s, the fact that a play was a Broadway or London hit was an important selling point in Alberta, where productions were sometimes advertised as being as "near a duplicate of the New York presentation as is humanly possible."[46] In the case of vaudeville, most of its content and most of the performers were American, although it was not deliberately exclusionist and its managers used whatever talent would draw the crowds. In 1924, the Pantages in Calgary hired two local cowboy stars, Guy Weadick and his wife, Flores La Due, to put on their show *Riddles* as part of the programme. *Riddles* had also been featured on the Orpheum circuit and was "always a winner." The crowd was invited to participate and prizes were awarded to the best dressed cowboys and cowgirls under sixteen years of age.[47]

Chautauqua was another type of touring show that brought many communities an outstanding summer and fall leisure event. It toured Alberta from 1917 until 1934 and was essentially a high quality travelling variety show which included lectures, music, dancers, comedians, and plays among its many features. Originally another American phenomenon, it began operations in

Canada in 1917 when the Dominion Chautauqua was formed, with its headquarters in Calgary. The Dominion Chautauqua arranged bookings and handled the business affairs of the tours.[48] With these arrangements, Chautauqua provided an entertaining and educational programme and enriched the lives of many rural prairie people who otherwise had few such opportunities.[49] Not only did it bring entertainment to remote communities, it also reinforced the standards of the dominant culture. As the *Edmonton Journal* correspondent in Viking observed in 1921, "we get far too little of real high class lectures and entertainment in the average Western town. Everyone should be ashamed to admit that they do not believe in Chautauqua. It shows a real lack of appreciation for the good things in educational and entertaining lines."[50] The Chautauqua neatly accorded with the aspirations of the dominant culture: the programme was in English, it was useful because it was educational, and its programme often contained high culture. Indeed, readers of the *Edmonton Journal* were told in 1921 that Chautauqua "should receive the strongest moral support from Church and State, for it is an ally of both."[51]

Because the Chautauqua programmes changed annually, a "veritable army of lecturers, musicians, orchestral groups, dramatic companies and assorted other artists and entertainers travelled the Canadian circuits."[52] The variety of Chautauqua was so great that it escapes generalization, except that it consciously included Canadian content. The many lecturers of note included the English suffragist, Emmeline Pankhurst, the social gospel preacher, Salem Bland, and the theorist of the UFA, Henry Wise Wood. On the other hand, the impact of the lecture on prison reform and citizenship by Dr. J. Rivers, the warden of the Lethbridge jail, was such that "no box office records would be smashed with the Doctor on the bill of fare."[53] A bewildering variety of musicians, from a "Hawaiian" group through to the Schubert Quartet of Toronto, a "Cossack Chorus" and soloists of various sorts, graced Chautauquas over the years.[54]

The breadth and variety of Chautauqua's programmes ensured their popularity in isolated communities, but the involvement of local citizens in their financing also promoted commitment and prevented the central organization from overextending itself. A local committee guaranteed each Chautauqua, contracting in advance with Dominion Chautauqua to pay any shortfall that the local programme might suffer. The central organization remained financially strong and an influential and supportive vested interest group emerged in every community that Chautauqua visited.[55] The guarantors were usually the leading citizens of a town, people who could afford to make the guarantee and who also, in theory at least, were interested in raising the cultural level of their community. In some cases, the guarantors did have to pay a shortfall. At Cadogan, near Wainwright, poor crops led to low attendance in 1924 and the guarantors were forced to make up $110.[56] Critics charged that the Chautauqua was draining capital out of the province and that the Dominion Chautauqua was a money-making operation, masked by talk about public service and education. As the deputy provincial secretary somewhat bitterly observed in 1928, "the lecturers and artists are highly paid and those at the head of it are not in it for their health or as a line of education."[57]

Each Chautauqua was staged in a tent, making the shows "independent of the limited hall and theatre accommodation" of small western communities. The shows could be produced "with exactly the same efficiency in the smallest as in the largest centres in Western Canada" and could thereby "bring to the doors of farmers a class of talent that ordinarily would only appear in two or three of the larger cities."[58] The same programme seen in Edmonton was also carried to small communities like Tofield, Ryley, Cereal, Bow Island, Barons, and Coaldale. Although Chautauqua was never as popular in Alberta as it was in Saskatchewan, in 1927 alone it visited fifty-eight towns in Alberta.[59] After 1934, however, the Depression ensured that people could not afford the admission and guarantors could not be found. Further, movies and radio by that time provided alternative and inexpensive leisure activities and were beginning to change standards and taste in entertainment.[60]

The collapse of the Chautauqua spelled the end of almost all forms of touring professional stage entertainment in the province. However, as in the rest of Canada, people in Alberta, both urban and rural, actually had more opportunities to see drama during the 1930s because of an upsurge in amateur productions. In some respects, this collapse strengthened the tradition of amateur theatre, although the organizing sponsors had changed since the 1890s. Many of the early plays served as fund-raising events for churches and other organizations, and some were community efforts designed solely for pleasure, like the melodrama *Vildac* and the comic burlesque *Love of a Bonnet* presented in the Fort Saskatchewan school house in 1895.[61]

By the late 1890s some amateur drama companies were being organized. The talented and ambitious Edmonton Amateur Dramatic Company, established in 1896 to put on light drama, toured Calgary, Canmore, and parts of British Columbia under the new name of La Cigale.[62] Following a popular touring show tradition, La Cigale's orchestra played for a dance after each play. La Cigale collapsed in 1897 when its director moved away from Edmonton, and although other dramatic companies were subsequently established in Edmonton and in other parts of the province, the greatest growth in amateur drama occurred after the war. In Calgary, the Paget Players, directed by Max Bishop, operated from about 1918 until they were succeeded by the Calgary Little Theatre group in 1924. The Green Room Club, founded in 1929, and the Calgary Little Theatre amalgamated in 1935 to form the Calgary Theatre Guild. The Guild disbanded in 1940 because of wartime conditions and was followed in 1944 by the highly successful Workshop 14 Theatre.[63]

This pattern of dissolving and reforming drama groups was typical and showed both the problems inherent in amateur drama and the existing level of commitment to it. Twenty-one drama groups functioned in Edmonton in the early 1920s. The Little Theatre was the largest and many of the others were associated with service clubs, community leagues, churches, and organizations such as the Jewish Young People's Society.[64] The Rotary clubs frequently put on plays at their regular luncheons, mounting in 1927 a patriotic one-act play, *Fathers of Confederation*.[65] Similarly, members of the Wauneta Club, a women's group at the University of Alberta, put on plays at their meetings.[66] Such sponsorship suggests that most amateur theatre was organized by English-speaking middle and upper middle-class people. In 1924, the Calgary Little Theatre counted among its active supporters and organizers "many of Calgary's well known citizens," including Mayor Webster and Judge Winter.[67] Nevertheless, a number of groups met the need for theatre in a language other than English: the first Francophone theatre in Alberta was established in Edmonton in 1912; the Polish Canadian Society, established in Edmonton in 1927, had a drama club which took its plays to Polish communities throughout the province; and a Chinese theatre group was active in Edmonton in the 1930s.[68]

Support for amateur drama in the interwar years was based upon several considerations; it gave pleasure to participants as well as to spectators and was considered to be socially useful. Except for some criticism of "godless" plays on Alberta stages,[69] people generally saw the theatre as a positive force that improved diction and speech, reinforced self-reliance, created fun, countered "modernism," and asserted humanistic values in a machine age. According to one observer in 1933, amateur theatre was important for self-development and resourcefulness.

> Just at this stage of the world's growth we seemed to be relying so much on being entertained, our pleasures were becoming vicarious and we were losing the ability to do for ourselves. Of course, it is easy to see why we were drifting to that state, as the gramophone, the movie, the radio and the car had all tended to do this.[70]

Precisely when these factors and attitudes gained impetus, the final collapse of commercial touring stage shows and the onset of the Depression forced people who wanted to see drama to be more self-reliant. Fortunately, amateur productions were a cheap and accessible form of entertainment,[71] while their local character gave added legitimacy. These amateur groups were best typified by little theatre, a somewhat vague term which was often applied to any formally organized and relatively permanent amateur civic theatre group that emphasized local production, direction, and actors.[72] Everywhere in Canada there was a surge in amateur theatre in the interwar years, and amateur theatre groups performed regularly in Calgary, Medicine Hat, Edmonton, and other places in the province during the 1920s. Further encouragement was given in 1929 when the famous British actor, Sir Barry Jackson, toured the country to promote the concept of little theatre. As a result, some new theatre groups appeared in Edmonton and elsewhere, while the Lethbridge Players, Calgary's Green Room Club, and a Medicine Hat theatre group increased their local support. The Medicine Hat group was under the direction of Norman Davis, who "had developed talent there to a point where his productions were always sure of a favorable audience."[73] As the Depression deepened, amateur drama increased, and by 1936-37 there were little theatre groups in Canmore, Red Deer, Camrose, Innisfail, Clive, Lethbridge, Edmonton, and Calgary. The group in Clive was active throughout the 1930s and by 1936 had fitted up the local community hall as a serviceable theatre space.[74] Similarly, various drama groups in Innisfail formed themselves into a guild, bought an old barn and converted it into the Innisfail Community Theatre, where in 1934 many people spent "their leisure hours studying, rehearsing, making properties, costumes and scenery."[75]

The success of many of these drama groups was largely due to the social and economic context of the Depression and to the collapse of touring companies, but a number of agencies also offered assistance and support. Especially valuable was the University of Alberta Department of Extension, which not only maintained a lending library of scripts made available for the cost of postage, but also provided assistance in the selection of appropriate plays, generally "serious comedy, light comedy or farce" suitable for amateur production.[76] Scripts were sent to 241 communities in 1924, but only to 140 in 1928-29. In 1930-31, the number increased to 348 and by 1933-34 it had grown to 483. For groups that were undecided, the Department of Extension sent "five or six plays. . .from which one or more may be selected."[77] The department gave further assistance by providing training. By 1933-34 this included summer programmes at Banff and Edmonton, instruction and advice by correspondence, and lectures in various communities. In 1934 the department lectured and provided assistance in play direction in forty-four communities and in other cases lent lighting equipment, gave instruction on how to make such equipment inexpensively, and provided information on the use of readily available materials for costumes and sets. Schools, drama societies, church groups, UFA locals, Women's Institutes, Little Theatre groups, lodges, and service clubs mounted the plays.[78] Further, the university and the provincial Department of Education jointly offered drama classes in Edmonton during the summer of 1933. They provided instruction to 125 people on the history and literature of drama and technical training in make-up, voice, acting, lighting, and design and culminated with the production of several plays. The university offered similar classes for 230 people who enrolled at Banff.[79] By 1936, the expansion of this programme justified renaming the Banff School of Theatre the Banff School of Fine Arts.[80]

The university's training programmes in drama, which provided incentive and practical training and helped to enrich the cultural life of many communities throughout the province, would not have been possible without the financial support of the Carnegie Foundation. In 1932, the foundation gave the University of Alberta thirty thousand dollars to develop a three-year programme in the fine arts, and additional funds were granted in 1935 to extend the programme for two years. After 1937, the drama programmes established with the Carnegie funds were maintained by the

Department of Extension.[81] These drama programmes helped to establish "community theatre as one of the most important cultural forces in the community life of the Province," especially in rural and small town communities.[82]

In 1937, drama was added to the public school curriculum after almost a decade of intense work by lobbyists who claimed that drama was effective in helping children to "live a more happy, joyous and complete life."[83] In part, this was a response to "progressive" ideas on education that became current during the 1930s, but it also reflected the impact on school teachers of the drama programme of the Department of Extension.[84] In some cases, school drama suffered from uninspired and parochial teacher direction, ignorant and uncaring students, and public criticism that only the three Rs should be taught in public schools. Nevertheless, it was important because, overall, it helped to raise provincial standards of theatre production, provided amateur theatre to communities that would otherwise have had none, and it created interest in drama among many students.[85]

Amateur drama received added stimulus and incentive from drama festivals where participants could learn better techniques and meet and associate with others of similar interests and commitment. Albertans first competed in a national festival at the Earl Grey Musical and Dramatic Trophy Competitions at Winnipeg in 1911. The competition aimed to encourage respectability through stimulating the use of "beautiful and refined speech in daily life" and amateur drama of a "higher order" than that seen in "the ordinary commercial playhouse." The Edmonton Amateur Dramatic club entered a comedy, *The Tyranny of Tears,* and won first place. Its success was a "genuine surprise" to the judge who noted that such excellence was not expected "from a town so far away as Edmonton, where opportunities for studying the best theatrical models are almost non-existent."[86] Despite the Earl Grey competitions, drama festivals were rare before the 1930s and Alberta groups could not afford to enter those held in central Canada. When the Alberta Drama League was established in 1929 as the first in the country, it promoted drama clubs and sponsored provincial festivals. After the Dominion Drama Festival was organized in 1932-33, the Alberta Drama League helped to organize the provincial festival at which Alberta's representatives to the Dominion Festival were chosen.[87] In 1933 the Alberta Drama Festival, which had been operating for several years purely as a provincial festival, became part of this network. Two plays were selected at the provincial trials held in Lethbridge and sent to Ottawa.[88]

For western Canadian drama groups, the Dominion Drama Festival was a mixed blessing. Although it gave national exposure and training and the chance to compete against the best talent in the country, the trip to the finals was expensive and some drama groups refused to enter the regional contests lest they be placed in the "false position" of having won their "way into a Festival to which they could not afford to travel." More commonly, however, local drama production suffered because the competitive urge was too strong and groups frequently:

> compete but husband their resources by cutting down their own local production schedule in order to have the funds to travel if successful. Thus it is that, at least in the West, the D.D.F. [Dominion Drama Festival] may indirectly result in less dramatic productions in an area than would be the case if some finances were behind this national festival.[89]

A number of local, often noncompetitive drama festivals unconnected to the Dominion finals were held purely for the pleasure of producing plays. These included school drama festivals and others such as Grande Prairie's drama and music school festivals which were the largest in the province.[90] An important and well-known festival sponsored by the Coleman Lions Club was established during World War II, "at a time when many dramatic organizations were suspending operations" on the grounds that wartime conditions made festivals impossible. The Coleman Festival, however, proved the opposite because it had

> a real community spirit behind it. Handbills advertising it were everywhere; all seats had been sold many days in advance, and on both evenings many persons were turned away at the doors; in stores, cafes, on the streets, both before and after the performance, I heard miners, housewives, boys and girls discussing their festival as they would a hockey match or a bonspiel.[91]

In 1947, the provincial government created the Alberta Drama Board as a part of postwar reconstruction plans to enrich the quality of life in Alberta. It was an important development, and, as was observed by one commentator in 1948, a much needed one, for "certainly something more must be done to foster that essential development [of the arts] in the future, than has been the case in the past." In this connection, it was noted that the Alberta

Drama League had struggled and worked alone "with practically no assistance from anyone" for the past twenty years.[92] The Alberta Drama Board represented a turning point, and after 1947 government coordination and sponsorship gave drama a broader scope and a more stable environment in which to operate than it had enjoyed in previous years. In the first two years of its existence, the Board sponsored an exchange of plays between Calgary and Edmonton drama groups, assisted the Alberta Drama League to stage drama festivals, sponsored a provincial tour of the University Provincial Players, and assisted rural groups to enter drama competitions.[93]

The increasing success of amateur drama in the 1930s did not mean that amateur drama groups did not face difficulties. Neither Edmonton nor Calgary amateur theatre groups had proper facilities in which to practice or present their plays. The Edmonton Little Theatre usually rented the Empire Theatre for its productions, but at a cost prohibiting any more than single night stands. Similarly, the Paget Players, the Calgary Little Theatre, and the Green Room Club in Calgary staggered along with unsuitable facilities during most of the 1920s and 1930s.[94] An even greater problem lay in the typical reliance upon a single key volunteer or perhaps a handful of people at best. This was, of course, an old problem—La Cigale had collapsed in 1897 when its director moved away. The Paget Players in Calgary depended heavily upon the work of Max Bishop who, exhausted, was "glad to retire in favor of the Calgary Little Theatre." But the latter group experienced the same difficulties and dissolved temporarily in the face of internal bickering and the illness of its director in 1928.[95] Similarly, the drama group in Clive, which won the Alberta Drama Festival in 1939 and shone at the Dominion Drama Festival, disbanded when its director moved to Edmonton and Clive was "heard of no more in the field of dramatics."[96] In other cases, drama groups dominated by cliques lost vitality and bored their audiences.[97]

Another problem lay in the scripts available. Some proved weak, especially in relevance to the community, since few good Canadian plays were written. While many Canadian plays were available, they were often "too derivative, too cosmopolitan if you like...their subject matter had little or nothing that could be called specifically Canadian." Thus, "Canadian dramatists of the 1920s and 1930s destroyed their own best market."[98] Theatre people in Alberta recognized the lack of indigenous play writing and looked for remedies. The Department of Extension administered a Carnegie programme during the 1930s that rewarded and trained

Alberta playwrights.[99] Similarly, in the early 1940s the Alberta Folklore Project, administered by the University of Alberta, stressed the development of indigenous drama based upon Alberta myths, legends, and history. Among those whose talent was given encouragement and impetus through such programmes was Gwen Pharis Ringwood, whose one-act play, *Still Stands the House*, won the prize for the best Canadian play in the 1939 Dominion Drama Festival.[100]

Among the many influences on theatre in Alberta were radio and film. Movies had a major and probably negative impact on professional theatre. Many people began to attend movies, and if the decline in professional touring theatre can be attributed, at least partly, to the advent of movies, then the growth in amateur theatre to fill this gap may have been another consequence. However, this benefit to amateur drama may have been offset by the impact of movies on the public's taste in theatre. In 1944, it was noted that theatre in Alberta was characterized by "the overwhelming influence of Broadway, and still more Hollywood." The public now demanded "the latest Broadway success or the stage version of some great Hollywood pageant" and amateur theatres in Alberta had neither the money nor the expertise to match movie production standards. Nor could amateurs or touring actors compete with Hollywood stars for "after all, the Greer Garsons and Robert Taylors are usually more talented and more alluring than. . .Maggie from the farm. . .or Jack Evans from the airport."[101]

Movies thus presented a major challenge to theatre, but radio presented a quite different situation. Indeed, in many respects, radio encouraged and gave new vitality to drama. Here, the University of Alberta and the Canadian Broadcasting Corporation (CBC) played important roles.[102] By 1930, the University was broadcasting drama as a regular feature on its radio station, CKUA. Initially, CKUA's production facilities were poor—"one play was almost ruined at its commencement by the power-house steam blowing off for five minutes." CKUA broadcast plays mounted by the CKUA Players and in 1931 they broadcast four of the Alberta Drama Festival plays from Convocation Hall.[103] In 1933-34 a Carnegie Trust Fund grant supported the production of a series of "historical sketches on Great Canadian Personalities," and in the same year, CKUA broadcast seven other plays; four mounted by the CKUA Players and one each by the University Dramatic Society, Edmonton Little Theatre Players, and the Dickens Players.[104] The station also broadcast lectures on techniques for

producing plays. Ten years later, CKUA's efforts were complemented by the drama club set up by station CJCA in Edmonton.
The club had a "permanent call list of thirty trained personnel,
and almost as many taking regular classes." The performers were
paid for all broadcasts in which they took part. CJCA saw this
programme as a contribution to drama in Edmonton and employed
a trained director to run the programme. The club successfully
broadcast a number of plays on the national network of the CBC
and also produced a series for the Canadian Chamber of Commerce for broadcast over private stations across the country.[105] The
CBC also frequently commissioned and broadcast plays, making
radio drama a specialized type of theatre, emphasizing Canadian
content, and providing crucial incentive and support for national
theatre.[106]

A homesteaders' band at Thorhild in 1910. (PAA A.7642)

Many of the patterns seen in the history of drama in Alberta also
applied to music. An immense variety of amateur musical events
prevailed alongside a good deal of professional activity, though
professionalism was less clear cut than in stage events. Many paid
musicians would never have defined themselves as professionals,

normally receiving an honorarium rather than a fee. This was frequently the case with Saturday night dance bands made up of local musicians. Consequently, "professionalism" does not provide a consistent reference, rather attention to the receptive or participatory nature of musical experiences proves more useful. On the one hand, people often attended musical events such as recitals and concerts to listen to the music. On the other hand, many participated, either by performing the music or by taking part in some other activity contingent on music, such as dancing.

Tipp's Orchestra provided the music for dances in Edmonton in 1923. (PAA A.8149)

It was commonly held that music could counter the miseries of the world. "Through the ages," one analyst generalized in 1927, "song has been an expression of our feelings of joy and triumph and a comfort when we are sad." Moreover, the power of evil could be mitigated through the inherent wholesomeness of music, for "the boy or girl, man or woman who is heartily singing is seldom planning an unkind act."[107] Whatever the attraction, dancing maintained the greatest popularity and provided the main form of collective entertainment in many Alberta communities. In 1923, dances were reported to be the chief winter social event in the area east of

Vegreville.[108] Clubs often put on dances to raise funds, but most were organized with no other motive than enjoyment. People with sufficiently large houses and phonographs or musical friends or family held dances in their homes. More commonly, dances took place in community halls or schools. In urban areas, commercial dance halls were common by 1920. Edmonton, "remote and isolated as it then was in the 1920s and 1930s, had 2 dozen places where one could go dancing on Saturday nights."[109] While some held that dancing was immoral and frivolous, such views had little impact.[110]

For some people, dancing was justified on the grounds that it was good exercise. In 1916, the Red Deer newspaper reported an American psychologist's findings that the "present day dancing craze" was not an example of declining morality but of an "increasing need for relaxation" because of the "strain of modern life." Dancing was "ultra primitive" in its rhythm and movement and was healthy exercise. Nevertheless, some people danced in unhygienic surroundings such as "overheated, overlighted, underventilated and dirty rooms." Thus, while dancing in moderation was good exercise, "its devotees can and frequently do defeat its beneficent purpose. They actually cause it to unfit them, instead of allowing it to fit them better, for the tasks and duties of life."[111] While the familiar argument that leisure should restore the individual for work received support among Albertans, many judged the amount of dancing necessary in rather liberal terms. Efforts to control the time spent dancing did, however, achieve success. In 1931, the UFA resolved that the late hours kept at country dance halls were "detrimental to health and sometimes to morals" and recommended that dances end at midnight.[112] In 1933 the government responded more directly to the specific report of "dissipation" at Sylvan Lake by prohibiting dancing on Sundays, after 12 midnight on Saturdays, and after 1:00 A.M. on other nights. It seems that these rules were generally obeyed although in 1937 parents in the hamlet of Glendon, near Bonnyville, complained of late Saturday night dances and demanded they end at midnight. "Once their children have been dancing all night," it was reported, "they are not in a position to attend any church services on Sunday."[113] To this limited degree, the state was perceived as useful in establishing the control that the family obviously could not.

The ubiquity of dancing suggests that it was a natural part of growing up. This was not always so, however, and learning to dance was often bound up with feelings of inadequacy and awkwardness, a situation that sustained commercial dance schools. One advertisement argued that after commercial instruction, "no longer will you have to remain at home all evening" because of an inability to dance. Furthermore, the advertisement observed, "at all social gatherings, someone is sooner or later going to suggest dancing." And here the fear became palpable: "when the others gather around for the fun, the one who cannot dance feels hopelessly out of it—a wall flower—a mere looker-on."[114] Lessons to overcome such critical social inadequacy were available by mail order or by personal instruction. Mail order dance lessons used charts and diagrams and claimed that "success was absolutely guaranteed" in the fox trot, one-step, two-step, waltz, and the "latest society dances." Anonymity was also ensured because "everything comes to you by mail in a plain envelope." Dancing schools providing personal instruction were always discreet as well; many promised "private rooms for beginners" and "special attention to out-of-town pupils," all of whom would "learn to dance in 3 days, or no charge."[115]

There had been dance schools from the turn of the century,[116] but their popularity increased during the 1920s. In 1903, dancing was apparently the most popular social activity in Calgary and the "non dancer is slightingly referred to as either a stick or a wall flower, with the result that he or she is considered desirable at only a very small percentage of social gatherings."[117] This pressure seems to have increased in the 1920s, perhaps building on the positive portrayal of dancing in mass circulation magazines and films. A Calgary newspaper in 1927 quoted Joan Crawford, the American movie star, as saying, "if you don't enjoy dancing, you don't enjoy life to its fullest!" She advised "every young person, especially every girl, to study dancing, even if she knows that she will never put it to any so-called 'practical' use."[118] Ability on the dance floor was firmly a sign of modernity and style.

Variety had always characterized Alberta dances. At the Edmonton "Old Timer's Ball" in 1896, the dance programme included the waltz, reels, gallop, jig, schottische, polka, cotillion, reel of eight, and others.[119] The most consistently popular dances throughout the period were waltzes, the one-step, two-step, fox trot, polka, and schottische,[120] but fads often touched the province and sometimes challenged respectability as well as these traditions. The Charleston was said to be unpopular in "polite drawing rooms" in Calgary, in part because "its steps are considerably more intricate than those of the well-established favorites," but "in modified versions" it had a "number of accomplished and dextrous exponents here."[121] Square-dancing was also widely popular, and while it was never practiced in "modern dance halls" during the 1920s and 1930s, it did experience a revival during the 1940s.[122]

With few exceptions, the history of ethnic dances in Alberta has not been effectively recorded. Ukrainian settlers who had immigrated between the 1890s and 1930 continued their traditional dances into the 1940s. Dancing among Ukrainians illustrates well the transformation of immigrant culture and leisure facing North American forces. Traditional Ukrainian dances fell into two broad categories: group dances and couple dances. The group dances included the Kolomyika type dances and the Arban, a men's dance. Dances for couples were more popular, highly variable, and subject to vagaries of fashion.[123] Learning new dances was part of the experience of the new world: Poles in the Crowsnest Pass were taught the waltz and the fox trot by two men "said to be from the United States," and, similarly, Ukrainians learned new dances in Canada. Among them were traditional dances taught by Ukrainian folk dance teachers as part of a Ukrainian cultural consciousness, but these never became important recreational dances. Instead, the dances of the Canadian dominant culture, such as the waltz and fox trot, became popular in the 1920s among second generation Ukrainians and the two-step was especially popular during the next decade. Traditional instruments disappeared and were replaced with the accordion, banjo, and clarinet, but some traditional dances survived at least into the 1940s, especially at wedding celebrations, which were particularly resistant to acculturation.[124]

Local musicians usually provided the music at dances throughout the province. Many times, a band was formed on the spot from among the available people.[125] At urban dance halls, orchestras played on a regular basis, some on a particular night each week for several years running.[126] Similarly, it was common for the same bands to play at country dances for many years. In Rycroft, Ma English and Bud Halverson were "the mainstays for music for dances for years," although other musicians frequently joined them, and other bands would play on occasion.[127] Many dance bands provided dance music of high quality. Ma Trainor's Hillbillies, based in Calgary, travelled throughout the southern part of the province during the 1930s and 1940s playing "Western" dance music. The Hillbillies were a widely popular band and Ma Trainor was legendary by the 1940s as a talented, amiable, but no-nonsense band leader.[128] The Calgary-based Bon Ton Dance Orchestra, a three-piece band with a fiddler, pianist, and drummer, played regularly during the 1920s.[129] For other tastes, jazz bands, such as

Bone's Acrobatic Jazz Orchestra, played for "modern" dances in the mid-1920s.[130]

Ma Trainor and the Hillbillies were widely popular in the latter part of the 1930s and the 1940s. (GAI NA-856-3)

The enjoyment people experienced at dances was equalled by the pleasure they gained from listening to musical performances. Amateur concerts and variety shows always included musical presentations of local talent, but various performers and groups also travelled throughout the province. Such tours were of greatest importance in Calgary and Edmonton, and unlike variety and touring stage shows, they did not suffer a serious decline in popularity during the 1930s. These itinerant musicians played music of immense variety. In the years before World War I, the most popular shows were musical comedies and performances by notable soloists or orchestras staged by concert companies. Madame Albani, the greatest Canadian soprano of the time, visited Calgary in 1897 and Edmonton in 1901 and 1906.[131] In 1910, the upcoming visit to Calgary by the famous Australian diva, Nellie Melba, proved to the editor of the *Calgary Herald* the city's "prosperity and growth" and a cultural triumph as well, for Melba was "interesting to people of our nationality as the first artist of British birth and parentage to reign supreme among the singers of the world."[132] Typically, these performances blended famous operatic arias with popular songs: Albani's rendering of "Home Sweet Home" in 1897 apparently brought Calgarians to tears.[133] Also popular in the early years of the century were Irish, Welsh, and Scottish theme concerts. On one occasion in Red Deer, the Kilties presented a "famous male choir of 16 trained voices, 6 celebrated Scottish dancers, 5 Bagpipers, [and] soloists." They also provided the common promotional gimmick of a "grand regimental parade at noon in full highland costume."[134] Another popular type of travelling concert at this time featured precocious little children who danced, sang, and played musical instruments.[135]

While performances by children endured, Scottish, Welsh, and other theme concerts gradually disappeared after the war. The number of high quality performances, especially in classical music, increased. In 1918 Calgarians heard Leopold Godowsky in a programme of Schubert, Chopin, and Liszt. Such tours were common, and in 1937 audiences in Edmonton heard Josef Hofmann play Chopin, Haydn, and Beethoven.[136] A number of light opera troupes also visited Edmonton and Calgary. Many tours were arranged by international booking companies. The Ellison and White Musical Bureau of Portland, Oregon, often booked performers into Calgary, and during the 1930s, the Celebrity Concert Series headquartered in New York booked musicians of international stature into Calgary and Edmonton as part of a prairie circuit which included Saskatoon, Regina, and Winnipeg. Groups such as the Calgary Women's Musical Club often provided local management for the circuit.[137]

Local clubs had other important functions in the musical scene in the province. Musical clubs were important everywhere in Canada for focussing and giving structure to musical life. [138] Such clubs took different forms, but most were broadly distinguished between those that provided a venue for the members to perform and those which aimed to foster music appreciation and training. An early musical club formed in Edmonton in 1893 included sixteen musicians who regularly practiced together and offered public concerts.[139] The Calgary Women's Musical Club, established in 1904, sponsored musical programmes for its members and also arranged various public functions such as lectures on music.[140] In 1908, a Women's Musical Club (initially called the Ladies Musical Club of

Edmonton) was established to encourage local artists and sponsor concerts. Similar clubs emerged in Red Deer in 1918 and in Lethbridge in 1932. The Red Deer club sponsored concerts and recitals featuring local artists and outstanding pupils of local music teachers, and tried to cultivate "a knowledge of, and a taste for, more of the music of the great masters."[141] Student recitals had a long tradition in both Edmonton and Calgary, and during the 1920s and 1930s, they were often introduced by typeset programmes similar to those used for international stars like Godowsky and Hofmann. Similarly, music students of Mount Royal College in Calgary put on public concerts,[142] and the annual music festivals also served as public concerts in classical music.

St. Andrew's Presbyterian Choir concert, Edmonton, 1929. (PAA A.3114)

Choral groups were also active in most towns in the province. Most churches used choral music in their services and encouraged and sanctioned its public performance. Choral groups associated with churches often presented public choral programmes as fundraising events.[143] Numerous secular choral groups put on concerts as well. The first Glee Club in Edmonton was established in 1887, and by 1907 Calgary had three "strong choruses, apart from its numerous choirs."[144] The CPR workers in Calgary formed the Canadian Pacific Male Voice Choir in 1922, and by 1932 they had presented eleven annual concerts in the city. And in 1909, Red Deer's

Choral Society staged a two-part programme highlighting an oratorio, *The Daughter of Jairus*, and a selection of shorter pieces. While the audience seemed to be appreciative, they demonstrated a "frenzied rush to get the out-clothes on before the music stopped," a problem the *Red Deer Advocate* believed could be solved if "the leading people" of the town would "stay with it" and through example teach the public some manners.[145] In other contexts, choral music often expressed ethnic continuity. Welsh settlers near Ponoka established a religious singing festival in the 1920s, and choral music played a large part in Estonian life in Alberta. In 1930, the Ukrainian Choral Association of Edmonton put on public performances of folk songs accompanied by a dance troupe of "small boys and girls in native costume."[146] Another notable Ukrainian choir, the Ukrainian National Choir of Mundare, performed in 1930 at the Great West Folksong and Folkdance and Handicraft Festival sponsored by the CPR in Calgary.[147]

During the 1920s and 1930s, numerous local groups produced light opera, opera, and symphony music. Before 1945 there was little grand opera performed in Canada and it was mainly available through the Metropolitan Opera radio broadcasts. Outside Toronto and Montreal, Gilbert and Sullivan operettas were the staple of musical theatre until after World War II.[148] In 1920, the Edmonton Kiwanis Club began mounting light opera and its performances were an annual feature of Edmonton's musical life by 1928. The Edmonton Civic Opera Society, established in 1935, was staffed entirely by volunteers and its operas featured local amateur talent. Between 1935 and 1949, the society had presented twenty-two operas and was said to be the "only continuing opera society between Ontario and British Columbia" that had presented

> to the public a continuous series of musical operas charging a consistently low admission price that makes it possible for people with moderate incomes to attend the performances and enjoy a presentation always equal to, and often surpassing, the standards of visiting organizations whose admission prices are usually twice as high as ours.[149]

The first symphony orchestra in Calgary was established in 1912 with just over fifty artists, "chiefly local," but including some from Chicago "on the more unusual instruments." Six evening and six afternoon concerts made up the symphony's first season, and the programme for the first concert was a "well-bound 20-page" effort

240

"got up in approved New York or Boston style." The orchestra disbanded because of the war, and its successor, which operated between 1928 and 1939, achieved only limited success due to poor facilities, too few concerts each year, and too little money.[150] Another orchestra was not organized until 1949. In Edmonton, the orchestra established in 1915 became the Edmonton Symphony in 1920, relying mainly upon local volunteer musicians and rented theatre space for performances. It collapsed in 1932 because of the Depression, not to be replaced until 1952.[151]

An undated photograph shows an Elks Band playing in a town in central Alberta. (PAA BA.551)

While concert life in the province was dominated by classical music and relatively "small and select circles," most people liked popular music.[152] Band music and folk and traditional songs gained most favour, and modern pop music, which was often called jazz, grew in popularity during the interwar years. Most of the music in vaudeville was of the popular sort, as was some of the music presented at the Chautauqua and by dance bands. Much of it originated in the United States, but the American influence on music in Alberta had begun well before the twentieth century. Because of isolation and the ethnic mix on the prairies, conditions "were not conducive to the preservation of folk songs." Moreover, the folk music traditions that existed were ignored and trivialized, and with few exceptions, folk song traditions rarely evolved into popular expressions of the new land.[153] One exception was American folk music; in the late nineteenth century, American cowboys working in southern Alberta had brought with them popular songs of the American southwest. Later, homesteaders drew upon American music and sometimes adapted the wording to prairie conditions, such as when "Greer County Bachelor" became "The Alberta Homesteader." These American influences later shaped some popular music in Alberta; during the interwar years, the best known local composers of popular music were country singers Stu Davis and Wilf Carter. Wilf Carter moved to Alberta in the mid-1920s and sang at dances and at events put on for tourists in the Rockies. He was featured as the Yodeling Cowboy on Calgary radio stations CFCN and CFAC, and in about 1932 he began recording for RCA Victor. Stu Davis was just beginning his career when he moved to Calgary in 1945, and in the following years he became an important local entertainer.[154]

The Cloverleaf Band of Czar, Alberta, photographed between 1911 and 1913. (PAA A.7360)

Before World War II, popular music was also played by brass bands frequently made up of musicians from the local fire brigade or police department. These were often sponsored by local businessmen, clubs, or the town council, and along with public subsidy came public criticism. Calgary had provided $325 to the Citizens' Band by 1909, and in response to public complaints about the quality of its performance, the mayor reprimanded the band by pointing out that the citizens wanted music and the city "wanted the revenue which music would bring, in the form of increased street car receipts."[155] Despite the carping, the Calgary Citizens' Band continued to operate until 1921 when the Calgary Elks Club took it over and carried it on until World War II.[156] In Camrose, the "town council in its liberality" made "ample provision" for band equipment, but the citizens soon became "accustomed" to "a band that never plays, to instruments that are never tuned and to uniforms that are never worn." Such was the fate of many citizens' bands: criticized when they were active, censured when they were not, yet lamented when they disbanded.[157]

In the years before World War I, popular music was played from sheet music and on phonographs and could be heard at dances, vaudeville, and road shows. In the interwar years, its reach broadened considerably through radio and film. Much of this music was termed jazz, which could be "rhythmically exhilarating, nice to dance to, lilting and a pleasant background for light entertainment, or it may be loud, vulgar and tedious."[158] In some circles, jazz was criticized on the grounds that it neither required skill nor exhibited good taste—that most elusive of qualities. In 1926, a Calgary theatre owner defended poorly played jazz because mistakes in jazz were "easily accepted as a new variation."[159] Other critics deemed jazz an improper modernism that right-thinking and serious people should reject. In 1925, the organizer of the annual Rose Ball sponsored by the Red Deer IODE was congratulated for her taste, the splendour of the decorations, and the quality of the music. According to one revealing assessment, "as might have been expected from a musician of the training and culture" of the head of the local IODE chapter, the music was "bright and dignified . . . and jazz was conspicuous by its absence."[160] Even so, such rejection of popular music was by no means absolute, and its wide acceptance was underlined by World War II when it was used for patriotic purposes. In 1940, the proceeds of Gracie Fields's western tour went to the Navy League. Fields attracted enormous crowds, which loved singing along: " 'There'll Always Be an England' was given with great spirit and in ear-splitting volume everywhere."[161]

The development of musical talent and events in Alberta did

occasion some official support. The University of Alberta Department of Extension offered music training programmes during the 1920s and 1930s and music was also included on the syllabus at the Banff School in 1936.[162] The provincial Department of Education provided grants for music festivals and bursaries for students "taking the examination of the Western Board of Music."[163] In 1946, the provincial government established the Alberta Music Board as one part of its postwar reconstruction programme. The board promoted music through various programmes, the most important of which was the sponsorship of concerts by Alberta artists, including a 1947 provincial tour by eighty members of the university mixed chorus. In seven towns in southern Alberta, fifteen hundred people turned out to hear the chorus.[164]

Music and the stage provided fantasy, laughter, and variety in people's lives and lifted them above their routines and their problems. In the heyday of the touring shows, people in Edmonton and Calgary could be entertained at a great variety of stage events. Between 1910 and 1925, patrons of the Grand Theatre in Calgary were able to watch almost every conceivable kind of stage entertainment available in North America, and this was only one venue of many in the city.[165] Although there are no means of assessing the composition of audiences, vaudeville, for one, advertised itself as family entertainment. Even so, it was commonly argued before World War I that young single men were an important part of the audiences. While the class and ethnicity of the audience remain unknown, the range of prices ensured that almost everyone could have attended many touring shows and musical events, save for the performances of such stars as Forbes-Robertson, Albani, Melba, and Bernhardt.

Vaudeville shows were American and their cultural context lay in the United States. They had little reference to Canadian conditions, let alone those in Alberta, and this must have been an important factor in the formation of provincial culture. They presented American standards of entertainment as the apogee of sophistication and fashion, which Albertans clearly appreciated. Yet, because only Edmonton and Calgary had the facilities to mount such shows and large enough populations to draw paying audiences, vaudeville and other touring shows remained largely an urban phenomenon in Alberta, and in the first part of the century it was the urban population that absorbed American practices, standards, and taste in entertainment. Although some custodians of the dominant culture in Alberta disapproved of vaudeville on moral grounds, it was never subject to the public restriction that would later be applied to films. Perhaps vaudeville was indeed more innocent than film, but the greater extent to which theatre owners and employees, hotel keepers, and others benefitted from vaudeville probably helped to mitigate negative views.

The American model for stage events was not absolute however; the upsurge in organized amateur drama in the 1930s, while infrequently using Canadian or Alberta scripts, nevertheless asserted local talent and ambition. But amateur drama experienced a serious handicap in comparison with the commercial operations: amateur groups could not afford permanent and attractive facilities and so could never fundamentally challenge the preeminence of the commercial stage with its star system. Indeed, it seems that by 1914 the standards of the commercial stage had become normative in urban Alberta. Nor could amateur groups meet the glamour and style of American film in later years. The lack of a permanent home in which to practice and mount productions meant that amateur drama companies were always marginalized in the entertainment world. However, since commercial touring shows, with the exception of Chautauqua, would rarely visit towns without adequate facilities, amateur drama in small towns in Alberta was in part a product of relative deprivation. So, too, was the upsurge in amateur drama everywhere in the province during the 1930s, stimulated by the general slowdown in the economy and the disappearance of the commercial stage.

Although musical productions shared many of the same characteristics and conditions as theatre, they differed in their ubiquity, greater tolerance of amateurs, their almost universal audience, and their infinite variety. Dancing was the most popular focus for music, breaking with the historic hostility to dancing in some of the Protestant churches of the dominant culture. Where dancing was so important, indeed, where it was often the only form of recreation, this was perhaps not surprising. The nature of musical productions, as in theatre, was often different for urban and rural people. Rural and farm people were forced to be more self-reliant and could not expect to enjoy performers of as high a standard as could those in urban centres. Yet high standards in urban areas meant a high degree of commercialization, and this sometimes meant restricted access. Although small-town Alberta had a richer concert than drama experience, the university's Department of Extension took note of the differences between town and country and promoted drama and music in its effort to encourage and provide educational leisure for rural people. The state was also directly involved in subsidizing music and drama festivals, although its major involvement in this area did not begin until after World War II.

In the end, the greatest influence in both drama and music was technological change. Modern transportation made possible the touring shows of the first part of the century, while developments in communications technology in the form of film and radio had a profound impact upon that older leisure tradition. The technological change that radio and movies represented was crucial for public entertainment, and if one sees the movie as part of the tradition of the stage, the historical role of the stage in Alberta entertainment remained central.

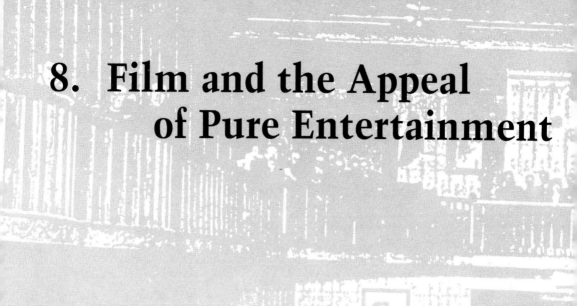

8. Film and the Appeal of Pure Entertainment

Motion pictures were especially important for urban Albertans, but they also provided rural people with inexpensive, satisfying entertainment. Although the introduction of sound track films in 1928 rendered silent films with subtitles and live or recorded music obsolete, both were commercial products intended for mass consumption. As an especially powerful medium of communications, with increasing potential during the interwar years to undermine the dominant culture, film came under close scrutiny and two forms of state control were instituted: censorship to restrict content, and, later, classification to restrict access by age. Because the content of movies and American domination of film making were thought to present a challenge to social authority, the dominant culture, and, in some extreme cases, the state itself, Alberta's approach to censorship both focussed and mirrored the issues that movies raised in the province.

In Alberta, entertainment by projecting a photographic image onto a screen began in the late ninteenth century. "Lantern" shows and "stereopticon" shows were available as early as the 1880s. Stereopticons were small hand held viewing instruments that blended two images into a single three-dimensional image. Lantern or magic lantern shows, by projecting slide images onto a screen in magnified form, prepared the way for motion pictures. Some Edmonton church socials in 1883 featured lantern shows accompanied by piano music, presenting travel and nature pictures or illustrated religious stories. Itinerant showmen and musicians also staged lantern shows commercially.[1]

Early lantern slides were often dangerous because they were highly flammable, but they became safer and easier to handle by the 1920s.[2] During the interwar years, lantern slides continued to be popular, especially in rural areas. In the 1930s, the Alberta Wheat Pool showed lantern slides of terminal elevators, grain handling, and prominent Wheat Pool personalities to gatherings throughout the province. Reports of these events emphasized both education and entertainment.[3] The UFA followed the same practice. In 1928, the UFA Juniors at Ardenode, near Strathmore, showed slides borrowed from the University of Alberta Department of Extension as a prelude to a dance.[4]

By the turn of the century, however, lantern slides had become old-fashioned because of the development of moving pictures. Only ten or fifteen minutes in length, early silent movies simply presented pictures of current events, landscapes, and birds and animals. Not yet an effective substitute for a vibrant and sound-filled stage, they were usually presented as part of vaudeville or variety shows well into the 1920s.[5] The Edison Motion Picture and Novelty Show travelled through Alberta in 1909 setting moving pictures into a variety show, and in Calgary the Allen Palace Theatre (a cinema) was still combining movies with a stage show as late as 1922. By this point, however, the movie was ranked as the "feature presentation."[6]

The Palace Theatre, Calgary. (GAI NA-2647-1)

Movie houses also maintained the link to the variety show tradition by employing musicians to enhance the entertainment. Even when recordings increasingly accompanied films in the 1920s, many movie houses still provided live music between features or for "getting the people in and out" of the cinema: stage bands, orchestras, and pipe organists were in vogue at various times.[7] These musicians sometimes did much more as well. In 1926, those from the Palace Theatre in Calgary, along with a few other local musicians, put on free Sunday evening concerts in the theatre and performed for broadcasts on a Calgary radio station.[8] In 1928, on the eve of the introduction of sound movies, there were forty-five theatre musicians working in Calgary, thirty in Edmonton, and ten in Lethbridge. As Premier Aberhart remarked in 1936 when informed that many of these musicians from Calgary were on relief, "there is perhaps no better example of the replacement of human services through the introduction of machinery. . .on account of modern developments in theatrical and moving picture technique."[9]

The persistence of variety show traditions helped to obscure the transformation taking place in commercial entertainment. While variety show traditions prevailed before 1928, movies had nevertheless become a primary entertainment feature even before World War I. By about 1908, theatres were renovated to accommodate regular showings of motion pictures and cinemas were being built, even though many were makeshift affairs located in renovated stores or office buildings. One Edmonton cinema of 1908 was located on the second floor of an office building that also housed a dye works, a jeweller, various other businesses and offices, and the Christian Scientist Reading Room, whose adherents rented the theatre space for Sunday services.[10] While makeshift facilities suggested an uncertain future, their proliferation signalled their appeal. In 1911 eight cinema licences had been issued for Edmonton, though only five were operating.[11]

Movies were shown to an appreciative audience at the Innisfail Opera House in 1910. (GAI NA-1709-23)

Some of these early cinemas were unsafe and in 1912 Calgary's chief of police pointed to the danger of "converting long, narrow stores into moving pictures theatres" because the patrons could not be easily evacuated in case of fire. Into poorly designed halls, theatre owners packed as many people as could sit and stand in seats and aisles.[12] Regulations were established in 1919 to control such practices, for as George Hoadley, the Leader of the Opposition, observed, many cinemas were like the "Black Hole of Calcutta."[13] While the general tone of these early cinemas suggests that movies provided neither respectable nor comfortable entertainment before 1918, their novelty had strong appeal.[14] As Bob Edwards quipped in 1915, "one of the most pitiful sights in the world is a highbrow person trying to conceal his delight in the low comedy of a movie show."[15]

The Gayety cinema, Brooks, 1912-13. (GAI NA-3250-28)

By 1920, movie houses had become both widespread and respectable. In 1921, there were 118 licensed cinemas in Alberta, and while this number declined to 101 in 1922, the movie had arrived as an entertainment event. The number of available films grew and theatres, many of which were fine buildings, were renovated to serve as cinemas.[16] The fifteen hundred-seat Grand Theatre in Calgary was converted into a cinema in the 1920s, although it continued to host variety shows until 1928. Such buildings provided effective exhibition space for both silents and talkies, but many less imposing facilities were judged insufficient for the new style and glamour of talkies. Famous Players built a new Lethbridge theatre in 1929 at a cost of $140,000,[17] and the private owners of Edmonton's Rialto rebuilt it in 1929 with "deep upholstered opera chairs" from which to "enjoy to the full the splendid programme."[18] By the 1930s, the transformation was complete and architectural theory recognized "that the moving picture theatre is a distinct type and not a smaller and less important theatre."[19]

The number of cinemas in Alberta stablilized after 1930: there were 85 in 1930 and 78 in 1933. Of the latter, the 6 in Calgary could accommodate 7,668 patrons, the 8 in Edmonton had 6,515 seats, while those in the rest of the province provided a total of 18,709 seats. The number of Alberta movie houses increased during the late 1930s to 140 in 1940.[20] In the cities, cinemas began to be located in the suburbs and by 1949 Calgary had six cinemas in the downtown area and six in the suburbs. In response to the diffusion of automobiles, the first drive-in theatres in Alberta were opened in Calgary and Edmonton in 1948 and 1949, each equipped with all the latest devices and capacity for 650 cars. At the beginning, they operated year-round, but by 1951 they were open only from spring to fall.[21]

Theatre patronage was heavier in urban than in rural areas. In 1933, Edmonton and Calgary, with about 22 percent of Alberta's population, recorded four million admissions, or nearly 67 percent of the provincial total. This corresponded roughly with national estimates in 1934; while Canadians over the age of five years averaged a movie a month, city dwellers averaged twenty to thirty times a year.[22] This greater use of urban theatres was reflected in their hours of operation and in the variety of features they presented. During the late 1920s, many urban theatres in Alberta changed programmes once or twice a week. By 1929, the 1,610 seat Capitol Theatre in Edmonton operated ten hours per day, six days a week.[23] The hours of operation were far more limited in small towns. In 1921, movies were shown every night in many small town cinemas, but within a year screenings at many places were reduced to one or two nights a week. In 1927 small town cinemas were often open only on Saturday nights, and in some cases only once every two weeks. Although their hours of operation gradually increased, even by 1940 many such theatres were open just a few days each week. The Elite Theatre in Wainwright, open only three days a week in 1930, retained the same schedule ten years later, "as the revenue is simply not here." By 1949, however, the movie theatre in Hanna was presenting two different features each week, and it appears that cinemas in rural areas had established a relatively frequent schedule by the late 1940s.[24]

Movies were accessible to a great many people because they were inexpensive. In 1910, the popularity of movies in Calgary was attributed to "their cheapness and entertaining features." The ten and fifteen cent admission to Red Deer theatres in 1916 ranked movies among the cheapest commercial entertainment available in the town.[25] Admission prices rose during the 1920s, and it became common for theatres to charge higher prices for epics and better quality films.[26] Nevertheless, during the 1930s it was frequently argued that movies provided "the only remaining form of amusement that is within the reach of the pocketbook of the average citizen,"[27] but even so, theatres were forced to use gimmicks like raffles, premiums and bathing beauty pageants to attract customers. In 1927, Miss Calgary was chosen by the audience at the Capitol Theatre. Fourteen contestants paraded "individually before the audience," which then chose the winner by secret ballot before viewing a romance about a woman "who, once despised by a man who called her a thief, won his love."[28]

The economic problems of the 1930s led to a decline in the annual per capita expenditure for movie tickets in Alberta from $3.28 in 1930 to $1.90 in 1934.[29] This decline was due in part to a decrease in ticket prices. In order to increase attendance, a number of movie houses lowered admission prices in 1931 and again in 1933.[30] In 1931, admission to a first run theatre cost 50 and 65 cents for an evening show, and 25 and 35 cents for a matinee. By 1933, first run movies in Edmonton cost a maximum of 50 cents for an evening show, and at less expensive second run theatres, one could see a film for 10 cents at a matinee and for 35 cents in the evening.[31] The lower prices, however, were not substantial enough to account for the overall decline in per capita expenditures, to which falling attendance must also have contributed.

Despite the difficulties of the early 1930s, movies became more important in establishing standards of entertainment than ever before, particularly after the introduction of sound pictures in the late 1920s. The first commercial talkie was produced by Warner Brothers and was shown in New York in August 1926. By late 1928, a scant two years after their world premiere in New York, Alberta audiences could see talkies at the Capitol Theatres in Calgary and Edmonton.[32] The talkies were the wonder of the age for "gesticulating figures no longer strut dumbly" across the screen. "Instead, the actors speak to you, sing to you, and the theatre fills with all those sounds which are associated with the living, moving world." This new technology was installed as soon as possible in movie theatres everywhere; the cinema in Stettler installed talkie equipment early in 1929.[33] The Capitol and the Empress, the two largest theatres in Edmonton, were showing only talkies in 1929 and while a few silents could still be seen at the Rialto and Monarch, both theatres installed talkie equipment later the same year.[34]

By 1930, nobody wanted to see silent pictures. The *Edmonton Journal* reported on the conversation of two Edmonton women overheard on their way home from a movie. One contended that she would not have gone had she known it was a silent movie and her partner agreed that the film had seemed "tame and flat after the talkies." Indeed, the *Edmonton Journal* somewhat naïvely estimated that "the movie house showing nothing but silent films will be as extinct as the dodo" within ten years.[35] Not only were silent movies becoming extinct, so too were vaudeville and the touring variety show and in 1930 there was only one theatre left in Alberta that offered both live performance and movies in the same programme.[36] The world of film also finally appropriated the use of the word "theatre" and earlier terms, such as cinema, movie house, and motion picture theatre, fell into disuse. Talkies also quickly increased public expectations of technical quality; in 1929 in Edmonton, audiences became annoyed when the sound was poor, too quiet, or "too loud and squeaky."[37]

The popularity of films and the growing number of theatres made movies big business, increasingly foreign controlled and, in the years before World War I, tending towards large theatre chains, especially in first run theatres. During World War I, the new Canadian owned Allen Theatre chain advertised that it provided "Canadian Pictures for Canadian People." In 1919, it had two theatres in Edmonton (the Allen and the Monarch) and one in Calgary. Allen's main competition came from Famous Players Canadian Corporation, an American company. In 1923, Famous Players bought the Allen chain and obtained effective control of the Canadian first run market, which it kept until the late 1930s when the Odeon chain was established.[38] American control had thus begun well before the talkies, but it was confirmed and entrenched by the introduction of sound pictures. The increased costs of installing and maintaining new equipment made theatre management more capital intensive. Silent movie projectors could not be used for sound film because they scratched the film, and "one slight scratch will cause a discordant sound all through the running of a picture."[39] One of the two types of early sound film equipment, the Vitaphone system, synchronized the projector with a phonograph machine. The alternative Movitone system produced sound from a sound track on the side of the film. In either case, the sound was automatic[40] and only its level had to be regulated. Theatres were forced to install both types of equipment in order to handle all types of film. All of this equipment was made in the United States, and rumour, apparently unfounded, held that each theatre had to pay a royalty of 10 cents per seat per day to the American manufacturer.[41]

The new equipment was expensive. In 1929, the Monarch Theatre in Edmonton spent five thousand dollars on new projection equipment alone.[42] The purchase of new equipment was purported to have led to the near bankruptcy of many small town theatres, and the Alberta Theatre Owners Association complained that the increased capital costs "resulted in many theatres in this Province being forced to close."[43] Sound equipment also required costly weekly servicing to maintain quality projection. There was almost no competition in this field because Northern Electric, which dominated the Canadian market, demanded that only their personnel adjust the equipment.[44] Not only did higher costs allow Famous Players to take the lead in installing sound equipment in its theatres, but the results presented Famous Players with the opportunity to gain a near monopoly of Alberta first run theatres by the mid-1930s.[45]

The American stranglehold was further intensified by the film distribution system, a big business "directed from the New York offices" of the film companies.[46] In 1934 the sixty-four film exchanges in Canada earned $ 7.6 million, or almost 10 percent more than the year before.[47] Earlier, the deputy provincial secretary had viciously remarked that most of these profits went "out of the country for the benefit of Yankee Jew interests."[48] The growth in the number of film exchanges parallelled the increase in the popularity of movies: two exchanges in Alberta in 1913 grew to nine by 1935, all located in Calgary. Almost all of the large movie corporations, such as Columbia, Fox, Paramount, United Artists, and Regal, owned their own exchanges and used the distribution system to promote their films. The Palace and Capitol Theatres in Calgary and the Empress and Capitol in Edmonton were first run theatres "owned and controlled by the big interests in Filmdom." After first bookings in these theatres, the films might then be sent to Lethbridge and Medicine Hat, but often they were sent for first run showing to another province before returning to Alberta a month or so later for exhibition in the "smaller country places" and the smaller theatres in Edmonton and Calgary at reduced rental fees.[49] These time and cost differentials illustrate significant differences in urban and rural or small town leisure.

Most people went to see films in theatres, but organizations like the Edmonton community leagues on occasion and rural community groups more frequently showed films in community halls. In an effort to combine education with entertainment, these films came mainly from the University of Alberta Department of Extension and, to some degree after 1915, from the provincial Department of Agriculture and the Department of Public Health.[50] Whether or not such films created a taste for useful leisure, they did habituate people to watch movies even before the purely entertaining films became available. In 1921-22, the university sent out 295 film programmes which reached thirty thousand people.[51] It also lent projectors operated by battery or line current. Before 1930, the university had lent 28 mm. film, but this was replaced in the early 1930s by 16 mm. film which was safer, cheaper, and more effective. By 1939, all of the film circulated by the Department of Extension was 16 mm. and much of it was silent film on travel and geography.[52] The National Film Board, established in 1939, also showed films in rural Alberta, beginning its first circuit in 1942. It showed films once a month in each community on the circuit and reached forty-five thousand rural Albertans by 1944. Film board personnel travelled by car and the projectionist brought along film, screen, projector, and a portable generator. Two circuits operated in the area north of Edmonton, one in French and the other in English. The films were shown in whatever facility was available, even a pool hall in one case, and each lasted eighty minutes. To promote the educational objective, literature about each film was sent out in advance and each presentation was followed by a discussion.[53]

Commercial itinerant road shows were even more important to rural leisure, but little information is available about the movies screened or the frequency of screenings. It is clear that a number of such shows operated regularly in Alberta by the end of World War I: one itinerant mounted films at the Rex Theatre in Red Deer in 1921.[54] During the 1930s there were usually fifteen to twenty itinerant exhibitors showing films at various places throughout the province.[55] One itinerant began showing movies in 1935 in Drayton Valley when the community hall was opened. He charged thirty-five cents,[56] which was at the high end of prices at second run city theatres. In 1931, the Bentley Community League contracted Mr. Sharp of Didsbury to show movies in the community hall to raise funds and give people a chance "to see and hear sound pictures." Remarkably, only five years after sound movies premiered in New York and three years after their first showing in Edmonton and Calgary, Sharp found that he had to use two projectors because "the public can only be attracted when a picture is continuous."[57] The new technology had spread so rapidly through both rural and urban society that expectations of performance had changed everywhere.

Road shows rented films from the film exchanges in Calgary. When some of the exchanges stopped these rentals in 1935, they limited "the type of picture that could be exhibited in village and rural communities." Then, in 1936, all of the exchanges "adopted a policy of absolutely refusing" to rent films to itinerants, effectively killing the shows for a time. The exchanges argued that the itinerants damaged the film, but the real problem lay in the itinerants' ability to compete with regular theatres by operating outside of the geographical areas specified in their contracts with the exchanges.[58] It is unclear how this dispute was resolved, but by the late 1930s the itinerant shows were operating once again. By the early 1940s they were being squeezed out by technological change, and in 1942 there were only nine itinerants operating in the province.[59] As an example of this process, itinerants who owned their own generating equipment regularly showed films at the Rycroft Community Hall, but when electricity was installed in Rycroft in 1944, the community hall was renovated "to provide for a regulation projection room" and the Hall Association purchased two 35 mm. projectors at a cost of nearly twenty-four hundred dollars. Without reference to itinerants, Rycroft was thereafter presented with "a good class and mixture of film...including many outstanding feature pictures such as 'Going My Way,' 'Gone With The Wind,' etc."[60] Such shows, as well as those provided by itinerants, the University of Alberta Department of Extension and the National Film Board, all habituated the rural population to watching film. As the Alberta Censor observed in 1936, "the occasional showing in a rural centre simply creates interest, and going to pictures is largely a habit."[61] Although movie theatres did not follow in all areas, the habit of watching film was certainly confirmed in the next generation through television.

The maturation of the movie into a self-contained leisure event was a long process. It began before 1910 when silent movies employing plot and characterization extended film's entertainment potential well beyond simple pictorial images. In 1910, Calgarians watched *Lost in Siberia,* which included "bomb throwing, a mutiny in the mines, a thrilling escape" and other exciting scenes. In the same year, people in Red Deer saw *Joan of Arc,* a film about patriotism and faith; and as part of the same package, they also saw two comedies about marital life plus the "thrilling, dramatic" film, *The Lion Tamer.*[62] All of these films were short; *The Lion Tamer,* the longest film at one thousand feet, would still have lasted less than twenty minutes,[63] but a selection of short films grouped together provided satisfying and novel entertainment.

Characterization and plot, along with astute marketing, also led to the creation of movie stars who, by their name, looks, and ability, could draw audiences to a movie. One of the earliest and perhaps greatest of these stars was Mary Pickford, the Canadian who became a star through her portrayal of female innocence. She had a "host of admirers" in Alberta and when her picture *Less Than Dust* was shown in Red Deer in 1918, her fans eagerly lined up to buy tickets to see a romance set in India with "big scenes that carry real thrill."[64] During and immediately after World War I, thrills were also found in war propaganda films that depicted the evils of the enemy with violence or humour. One such film, *The Hour Will Come,* was a comedy about the "cruel Kaiser" and another was entitled *The Claws of the Hun. To Hell With the Kaiser* portrayed the evils of the enemy in such graphic detail that it "makes the blood boil with righteous indignation."[65] Since the main business of war was violence, these movies often depicted fighting. *From Trench to Trench,* a war film produced in France, was shown in 1916 in Alberta and featured "marvelous scenes taken right in the thick of sharp battle. Hand grenade warfare will be shown with all its deadliness, also the battlefield from a bullet proof observation post during an engagement."[66] Film stars also worked for the war effort: Mary Pickford, for example, did "her bit for her country" in the 1918 Victory Loans Campaign by starring in a patriotic movie designed to "draw money for war purposes from the hiding places and savings banks."[67]

In the 1920s, movies became longer and characterization and plot rapidly developed to a level that would be recognizable to modern movie goers. Among the stock silents were romances, comedies, and action and drama films. *The Sky Pilot,* a Canadian film based on a Ralph Connor novel, was a romance advertised in 1921 with the rhetorical question, "But did he marry her? Yes or No?" *The*

Face of the World, an action film shown in Alberta in 1925, was popular for its "big moments" like "the wrecking of a high powered racing car" and "the burning of a three storey building and a rescue from the flames—which, by the way, almost cost Edward Hearn [the actor] his life when the scene was being photographed." The emphasis on the actor as hero had more to do with the star system and the movie's promotion than it did with the merits of the film. Films could also be sold by stressing technical innovation like the "natural colors" and "amazingly beautiful" filming of Zane Grey's *Wanderer of the Wasteland* in 1925. Another promotional technique, particularly in the age of silent movies, was serialized films. Among the most famous were *The Perils of Pauline*, which showed in Calgary in 1915, and the fifteen-part *Lucille Love*, which played in many places in Alberta the same year. Occasionally, the movie's plot was serialized in a newspaper before its screening.[68]

Comedy, although popular, presented real problems in the era of silent films. The format for comedy was limited and usually imitated the idiom of vaudeville slapstick, and only a few artists, such as Charlie Chaplin, were able to create enduring images that lifted slapstick above banality. The lack of spoken dialogue and the need for easily understood subtitles often ruled out subtlety in plot or characterization in any film, whether comedy or drama. Thus, most of the silent films centred around themes that could be easily dramatized and in which continuity could be maintained through subtitles and live music. Many were burlesques, epics, and westerns; few film makers of silent movies were able to overcome these limitations and achieve excellence. One director able to conquer these barriers was D.W. Griffith, whose 1915 epic, *Birth of A Nation*, excited audiences everywhere, including those in Calgary and Edmonton. Nonetheless, most silent films were too limited and too poorly conceived to establish a tradition of film making.[69]

The talkies, however, changed everything. As early as 1929, it was estimated that 85 percent of the movies shown in Edmonton were "dialogue" films in which dialogue took precedence over elaborate sets, costumes, and visually dramatic plots.[70] Dialogue films often explored "sophisticated" themes; a term used by the film industry to describe films which dealt with sex or other popular but publically hazardous topics. Many "sophisticated plays of Broadway," reworked for the screen, contained primarily conversation.[71] Some early talkies, such as *Faithless* (1932) and Clara Bow's *Call Her Savage*, dealt with the "sophisticated" topic of prostitution. In the case of *Faithless,* the story shocked some Albertans by portraying "a wife fitting herself out. . .and practising prostitution to support her husband, and actually soliciting her brother while plying her trade."[72] However, traditional love stories, musicals, and dramas were more typical and were immensely popular, building upon the traditions of fiction. As the *Calgary Albertan* observed in 1929, fiction required plot and the "clashing of wills and a happy denouement. Love and crime are the most ready bases for these elements," and since people loved mystery and being "pleasurably terrified," such themes provided consistently popular entertainment, whether in silents or talkies.[73]

Romance, action, westerns, and comedy thus continued to be popular. When the Monarch Theatre in Edmonton began showing talkies in 1929, an action film, *Wings,* and a drama, *The Toilers,* were among the first features. *Wings,* starring Clara Bow, revolved around World War I aviation and "the young knights of the clouds." It was billed as a movie of "high courage, the bravery of unselfish and unheeding youth, the splendor of youthful sacrifice and [the] beauty of human comradeship."[74] Clark Gable and Norma Shearer (who starred in *Strange Interlude* shown in Alberta in 1933) and Kay Francis (who starred in *Mary Steven, M.D.*) were also very popular in Alberta during the mid-1930s. The objections of some to the moral tone of these films had no impact on the popularity of the genre and the actors.[75]

Musicals were among the first sound films produced, and the musical *Rose Marie* was among the first talkies shown in Edmonton. A "musical melo-drama-comedy" about love and Mounties starring Jeannette MacDonald and Nelson Eddy, it was advertised as a film with a "strong plot with situations in which anyone might find himself or herself" were they to go into "rough wild country." Viewing a story supposedly set in Quebec, but featuring the Canadian Rockies,[76] Canadians, in an intriguing example of cultural colonialism, apparently accepted with little comment the convenient relocation of their landscape by American film makers. The first talkie shown in Lethbridge was also a musical starring Al Jolson in *Sonny Boy,* but it was the 1929 film *Broadway Melody* that set a lasting standard for American musical films. Others that followed include the now famous 1933 performances of Fred Astaire and Ginger Rogers in their first film, *Flying Down to Rio,* and Judy Garland's 1944 performance in *Meet Me in St. Louis.*[77] Gangster pictures of the early 1930s were followed in about 1935 by "G-Man" movies, both of which featured "the thrills of raids, machine gun firing, shooting and all the rest."[78] The gangster films were an important genre. While violence had commonly been depicted in films for many years, the gangster films' use of fast, innovative camera work and tight, blunt language profoundly modified the "theatre dialogue" format of many of the early sound films.[79] Other thrills could also be had through terror: two 1931 movies, *Dracula* with Bela Lugosi (a film that "will thrill the audience through and through," said the *Calgary Herald*) and *Frankenstein* with Boris Karloff (who had gained his acting skills working in stock shows in prairie Canada),[80] established a pattern for horror films that remained powerful for at least the next two decades. Other important "suspense" films of this period included those by the expatriate British film maker, Alfred Hitchcock, whose 1935 movie, *The 39 Steps*, established a pattern for yet another genre.[81]

The talkies were revolutionary and put film in a preeminent position in public leisure. Nevertheless, there was a consistently expressed fear that movies, whether silent or sound, threatened the basis of social authority and the British character of Alberta. Such apprehensions led to demands for restriction and control of movies shown in the province. In 1910, Mayor Jamieson of Calgary argued that films, especially those showing violence and crimes against property, "should be banished from local moving picture theatres." Others objected to the influx of American propaganda. In 1912, Alberta police canvassed for their opinion on film censorship all agreed that it was essential. Their commonest complaint deplored "too much display of the American flag" and too few scenes of Britain or Canada which would help to develop patriotism in the audience. Movies were thus expected to serve the cause of implanting a British society in Alberta, and not unrelated to this concern, the police also faulted movies for excessive depictions of crime, lawlessness, and sex.[82]

The *Calgary Herald* was particularly concerned about sex; it found one film, *An Exposure of the White Slave Traffic*, which had been shown throughout southern Alberta in 1911, especially disgraceful. The film was technically poor, being made up "of reproductions from picture post-cards, patched together indiscriminately in a disjointed mass" and, aside from its "insidious suggestiveness," was not worth the price of admission. The movie showed the interior of a brothel with the occupants drinking and "in a state of deshabille." These "filthy details" were explained by a "slimy lecture" in case the audience "should fail to understand what these sordid details meant." Without censorship, the exhibition of such trash could not be stopped, and the public could "only grin and bear it." Making matters worse, the *Herald* found the number of children in the audience especially shocking.[83]

In response to the chorus of complaints and the precedent set by Ontario, which had brought in censorship in 1911, Alberta enacted statutory authority for censorship in the session of 1911-12 and established regulations for censorship by Order in Council in February 1913. Before 1920, however, not all movies were reviewed, nor were government facilities for screening films in place. Rather, arrangements were made with a theatre in Edmonton "to screen any pictures that might require attention." Subsequently, censorship was regularized with a Provincial Censor Board under the direction of Howard Douglas as chief censor. While 16 and 28 mm. film remained exempt, the board was "passing" all 35 mm. film shown in the province.[84] In 1920, 5,443 reels of film entered the province, of which 3,379 were screened by the Provincial Censor Board and 2,064 were passed without examination. The latter had been censored in eastern Canada and were automatically accepted for screening in Alberta.[85]

The belief that censorship was necessary to protect the ideals, standards, and morality of the province originated in the premise that environment influenced human behaviour. Since it was accepted that the mind (especially of children and youths) was highly impressionable and malleable, censorship aimed to control the political and moral content of images that could so easily influence human behaviour. This reasoning remained the central justification for movie censorship until the end of the period under review. In his 1927 report to the Alberta government on juvenile delinquency, Gerald Pelton, a Calgary lawyer, noted that movies were "full of suggestions to the child mind." He believed that if a child saw a "hero getting away" with crime and "receiving applause in his success in eluding detection," such an image would frequently find its "reflex in the operations of young desperados," who became convinced that a crime was not a crime "unless you get caught." Thus, the problem was more than mere emulation, and Pelton's use of the term "reflex" was a significant measure of contemporary views about the link between environment and behaviour, especially in the case of impressionable children and youths. The general faith in causal and rationalistic explanations for behaviour meant that, to use Pelton's words again, "every act of every individual is the expression of a corresponding thought." Given this assumption, it was clear that in movies, with their powers of depiction, "the presentation of unwholesome mental impression in any form is inimical to the young mind."[86]

Tied to this ambition to restrict and control films for behavioural and moral reasons was an effort to make leisure useful and socially productive. This issue was especially relevant to movies because theatres were open to everyone, "to the wise and the foolish, the sophisticated and the unsophisticated, the young and the old." Such universal entertainment needed to be controlled and shaped into a useful and socially sustaining force that would entertain, educate, and "lighten the burden of this unintelligible world." Before World War I, "some well-meaning people," especially those of "strong religious tendencies," simply put movies in the same class as card playing, dancing, and variety shows as inherently frivolous and morally corrupting.[87] Given the accessibility of films, such a categorical rejection was impractical. In 1912, it was argued that censorship should aim to promote films "which will have an educational function" and to "obliterate" those which "would have the effect of disturbing the morals of the population in any way." In 1922 the Alberta Censor said of movie entertainment that its "integrity should be protected as we protect the integrity of our churches, and its qualities developed as we develop the quality of our schools."[88]

Standards for censorship were difficult to establish, and, then as now, censors seem to have relied upon their perception of publicly acceptable standards of behaviour and morality. No national standards for censorship were enforced, nor was it possible to create them because "each Province has a different class of people to deal with."[89] Nevertheless, the censors of the four western provinces met in 1919 and drew up standards providing detailed criteria to either "condemn" or "disapprove" films. The targets for condemnation included a whole range of sexual topics such as "white slavery, unless a true moral lesson is conveyed," seduction, common-law relationships, and abortion; depictions of violence, violent death, and the exploitation of "notorious characters"; and scenes of drunkenness, "especially if women have a part in the scene." The topics for disapproval were a rather miscellaneous group including "the drug habit," depictions of women smoking, all forms of crime against property "which may put like action into the minds of those of evil instincts," gangsterism, "vulgarities," and ridicule of religion.[90]

Given the number of films passing through censorship and the breadth of the censorship standards, it is difficult to determine whether censorship was consistent. It is apparent, however, that the standards set by the western provincial censors did illustrate the general attitude to censorship in Alberta. In 1922, eight films were condemned for depicting lawlessness and murder, thirteen for immorality, eight for vulgarity, one because it was gruesome, eight because they were suggestive, and three because they presented a travesty of religion.[91] In articulating the aim of censorship in 1932, the chief censor used almost the same language that had been current a decade earlier. He observed that censorship in Alberta aimed to "eliminate as far as possible" those things which "flaunt our laws, that which would be easy of imitation by young people, excessive drunkenness, vulgarity, nudity, [and] stimulating in sex appeal"; all the things that would, by "direct scene or statement or by suggestion, influence people to immorality or wrong doing."[92]

The coming of the talkies complicated censorship further because the use of language and sound had to be judged as well. The "double meanings" of words were scrutinized by the censors and were cut from a film if they were considered to be risqué. Nonetheless, some words made it past the censors, only to be eliminated after the film's release because "certain members of the audience emphasized the objectionable side of the statement."[93] The problem frequently was seen as transcending just the use of certain words. "The coming of the talking picture," the chief censor noted in 1932, "has made possible the producing on the screen of a large number of rather sophisticated plays that have run successfully on Broadway, but which deal with problems of life that are not always acceptable as entertainment to the family trade that frequents theatres in Alberta."[94]

From 1930 to 1932, almost ninety sound films were rejected by the censor. As well, the number of excisions increased dramatically. According to Robert Pearson, Howard Douglas's successor as provincial censor, although there had not been as many total rejections in 1932 as in 1930 and 1931, pictures were becoming worse "from a moral standpoint" and "never. . .have we had to make so many eliminations."[95] Nevertheless, the percentage of condemned films generally decreased in the period from 1928 to 1938, except in 1930 and 1931. Then, in 1932 and 1933, the number of eliminations increased significantly. By 1935, the censor's scissors were less sharp, and the number of eliminations and condemned films steadily decreased.[96] This might indicate that films had become more acceptable, but it is more reasonable to suggest that the censors had initially overreacted to the talkies, so different in their presentation from the silents as to make them seem especially threatening. Once they became commonplace, changes in taste became less noticeable. In any event, there was a limit to how far censorship could go, before either mangling the film to the point of unintelligibility or unreasonably restricting the number of available films.

In reality, censorship was a pragmatic effort, and as Robert Pearson observed in 1932, if only films which "present the idealistic, or which are based on sweet and pure scenes free from any moral lapses" were passed, not 10 percent of the movies could be shown. By the mid-1930s, censorship seems to have become more flexible and accommodating, and the censor took an almost creative pleasure in adapting films to provincial standards. As Robert Pearson told a Calgary IODE meeting in 1937, the Provincial Censor Board "married couples in pictures by inserting captions, eliminated corpses and cocktail parties, and even took the sound out of dagger thrusts so as not to offend sensitive movie goers."[97] All of this must have taken place at some cost to continuity. Since the sound track was embedded on the side of the film by 1930, the cutting of frames would have broken the sound, although blank frames were substituted for those cut so the duration of the film would be synchronized in sound and image.

Censorship was also sometimes influenced by local opinion. At the end of World War I, the theatre in Lethbridge sometimes sought approval from local leaders of opinion for potentially controversial films that it planned to show.[98] Special interest groups or lobbies throughout the province brought their particular views about society to bear on the censorship of films, and the degree of their success was a good measure of their authority and power in Alberta society and their influence on the state. Some people demanded the banning of films they had never seen or had never been released in Alberta. In 1932, the censor "found that people have read in American religious journals, commendations [sic] of pictures, and made quotations about the dangers of these pictures, not knowing that the pictures referred to, had been condemned in Alberta."[99] Other demands were more specific, in terms of class or social interest. The power of businessmen, even when a farmers' government ruled in Alberta, was shown in 1932 when the Calgary Board of Trade demanded that all gangster movies be banned because they "glorified" crime and corrupted Alberta's youth. In "the interests of business in general and for the protection of the business man," gangster pictures should be banned so that Alberta businessmen would never "be subjected to racketeer and gangster terrorism." The government agreed fully, and the Alberta Censor noted that he, in any event, had never passed a film that "would make a hero out of a gangster"; indeed, "we never allow even the word kidnap to be mentioned in any picture, or any scene that would show how a crime could be committed."[100] Nevertheless, the whole genre was proscribed in Alberta, and the Provincial Censor Board "promised our superiors here as well as certain public organizations that we would not pass any more gangster pictures and [we] have held firmly to that policy."[101]

Other groups were not as successful as the Calgary Board of Trade. The Alberta Association of Registered Nurses unsuccessfully attempted in 1934 to have a representative of their profession review all pictures "featuring nursing so that pictures which are distasteful to the nursing profession may be banned."[102] In another case, the National Council of Women and the Alberta Women's Institute resolved in 1937 that all scenes involving liquor should be cut from movies,[103] but prohibition sentiment had waned to the point that their request could be ignored. Similarly, the Roman Catholic Church was not satisfied with Alberta censorship because films or scenes dealing with divorce were not automatically banned or cut. Nevertheless, most Protestants were generally happy with Alberta standards of censorship,[104] and they were the most influential group in the province.

Those who defended British standards in Alberta argued that leisure, and movies in particular, should not disrupt the state and lines of authority in society. This objective could be fostered by creating and preserving a British and Christian society in Alberta. In 1922, the Alberta Censor praised all films supportive of the RCMP and argued that all adverse references to them should be deleted. Further, in the first six months of 1921, two films were banned for denigrating the Christian church.[105] As well, films made in Germany inevitably came under close scrutiny. They were subjected to an outright ban during World War I, but a paranoia about German propaganda persisted even after 1918, and the provincial censor advised in 1922 that "particular attention be paid to any propaganda" in German films. Later, appeals from German officials were rejected on at least three occasions in 1936 and 1937 when the German consul in Winnipeg asked that certain films be banned in Alberta because they supposedly promoted hatred of Germany through their portrayal of Nazi Germany's role in the Spanish Civil War.[106]

Concerns about left-wing messages in films also arose, for the first time in 1924 over a Russian film that contrasted the USSR with Germany. Although bourgeois society was shown in a poor light, the deputy attorney general felt that "the film does not contain anything of an objectionable nature apart from its advocacy of Russian communism." He therefore felt that it was neither seditious nor would it "endanger the peace of the Province." The cabinet, however, decided to ban the film "on the ground that we should not encourage any organizations, communistic or otherwise, outside of our own state, to manufacture and send into Canada films intended solely for political propaganda."[107] The same issue arose after World War II with respect to 16 mm. films that were said to be procommunist. To prevent this "menace," the provincial government asked the RCMP to investigate individuals who were involved in showing films as part of the "cultural work" of the "Ukrainian Labor Farmer Temple Association and its successor, the Association of United Ukrainian Canadians (formerly the Association of Ukrainian Canadians)." The government claimed that "at least 90%" of these films, primarily from World Films in Toronto, were propaganda about "the glories of Soviet Russia and the Communist State."[108] In 1946, in response both to postwar anticommunist hysteria and to technological improvements in 16 mm. film, the censorship regulations were amended to cover all film, not just 35 mm. film. Despite protests from a large number of groups,[109] 16 mm. films were subsequently censored for immorality, violence, or holding "up to ridicule recognized and religious ideals." As well, no foreign film, defined as any film in other than English or French, could be released without review of a "certified translation of the entire script." Further, all "propaganda" films, except those promoting tourism, were required to carry a prefix and suffix identifying them as propaganda.[110] It was a peculiarly naïve and paternalistic approach that sacrificed individual judgement out of fear that people would be duped by outside forces.

Far more important to the campaign for British traditions was the display of patriotic symbols and the singing of "God Save the King." In 1932, the National Council of Women demanded that the Union Jack be shown and "God Save the King" be sung "during at least one performance in each theatre each day." Ironically, investigation showed that only the American-owned Famous Players theatres used a daily trailer featuring a picture of the King during the playing of the national anthem. They had at one time played the national anthem "in the middle of the evening performance, but...people seemed to resent being disturbed in the middle of their visit to the theatres, and much prefer to rise at the close." Other theatres in Alberta ignored several options; a good patriotic sound trailer available from Associated Screen News of Montreal or, for those theatres without sound equipment, a disk synchronized with a silent trailer offered by the Victor Talking Machine Company. The campaign was successful, and by 1934 most urban theatres ran a patriotic trailer at the end of the last show of each day.[111]

Patriotic trailers and flags, however, were not the solution to the excess of American propaganda in films made in the interwar years, a result of the American domination of English language film making. Given the nationalism that permeated American cultural productions, American movies were from the beginning full of flag waving and self-congratulation. American film makers, concerned only with the profitability of their films in the urban United States market, naturally disregarded the sensibilities of non-American viewers. Since Canada was seen as a part of the United States domestic film market by the early 1920s, American films were forwarded to Canada without any alteration. According to Alberta censorship officials, 90 percent of the movies shown in Canada were American,[112] but only 3.5 percent of the total earnings of a movie came from Canada. Consequently, Alberta's, and indeed the whole of Canada's, circumstances were irrelevant to American producers who made films for the "larger and sophisticated audiences of the great American cities" rather than the "smaller towns and rural communities of Alberta where families constitute the largest" audience. This neglect of Canadian sensibilities could be countered only through censorship, which was forced to go "further" in Alberta than in many other parts of North America because of the special nature of Alberta society.[113]

The control of American propaganda in films had been part of the argument for censorship before World War I and remained important in the years after the war. In part, it was argued that the protection of the moral tone of films would keep Canada a "strong and energetic nation." More particularly, it was said that American images and propaganda would weaken Canadian commitment to and understanding of the British identity of Canada.

Colonel Gibsone, colonel commandant of Military District 13, wrote to the premier in 1925 complaining that the Capitol Theatre in Calgary was running the Pathe Gazette vignettes, *Our America,* featuring United States cities. One in particular rankled: Richmond, Virginia, was captioned *The Pride of Our Dominion,* and in the colonel's mind, "these misleading titles will have an adverse effect on the minds of subjects of the British Crown living in Canada."[114] The provincial censor reported that the board had passed the films in question and had rejected only those demonstrating "an extra amount of flag showing." "We do not," he concluded, "consider it propaganda," but he undertook to review the films and have them "looked over by some of the principal military officers" in the province.[115]

Feature length films provided the central problem in controlling American propaganda. From 1929 until the end of 1934, a total of 10,594 films had been screened by the Alberta Censor, 10,337 of which were American, 249 British, and 8 "foreign."[116] In 1930, 90 percent of films shown in Canada were made by Americans, and most were set in the United States. Only one was set in a "North Country—Canada."[117] When American film makers did make films about Canada, they stereotyped the country as a place of criminal Métis, jolly but roguish French Canadians, violent Indians, and noble policemen occupying a geography and climate unrecognizable to anyone who lived in the country.[118] To complicate the problem further, American content in news reels proved to be another area of concern. Although Associated Screen News, a CPR owned company, produced Canadian news reels after 1920,[119] American news reels emphasizing American news predominated. In one ten-day period in 1930, the Censor Board reviewed fifteen newsreels containing fifty items of American news and thirty-eight of news from other countries, including just seven on Canadian events. In 1929, the different provincial Censor Boards had recognized this imbalance at their annual meeting and had notified the "Motion Picture industry that they would expect 30% of the News Reels to be devoted to events within the British Empire." In addition, the censors promised that they would also "eliminate all pictures giving wrong versions of history, as well as many other undesirable features."[120]

The American stranglehold on the Canadian movie market represented an intractable problem. One alternative was the encouragement of British or, better still, Canadian films. A 1922 report stating that Canadians were annually paying $4 million to

American companies for films anticipated a better future when Canadians would no longer have to be "passively content with the California fruit" because Canadian films featuring Canadian scenes would soon be available. These Canadian films would transcend mere scenery and treat cultural and moral issues in a way that would counteract Hollywood's immorality and wickedness. As the provincial censor remarked, Canadian film corporations would be the beneficiaries of the stories about sin in Hollywood, for if they employed "only cultured and clean living artists in the production of Canadian pictures," their films would be popular with Canadians.[121] Whether this would have been so was never discovered in Canada's limited film industry, one that frequently operated as a branch plant of American studios.

Nevertheless, some Canadians did make films. Railway companies and governments produced the earliest movies to promote the benefits of settling Canada or of buying Canadian goods. In 1912 a number of Canadian film makers began to produce Canadian drama. The surge in Canadian nationalism around World War I led to the production of a number of Canadian films, including *None Faultless*, a drama filmed in Edmonton.[122] Among the early Canadian productions that continued to appear until the early 1920s were the films of the expatriate Canadian producer, Ernest Shipman, who shot the film *Back to God's Country* in Alberta in 1919. Based on the James Curwood novel, *Wapi, The Walrus*, the film was financed in Calgary and was hugely successful both in Canada and abroad.[123] It set new attendance records in Edmonton where it was advertised as "the season's film sensation made by an Alberta company." It was filmed near Grouard on Lesser Slave Lake and told the story of Delores, "the swimming girl of the Canadian Northland, whose love of animals makes them her friends and protectors from men of prey more heartless than the beasts themselves."[124] *Cameron of the Mounted*, based on a Ralph Connor novel, was filmed in southern Alberta in 1922, and it was remarked that "for once a Canadian scenario will be correct in every detail."[125] In 1922, a company called Alberta Motion Pictures Ltd., a short-lived American branch plant, produced only the NWMP drama, *The Scarlet Keeper*. In 1923, an all Canadian film was made from yet another Ralph Connor novel, *The Man from Glengarry*.[126]

While it had been hoped that these feature films would launch an enduring Canadian film industry, such hopes were not realized despite the enthusiastic reception that Canadian films always received in Alberta. In the 1920s, only the CPR continued to sponsor film production designed, like their earlier films, to lure immigrants to Canada.[127] Otherwise, there was little film making in Canada. Unlike the governments of almost all European countries, the Canadian government did nothing to protect its film industry in the interwar years, nor did it encourage or protect Canadian films in the domestic market in the years immediately after World War II.[128]

In the interwar years, the lack of Canadian films led some people to emphasize British films as an alternative to American ones. While they sometimes seem to have been supported by the Alberta Censor simply because they were not American, this preference for British films represented a conscious cultural policy. Theoretically, British films would sustain the British ideals of the country. In 1919, the Allen Theatre chain formed British Films Ltd. to import, distribute, and show British films in their theatres and promised to reduce their use of American films by 20 to 30 percent. This move was welcomed by some because "all these films will breathe the spirit of British liberty and British nationality. They will focus the minds and hearts of the spectators upon British achievements and British institutions."[129] This attempt to replace American with British propaganda was not successful and Famous Players bought the Allen chain in 1923. In the late 1920s, Alberta, along with Ontario and British Columbia, enacted legislation that permitted "the establishment of a quota for British films," but no steps were taken to implement such quotas.[130]

The support of British films was a futile effort in the face of American domination of film in North America and the popularity in Canada of the American style of film making. Canadian film distributors rarely imported British films, which were said to be of poor quality and unpopular with Canadian audiences.[131] The American film companies that controlled the film distribution system in Canada argued that few British films were available. In 1926, film distributors in Canada made only thirty-nine British films available, which the president of the Picture Distributors and Exhibitors of Canada claimed was "evidence that we have been reasonably anxious to get everything that could be marketed in this country."[132] Given these conditions, the preservation of a British society in Alberta was thus forced to rest upon censorship. The Alberta Censor Board cut as much American propaganda as possible from feature length films, and the chief censor observed in 1930 that this represented the only "effective method" of meeting the United States onslaught in the absence of a Canadian film industry.[133] In addition, the Alberta Censor Board looked to the British Censor Board as a model and during the 1920s proudly noted that Alberta's and British censorship rulings often coincided.[134]

The cultural implications of film were acute for the raising of children. In many respects, movies crystallized the growing differentiation between the leisure of children and adults. While this difference was implicit in the view that the mind of a child was more malleable than that of an adult, commercial movies provided a point of reference that was in many ways unique. The traditional role of the parent, the family and the community in providing children's leisure through the home, church and school did not operate in the case of movies. Because of their accessibility and independent presentation, movies represented a new form of leisure not entirely subject to traditional forms of control. This was especially alarming because motion pictures were said to stimulate many wrong tendencies in children. In 1913, the Reverend A.D. McDonald told the Naomi Mothers Society in Calgary that movies encouraged smoking, drinking, "reckless-ness," and a distaste for school and "the regular duties of life." He believed that censorship would be a "safeguard" to make films "clean and wholesome."[135] Such hopes proved to be naïve, and by the end of World War I censorship alone seemed unable to render all movies suitable for everybody, regardless of age. As Alberta Attorney General, J.R. Boyle, observed in 1919, some films that were perfectly acceptable for adults were unacceptable for chil-dren. Yet children were "indiscriminately" admitted to movies and "it was especially bad for them to see certain kinds of rough play which might contain a moral for adults, but the children only saw the obvious." The solution was to prevent children from seeing some films; indeed, it would better if films were banned altogether than to "have them under the present circumstances" of unres-tricted admission.[136]

In the mid-1920s, lobbying by various social reform groups such as the Calgary Council on Child Welfare and its parent organiza-tion, the Canadian Council on Child Welfare, heated up this debate over age classification.[137] The provincial censor opposed classifi-cation, arguing that film makers had found children's movies unprofitable because the market was too small. The Canadian Council on Child Welfare drew up monthly lists of films which had no "objectionable parts," and he advised parents to use these lists rather than rely on state directed classification; in fact, he concluded that if pictures were advertised "as suitable for adults only," such notice would be a better way "to fill the house with all classes than any other method of advertising."[138] Among other opponents, a theatre owner in Okotoks claimed that parents already regulated their children's attendance at movies, and since movies were officially censored, classification was unnecessary. Similarly, the Motion Pictures Distributors and Exhibitors of Canada disliked classification and circularized all theatre owners to exercise special caution in what they showed at children's matinees. Since only about 20 percent of pictures gave rise to criticism, if such movies were eliminated from matinees, "we shall hear less about the desirability of classification."[139]

Although the advocates of classification agreed that parents should supervise their children's movie-going, they felt that voluntary control was not enough. Mrs. Riley of the Calgary Council on Child and Family Welfare argued in 1928 that movies were "often destructive in the character building of children, and even if they are chaperoned, this form of amusement often becomes harmful."[140] This was the culmination of the debate, and the same year the provincial government responded with classification by Order in Council. Some movies were henceforth classified as "Passed U," suitable for "universal exhibition" as "family pictures." No child under the age of fourteen could attend a film that was not classified as "U," except news films, unless accompanied by a parent or "bona fide guardian."[141] Keeping in mind the chief censor's apprehension that the identification of movies as "adult only" would merely serve to advertise a film as risqué, only the "U" classification was advertised and all others were automatically defined as "adult." The system was refined in 1941 and two slightly different classifications were introduced: "Passed" films were for adults, and "Passed U" films were for families and children. Only in the late 1940s did the Provincial Censor Board begin to use the classification of "Adult Passed" instead of "Passed," for movies that were "too tense, [and] too emotional."[142]

Classification was an attempt to mitigate the evils that might develop from modern commercial leisure. Yet it was impossible to police effectively and created recurrent problems for the Provincial Censor Board. As the provincial censor noted in 1934, classification was difficult to enforce in towns and rural communities because "theatre owners do not like to turn down anyone who has a nickel or a dime they wish to give in at the box office."[143]

Further, a stream of complaints about children getting into adult films through various subterfuges all had to be investigated by the censor board. In 1935, for example, the Calgary Local Council of Women complained that newsboys were taking "the younger boys who assist in delivering their papers to moving pictures not passed 'U.' The newsboys purchase the tickets themselves, thus permitting the younger boys to attend a show they should not be allowed to see." Such scams appear to have been a popular form of entertainment for children, and for a time this "problem" was said to be "quite bad in Calgary."[144] As well, children often hung around outside the movie theatres and asked adults to take them into the adult movies. After they had been successful in finding someone to get them inside, "they naturally break loose from the adult who takes them in."[145] Further complications arose in 1937 from a ruling that no child under age fourteen could go to a movie unless the whole programme had been passed "U." In other words, not only the feature film, but also the shorts, news films, and previews all had to be passed "U." The provincial censor admitted that this rule was "impossible to enforce" because many films which were fine for a family could not be advertised as such because the whole programme was not known in advance. A card placed in the window of the ticket booth to announce whether the programme was passed gave insufficient notice to many families lacking the time or the inclination to shop around for the passed "U" programme.[146]

In part, the difficulties surrounding the admittance of children to movies arose because relatively few children's movies were made, and fewer were profitable. According to the manager of the Palace Theatre in Calgary, because only a few children attended movies, the theatres aimed to satisfy adult tastes in films.[147] Although the Calgary Council on Child and Family Welfare sponsored children's films at Christmas, the onus for showing children's films otherwise fell upon the theatre owners, who usually presented them at Saturday morning matinees. As late as 1936, children's matinees in Calgary commonly showed silent movies as well as animated cartoons like *Mickey Mouse*, "Western" movies, films which featured child actors, and juvenile films, such as *Skippy* or *Cats Paw*.[148] Running only for a day, these films were not as profitable as other films. The children's film, *Alice in Wonderland*, could not "even be booked in several towns in Alberta" because "it was felt that its appeal was solely to children" and was not "commercially profitable."[149] The persistence of classification in the face of the assorted difficulties illustrates the strength of the concern about moral standards and the protection of children from undesirable models of behaviour.

A poster advertising *The Apache's Vow,* possibly an itinerant show, appeared outside the Peace River Post Office, sometime between 1914 and 1915. (PAA A.6736)

While movies broadened entertainment options for Albertans, the early and consistent pressure for control and regulation by the state expressed a reaction against a foreign and uncontrollable force that challenged the dominant culture and the British character of Alberta. The steps taken in response were derived from the prevailing assumption that behaviour was largely a matter of patterning and imitation and from a sense that there were no alternative ways to channel movies into an acceptable format stressing usefulness and particular moral standards. Not only was the movie industry unresponsive to local pressures, it had few local allies at the official level. The theatres, the distribution system, and the production and marketing of films were for the most part owned and directed from outside the country. An important vested interest group never arose in the province, nor did the movie industry need it. The industry seems to have treated censorship as something to be lived with, since censorship did not significantly diminish its attractiveness, its profitability or its right to distribute films in the province.

And movies were a pervasive force in the society. Although urban people had the most consistent access to movies, rural people could also see and enjoy them. The influence of film thus transcended many of the geographic, economic, and social distinctions of Alberta society, and their impact was increased through technological improvement. The move from silents to talkies was one of the very few examples of technological change seen as a threat to the dominant culture. Whereas the auto, the telephone, and radio all represented salutary opportunities for the extension of the dominant culture, movies threatened to replace it with an Americanized and immoral alternative.

Movies also focussed and crystallized an increased emphasis on age distinctions in leisure. Created and displayed outside the family, the home, and the institutions of everyday life, movies called for state intervention through legislation that entrenched distinctions between adults and children. In another respect, movies, especially the talkies, had a general impact on leisure by making it more personal and individualized. Sound tracks made the illusion of film complete: one could escape, for a time, into a completely different world without reference to one's place in time or space. What silent film approached, talkies realized to a far greater degree by integrating dialogue, music, and a visual image. Although most people went to movies in couples or in groups and sat in large audiences, interpersonal relationships were temporarily replaced by an intensely personal integration of the individual with the film. Indeed, some people even complained that this solitary communion was disrupted by their more gregarious fellows. One disgruntled Edmontonian chafed in 1938 at chatter, children squirming, and the presence of "the fiends who carry paper bags which never cease to russle." And in the days of the silents, there had been the "conversationalists" who, "under the kindly but mistaken idea that you couldn't read, informed you of the captions as they appeared and occasionally made comment on them. Then came the talkies and under the impression that you were either deaf or inattentive, they repeated fragments of the dialogue."[150]

Movies, restricted though they were to a degree by censorship and classification, greatly influenced ordinary Alberta life. They helped to change language, or at least they popularized the use of certain words and figures of speech.[151] They must have influenced fashion in clothes, dances, hair styles, houses, cars, and the whole panoply of modern consumerism that defined status purely in material terms. They presented a bewildering array of new models of dress, behaviour, and personality. To these models, however, the talkies added the dimension of language with all of its emotive and cultural implications. As Northrop Frye suggests, the texture of language "enters into the mental processes of all native speakers of the language." That the great majority of movies shown in Alberta were American was therefore crucial, not only for models of behaviour, but because English, and specifically American English, was reinforced, again in Frye's term, as the "culturally ascendant language."[152] Nonetheless, movies were only one part of a new age in which ideas and images were available in an unprecedented manner to almost all people, and the impact of such innovations as radio often seemed to be forgotten by those who saw modern social change as the "fault" of movies. Movies certainly provided powerful models, but other forces too were at work.

9. On the Edge
of History: Radio

Marconi received the first radio signal to cross the Atlantic at St. John's in 1901. The signal was in Morse code, but by 1920 the Marconi Company was transmitting scheduled human voice programmes over station XWA in Montreal.[1] The first station in Alberta was established in Edmonton in 1922 and, later the same year, two more stations were established in Calgary. The social impact of radio was wide-ranging because of its very nature. When a message was produced and broadcast, it could be received by anyone within range who had the proper equipment. This allowed wide distribution of another form of American entertainment in Alberta, either directly from American stations or as carried on Canadian stations. As the development of national public broadcasting in Canada demonstrated, radio raised not only cultural but political issues.

The possibilities of radio elicited early comment. E. A. Corbett of the University of Alberta Department of Extension saw radio as a promising technique for education. "Someday," he wrote in 1930, it would be possible to "place within reach of everyone who cares to listen, courses that will, in full, be equivalent to a course at the University."[2] And in the mid-1920s, it had been common to argue that radio would be a means to preserve the family farm by lessening rural isolation and making farm life more attractive.[3] The idea that radio would confirm the home as the centre of leisure was expressed most precisely in advertisements for the radio as "the new heart of the home":

> in this day when the mad rush for pleasure tends to scatter families—when the home is in danger of losing its sacred meaning... a new influence has come into the lives of people, an influence that will make the home once more a place where desire for pleasure and entertainment may be fully gratified. This influence is radio.[4]

Unlike film, the other great modern form of communication, radio was seen as a positive social force. Radio was exciting and new, and it confirmed the value of technological change; change that would serve Alberta's needs and priorities. Traditional values and relationships were not threatened by radio since most radios were located in the home and access could be controlled by the family.

Statistics on the number of radios in the province are uneven, but early federal government licensing records provide a general estimate. The Canadian government licensed 2,769 radios in Alberta in 1923-24 and 21,456 radios by 1929-30. A steady increase during the 1930s, particularly between 1933-34 and 1938-39, brought the total to 81,238 radios by 1939, and the pattern of expansion continued during World War II.[5] More detailed statistics on the number of Alberta farms with radios are available, but for 1931 only. The 1931 census defined a farm as one acre or more in size, and in that year the farm population (as distinct from the rural population) was calculated at just over 51 percent of the total provincial population. Radios were reported only by about 17 percent of farms, the greatest number of them close to Edmonton and Calgary.[6] Although the statistical data are not categorized in the same way for later periods, the census of 1941 reported that 72 percent of rural households and 89 percent of urban households had radios.[7]

The greatest growth in radio ownership thus took place in the mid-1930s and the early war years. While the number of radios on farms was low in 1931, it had increased dramatically by 1941, when radio ownership on both farms and in urban areas had become typical. According to Francis Martin of station CJCJ in Calgary, "it wasn't until the 1940s that radio really started to move" in western Canada, because people were eager for war news and "stayed glued to their sets for the latest news from the front, and they developed habits of listening that stayed with them."[8] Other evidence confirms that radios were not common in rural areas at least until the early 1930s. John Blackburn recalled that few farmers could afford a radio during the mid-1920s, and those fortunate enough to have one enjoyed a steady stream of visitors who came to listen to it. Carl Buchanan, who grew up near Waskateneau in the early 1930s, also recalled very few radios in that area at that time.[9] Indeed, G.R.A. Rice, one of the pioneers of radio broadcasting in Alberta, observed that the rural population was often mystified by radio. During the mid-1920s, CJCA in Edmonton sent a display to the rural areas in order to stimulate interest in radio. In one area, Rice recalled, they set up their display in a hall and tuned in a broadcast. In the middle of the demonstration, some of the people "decided it was all a hoax and that we were really using a gramophone. They stormed the stage and tried to find it. Radio was so new, they were positive it was just another carnival trick."[10] Even so, people needed to be cautious: salesmen were known to circulate small towns selling fake radios. In Castor in 1922, for example, "a fakir" arrived in town, set up a "radio" in the hall, attached it to a gramophone in the basement, and demon-

Radio helped lighten the chore of laundry for this Calgary-area woman in 1922. The first CFCN daytime broadcast was aired in May or June 1922, and the first evening broadcast on May 18, 1922. (GAI NA-1319-1)

strated a musical "broadcast." When the fraud was exposed, the angry citizens smashed the equipment.[11]

Radios were commonly available from mail order houses, local merchants, and by mail from the general distributor. It was a popular hobby by 1925 to build a radio at home from purchased kits, and magazines and newspapers also commonly printed instructions for building radios.[12] Hobbyists also organized clubs to build and to listen to radio, but most people purchased one factory-made. Radio dealers in the 1920s commonly used the ploy of providing a radio in a home on approval, knowing that once it was in the home "few people would do without it."[13] Radios were usually sold for cash, and in at least one case, a false rumour that an Edmonton dealer was selling them on the "installment plan" created a flurry of hopes in one community. The "cash only" rule was significant because radios were expensive, but the desire to own one was so great that, as John Blackburn recalled, "the purchase of necessities" was often postponed to buy one.[14] The cheapest radio sold by Macleod's in 1927 cost $79.50 and cabinet models started at $105. By 1930, prices had dropped somewhat and a table model could be purchased for $49.95, still a large expenditure for a typical Alberta family. Cheaper sets were unsuitable for Alberta's dispersed population and its great distances. By 1930, Macleod's sold only five and six-tube sets because the cheaper ones, with two or three tubes, were "not suited to this country," and by 1938 a six-tube battery powered radio was considered standard in Alberta.[15] Electric radios were common only in urban areas because most farms did not have electricity until the decade after World War II.

The initial set-up costs included not only the purchase price of a radio but the cost of an antenna. In the 1920s, headphones were also often required to overcome poor reception. All radio owners were required to pay an annual license fee to the federal government, initially to the Department of Defence, but after 1923 to the Department of Marine and Fisheries. The fee was $1.00 per household during the 1920s, but rose to $2.00 in 1932 and to $2.50 per radio per year by 1937.[16] Licenses could be obtained from post offices and radio dealers, but it is unclear if the fee was consistently collected. The government ran advertisements warning radio owners to pay their license fees and, presumably, all dealers issued a license with each radio sold. Further expense was occasioned by upkeep. Although tubes (and usually batteries as well) were included in the purchase price of a radio, they had to be maintained and replaced. A typical radio needed four batteries which would last about a year if used for two hours per day.[17] Their life could be greatly extended through regular recharging and proper maintenance, which involved maintaining the water level. All of this necessitated equipment such as hydrometers, amperemeters, and voltmeters. Recharging was accomplished with a "small windmill" that generated a charge,[18] but, ultimately, batteries as well as tubes had to be replaced.

An extraordinary number of radio tubes were sold in Alberta each year: one hundred thousand in 1938-39 alone. Since the cheapest tube cost about $1.30,[19] the purchase of tubes represented a large aggregate expenditure in the province. The tube was crucial because the radio's quality "depends upon the merit of the tube. The radio set is adapted to the tube, not the tube to the set."[20] It was widely believed that tubes were unnecessarily expensive and of poor quality, and in 1939 the Social Credit government established an inquiry into the cost of radio tubes. Because one company, Thermionics, held Canadian patent rights for all radio tubes and enjoyed a monopoly in the marketplace, the inquiry concluded that this resulted in higher prices and probably in planned obsolescence. It recommended that the provincial government undertake, through the Provincial Marketing Board, the distribution of radio tubes in Alberta.[21] Expenditure on radio tubes was, however, more than just a matter of corporate manipulation of the market. By 1939, people's standards had changed and although a five to six-year-old tube still worked at 50 percent efficiency, it was often replaced since "the radio listener wants continued high efficiency service." While early replacement was not strictly necessary by this point, because radio stations were more powerful and broadcasting was of better quality,[22] consumers insisted on the best possible performance, another example of changing expectations.

High quality performance was not all that listeners expected from their radios. They also wanted style, and by the end of the 1920s radios were commonly sold for appearance as well as performance. Cabinet radios cost more than table models and probably gave their owners greater social status. Cabinet radios were generally finished in walnut, mahogany, or other hardwood veneers and came in a variety of styles to satisfy different design preferences.[23] The use of cabinet radios reflected the growing focus on radio in home life, where it had a higher status than a mere piece of machinery. Encased in veneer, it had broken into the home as "furniture," a status given to few machines. By the late 1930s, radios had been totally integrated into advertisers' pictures of home life and domesticity, with the family grouped around its cabinet radio.

During the 1920s and for most of the 1930s, programme reception suffered from a variety of problems, some of which could be minimized, but not eliminated, through good antennae, batteries, and tubes. Most early radios provided poor channel separation, which was complicated by technical problems in radio transmission and poor studio design. Static, fading, and other problems often meant that eager listeners heard only part of any given programme. In 1930, H.J. Macleod, professor of electrical engineering at the University of Alberta, provided a concise summary of these problems according to the current understanding of radio broadcasting technology. Macleod explained that once sound waves entered the microphone in the studio, they were amplified and sent via a telephone line to the station's broadcast antenna. The energy provided to this antenna, or the wattage of a station, radiated these waves into space. The waves were very strong in the immediate vicinity of the station but weakened rapidly and then stabilized at that strength for long distances. Beyond one hundred miles, the wave picked up by a receiving aerial was extremely weak and had to be amplified millions of times before it could operate a loud speaker. A number of factors could create poor reception. The transmission from the station could be faulty or the power in the mast could be too weak to transmit sound waves properly. Problems could also occur in the receiver itself. "Fading" was the result of waves from the same station reaching the receiver "by different routes." This was a common problem for those far away from the station, sometimes "at a distance of 100 miles," but more frequently at greater distances. The radio waves could also encounter static or electromagnetic waves in space. Power and telephone lines and street cars, for example, created static for urban listeners, but electrical disturbances in space were the greatest source of static and could not be "tuned out by a receiver." Weather could therefore be an important negative influence, but it could also work to the listeners' advantage; in winter, for example, "when static is negligible, a 5000 watt station may be clearly heard 1000 miles away, but on a summer day its range of good service may be only 100 miles." Macleod assumed that these problems were insoluble;[24] within a decade, however, sufficient research had been completed in ground conductivity and other areas to surmount many of the worst broadcasting problems.

Reception of distant stations, in part due to climactic factors, was sometimes astonishing. Albertans received programmes from stations throughout North America and sometimes from even further afield. T.J. Allard, an early Alberta broadcaster, acknowledged that Alberta's cold winter nights helped, but he also observed that "the spectrum was so uncluttered it was not uncommon" in northern Alberta to pick up radio signals from Russia, Australia, and other exotic places.[25] In 1922, a Mr. Taylor of Red Deer proudly reported having received forty-seven different stations, the furthest being Schenectady and Atlanta, two thousand miles distant. Given the right conditions, thought Taylor, "one in his own home can by radio get in touch with the rest of North America. . .What will be next? A programme from Europe? and Lloyd George speaking to the world? Nothing surer."[26] The magic of radio was manifest: people were on the edge of history.

Radio station CJOC, Lethbridge, 1929. (GAI NA-1111-21)

The novelty and romance of receiving distant stations gave rise to a new hobby. It began, according to Allard, by noting the time of reception and "anything that would give certain identification." The listener then "wrote that station which sent you back a DX Postcard, for verification. People collected these things the way we would collect rare coins today." Perceptively, he noted that the DX card craze was possible because "lives were less cluttered in those days. I suppose in a way, radio was the beginning of clutter. Suddenly, there was all this stuff coming into their homes from the outside—some of it good; some of it not so good."[27]

Alberta broadcasting burst into activity during the 1920s. Ownership of stations was diverse and many changed hands frequently, especially in the early years. Some were established by gifted hobbyists who translated their fascination with radio into a business, notable among them W.W. Grant, who established and ran CFCN in Calgary; G.R.A. Rice, the general manager of CJCA in Edmonton (and who later purchased CFRN in Edmonton), and Joe Palmer of Lethbridge, who set up a ham station in his home in 1926 and soon translated it into station CJOC.[28] Commonly, newspaper interests established or owned radio stations. The *Edmonton Journal* established CJCA in Edmonton in 1922; the *Calgary Herald* owned station CFAC and the *Albertan* purchased station CJCJ in 1930. In Canada, newspaper interests saw radio as a means of boosting newspaper circulation and broadening and maintaining their commercial viability in the face of new communications technology.[29] While the ownership of radio stations by newspapers seems generally to have been uncontroversial, it sometimes created concern. In 1948, the CBC Board of Governors considered a former CJCA employee's complaints about interference by management of the *Edmonton Journal* in CJCA's broadcasting policies, particularly in respect to the strike by printers at both the *Journal* and the *Bulletin*.[30]

A number of other stations in Alberta were created with special purposes in mind. From 1927 to 1933, the Alberta Pacific Grain Company operated its own station, CKLC in Red Deer, to broadcast grain prices to its elevator agents. Previously, each elevator received grain prices by telegram, sometimes as many as five a day. Radio was a more efficient and ultimately cheaper method of communication; when grain prices were not being sent, the station broadcast other programmes when available. CKLC's reception was good in almost every part of the province, and it has been judged that "Alberta has never had a station with coverage equal to that of CKLC."[31] In another realm, the University of Alberta set up CKUA in 1927 to produce and broadcast educational programmes as part of the university's extension programme.

Distinguishing early Alberta stations from one another was sometimes a difficult task: call letters were occasionally reassigned and sometimes a number of stations would share the same channel. During the 1920s, Calgary had at least nine stations, some of which broadcast for only a year or so. Of the survivors, CFAC, CFCN, and CJCJ (later CKXL) shared the same channel—7800 kc.[32] Before 1933, further confusion was created because direct advertising was prohibited in Canada. One way around this rule was the creation of "phantom" stations. An advertiser leased the "facilities of a station" and used "his own call letters while his programs were being broadcast. Though the equipment and technical staff were identical, the program staff was usually different." This system was said to have been devised by W.W. Grant of CFCN, and at one point, CFCN "had ten different phantoms for as many different advertisers." Abolished in 1932 by the federal government, phantoms appear in retrospect to be confusing, and listeners at the time would have agreed: some people apparently argued that reception was better when a particular phantom took over a station.[33]

These early stations were often poorly capitalized. In 1927, it was estimated that a "tailor made" 500-watt station would cost about $25,000, including transmission masts. A more powerful station would cost much more, and in 1931 it was estimated that a 5,000-watt station would cost about $125,000.[34] Consequently, many early stations improvised equipment that often resulted in poor programme transmission. A gramophone was often used to provide the music and a telephone frequently served as a microphone, even though it "didn't pick up all that well except for the voice."[35] Properly designed and soundproof studios were expensive, so stations improvised or did without. Although most stations had properly isolated studios, the *Edmonton Journal* station, CJCA, was located in a corner of the newsroom. At CKUA, the studio was soundproofed by nailing burlap around the room, but this was only partly effective and some programmes were interrupted by the whistle of the trains on the High Level Bridge or by the sound of steam being blown off by the university power house. Some studio control equipment in both Calgary and Edmonton was manufactured by local radio enthusiasts such as W.W. Grant of Calgary who in 1927 built the studio equipment for CKUA, the University of Alberta station.[36] Transmission masts made up a considerable part of the cost of a station, although some improvisation was possible. CKUA attached twenty-foot masts to the nearest and highest windmill towers, which happened to be near the residence known as Pembina Hall. Powerful transmitters were generally out of the question because of cost and, later, because of regulatory restrictions tied to the development of a national broadcasting system. CKUA broadcast from 1927 to 1940 at 500 watts, and CJCA in Edmonton started in 1922 with 50 watts, which would have given consistent coverage to little more than the city.

Cooperative programming arrangements among stations — in effect, a form of network broadcasting—could overcome the problem of low wattage. In the early 1930s, CKUA and stations in Lethbridge and Calgary established the Foothills Network, linked by Alberta Government Telephones (AGT) lines, and broadcast classical music, debates, sports, and current events. CJCA in Edmonton soon replaced CKUA as a member of the network, although it seems that CKUA continued to use AGT lines for transmission of its programmes to a number of stations in Alberta.[37] In subsequent years, CFGP in Grande Prairie also joined the network, which was operated by Taylor, Pearson and Carson Ltd., a company started by Calgary auto parts dealer Harold Carson who was a major figure in prairie broadcasting.[38] Not all stations, however, needed network arrangements. Radio station CFCN, "The Voice of the Prairies," owned by W.W. Grant, became the exception to the usual low power Alberta and Canadian stations when it was granted the right in 1931 to increase its power from 500 to 10,000 watts. For a time the most powerful station in Canada, CFCN could transmit to the most populated areas in Alberta and Saskatchewan and to much of the British Columbia interior.[39] By 1940, broadcasting conditions and equipment had generally improved at all stations and even CKUA installed state of art equipment and increased its power to 1,000 watts.[40]

In the interwar years, all stations in Alberta were forced to compete with American and Mexican stations. The American programming that was so exciting for Alberta listeners also produced chaotic broadcasting conditions because of the low power of most Alberta stations and the lack of agreement between Canada, the United States, and Mexico on the allocation of radio wave lengths. Alberta stations were soon blanketed by powerful American stations on or near the same channels and by the 50,000-watt stations being built in Mexico by 1931.[41] In 1932, the total power of American stations penetrating Canada was twenty-one times greater than the total wattage of all stations in Canada, and while "every radio receiver in Canada could pick up an American station, only three in five Canadian radios could receive a Canadian station."[42] In 1931, of ninety-six broadcasting channels in North America, ninety were American and six were Canadian. These six channels were inadequate for Canadian needs, and "after long negotiations," Canada borrowed twelve channels from the United States for a total of eighteen.[43] By 1937, the number of Canadian channels had increased to twenty-four "shared" and six "clear." Even these were subject to foreign interference, although this occurred mainly during the winter and in the evenings. In most urban areas in the province in 1936, it was almost impossible to receive American programming in the daytime,[44] although evening broadcasts from the United States could generally be received during the winter. In 1936, Edmonton was characterized as one of several Canadian cities "seriously affected" by foreign interference,[45] and as late as 1940, complaints that western Canadian stations were suffering interference from American stations were still common.[46] The North American Regional Broadcasting Agreement (the Havana Treaty), negotiated in 1937 and fully implemented in 1941, established station classifications for the whole of North America in order to protect radio transmissions from interference. Frequencies, or channels, were changed to create separations and protection was provided to a station "to that point where its own signal is twenty times the strength of all interference." The treaty gave Canada fourteen clear and forty-one shared channels.[47]

A souvenir of the first CNR national radio broadcast, December 27, 1928. (GAI NA-3543-1)

Despite the chaos caused by foreign interference, important developments affected Canadian broadcasting during the 1920s and especially the 1930s. Encouraged by the passion for radio of its president, Sir Henry Thornton, the Canadian National Railway

(CNR) created Canada's first network in 1923 to promote CNR rail and hotel services and to lure travellers onto the trains. Big Victor radios and loudspeakers boomed programmes through the passenger cars. Earphones were used if someone objected to the noise.[48] By 1929, CNR had established "regular coast to coast broadcasting on a daily basis" and handled programming until 1933 either through CNR radio stations in Toronto, Montreal, and Vancouver or through phantoms that inserted CNR call letters during the broadcast.[49] In Alberta, CNR used CFAC in Calgary, CKLC in Red Deer, and CJCA in Edmonton as its phantom stations. G.R.A. Rice of CJCA remembered "a big locomotive bell which we had to ring on the air to provide CNR identification."[50]

Many programmes were broadcast live from the ballrooms of CNR hotels, which imparted a very stylish and glamourous aura. The CNR network extensively broadcast classical music through an exclusive contract with the Hart House Quartet, the best known classical group in Canada at the time, and a 1929 contract with the Toronto Symphony Orchestra for a series of twenty-five broadcasts. The network also did pioneering work in the production and mounting of radio drama.[51] These broadcasts were aired for a few hours each day during the times that passenger trains passed through each locale. Because the broadcasts were not "wired" (on cable), everyone in the area could listen to them. In 1925 a CNR broadcast from Calgary, with the call letters CNRC, "performed what might well be included in the great radio feats in the world in making itself heard in the Fiji and Samoa Islands."[52]

The CNR network showed that Canadians could compete with American broadcasting and demonstrated that national public broadcasting was feasible. The long-standing hope that radio could become a forum for national expression was further bolstered in 1927 by a trans-Canada broadcast to celebrate the sixtieth anniversary of Confederation. The Canadian radio event of the decade, this first coast-to-coast broadcast in North America was a cooperative venture among CNR, Bell Canada and all the provincial telephone companies.[53] In places where no telephone lines existed to transmit the programme, wire was strung on fenceposts. The programme included political speeches and the sounds of the bells on Parliament Hill. The sensational achievement seemed to herald a new age for Canada because people "from coast to coast will be listening to the same celebration at the same moment, no matter what their occupation or location might be."[54]

The Diamond Jubilee broadcast proved that national broadcasting was possible, and many Canadians insisted that it was necessary in the national interest. Canadians were listening to more American than Canadian radio programmes because the small size and poor capitalization of stations, especially in the west, prevented the regular production of appealing Canadian programmes. It was in this climate that a dispute over the cancellation of the broadcasting license of the International Federation of Bible Students (an organization sponsored by the Jehovah's Witnesses and which operated a number of stations including one in Edmonton) created a furor over broadcasting policy. In response, the federal government established a commission of inquiry, chaired by Sir John Aird, to examine the whole question of broadcasting in Canada. In 1929, the Aird Commission reported that it had found unanimity in Canada on one point—"Canadian radio listeners want Canadian broadcasting"—and recommended a national public broadcasting system. In the national debate that followed, strong support for public broadcasting came from the United Church of Canada, the Anglican church, the Roman Catholic church, the Imperial Order Daughters of the Empire (IODE), Federated Women's Institutes, the Canadian Legion, and the United Farmers of Alberta (UFA). The strongest opposition came from private station owners, the Canadian Pacific Railway (CPR), and others in the deeply divided business community. The *Edmonton Journal* and the *Calgary Albertan*, both of which owned radio stations, opposed public broadcasting, but the *Calgary Herald*, which also owned a station, the *Edmonton Bulletin*, and the *Lethbridge Herald* supported it.[55] National support was focussed by the Canadian Radio League, which had a number of Alberta members and apparently strong Alberta support. The membership of the league, whose most notable spokesman was Graham Spry, argued that Canadians were subject to too much American programming, that Canadian unity could be created through national public broadcasting, and that the cultural survival of Canada depended upon public broadcasting emphasizing the Canadian experience. Moreover, the American ownership and domination of other cultural institutions, such as movie theatres, meant that Canadians should prevent such foreign ownership in radio. Spry's revealing slogan was "The State or the United States."[56]

Public broadcasting was implemented in 1932 through the creation of the Canadian Radio Broadcasting Corporation (CRBC). The CRBC was publicly funded, for the proceeds from radio licenses (at two dollars per year in 1932) were supposed to support the corporation.[57] In 1933, the CRBC purchased some of the assets of the CNR network and leased additional facilities. To ensure service throughout the country, it identified "basic" stations which were paid to carry its programming. Use of its programmes by other stations (which were referred to as "cooperating" stations) was optional.[58] At the beginning, the CRBC broadcast only a few hours each week but by 1936 it was broadcasting six hours per weekday and eight and one-half hours on Sunday. The basic stations were required to "carry a minimum of 2 hours of public service programs daily."[59] The CRBC increasingly produced its own programming, saving the basic and cooperating stations the production costs. Thus, the CRBC offered "substantial economies" and increased audiences to private stations "working closely with the Commission." Moreover, "the value of the time immediately prior to and following the programmes broadcast by the commission will be enhanced. Though no higher rate may be charged for it, generally speaking, that time should become more readily saleable."[60] In 1935, the CRBC relied upon CFAC in Calgary, CJCA in Edmonton, and CJOC in Lethbridge as basic stations, and CFRN in Edmonton and CJCJ in Calgary as cooperating stations.[61] Regular CRBC programming was thus available to most people in Alberta by the mid-1930s.

Although the CRBC made some progress in implementing public broadcasting in Canada, it was hamstrung by its administrative structure and its lack of money and staff. In 1936 public broadcasting was reorganized through the creation of the Canadian Broadcasting Corporation (CBC). The CBC's mandate, like the CRBC's, was wide: it was the "trustee of the national interest in broadcasting," and in addition to producing and presenting Canadian radio programmes in both French and English, it regulated broadcasting in Canada. The Board of Governors of the CBC had authority to make recommendations to the Minister of Transport on license applications and proposals to increase the power of private radio stations.[62] While its critics complained that this combination of programming and regulation gave the CBC the power to regulate its private competitors,[63] it has never been established that this was a bad thing for Canadian broadcasting.

The CBC created a network of stations across the country and for those areas without direct CBC coverage, it continued the CRBC's system of affiliation with private stations.[64] Put simply, the "basic" stations were obliged but also paid to carry some noncommercial CBC programmes, called "sustaining" programmes, and they received a portion of the revenue from commercial programmes. Because this was a lucrative proposition for private stations, by 1940 nearly every part of Alberta was receiving at least some CBC coverage through affiliated stations.[65] In 1939, CBK, with a 50,000-watt transmitter in Watrous, Saskatchewan, opened to serve most of Saskatchewan, Manitoba, and Alberta. The distance was too great, however, for CBK to reach Edmonton, among other outlying communities,[66] and most Alberta listeners continued to receive CBC coverage through affiliated stations. In 1948, the CBC established CBX with a 50,000-watt transmitter at Lacombe to cover all of Alberta, but its transmission was poor because of various technical problems and so a relay station was built in Edmonton. Even then, CBX reception was the poorest in the city.[67]

Between 1922 and 1945, there were major changes in broadcasting content. During the interwar years, programming drew from the traditions of the variety stage and vaudeville, presenting short self-contained pieces of entertainment "rigidly structured in hourly, half-hour and quarter hour formats." Only in the 1950s did radio begin to offer a "rolling format." During the 1920s, programming at many stations was close to chaos. CJCA shared facilities with "two or three other stations" and gave little thought to programme coherence: a bible broadcast might be followed by sports and then by a university lecture. Each station employed a pianist who filled in gaps in the programming with "old time" and "dance" music.[68] When stations were established, few if any thought seriously about programming: one observer noted in 1927 that Alberta radio stations had "started something without knowing where they were going, and they are now unable to keep up interest and suitable programmes." As A.E. Ottewell wryly commented, programming was so scarce in the 1920s that "even lectures by University professors were welcomed."[69]

Programming problems were especially acute in western Canada where the Toronto and Montreal options of purchasing programmes by wire from NBC and CBS in New York were unavailable. This would have been too costly in any case and one solution was to pirate American programmes. In 1931, CJCA set up receivers outside of Edmonton and picked up the World Series for rebroadcast through its station.[70] In Calgary, one station rebroadcast American programmes picked up through receivers that it had set up on the hills south of the city. Though pirating was outlawed in 1933, it was understandable if not excusable to Austin Weir, an early figure in Canadian broadcasting, because the western "stations were struggling to stay on the air, under desperate conditions, with revenue virtually non-existent."[71]

In the 1920s, stations were typically on the air only a few hours each day,[72] and as late as 1931 Canadian (and Alberta) private stations broadcast for an average of only 6¼ hours per day. Usually, noncommercial live talent filled 1¼ hours, phonograph recordings 3¼ hours, and sponsored programmes 1¾ hours.[73] The broadcast schedule was not continuous through the day, and CFAC in Calgary, for example, averaged merely one hour daily in 1929. The schedule for March, 1929 included only news, livestock reports, and football results on Saturdays; an evening church broadcast on Sundays; and news at one o'clock and a one-hour music broadcast at 3:30 on Tuesdays. The busiest day was Thursday, with four different programmes.[74] However, CFAC did share its channel with two other stations (not phantoms) and the total hours of broadcasting available in Calgary would therefore have been much higher. During one week in June 1930, CKUA broadcast on only two days, although it provided up to six hours of continuous programming on each day.[75] By the late 1930s, these schedules had filled out and CKUA, for example, was broadcasting about eight hours every weekday and about three hours on Sundays.[76]

Information broadcasting was an early feature of radio and news was an important part of early programming. During the 1920s and early 1930s, radio news tended to be rather haphazard; at CJCJ in Calgary it was simply taken from the newspaper. Since Canadian Press initially would not extend wire service to radio stations, they turned to the four daily transmissions of the British Universal Press service for international news. Local and provincial news was gathered by telephone and they "scalped the rest from the newspapers."[77] In 1934, CJCA began buying the Texaco Newscasts and broadcast them at 10:00 each evening. Although these broadcasts did not contain any Alberta news, they were immensely popular, often serving as pure entertainment, and some people built their evening routines around them.[78] Then, in 1935, CFCN set up what is claimed to be Canada's first private newsroom with John Stout as editor.[79] The habit of listening to the news was clearly well established by 1939, but the war gave the "news habit" a great stimulus. The CBC established an overseas programme unit to produce war news broadcasts and news was increasingly featured on the regular programming schedule of the CBC. In addition to the daily British Broadcasting Corporation overseas newscasts, news was featured for fifteen minutes at breakfast, lunch, and dinner times and in a final broadcast at 11:00 P.M.[80] In the 1930s, newspaper publishers feared that sales would suffer because of radio news, but the exact opposite happened. Newspaper circulation benefitted during the war from radio's "whetting of the public appetite for news."[81] As well, radio news was said to be "generally disappointing to all who have access to daily papers" and people continued to rely upon the press.[82]

Early forms of information broadcasting did not stop at news clips. Among the first current events broadcasts in the province was CFAC's coverage of Donald MacMillin's Arctic exploration by ship in 1923. On-the-spot reporting increased and in 1937 coverage of the coronation events was broadcast by CJCA from 2:00 A.M. until nearly 6:00 P.M.[83] Another information service involved broadcasting messages to people in remote areas. In 1926, CJCA in Edmonton was permitted to broadcast "private" messages to people in isolated parts of Alberta and the Northwest Territories.[84] Later, the personal style was brought to radio in the form of news commentary programmes. One such programme created by CJCA in 1944 was designed to be controversial, to whatever extent that was possible under the station's rules preventing the host from dealing with politics or religion.[85]

The farm broadcast was an especially relevant information format to Alberta. CFAC in Calgary carried a livestock report as early as 1923,[86] and similar broadcasts developed during the 1930s into comprehensive programmes covering a range of farm topics. During the 1930s, CKUA produced a noon-hour farm broadcast which was carried by other stations throughout the province. Similarly, the CBC began in 1939 to produce a farm broadcast with agricultural news, market reports, and "recommendations concerning agricultural production under war conditions." In 1942 the Alberta Department of Agriculture, in association with CKUA and CFCN in Calgary, launched a regular programme called the Alberta Home and Farm Forum.[87]

Farm reports, news, and other forms of information broadcasting often had, in addition to their direct objectives, an entertainment function, although it is difficult to separate the two. Similarly, political and institutional broadcasting served a dual purpose. The UFA broadcast its annual conventions in 1926 and 1928, the latter consisting of about nine hours of programming.[88] The Alberta Wheat Pool provided information on Pool policies over CFCN, CFAC, and CJCA during the winter months from 1927 until at least 1931. In 1928, the Alberta Wheat Pool organized a glee club among its Calgary office staff to contribute an especially popular feature.[89] In its planning, the Pool somewhat naïvely asked its listeners to identify the times most convenient for receiving the broadcast. Of course, no agreement could be reached, but a number of listeners were opposed to Friday nights "as many people want to go to dances."[90]

The Social Credit movement, however, perfected broadcasting for political (and religious) purposes, and William Aberhart's broadcasts from the Alberta Bible Institute have become one of the clichés of Alberta history. After the election of a Social Credit government in 1935, the organization continued to run its weekly broadcasts with strong religious content and individual or Social Credit group sponsorship. Entertainment was freely mixed with politics; the Camrose Social Credit group paid for one broadcast in 1939 and provided the music by "some local singers" who sang a couple of "sacred pieces (they don't sing the other kind)."[91] Although the Social Credit programmes were a regular part of Alberta broadcasting in the 1930s, political broadcasting in general was a delicate issue over which the regulatory authorities kept a close watch.[92] The CBC established policies in 1936 to govern political broadcasting, prohibiting dramatized political programmes that had been a Social Credit specialty, and tightened the regulations further during the war.[93]

The political nuances of broadcasting sometimes went beyond regulatory issues, as was the case when some Social Crediters purported to see conspiracies behind the uneven reception of some Social Credit broadcasts. In 1937, Aberhart used the *Edmonton Journal* station CJCA for his political broadcasts. That the *Journal* had little sympathy for Social Credit or Aberhart explained the poor reception for one listener in Spirit River who wrote to Aberhart that "for some time I have been suspicious that your broadcast was unnecessarily weak so much so that we here can not possibly get any good of your broadcast." Aberhart was blanketed by a Mexican station and the listener fiddled with the dials to no avail. Here was proof that CJCA was deliberately suppressing the great man's message, for "when I see what the Journal will print about you I am not the least surprised to know that they would do this too." He, however, did not need the broadcast himself, because "we are already convinced but we want the message to go forward."[94]

The University of Alberta's station, CKUA, used radio extensively for educational broadcasting, despite poor facilities and a low budget. Even before the provincial government took over the station in 1945, CKUA provided a pioneering range of educational and "serious" lectures on such topics as agriculture, handicrafts, literature, science, economics, current affairs, and history. The station regularly produced radio plays, presenting twenty-seven in 1933 alone.[95] In addition, CKUA served as an outlet for many CBC programmes during the late 1930s and early 1940s, carrying the Metropolitan Opera, the New York Symphony, and the CBC Farm Broadcast, among others. In 1943-44, CBC programmes made up about 45 percent of CKUA's schedule, the balance including local programmes such as lectures, musical programmes, and school broadcasts. CKUA was careful to ensure that its programmes were "worthy of a University station," and it refused to carry prize fights, "swing music, crooning, and 'thriller' plays." Nevertheless, they recognized and met popular taste by carefully interspersing their programmes with "light entertainment."[96]

Educational, religious, political, and information programmes constituted leisure options, but more people enjoyed the large number of programmes designed purely for entertainment. In 1938, the *Farm and Ranch Review* asked its readers about their "radio listening habits." The replies "left no doubt" that people primarily looked to their radios for entertainment. A Mr. Ellis of Cherhill had to "confess that our chief desire is to be amused. To be made to laugh as heartily and as often as possible." Another respondent from Viking observed that "after a hard day's work, we rural people like a little amusement." Indeed, in the general view, radio was the "chief form of entertainment for the farmer and his family in the winter months."[97] Only in the justification that it was a reward for work and isolation was there any hint that radio entertainment had to be useful.

Music was a large part of early entertainment programming and it continued to be important. During the 1920s, most programmes consisted of performances by local musicians performing live at the station. Many musicians worked gratis or for low fees in the hope that a radio performance would help their careers. While some stations, even in the 1920s, used recordings,[98] most record companies discouraged the broadcasting of their records because they feared that it would reduce record sales. At CJCA the use of recordings did not become important until about 1929, the same time as sound movies were introduced in Alberta.[99] Thus, the crisis for Alberta musicians created by the death of the silents was further exacerbated by increased radio broadcasting of recorded music. Nevertheless, live performances continued, although at a reduced level, to be part of radio programmes up to 1945. In 1933, CFCN in Calgary proposed to use local talent to produce a number of programmes for the CRBC, drawing on many talented local musicians including "the yodeling cowboy, Wilf Carter," the Native Sons Band, the Shriners Band, and Hopkins Old Time Orchestra.[100] The music of "Mart Kenny and his Western Gentlemen," another successful Alberta band, was first produced by CJOC in Lethbridge on a remote from Waterton Lake that was then fed into the CRBC network.[101] Kenny continued to be a popular radio performer throughout the 1930s.

Alberta radio stations broadcast a good deal of classical music, although there would have been much less without CKUA, the CRBC, and the CBC. Along with some live broadcasts, CKUA's library of eight hundred recordings of classical music received from the Carnegie Foundation formed the basis of its classical programming.[102] The CBC also broadcast classical music on a regular basis and many of its broadcasts were carried by the private stations as noncommercial CBC programming. The weekly Metropolitan Opera and New York Symphony programmes were two of the longest running examples.[103] The CBC also marked Christmas and Easter with special musical programmes; by 1944, Handel's *Messiah* was a traditional Christmas feature.[104]

Increasingly, however, radio stations moved away from live musical broadcasts to recorded popular American music. Contempt was sometimes expressed for the amount of swing and jazz music played on Alberta stations, but it remained highly popular. American musical and variety programmes broadcast in the 1930s were also immensely popular with those who could receive them on American stations. The CBC was not immune to their popularity either, and its prime hours in the late 1930s were dominated by these American programmes, which were encouraged after 1937 when the corporation allowed their sponsorship on the network. In February 1938, the CBC carried 57¼ hours of unsponsored Canadian programming, 3¼ hours of sponsored Canadian programmes, 17½ hours of unsponsored American programmes, 8¾ hours of sponsored American programmes, and 12½ hours of unsponsored overseas programmes. Most of the sponsored American programmes were variety or musical shows mixing music, humour, skits, and chatter. In the late 1930s, popular shows included the "Jack Benny Show," "The Kraft Musical Hall" (Bing Crosby's programme), and "Fibber McGee."[105] One Canadian variety programme, "The Happy Gang," began in 1937 and became one of the longest running and most popular variety shows in the country.[106]

Radio drama was equally popular. One individual at Daysland remarked in 1938 that listening to the American programme, the "Lux Radio Hour," was "just about as good as seeing a picture show."[107] In radio drama, however, it was the CBC that excelled, and the Canadian tradition of excellent documentaries began with the CBC. Among the earliest and most notable, the "Night Shift" series made on location in 1937 explored the experiences of people who worked at night. In 1939, about 50 percent of CBC radio drama was written by Canadians, and Canadians listened to Canadian-produced radio drama that was probably the best in the world.[108] Some local stations, like CJCA, also produced radio drama of high quality.[109] Beginning in 1945, CFRN in Edmonton carried the privately produced documentaries, "The Northern Electric Hour," which were designed to "foster Canadian unity" by featuring a Canadian city, province, or region.[110]

This street billboard for CFCN, Calgary, photographed circa 1937-38, was located at 1433-17th Avenue SW. (GAI NA-2771-3)

The balance of radio programming consisted of sports coverage, morning talk shows, children's programmes, and amateur hours, many of which were locally produced. In 1928, CKUA presented what was reputed to be the first live broadcast of a football game in western Canada, and local hockey games were broadcast in the province by at least 1930.[111] Prize fights were also broadcast, although many considered them especially deplorable programming. By 1939, the range of sports broadcasts had increased tremendously, including national coverage of final and semifinal events in tennis, hockey, baseball, and skiing.[112] By 1938, the Saturday night CBC broadcasts of National Hockey League games, sponsored by Imperial Oil, had become a Canadian tradition. Other programming included morning shows such as CFAC's "Toast & Marmalade" and CJCA's "Breakfast Brevities." Both were developed in the 1930s and were breezy, chatty and widely popular. In 1934 CJCA also produced "Morning Meditations," a "restful" programme of music and reading. Both local stations and the CBC developed children's programming: CJCA produced "The Farmer's Show" during the 1930s,[113] and by 1939 the CBC was producing "Maggie Muffins" and "Just Mary." The latter proved to be so popular that the CBC published a selection of the stories in 1944.[114] Most stations also organized amateur hours, inviting children and adults to sing, dance, and recite their way onto the airwaves.

The reaction of the public to all of this programming is difficult to gauge. The trustworthiness of available statistics on listenership is questionable, as it is not clear how these statistics were gathered or what sampling techniques were used, and estimates of popularity and value therefore remain highly subjective. The UFA loved CKUA because the station was a form of public broadcasting and because it was also heavily involved in agricultural broadcasting.[115] CKUA had other ardent supporters as well. In 1927, a Mrs. Stop of Cold Lake wrote CKUA a touching letter praising the horticulture broadcasts that gave her so much pleasure and knowledge. She had followed their instructions on tomato culture, writing: "How I wish you folks could see the wonderful tomatoes, and I have them by the bushel." She had also followed their advice on "everlasting flowers and [we] will have large bouquets all winter." But not all Albertans were so sympathetic to CKUA. "A Christian" wrote to Premier Aberhart accusing CKUA of "making itself an agent and propaganda" for communism, atheism, and "irreligion," as shown in its broadcasts about the Spanish Civil War and its supposed praise for Soviet Russia.[116]

While CKUA's aim was never mass broadcasting, it is apparent that the large private stations, as well as the CBC, strenuously pursued large audiences in order to improve their balance sheets and to keep their advertisers happy. The CBC accommodated the needs of the private stations because they often carried a wide range of CBC programmes,[117] and these conditions gave advertisers power in determining broadcasting content. The "sponsors," commented one observer in 1939, were reluctant to buy time following a "programme which, because of its restricted audience appeal, has caused listeners to turn to another station."[118] By 1942, another critic thought the CBC was concerned only with commercial objectives. This

> means that their policy has always been subservient to the interests of the advertiser and the station owner who insist on the highest possible audience and the greatest volume of sales. It is a matter of common knowledge that the largest audiences as indicated by surveys and "box-top" returns are for programmes which are purely entertainment or whose educational content is either very low or even negative. Examples are Fibber McGee and Lux Radio Hour for entertainment and the soap operas for the "box-top" returns.[119]

Despite these opinions, it is unclear if programme content was the main reason why people listened to a broadcast. Presentation became vital, and it was in this respect that the American model proved so important for Canadians. By 1936, it was evident that Canadian listeners had "grown accustomed to the highly expensive broadcasts produced in the United States and regard these as a normal standard of entertainment." In slick American radio, content was secondary to form.[120] As G.R.A. Rice frankly admitted, "it is an established fact that most people will listen to anything that is well done, but few if any, will listen to anything poorly done."[121] This fact made advertisers powerful. Sophisticated production was expensive and since Canadians were unwilling to provide enough public funds to meet such production requirements, advertising money became crucial to a station's ability to mount attractive programmes.

This leads to the conclusion that the impact of radio on Alberta society was a mixed one. To suggest that the society came to prefer form over content is not heartening. It is also reasonable to assume that a barrage of advertising resulted in a more commercialized and materialistic society. Yet it can be suggested that Alberta, like the rest of prairie society, had a very materialistic bent from the beginning of settlement, and while radio may have confirmed these tendencies, it did not necessarily create them. Radio advertising had the power, however, to change people's preferences and, with constant repetition, to make them needs. It can be argued that modern advertising is built upon conformity, the rejection of anything old, and unqualified support for anything new.[122] This had an important impact upon the authority of the family as well as on self-esteem. As one correspondent only half humourously wrote to the *Farm and Ranch Review* in 1929, "it is annoying to have the merits of gum and tobacco dinned in the ear of your offspring when in your household chewing gum may be the forbidden sin." Moreover, "it is positively distressing to be urged to buy a 'Helluva' watch when you have not the wherewithal for a nickel 'Harvester'."[123]

Radio also had other implications. For those willing to listen, certain programmes, such as the productions of CKUA, would widen intellectual horizons and stimulate new interests. Citing a radio broadcast also became a form of intellectual authority. One unhappy Social Credit supporter, who did not have a radio, informed Aberhart that political arguments were always settled in favour of those with radios because they would "say 'well, thats what came over the radio' which leaves one no ground for argument if he hasn't also heard the speech."[124]

Radio probably also played a significant part in both the commercialization of sport and the growth of its importance as a recreational activity because it presented higher standards of play for public emulation and fostered the growth of the sports star system. As well, radio was doubtless a boon for Alberta farmers. It replaced the frequent boredom and isolation of winter evenings with laughter and pleasure, however fleeting; and it replaced the uncertainty, although not the pain, of knowing commodity prices in advance. On the other hand, since some tractors were now equipped with radios, journalist Miriam Green Ellis wondered in 1940 what that meant for the traditions of the " 'thoughtful plowmen'. . .with the radio retailing 'swing' or war news, what chance has a man to think of the 'heavens and the earth, and all that is in them.'" She believed that radio had made life more regimented, more predictable, and less original because radio's devotion to precision and form would not tolerate the unexpected. Programmes, she wrote, "come with all the precise arrangements of an undertaker. . .[and] have the hard mechanism of a pianola. There is no adventure of the unexpected."[125]

Radio also had an impact on language. The CBC recognized "the great and growing influence that radio exercises on the speech habit of the community," and consequently it rigourously enforced standards of speech in its programming.[126] In fact, it came to be popularly accepted that pronunciation by CBC staff was perfect, which meant that some would accept a mispronunciation by a CBC broadcaster as correct.[127] Radio also placed a premium on a good understanding of nuance and, in some cases, on the colloquial use of English. Radio announcers were told to use "ordinary conversational terms," such as contractions, in order to create familiarity with the listeners.[128] Moreover, before World War II, almost all broadcasting in Alberta was in English and this must have had a major impact upon people whose first language was not English or whose English was poor. Doubtless, it served as another force leading to the abandonment by non-English Albertans of their first language.

These radio announcers at CFCN, Calgary, were inundated with mailed responses to a contest sponsored by a manufacturer in the 1940s. (GAI NA-2771-9)

For French-speaking Albertans, the Association Canadienne française de l'Alberta sponsored bimonthly concerts over CJCA in Edmonton in 1930, but this was, to all intents and purposes, the limit of French broadcasting in the province. In 1933, the CRBC produced some French language broadcasts carried over its affiliates in Alberta. W.W. Grant reported that the first such broadcast was "very popular, it being something new and as there was not too much French talking, it was very acceptable." He did, however, note that the commission should be careful not to "overdo this" because subsequent French language broadcasts had created a "very bad reaction" in Calgary.[129] A French language station was not established in Alberta until the late 1940s—and then only over the protests of the provincial government and organizations such as the Loyal Orange Lodge. In support of their argument, the Orangemen claimed that the creation of a non-English radio station was a threat to "national unity" through the encouragement of "racial segregation."[130] The French Canadian community in Alberta was embittered by this dispute. Father Bréton, the editor of *La Survivance*, wrote that Franco-Albertans would not submit to Anglicization: "we are Catholic and French and, for all their opposition, we fully intend to stay this way." This quarrel over broadcasting showed that "we must rely upon ourselves above all else. Once again, we have seen that we cannot trust the declarations of good will, understanding and fair play, the British tenets of democracy professed by our Anglo Saxon fellow citizens."[131] Radio thus showed more potential for focussing old battles than for bringing French and English together in Canada.

The role of radio in promoting American standards of taste in Canada was more ambiguous. It seems clear that Canadians wanted American programming and increasingly wanted American style programming. This in turn must have helped to make American speech patterns, style, and attitudes acceptable to Canadians. The cultural implications of this are difficult to assess because radio, unlike film, had some Canadian content and a Canadian viewpoint expressed through public broadcasting. It is apparent that significant Canadian content would not have been provided in Alberta without public radio; most of the private stations during the interwar years could not afford to produce anything except the cheapest local programming. Moreover, their concern with profit through advertising raised the appeal of American programming. The CRBC and the CBC therefore spoke a great deal about their commitment to Canadian content and did much to encourage it, but because much of it came from other parts of Canada, musicians and other performers in Alberta largely found this meaningless. In 1936, the CRBC was criticized for ignoring Alberta musicians and assuming that Calgary, in particular, "can do no better than furnish a poor imitation of an American dance band." There were no CRBC broadcasts originating in Calgary that had "any cultural value or much entertainment value" and the Calgary Symphony, for example, had been hired only once by the CRBC for a broadcast.[132] Similar complaints continued; in 1950 the Alberta Music Board argued that Canadian content must mean more than music from only Vancouver, Winnipeg, Toronto, and Montreal. Because musicians from Calgary and Edmonton were never given a "chance to perform on network broadcasts," the description of CBC broadcasting as "Canadian" was a misnomer.[133]

Nevertheless, the existence of Canadian content helped to mitigate any criticism that listening to radio as a leisure activity might undermine the society. Yet the existence of public broadcasting only partially explains this reaction because, even before public broadcasting existed, radio was uncritically accepted by most Albertans. Although the reasons for this are not entirely clear, they may have arisen from the magical aura of radio; it was even more magical than film, for it had a disembodied quality that film did not have. The sound appeared as though from nowhere and became real in one's presence. It was also made real in one's home, which must have provided a sense that radio could be controlled and integrated into traditional life where the family could play the central role. Thus, the argument that radio would not only preserve the family but would restore it to a central place in leisure must have been deceptively attractive. Yet radio was highly individualized because the radio programmes could only suggest an image, leaving each listener to create in his or her mind a visual context that was necessarily personal. Because of its abstraction, it could not always be easily communicated to another person. Interpretation was therefore of primary importance for the individual's appreciation and understanding of the programme. Radio thus abstracted and limited the cultural experiences shared by people in the same community or even in the same home, even as it brought them together in receiving identical messages. On the other hand, radio could easily be taken beyond the home to create a focus for community or travelling entertainment. People danced and held pie and box socials to the radio,[134] and by the early 1930s, they could drive and listen to the radio as well. Although car radios were not typical in Alberta even by the early 1940s,[135] their limited presence in cars indicated a broader potential.

The uncritical acceptance of radio owed much to its relatively non-threatening social impact. It never challenged the centrality of work in society; indeed, one could work or do something useful while listening to the radio. The favourite images in early advertisements for radios presented scenes of people reading, knitting, or at least being together as a family while listening to the radio. Furthermore, radio did not present explicit examples of controversial behaviour that could be imitated. Radio never offered "sophisticated" entertainment (in the way that movies used the term), but always wholesome "family" entertainment. The single cultural apprehension, about the dominance of American content, was dealt with through the development of national public broadcasting. Many stations were locally owned; indeed, they were often owned by local newspapers that could directly influence opinion.[136] Moreover, local control fixed radio within the familiarity of everyday life. This local quality gave radio a homey familiarity that made it acceptable without diminishing its magic.

The areas of life touched by radio were so various that it is impossible to describe its overall impact with precision. Radio was only the first stage in a wide-ranging communications revolution that had an immense impact on leisure. In the 1950s, television became the new innovation that radio had been in the 1930s and 1940s and added new dimensions to leisure patterns. In general terms, radio served as one of the first of several powerful forces that contributed to the transformation of social structures everywhere. As Egyptian President Gamal Abdel Nasser once observed, "radio now counts for more than literacy."[137]

10. Agricultural Fairs
and Rodeos

Fairs were organized in most parts of the province soon after settlement and rodeos became common after World War I. While rodeos were plainly designed for entertainment, fairs were always officially justified as educational opportunities for farmers to meet, show their livestock and produce, compare experiences, and listen attentively to explanations of efficient farming techniques, and measures to improve and reform rural society.[1] The agricultural fair was part of the Anglo-American inheritance of Alberta. First developed in Britain and the United States in the early nineteenth century, it was an accepted part of North American life by the 1840s. In Alberta, it largely expressed the educational ideals of English-speaking settlers, although at Edmonton the French-speaking community actively participated in the local fair.[2] Traditional fairs were mounted by agricultural societies, but government agencies promoted them as educational events in another assertion of Anglo-Canadian practice. Beyond such objectives, the fair clearly offered fun and enjoyment at the midway or sports events. Keeping the dual functions of educational leisure and simple entertainment in appropriate balance was sometimes a matter of public concern.

The territorial, provincial, and federal governments all provided grants, displays, judges, and speakers for agricultural fairs. Before 1905, the territorial and federal governments gave grants to agricultural societies equalling 60 percent of the total prize list.[3] After 1905, the provincial government granted sums equal to two-thirds of the previous year's prize list to a maximum of three thousand dollars,[4] and the federal Department of Agriculture continued to issue grants to medium and large-sized fairs where prize lists met certain specifications. For purposes of grants and general organization, all fairs were classified as A, B, C, D or E. The latter three classifications were usually simply referred to as C fairs. The categories were differentiated by various criteria, most notably the extent of the prize list. There were only two A fairs in Alberta (at Edmonton and Calgary), but the number of B and C fairs varied over time. While the federal government paid grants only for A and B fairs, the province provided grants for all categories of fairs.

The government grants were designed to promote agricultural education, not entertainment programmes. In 1932, George Hoadley, the provincial minister of agriculture, contended that he saw "no good reason why we should continue to build up large expensive plants, with equally expensive management, to entertain a holiday crowd." The "circus feature of fairs," which overshadowed the educational objectives, should be discouraged, and the province refused to support a "questionable kind of entertainment" for innocent boys and girls.[5] Still, agriculture and education sometimes took the back seat at many fairs. The Lethbridge Experimental Farm took a display to various fairs in southern Alberta, but for the more than thirty-five hundred people at the Raymond fair of 1915, "the sports, bucking, roping, racing etc were so good that the people had little time to look at the exhibits."[6] Government officials were always pleased when entertainment features were not prominent. The Alberta superintendent of fairs happily observed in 1913 that the Red Deer fair was "strictly" an agricultural show and "the attention of the people" was not distracted by "midway attractions."[7] Even the best educational efforts could be abused by a frivolous public. In 1906, the provincial Department of Agriculture recommended an admission charge of one dollar for its lectures at fairs, "thereby preventing the attendance of a lot of undesirables such as children and loafers."[8] Of course, not all government officials attempted to exclude entertainment from fairs. Most recognized a legitimate recreational dimension, as long as the carnival did not dominate.

The increasing number of fairs held in Alberta during the first fifteen years of the twentieth century did not indicate merely an appetite for agricultural knowledge or even for entertainment. Fairs were often organized to promote and enrich a town or locality. As early as 1882, the *Edmonton Bulletin*, which almost pathologically promoted Edmonton's growth, characterized the Edmonton fair as a means of boosting the economic growth of the town and region. While in comparison to the "great agricultural exhibitions of the east, our little show. . . may seem a very poor affair," the agricultural displays proved the great capacity of the district and advertised it to the world.[9] Such thinking was common and enduring. Three decades later, in 1914, the Edmonton Exhibition Association frankly stated that the annual exhibition was more important to encourage Edmonton's commercial growth than to stimulate agricultural improvement. The coming of thousands who would not otherwise visit Edmonton benefitted "many lines of trade and brings much money into the city," making it the "clearing house of business interests for the whole central and northern part of Alberta."[10] In their promotion of fairs, urban governments also discouraged interlopers from distracting the public from the fairs' entertainment features. In 1908 Red Deer would not allow Mr. Diller of Calgary to operate a merry-go-round in the town at the time of the fair, unless he did so on the fair grounds with the permission of the fair board.[11] Similarly, Edmonton used its licensing power in 1921 to prevent competition. Circus licenses cost $1,000 if mounted within thirteen days of the start of the Edmonton fair, but only $350 if staged at least two weeks before the fair or at any point in the summer after the fair.[12]

Boosterism involved not only specific commercial objectives but local rivalries. The plans for the 1912 Edmonton Exhibition aimed to confirm Edmonton's economic aspirations and celebrate its growing metropolitan status. The theme of the exhibition was the railway and celebrated four important events in local history: the completion of the Grand Trunk Pacific main line; the Canadian Northern Railway line to the Peace River country; the Edmonton-Fort McMurray (Waterways) line; and the entrance of the Canadian Pacific Railway into Edmonton over the High Level Bridge. At the same time, the fair board lodged a protest with the minister of agriculture over Calgary's "usurpation" of the title "Provincial" for its annual exhibition.[13] Similarly, according to a 1910 assessment, many small town fairs were held simply because of intertown rivalry. When one town held a fair, the merchants in a neighbouring town responded with their own fair because "it hurts them like everything to see what normally would have been theirs going into the coffers of their competitors." Inevitably, the respective townsmen, out of "loyalty together with the spirit of rivalry," boycotted each others' fair and soon two poor fairs were operating where formerly a good one had existed. Then, "after a year or two of barely living," both died "a natural death."[14]

The use of the fair as a commercial weapon alienated many farmers who, "as a class," were very "suspicious and full of mistrust." Although all fairs were organized by agricultural societies, the fair boards were usually dominated by townspeople. Some farmers refused to attend because they believed that they would "not get a square deal," and this town-farm split was an important limitation to the success of many fairs. Moreover, the domination of fair boards by townspeople led to poor planning by locally prominent men with too many social and business commitments to give much time to the fair, and an event that could have been a "profitable pleasant entertainment" was often "converted into a veritable chaos."[15] City fair boards were similarly dominated by the local elite: 50 percent of the members of the Edmonton Exhibition Association in 1909 also sat on the Edmonton City Council. The large urban fairs were saved by the employment of a full-time director and secretary which provided continuity and expertise. In 1903, the Calgary Exhibition Association hired E.L. Richardson as assistant manager and in 1907 he took over as manager. It was the beginning of a long and fruitful career for Richardson who, twenty-one years later, established the Calgary Stampede as the feature of the Calgary Exhibition and made it into one of the greatest annual events in Canada.[16]

The number of fairs held annually in Alberta fluctuated greatly over the years: 32 in 1908, 66 in 1913, 103 in 1922, 63 in 1928 and just 16 in 1934. At this point, the numbers stabilized between 16 and 20 until the end of World War II.[17] During the 1930s, Alberta had the least number of agricultural fairs among the prairie provinces.[18] Too many small fairs had been established for the wrong reasons, then were cancelled because of apathy and a lack of cash reserves to face economic downturns. In 1922, the Peace River fair attracted six hundred people but very few farmers participated, partly because they were harvesting, but also because they had little enthusiasm for the fair. The fair was essentially a sports meet with "baseball games drawing the largest share of the attendance on both days," and the next year, a fair was not held at all because of crop failure and a general lack of money.[19] In 1927, Fort Macleod cancelled its fair which had been gasping along for several years. As the secretary of the association said, "I am sick of this struggle to make it a success. The trouble is our farmers don't seem to want it, they have no pride in their stock or their farms."[20]

Small fairs also suffered from changes in transportation. Even before World War I, people often took advantage of railway excursion rates to city and large town fairs. To further encourage out-of-town visitors, fair associations often operated billeting offices that helped people to find lodging. In Calgary, the office was located near the CPR station and visitors could arrange accommodation upon arrival. In 1908, the Calgary association went one step further by converting schools, including the normal school, into "large hotels" where visitors could sleep for fifty cents per night. Such amenities were also available at some of the B class fairs. In 1919 the Red Deer fair association provided billeting services and converted local facilities into sleeping quarters for visitors.[21] These services made the larger fairs accessible to many rural and small town people as a relatively inexpensive form of entertainment involving a twenty-five to fifty cent cost of admission and variable costs of food, rides, and other attractions. With the increasing use of trucks and cars during the 1920s, the appeal of larger fairs broadened further. In 1931, George Hoadley noted that the "advent of the automobile makes it easier to go to the larger centres and farmers have consequently lost interest in the smaller fairs." By 1938 the "crowds, drawn mainly from the rural sections," were "enormous" at the Edmonton Exhibition.[22] Many of these visitors preferred camping over billeting, one indication that the income level required to attend a fair was dropping and that fairs were becoming more accessible for rural people. The Calgary Exhibition and Stampede provided camping facilities and in 1920 the Edmonton Exhibition Association advertised its fair as "the cheapest holiday you can plan," with a campground for "motoring parties," where a tent could be pitched beside the car. The campground featured a kitchen with running water and a stove, and campers could rent tents, straw mattresses, and cots. Tents rented for $4 to $7.50, in sizes ranging from 8-by-10 feet up to 14-by-16 feet.[23] Out-of-town fair visitors could also camp at the local auto camp, a commonplace facility by the late 1920s.

The Sunshine Auto Camp, Calgary, in 1930, was located opposite to the grounds where the Calgary Stampede took place. (GAI NA-3990-1)

By 1930, the province was littered with moribund rural agricultural societies, many lost to apathy and technological change, but many killed by an early provincial government resolve to reduce its annual number of fair grants. In 1920, the Department of

Agriculture began cancelling the charters of agricultural societies failing to mount a fair or a short course for two consecutive years. To save costs, and because motor vehicles allowed people to "get about easily and quickly, it was felt that a number of these fairs could be reduced." From 1920 to 1931, this ruling alone accounted for a 50 percent decline in the number of fairs and a reduction of almost one-half in grants.[24] Before 1922 a new agricultural society could be organized if it was at least ten miles from an existing one, but after further policy refinements in 1922, this was changed to a distance of at least twenty-five miles apart,[25] a clear indication that the definition of "community" was widening appreciably. The last blow came during the Depression when the UFA government decided not to pay any grants for fairs from 1932 to 1934. Although the Social Credit government restored grants in 1935, these were too small to support a prize list.[26] Fairs receiving federal grants subsequently dominated, and of the sixteen fairs held in 1934, eight received federal grants for their prize lists.[27] The fairs that survived the problems of the 1920s and 1930s had either a large enough physical plant to draw large crowds or some reserve capital with which to maintain their operations and prize lists. For the rest, their charters were suspended and their assets sold or turned over to other community uses. When the Taber Agricultural Society was liquidated in 1937, its buildings were torn down and the lumber used for a new community skating rink. In 1935, the majority of fairs were held in the northern half of the province.[28]

Of all the fairs in Alberta, the Edmonton and Calgary Exhibitions were the largest, richest, and most successful. In part, they owed their success to effective management and the good fortune of receiving financial and other support from the cities, but they also drew on large population bases and received revenues by the late 1930s from their race tracks and buildings. The large population base was important for maintenance of impressive grounds and multi-use buildings that could be rented out year round for public functions, thus producing some ongoing revenue.[29] Some small fair associations attempted to do the same, but insufficient population made this ineffective. That was nevertheless the objective of the Innisfail Fair Association's plans in 1906 to fence the fair grounds and dig a well in order to rent the grounds out for sports meets, horse races, and pasturage.[30]

Although the Calgary and Edmonton Exhibitions were the largest, other important fairs were held at Red Deer, Vermilion, Vegreville, and Lethbridge from the 1920s until the 1940s. These were one to three-day fairs compared with the four to six-day Calgary and Edmonton Exhibitions. Attendance was usually high. The Red Deer fair did well with around 6,000 people in 1934,[31] but the city exhibitions had by then long established their dominance. In 1910, the Edmonton Exhibition attracted 40,000 people over its four-day run, and just over 59,000 people visited the Calgary Exhibition. By 1931, Calgary attracted about 198,000 visitors and Edmonton about 87,000. After declines at Calgary in 1932 and 1933, almost 215,000 visitors attended in 1936, while Edmonton drew almost 128,000. In 1939, more than 240,000 attended the Calgary fair and more than 150,000 attended the fair in Edmonton. Even if a visitor went to the fair more than one day, these levels of attendance still exceeded the total populations of the host cities, and, in Calgary's case, attendance often exceeded two and one-half times the city's population.[32]

The Manufacturers' Building, Edmonton Exhibition, 1914. (PAA B.8786)

During both wars, there was some debate about the appropriateness of agricultural fairs during wartime. A minor issue during World War I, it claimed much more attention during World War II, when it was argued that fairs were neither useful in stimulating wartime production nor practical because of the rationing of gasoline, tires, and labour. Nevertheless, attendance at the Calgary Exhibition continued to increase and the largest number of visitors ever attended in 1941.[33] The Edmonton Exhibition was seriously affected by the use of part of the exhibition grounds for air training in 1941, and when the rest of the grounds were claimed in 1942, the fair was cancelled. When it was revived in 1945, almost 176,000 people attended, followed by nearly 214,000 in 1946.[34]

All fairs, regardless of size, offered certain basic features. The programme at a small rural fair would generally include agricultural exhibits, food concessions, sports, possibly a rodeo, and horse races. Some were little more than sports days with a local band playing on the grounds and a dance to end the day. The larger town fairs added a parade, a midway, and a grandstand performance. A more elaborate version of the same programme was available at the Edmonton Exhibition and in Calgary, except that Calgary combined its programme with a stampede after 1923.

A commercial display at Vegreville Fair, 1927. (PAA B.2659)

An attractive overall programme cost money, especially for entertainment. At the Calgary Exhibition in 1910, slightly more than one-third of the total expenditure was for music and attractions.[35] Since the government grant could not be used for this purpose, admission charges and volunteer work supported these features. Government grants could, however, be used to provide prizes for competitive exhibits, which were often considered recreational in themselves. The exhibits ranged from "ladies' fancy work" through agricultural produce, poultry and livestock, dogs and pets, to arts and crafts. Walking through the exhibition hall and looking at this huge array of displays enriched the recreational dimension of the day. Prizes were awarded for the best entries, even though judging was often a matter of debate and sometimes of dissension.[36]

Many fairs also arranged a variety of commercial exhibits, special displays, and contests. The 1909 Calgary Exhibition presented a butter making contest (which included milking the cow), the shearing of one hundred head of sheep by the United States champion sheep shearer, and an exhibit of two hundred paintings by "celebrated" European and Canadian painters. In the previous year, a special display of live wild animals from Banff National Park included buffalo, moose, elk, and deer.[37] When feasible, these special events were placed among the competitive exhibits. Even at the Edmonton fair of 1894, various distributors showed their commercial products, someone exhibited a cage of canaries, Mrs. J. A. McDougall showed off her magnificent spotted lily, and a Mr. Anderson of High River operated his phonograph, which continuously drew a crowd of people "who held their ears to the tubes" to listen to the music. The local band played at intervals through the evening while the crowd looked at the displays.[38] Exhibits soon became more numerous and the commercial displays multiplied. At the Calgary Exhibition of 1908, heavy machinery was displayed outside, while 130 manufacturers and dealers turned the Industrial Buildings of the Main Pavilion into a "blaze of beauty" with their exhibits.[39] Farm machinery was always a popular part of these heavy equipment displays, and by the late 1940s commercial exhibits at Calgary had grown to the point where not all applicants could be accommodated.[40] Commercial displays were more modest at the smaller fairs. In fact, they were positively lacklustre and correspondingly unpopular at the 1924 Red Deer fair, where displays from local manufacturers augmented just two out-of-town presentations, one by the Federal Poultry Division and another by an insurance salesman.[41]

It would have been surprising if an insurance salesman could compete with the other features of the Red Deer fair: a midway, music at the grandstand, horse races, a ball tournament, food concessions, and an evening dance at the armouries. Some of the parades opening the larger fairs were equally grand affairs. The 1908 Calgary Exhibition parade, celebrating both the fair and July 1, was led by a "Strokel airship" piloted by Captain Dallas, followed by a "historical representation" of western Canadian history that proved "highly instructive, even to the old timers." The parade included "what may be considered the greatest parade of Indians ever seen in Canada. More than one thousand aborigines had been assembled. . .and in their gay and gaudy costumes they presented a most picturesque sight." Cowboys, pioneers, Hudson Bay Company traders, and "other types intimately associated with the early history of the Prairie region" joined between fifty and seventy-five automobiles "owned in the city"[42] and a series of floats, the most outstanding of which was a model of Leif Ericsson's ship. The whole parade was described as "historic, educative and interesting."[43]

Entertainment was hardly the principal motivation for these spectacles. The Calgary parades of 1908 and 1909, for example, were organized by the board of trade to advertise the city. In 1909, the city's publicity department provided a one thousand dollar grant to make a publicity film about the parade, which raised the parade from "a local feature to a status even wider than that of Alberta itself."[44] The Edmonton Exhibition also utilized parades to good effect. The 1925 parade included floats from service clubs, boards of trade, and many commercial organizations including machine companies, meat packers, furniture stores and other retailers, as well as Indians, police, horses, children, and the whole of the midway from the fair. As advertised, it was truly a "monster" parade.[45] The 1938 parade theme publicized the sixtieth anniversary of the Edmonton Exhibition. Premier Aberhart rode in his car in the parade; but only his car was allowed, "because a string of cars spoils a parade" and there was "no room for other members of Government."[46] Here was a dramatic change from the earlier tendency to conscript every car in a town or city.

A midway was the big attraction at the larger fairs. The various midway companies active in Alberta, including C.W. Parker Shows, Conklin and Garrett Shows, the Moyer Amusement Company, and the Universal Amusement Company, provided rides, food concessions, and sideshows. In 1909, C. W. Parker Shows offered visitors to the Calgary Exhibition a ferris wheel, "a big carry-us-all," a trained wild animal show, a series of acrobatic acts, and

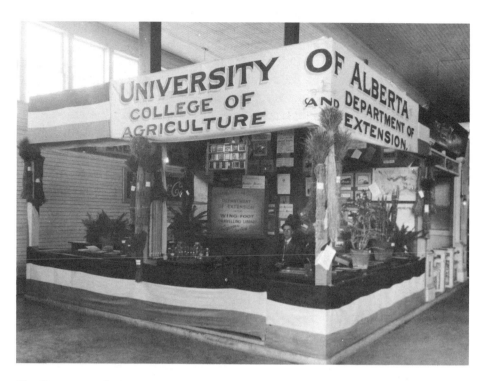

The University of Alberta booth at Edmonton Exhibition, 1926. (PAA A.8362)

various side shows such as "a representation of an Italian earth-quake," the "Johnstown Flood," and "Broadway Belles." Only the acrobats could be seen without paying admission.[47] Over the years, these presentations became more elaborate and the number of rides increased, although those at small fairs were always more limited. While most midways after 1914 came from the United States,[48] some Canadian ones operated in the prairies. In 1928, the Moyer Amusement Company, a small carnival show from Assiniboia, Saskatchewan, provided four rides including a ferris wheel and a carousel plus "several good, clean concessions." Such shows would have appeared at many small rural fairs throughout the prairies during the 1920s.[49]

Rides such as ferris wheels and carousels had been featured at Alberta fairs since the beginning of the century, but by the mid-1920s they were supplemented at the large fairs by more exciting rides. Nevertheless, the side shows continued as major attractions, often approaching circus status with their extensive use of animal and stunt shows.[50] In 1930, Circuit 2 of the Western Canadian fairs, which in Alberta comprised Lloydminster, Red Deer, Vermilion, Vegreville, Stettler, Wainwright, and Lacombe, negotiated with Conklin and Garrett Shows for the provision of the midway for all fairs on the circuit. Conklin and Garrett provided a ferris wheel, tilt-a-wheel, Merry Mix-up, "catterpillar" and, where feasible, a pony saddle track. They also presented nine side shows which included a freak animal show, a snake show, "Worlds Museum," "Unborn," and "Death on the Guillitine." The fair board received 10 percent of the gross receipts up to $2,000, and 15 percent of any receipts thereafter. Conklin also paid $200 for the right to set up a number of food concessions. Conklin provided the local fair board with posters and also agreed to supply, at extra cost, a calliope for advertising. Each fair board had to provide a minimum of 75 kilowatts per hour of electricity each night for the "lighting up of the midway."[51]

The sword swallower at Leduc Fair in 1906 attracted a large and curious crowd. (PAA B.2479)

The midways were the primary means by which the fair associations made money and drew the public, but they were sometimes criticized for being immoral and neither useful nor uplifting.[52] The *Farm and Ranch Review*, which was a strong advocate of educational fairs, particularly hated midways, and on one occasion it savagely criticized the side shows in an article entitled "Scum at Fairs."

The Edmonton Exhibition midway, pictured here about 1910, drew the public to its sideshows. (PAA B.8874)

"At some fairs," it noted, "the flim-flam artist and debasing show have become more noticeable than at others, and as a rule, the fewer real good exhibits there have been, the more brazen have been the riff-raff element," simply because exhibition boards had "an eye for the revenue." But even the *Farm and Ranch Review* had to admit that the public liked the midway, and almost unbelievably, "the side shows claim that farmers are their best patrons," who, like townspeople, showed little reluctance in parting with a dollar for "two bits of glass" which had "no intrinsic value whatsoever."[53] Others criticized the side shows because they were not socially respectable. There was nothing wrong with the rides, it was observed in 1922, but "why should we be willing to listen to a class of entertainers at a fair whom [sic] we would not admit in our own homes."[54] Some critics felt that the "games of chance" offered on the midways amounted to gambling, and over the years, the police did close some games for this reason.[55] These negative views, however, held little currency with the majority. The *Red Deer Advocate* even went so far as to characterize the midway shows as "educational, entertaining, clean, amusing and harmless, honorably conducted. . .and there is an air of splendor about them that is very pleasing."[56] This was more credit than was due, but it was an interesting application of the arguments about utility and demonstrated the continued potency of the belief that leisure should be useful.

In addition to a midway, a show in front of the grandstand augmented many fairs with diverse programmes of local talent or imported productions. At the Calgary Exhibition in 1909, an impressive grandstand show presented the Navasser Ladies Band of New York, "CeDora in the Golden Globe," the "Mizra Golems," comedians, and animal acts. The Navasser Ladies Band was touted as a world famous group that had played in New York, Paris, St. Petersburg, and now, Calgary. Indeed, it "surprised some people" that such a famous group would travel to Calgary. The reason, however, was simple and comforting: the ladies wanted to see the West, so westerners would see them at a bargain price. At Ashbury Park, New Jersey, "and other big pleasure resorts," the band commanded $3.50 for a reserved seat, but at Calgary it would cost only 50 cents—25 cents admission to the grounds and 25 cents for the grandstand. One of their "spectacular" performances was the "Anvil Chorus" from *Il Trovatore:* "six or eight of the Navasser girls are dressed as blacksmiths, standing by as many anvils which are connected with electricity. When these are struck, showers of sparks are thrown about." The other grandstand acts reflected equally well upon Calgary's status. People "down in New York City" had been watching CeDora in the Golden Globe "for several weeks past," and CeDora had also been a "heroine" in London, England. Her fame came from her performance of a "daring, sensational motor-cycle leap-the-gap act in a huge globe simultaneously with another woman and a man, all going in different directions." And the Mizra Golems, who performed acrobatic acts that were "the marvel of the athletic universe of 1909," were "coming directly to Calgary from the Court of the Shah of Persia" in Teheran.[57]

Over the years, both the Calgary and Edmonton Exhibitions continued to hire big name performers and celebrities. In 1916 and again in 1918, the Edmonton Exhibition brought in Katherine Stinson, the "premiere aviatrix of the world," whose 1918 flight was a dramatic event for the Edmonton audience. Once she was ready to take off, her "helpers stepped aside, and the crowd, which had been 'shooed' back by the police to make a clear track for the ascent, divided to the right and left like the waters of the Red Sea before the passage of the Israelites of old." The plane took off and "soared, bird-like upwards into space." Stinson ascended to about one thousand feet and "glided hither and thither and performed various evolutions" for about ten minutes.[58] Such events were immensely popular: parachutists leaping from balloons, aviation stunt flyers, and high wire and diving acts—all were stock items at many Alberta fairs from the turn of the century. At the Red Deer fair in 1919, Lieutenant George Gorman of May Aeroplanes Ltd. from Edmonton performed stunts—one of which was to dive at the grandstand "head on but a timely shift always cleared it." Gorman also gave private rides in his plane.[59] In 1921, the Edmonton Exhibition featured a high wire act as well as the "Diving Ringems," a star attraction in which a man dove off a 118-foot high platform into a tank of water.[60] Some critics, however, thought such stunts were perverse. Why, it was asked in 1908, should anyone take pleasure in watching a "dare devil feat" in which a man could be "crushed out of resemblance to all human form?" Especially horrible were "these senseless balloon ascensions" in which the crowd watched "with bated breath to see whether the parachute leaves the balloon and opens alright." And as soon as it did, "all interest seems to cease." There was nothing instructive or progressive about such entertainment.[61] Whatever unpalatable truths they forced upon critical observers, the crowds loved them.

Besides daredevil stunts, the grandstand shows at the larger fairs included vaudeville-type productions with music, dancing, trained animal acts, and comedians. Indeed, these productions proved to be the most enduring form of vaudeville in the province, still popular by World War II. They were often mounted by travelling shows working the Canadian and American fair circuits. In 1915 and 1916, all of the larger western fairs cooperated and engaged the same programmes in order to lessen transportation costs and "to obtain a better line of attractions."[62] The 1916 grandstand show put on by the Ethel Robinson Amusement Corporation of Chicago featured four trained elephants as well as gymnastics, juggling, and tumbling acts.[63] In 1930 Circuit 2 of the Western Fairs hired Conklin and Garrett to provide both the midway and the grandstand show for all of its fairs. The circuit preferred the Merrill Troupe of Jeffersonville, Indiana, but because the Merrill Troupe used trucks and cars to transport their equipment, it was "too risky to depend upon them in case of wet weather and the long jumps between the fairs." Conklin travelled by rail and charged $500 per fair, a considerably lower rate than the $675 charged by the Merrill Troupe. Conklin provided a one-ring circus consisting of two horse acts, a bucking mule, a pony drill, and a wire act, plus a clown, and "Pete Sodderburg in the Dive of Death."[64] Most of these shows ended with fireworks displays.

Local acts, especially beauty contests and musical performances, were part of many grandstand shows at the larger fairs between the wars. Many smaller fairs, and some larger ones as well, put together their entire grandstand show from local or regional talent. At the Lacombe fair in 1921, the grandstand show consisted simply of a baseball game, running events, and basketball.[65] When they used local talent, the larger fairs usually put together a more comprehensive programme. The Glovanile Entertainers from the Alberta Conservatory of Music in Lethbridge put on the 1924 grandstand show at the Red Deer fair and presented choral works, six little girls in a dance routine and "little Gwendolyn Smith of Calgary, with her clever costume dancing."[66] In another common grandstand feature during the first twenty years of the century, the local fire brigade demonstrated its tasks against the clock: the men hitched up the horses, raced around the track, and readied their equipment.[67]

some even spent a portion of each summer travelling around the province. Stanford Espedal, the physical education teacher at the Olds Agricultural School, trained some of his pupils to perform "an acrobatic act." They had "worked on C class fairs, theatres, beaches, the Edmonton Arena and as far as Los Angeles," and they hoped to work the B class circuit in Alberta in 1930.[68] In 1914, the Edmonton Exhibition Association utilized a folk dance show "prepared by the school children of the city" that "demonstrated the efficiency and crowd drawing force of home talent."[69] During World War I, military recruits presented drills and parades to entertain the crowd, engender patriotism, and boost recruitment. The Edmonton Exhibition still used local performers in 1946, when it sponsored the Edmonton Schoolboy's Band, which played on downtown streets in the mornings and on the exhibition grounds at special times.[70]

Native Indians took part in the Calgary Stampede parade in 1912. (GAI NA-4035-96)

Native Indians attracted attention at many fairs. At Calgary and Medicine Hat, officials encouraged exhibits of Indian arts and crafts, but most fair boards were more interested in creating a "wild west" ambience. Indians participated in the parades and put on dances at the fair grounds, and most boards gave free admission to Indians dressed in traditional clothing.[71] By about 1908, however, the Department of Indian Affairs actively opposed such participation, not because the Indians were being treated as curiosities to increase attendance, but because these events hindered the Europeanization of Indians by freeing them from the restrictions and control of reserve life for a few days. Moreover, the Indians were being encouraged to practice their traditional dances, songs, and rituals. There was, however, considerable support for such events from fair boards, the public, and even some missionaries like the Reverend Mr. John McDougall. Although it had no bearing on the final decision, the Indians also had no objections. In 1914, a compromise left the question of Indian participation to the discretion of local Indian agents. This meant that the issue was not resolved, but, generally, Indian performances and participation at fairs continued to be prominent.[72] In 1924 at Red Deer, the Indians "added a lot of colour and life" to the fair and put on a "pow-wow" in front of the grandstand.[73]

There is no doubt that the entertainment features attracted crowds, but so did the ambience of the fair with its glitter, noise, lights, and opportunities to eat hot dogs, ice cream, and candy. Food was an attraction in its own right, offered through concessions run mainly by local church groups and fraternal organizations. Sometimes, no outside concessions were allowed: volunteers manned the booths and directed all profits to the fair board.[74] In other cases, the right to operate a concession was sold to an individual. In 1949, the Edmonton Exhibition Association did both: it ran its own concessions while also allowing others on the grounds, all of which charged double the "city prices."[75] Food was always plentiful, and even at the small fairs people could buy hot dogs, ice cream, candy, soft drinks, popcorn, corn on the cob, baked beans, and citrus punch. Hot dogs and ice cream were greatly in demand. One individual who applied for a concession at the 1925 Crossfield fair argued that he needed the exclusive right to sell hot dogs because they were profitable: "everyone looks forward to seeing them on the Fair grounds."[76] At fairs with a midway, the midway operator also provided food, but by the late 1940s the public apparently no longer found this service appealing, although there is no evidence why this change took place or how it was met.[77]

Various sports events were also regular features at Alberta fairs. Some fairs, especially the small ones, presented sports as the main entertainment attraction. The first fair in Benalto in 1918 was dominated by horse races, baseball games, and various foot races.[78] Similarly, the 1910 Camrose fair presented silver cup trophies to the winners of baseball games, horse races, and a five and ten-mile foot race. Although the fair was advertised as a Sports Day and Agricultural Fair, the sports events had the upper hand.[79] The larger fairs also featured sports, more prominently in their early years. At the first Calgary fair in 1885, sports, horse races, and polo were the main attractions because it was difficult and expensive to find good grandstand acts for Calgary alone.[80] At the 1894 Calgary Fair, bicycle races drew a big crowd and competitors came from Edmonton, Medicine Hat, Lethbridge, Macleod, and Calgary.[81] Sports continued to be popular even after other attractions became available, and, of these, horse racing proved to be the greatest obsession.

Horse racing was tremendously popular from the beginning of European settlement in Alberta. During the 1880s, both impromptu and organized racing were taken very seriously. Timing was sometimes a contentious matter: a debate at the July 1883 races in Edmonton was stilled by the appointment as timekeeper of Mr. Huxley, who was "possessed of a stop watch."[82] The early races always presented the opportunity for gambling, in some cases for considerable amounts. More than three hundred dollars changed hands at a horse race held on the Big Lake Road in Edmonton in 1881.[83] The continued popularity of racing was shown by the organization of horse races by special groups, usually called turf associations.[84] The Claresholm Turf Association was organizing fall race meets by 1907, making the arrangements for the meet, setting the purses, and enforcing the rules. Such meets usually featured additional sports and an evening dance.[85] Horse racing was, however, hardly the monopoly of turf associations for it continued to be popular at fairs and other community events. It held a prominent place at the New Norway Sports Day in 1910 and, along with rodeo events, constituted the main attraction at the UFA picnic at Marquis Municipal Park in 1928. A common race featuring Indian riders was so popular before World War I that the grandstand at the Calgary Exhibition "literally goes crazy."[86] Indeed, horse races overshadowed all other events at many fairs, and in 1908 the Alberta superintendent of fairs observed that horse races were so popular that

> there is usually a large crowd around the show ring until such time as the racing starts, but at the sound of the bell everyone disappears excepting the exhibitor and the judge. We have even seen cases where the exhibitor was attending the horse race when he should have been showing some of his animals.[87]

Horse races at Medicine Hat, circa 1912. (GAI NA-4061-46)

This appeal of horse racing was never challenged, even by the machine. Automobile and motorcycle races became popular during and after World War I, but they were novelties that initially created great excitement simply because most people "had never witnessed events by racing cars and had no idea of the power of these machines or the daring of their drivers."[88] While such events became relatively widespread for a time, they never replaced horse racing in popularity. In Edmonton and Calgary, as well as in some of the larger towns in the province, the local exhibition association handled horse races either directly or through an affiliated jockey club. Those held by the Edmonton Exhibition Association were the most famous in the province. By 1914, their spring race meet was "the curtain raiser for the Western Fair Circuit." Edmonton had a good track, good facilities and a reputation for "clean racing."[89] The exhibition association guarded against corruption and organized betting on a pari-mutuel system to eliminate bookmakers, regarded as the greatest source of corruption. In pari-mutuel betting, a small percentage of all bets was taken for administration, and the balance was divided proportionately among the bettors according to their wagers.[90] Patrons liked the system because they stood a better chance at winning with it than with the bookies. In 1908 at Red Deer, the racing was controlled by the bookmakers and although "some leading citizens did not do so badly," the "average citizen was not treated with the same consideration." Calgary used pari-mutuel betting for the first time in 1911, and in 1913 Edmonton purchased pari-mutuel machines and rented them to other fairs on the same circuit: at Calgary, Brandon, Regina, Saskatoon, Yorkton, and Swift Current.[91] The Prairie Thoroughbred Breeders and Racing Association rules applied to the spring races and governed betting and entry requirements.[92]

Although gambling was considered to be a vice, betting on horses escaped much of the opprobrium. There seems never to have been any attempt in Alberta to eliminate betting on horses; it was so deeply entrenched in all classes of society that the only feasible way to deal with it was to ensure that it was clean.[93] Control benefitted the provincial government and the race organizers in turn through taxation of the betting pool. In the early years of pari-mutuel betting the exhibition associations made little profit from racing. In 1927, the province levied a new tax of 5 percent on the bets, and gained a fair revenue. It paid the race organizers 2.5 percent of the tax collected for administration, which effectively left the organizers with no profit.[94] When the province stopped paying grants to fairs in 1932, however, the quid pro quo was that the Edmonton and Calgary Exhibition Associations could take 50 percent of the provincial tax in lieu of the fair grants. This improved the associations' profits somewhat, but not by much until the end of the 1930s.[95]

The stakes were large, nevertheless, and amounted to a total of almost $500,000 at both Calgary and Edmonton in 1936. The pari-mutuel pools increased dramatically in subsequent years. The total of the Edmonton and Calgary pools was $516,523 in 1940, it increased to $1,311,319 in 1944, and by 1949 it had reached almost $2.5 million.[96] Betting was especially popular at the Edmonton Exhibition where the $125,000 bet in a single day in 1946 "broke all Western records outside Winnipeg."[97] Increased betting gave both the associations and the province substantial revenue by the late 1930s. In 1938, the provincial tax to be shared was $22,712, but by 1946 it had grown to almost $100,000. Of course, this did not result in pure profit for the associations since they paid for veterinary tests, track and stable maintenance, and other expenses such as salaries.[98] This increased betting also helped to improve horse breeding. Larger purse sizes encouraged horse owners to invest in better breeding stock. In 1931, of the 176 western Canadian thoroughbreds raced in western Canada, 129 were from Alberta, referred to as "the Kentucky of Canada."[99] The purses were often large: $40,000 was offered in 1926 at the Calgary Spring race.[100] Although the purses at both Edmonton and Calgary declined during the 1930s, they increased in the 1940s to almost $104,000 at Edmonton and Calgary in 1946.[101]

The enduring public appeal of events involving horses extended to rodeos. Unlike fairs, rodeos did not pretend to be educational; they existed solely for entertainment and competition for prizes. At the turn of the century, small rodeos took place in the south and central-east parts of the province. By the mid-1920s, the Calgary Stampede had become an annual event and rodeos appeared in the Peace River country and other mixed farming areas of Alberta. Although rodeos grew out of "simple contests among working men who had few other amusements," their popularity in Alberta developed long after the ranching era had ended. They were an exercise in a nostalgia[102] of little relevance to the history of most Albertans. In 1884, the *Bulletin* ran an article on the exotic and little known creature, the cowboy, "about whose exploits we hear so much in the United States papers."[103] In large part, interest in rodeos was stimulated in Alberta by touring Wild West Shows like the famous Miller Brothers Wild West Show that brought riding and roping acts and dramatizations of the "Old West" to Calgary in 1908. A similar show, the Oklahoma Wild West Show, visited Red Deer in 1913 and shows of this sort continued to be popular as late as the 1930s.[104]

Although the town of Raymond claims to have held Canada's first official rodeo on its main street in 1902,[105] the Calgary fair of 1894 featured bucking horse and steer roping events among its attractions. The rodeo events were among the biggest drawing cards and the *Edmonton Bulletin* reporter found them exciting:

To those unaccustomed to ranch life it was a thrilling sight to see wild, unbroken horses lassoed, bridled, saddled and ridden by these fearless men. The efforts of the broncos to rid themselves of their unwanted burden were vigorous and determined, though utterly unavailing. Not a rider was bucked off, though one or two had to jump off, their mounts going backward. To the uninitiated, they seemed all equally good.

In the steer roping contest, also known as steer wrestling, the cowboy threw and tied up a steer. Winners were declared on the basis of speed, but the cowboy was disqualified if his steer broke loose after being down for less than five minutes. The inventor of this sport in Canada was said to be John Ware, who competed in the 1894 Calgary Fair. Ware, the "coloured rancher of High River," threw and roped his steer in the "marvelous time of 54 seconds," but the steer broke loose in two minutes and "the $100 prize fell from this veteran's grasp."[106]

Bronc rider Walter Nelson on Gray Eagle, Carmangay Stampede, 1919. (GAI NA-2080-5)

By World War I, rodeo events were integrated with a number of community functions. The 1910 New Norway Community Picnic and Sports Day featured bucking horse contests and a "cowboy race,"[107] and the Millarville races in 1908 also featured a "cowboy, or stake race as it is now called." In this race, "two barrels were set up on the track and the field in a body made the figure 8 around them—a feat which called for clever manoeuvering on the part of horse and rider."[108] Rodeos and rodeo events retained an element of novelty for a number of years. At the first "real stampede" organized in Medicine Hat in 1917, the facilities were rudimentary: "at that time there were open benches to sit on like a ball park. You could park your cars around the infield outside the barbwire fence."[109] Similarly, at the first rodeo display in Edmonton, held in 1920 as the entertainment feature of the spring livestock show, two vaudeville stars from Calgary, Guy Weadick and his wife, Flores La Due, gave a demonstration of rodeo riding and roping.[110] Rodeo events became more common in the following years and, while still concentrated in the south of the province, were well known everywhere by the 1940s. In 1947, twenty-two rodeos took place in Alberta, many drawing large crowds and providing varied programmes.[111] Many were probably inspired by the Calgary Stampede, one of the major competitive rodeo events in the world.

The Battle River Stampede, near Hardisty, in the second decade of the century. (GAI NA-22-84-16)

The first version of the Calgary Stampede was held in 1912. It was sponsored by the "Big Four"—Pat Burns, George Lane, A.E. Cross, and the Honourable Archie McLean—who put up one hundred thousand dollars "to guarantee its success." Because the event also served to assert the ambition of the southern Alberta ranching elite to perpetuate its vision of a British Canadian society in Alberta, the stampede was a celebration of the ranching frontier and its British and Canadian traditions.[112] Guy Weadick, formerly with the Miller Brothers Wild West Show (an American operation), was appointed manager.[113] The 1912 Calgary Stampede lost money because the sponsors brought most of the horses and stock from the United States and bore the general expenses of contestants. Nevertheless, in every other respect, it was a great event, "the most spectacular and colorful Stampede, with more of the feeling of the Old West than any held subsequently."[114] Prizes for steer roping, races, riding bucking horses, fancy roping, riding competitions and others totalled an unprecedented twenty thousand dollars, and served to draw contestants from a great distance.[115] Many participants were American "working" cowboys, but a number of cowgirls competed in the steer roping contest, fancy roping, and in "girls bucking contests, but on picked horses and with tied stirrups." Hundreds of Indians were recruited (including about a hundred imported from the United States) to play a part in the events and were paid with "all the free meat they could eat, and a ration of tea, sugar and flour." Groups of "Cossacks" and Mexican rancheros joined the Cowboy Band of Pendleton, Ohio, who "played their instruments [while] mounted on horseback."[116]

According to Clem Gardner, who participated in this first stampede, the rules were "more severe" in 1912 than later. In bucking contests, for example, the rider stayed on until the horse stopped bucking. Later, the rule was amended so that the rider had to stay on for only nine seconds. The original rule was especially difficult to meet in 1912 because Cyclone, the fiercest bucking horse in the world, was brought up from Arizona for the competition. He "had to be thrown down and saddled on the ground, for if he were saddled standing up he would throw himself backwards." The rider therefore had to "stand over the animal with his feet in the stirrups and then they would let the horse up." Cyclone had a trick of "rearing, giving the impression that he was going right over, then coming down." Gardner rode this fearsome animal for thirty seconds before being thrown. Tom Three Persons from the Blood Reserve stayed on Cyclone and won the World's Bucking Horse Championship and the one thousand dollar purse.[117]

The 1912 stampede was not immediately repeated because it was not profitable and the war intervened. A second stampede held in 1919 was the main feature in the celebration of the end of war. Only after a stampede was featured as part of the exhibition in 1923 did it become an annual event. The exhibition had lost money from 1920 to 1922, and when the government announced that the grant for

1923 would be reduced from $10,000 to $8,000, the fair directors real-ized that the fair had to bring in more people or else be abandoned. The 1912 and 1919 stampede precedents were important, and the directors argued that if they "could add a really outstanding stam-pede as an exhibition attraction, we could recoup our losses and build up an institution which would be as important in building up Alberta as the Canadian National Exhibition is in Eastern Cana-da." With this objective, the first stampede "tried" in 1923 was splen-didly successful and attendance increased dramatically. In 1922, the Calgary Exhibition had attracted about 97,000 people; in 1923, the first year of the stampede, it drew nearly 138,000 and in following years attendance increased even more.[118] At the same time, the stampede was transformed into the image of American rodeo. The white stetson was appropriated from Hollywood cowboy movies as a symbol of Calgary, and "the cowtown mythology was capital-ized on and perpetuated for commercial advantage" by civic lead-ers. This ethos "only reinforced the American stereotype and the cultural assimilation that the original ranching community so feared." The success of the stampede thus contained not a little irony.[119]

Among other contributing factors, the consistently high quality of the programmes and an emphasis on advertising were especially important in the success of the stampede. Over the years, the programmes generally included the same range of events that had been staged in 1912, but in greater number and variety. By 1949, the stampede featured chuck wagon races, bucking horses (both sad-dled and bareback), calf roping, bull and steer riding, wild horse races, wild cow milking, steer decorating, trick riding, and trained horse and cattle acts. Of these events, the highly popular chuck wagon race was "essentially a Calgary development." In this race, an "outfit" consisted of a wagon pulled by four strong horses flanked by four outriders. Four outfits competed in each heat, plac-ing thirty-two horses on the track at one time.

> At the start of a heat the wagons are lined up in the infield racing away from the grandstand. At the sound of the starting horn, the stoves, tent poles and flaps are thrown into the wagons by the out-riders, and wagons and riders cut a figure 8 around the barrels, hit the track and the race is on. Travelling from start around the half-mile track the time varies from 1:10 to 1:15 . . .

In 1949, the purse for the chuck wagon event was seventy-five hundred dollars, the largest purse in Canada except for the King's Plate of horse racing.[120] While the size of the prizes drew contestants to Calgary, the fact that the stampede was a genuine contest and not just a show was of equal importance. Winning a trophy at the stampede was an honour in its own right; beginning in 1939, bronze trophies were made by the "cowboy artist Charles Beil of Banff" and, independent of their monetary value, were "probably the most sought after trophies offered in rodeo competitions." The management of the stampede ensured that the best judges were hired for the events and that excellent quality stock and horses were provided. As a result, by the late 1940s the Calgary Stampede was ranked as one of the three great sporting events in North America.[121]

Roasting buffalo for the barbecue at the 1923 Calgary Stampede. (GAI NA-3985-16)

The stampede programme did not, however, include only rodeo events. In addition to the exhibition midway, grandstand show, and exhibits, it featured a street parade, livestock exhibits, and other special events. In 1923, the public was invited to eat roasted buffalo cooked over a deep pit on the grounds. Street events included "cowboy" music, decorated store fronts, flapjack breakfasts, and even a horse branding on Ninth Avenue. The parades soon became famous for their size, quality, and varied content. In 1924, spectators at the parade were entranced to see Slim Moorehouse driving a thirty-two horse team hauling eight double-box wagons of wheat.

Slim Moorehouse drove a thirty-six horse team at the 1925 Calgary Stampede parade. (GAI NA-2367-1)

In 1925, the same feature was presented again—this time with a thirty-six horse team of percherons. It was a great hit and crowds followed Slim around the city to watch how easily he could handle such a team. By 1945, between 50,000 and 60,000 people watched the parade, and the morning of the parade came to be characterized by a mad scramble for good spots along the route. Both the parade and the street activities took over the downtown during the stampede, and in 1927 "visitors from a distance" were "amazed . . . that in this age, automobiles can be barred from the main business streets of one of Western Canada's biggest cities" in favour of "Indians, cowboys, [and] chuck wagons."[122]

Stampede personalities and their horses pose for the camera in front of the Hotel Alexander during the 1928 Calgary Stampede. (GAI NA-2365-8)

In the livestock exhibits, the stampede also showed the imagination that turned the tradition bound livestock parade into a unique spectacle. The livestock parade took place in the morning near the end of the stampede when

> some fifteen or sixteen thousand girls and boys, guests of the directors, and their parents arrive between 9 and 10 o'clock in the morning, have a sing-song, enjoy a couple of vaudeville acts, see hundreds of horses and cattle parade over the platform, and participate in a drawing for ponies, dogs and other prizes. As the livestock pass over the platform, the name of the breed, what the breed is for, and the prize the animal has won, is announced over the loud-speaker as an educational feature. This program has been a phenomenal success. . .[123]

The imagination of the stampede's management extended beyond its programmes to its publicity. Guy Weadick, who served as stampede manager until the early 1930s, was an indefatigable promoter, inviting prominent public figures to the event, promoting it through his vaudeville show and even persuading Hoot Gibson, the American Western movie star, to use the stampede as the backdrop for one of his films, called, not surprisingly, *The Calgary Stampede*.[124] From the beginning, more traditional advertising and promotion were also considered essential to the success of the stampede, justifying an expenditure of upwards of seventeen thousand dollars per year by 1927. Some of the promotional literature was reputed to be "the finest literature published by any fair on this continent," using good quality printing and photographs and imaginative and effective layout. Advertising of this quality was based on the recognition that Calgary was situated "in a sparsely settled district." In addition to drawing as many local people as possible, the stampede attracted visitors from further afield through the promotion of the stampede, Banff, and the mountains as a complete vacation package.[125]

The Alberta Social Credit League float took part in the 1935 Calgary Stampede parade. (GAI NA-2590-1)

By the early 1940s, the Calgary Exhibition and Stampede was by far the most successful fair in Alberta, if not the whole of prairie Canada. It presented an effective mix of entertainment and agricultural events within a credible context. It integrated the myth of the wild west into Calgary's self-image to the point that the stampede became a believable part of the city's history. Whether this was a wholly legitimate view of Calgary's past became irrelevant. The exhibition and stampede had its traditional serious components, providing an opportunity for the competitive exhibition of livestock, produce and "cowboy" skills, but their attractive integration with the entertainment of the rodeo produced an effective, sometimes eclectic, annual leisure event of broad appeal.

This recipe for success provides a significant measure of the place of leisure in Alberta. There was probably not a single fair in the province that had ever been viewed by the majority of Albertans as an occasion primarily concerned with education. As early as 1883, the *Edmonton Bulletin* suggested that "the most important, although not often the most prominent business of an agricultural fair is educational."[126] While the tension between entertainment and education never disappeared, successful fairs channelled the popular desire for entertainment in support of agricultural objectives. Success often depended on wealth and skill in attracting sufficiently appealing entertainment so that attendance would make the fair economically feasible. The scope of the organizing association also played a part: agricultural societies in Alberta were concerned almost wholly with fairs, whereas in Saskatchewan and Manitoba they had a wider concern with extension work.[127] Indeed, it might be suggested that this single-purpose quality of many Alberta agricultural societies contributed to their failure, while the enduring fairs, such as those at Calgary and Edmonton, maintained success by combining service to agriculture with public entertainment.

This became even more crucial in the interwar years because of changes in transportation. The automobile helped to destroy some of the small rural fairs that could not afford expensive entertainment packages to draw people or to distinguish them from sports days, picnics, and other community events. If it was simply a sports day with a few livestock and other agricultural exhibits thrown in as an afterthought, the fair had neither distinctiveness nor integrity to sustain it. Increased mobility gave people the independence to choose from a greater range of events. As well, the decline of the rural fair reflected the absence of a distinctive, self-sustaining rural tradition in Alberta. Rural people demonstrated the same preferences in leisure as urban people: because of modern systems of communication and transportation, they increasingly responded to the same stimuli with the same leisure patterns.

11. Hanging Around: Bars, Poolrooms, and Cafés

The steady commercialization of Alberta leisure during the twentieth century showed in stage, radio, movies, sports, and even the country fair, but nowhere was it so widely and consistently evident as in three establishments: the bar, the poolroom, and the café. These facilities not only raised social issues that often threw the value of leisure into question, they also focussed class divisions within the dominant culture and in society in general as did no other leisure activity. At one time or another, all of them achieved a similar notoriety among certain social critics who saw them as individual elements in a web of evil linked together by liquor and gambling. Slot machines also received related attention for a time, especially in association with cafés.

The interior of a southern Alberta bar, circa 1900. (GAI NA-2890-21)

Plainly, liquor played a prominent and often important part in leisure during the period under study. Its use cut across all class and ethnic lines in the society, and drinking was common among men at sports days, fairs, rodeos, dances, and picnics. Most legion and golf clubs in the province were licensed to sell beer and there were bars (and later, beer parlours) throughout the province. Of course, the place of liquor in community life did not go unchallenged; between 1890 and 1945, the liquor question, with particular emphasis upon the bar, was the subject of some of the most important and bitter political and social debate in the province. In part, this debate grew from a recognition of the social costs and problems caused by liquor, but it also stemmed from assumptions within the dominant culture about the role of environment in forming human character and about the source of rightful authority to shape the society.

Until 1892, liquor was controlled in the Northwest Territories through a permit system brought in by a Territorial order-in-council in 1873. Under this system, possession of liquor was allowed only to the holder of a permit. This legislation was aimed primarily at Indians, but Europeans were subject to it as well. The police, often unwillingly, attempted to enforce the law,[1] in part through arbitrary arrests, seizures, and searches. Even the use of liquor obtained by permit was restricted, and there was widespread resentment of the law. Administratively, the whole system was chaotic: bars were allowed to operate because it was permissible to deposit a bottle of liquor at a bar, along with the permit, and have a drink when convenient. Since the permits were not numbered or named, they in effect attached to the bottle, which could be conveniently refilled with cheaper bootleg whiskey. In 1892, abolition of the permit system led to an immediate upswing in the number of saloons. By 1900, every settlement had at least one saloon and public drunkenness was common; indeed, drinking sometimes seemed to be the only entertainment enjoyed by a large transient young male population.

While the enforcement of the permit system had been a headache for the police, in one assessment it was "probably favoured by the majority of the homesteaders from Ontario and by many of the Protestant majorities of the urban centres."[2] When the permit system was abolished, opposition within the dominant culture to liquor persisted since the idealized Ontario model meant the imposition of sobriety and restraint. The *Fort Macleod Gazette* pressed the case in 1892 for controlling drunkenness and wild behaviour in order to establish a decorous and polite society of which one need not be ashamed when entertaining visitors.[3] There was a religious bias in the prohibition mentality as well, for the attitude that liquor was evil was deeply rooted in Ontario and North American Protestantism. While Britain and other European countries had strong temperance movements, the enthusiasm for prohibition was peculiarly North American, led in Canada by Ontario Protestants, especially Methodists, Baptists, and Presbyterians. The important Roman Catholic and Anglican prohibitionists (as opposed to advocates of temperance) were exceptional, not typical.[4] Indirectly, the denominational division touched on the ethnic dimension of the debate about liquor. For many prohibitionists and temperance leaders, the bar stood for a wider problem associated with the increasing number of new Canadians who were said to lack "moralistic attitudes to alcohol." Thus, the debate about liquor overlapped with the one about assimilation of non-Anglo-Saxon immigrants.[5] As late as 1928, the Women's Christian Temperance Union (WCTU) articulated as its goal the "making of British subjects out of 257,000 people speaking 70 languages in Alberta. . .To implant respect for law, the spirit of fair play, religious tolerance. . .temperance. . .a stable government etc."[6] The religious and ethnic dimension was further reinforced by the temperance and prohibitionist forces' belief that liquor was one of the "disintegrating" forces in life which lowered self-control and led to crime, violence, and social misery. Drinking, of course, also interfered with work. Obviously, drinking on the job led to inefficiency, but the after effects of leisure time drinking too resulted in poor work habits.

The anti-liquor forces expressed different shades of opinion ranging from the acceptance of moderate drinking to complete prohibition. A steady movement towards the prohibition extreme received even greater support during World War I. Prohibitionists were able to capitalize on the tribal feelings the war engendered in English Canadians to elevate the arguments about liquor into matters of British-Canadian patriotism, social purification, and national efficiency. The military rhetoric favoured by prohibitionists became more extreme and pointed and their demands finally led to a referendum in Alberta in 1915, when a majority of Alberta voters followed the prairie pattern and endorsed prohibition. Pockets of dissent could be found in coal mining communities, in the northern part of the province, and among Franco-Albertans, but many Central Europeans, who traditionally opposed prohibition, apparently voted "dry" to prove their loyalty. The province enacted prohibition the next year, and Alberta remained officially "dry" until 1923.[7]

As Bob Edwards put it, prohibition "at any rate. . .made Alberta safe for hypocrisy."[8] People made liquor at home, bootlegging was common, and poolrooms and cafés were often suspected of being distribution points. The "temperance beer" (beer with 2 percent alcohol) that could legally be sold in Alberta was often mixed with stronger beer. Some of the liquor produced legally for "vendor use" as medicine and for export found its way onto the local market instead.[9] Because the province could not constitutionally restrict interprovincial trade, Albertans could and did import liquor by mail or railway express from other provinces like British Columbia. This was limited in 1918 by a federal order-in-council prohibiting the importation of liquor into any province that was "dry" so as to channel raw materials into useful war-related production and to reward the prohibition forces for supporting the "Unionist" government in the election of 1917.[10] When the war was over, however, importation was once again legalized.

The beer parlour in the Assiniboia Hotel, Medicine Hat, in the late 1920s. (GAI NA-2479-9)

However it came onto the market, liquor was easily available. By the beginning of prohibition in 1916, public taste had turned to beer, which replaced whiskey as the commonest drink in Alberta bars. Late in the nineteenth century, remembered one group of Alberta brewers, "we couldn't sell beer at all, everybody drank whiskey. It took. . .a long time to educate the people into drinking beer." Now, prohibition revived the appeal of whiskey, presumably because it was easier to bootleg and ship than beer, although in places "real" beer (more than 2 percent alcohol) was still commonly available.[11] Many people objected to the presence of any liquor. At Roselea, near Barrhead, one individual complained in 1922 that "we are annoyed by having so many drunken men, especially at dances."[12] At Pincher Creek in 1919, prohibition was "openly and brazenly violated." Not only were "blind pigs" flourishing,

> but drinking is done openly at public dances and unfortunately, men alone in this case are not the sole offenders. Many of those most guilty are women who are socially regarded as the "smart set." It has become so bad that self-respecting people will not attend these dances tho' they are given under the auspices of various clubs etc. . .Up to the present the local authorities have eyes but they see not as far as this matter is concerned.[13]

The fact that women were now drinking was a sign of the greatest change that took place during prohibition. Mixed drinking became more common and was often centred in the home. Despite his reputation, Calgary newspaperman Bob Edwards had been an advocate of prohibition, but he later became its opponent. Admitting his own drinking problem, Edwards observed in 1920 that "such drinking as we did was always amongst men. In twenty years residence in Calgary we have never had a drink in a private house, nor have we ever been to one of those drunken parties in the home that we hear so much about."[14] Prohibition was thus defiling and not strengthening the idealized home.

The UFA officially supported prohibition, and from 1913 until 1916 it was in the forefront of prohibition campaigns in Alberta.[15] After it formed the provincial government in 1921, however, it abandoned its prohibitionist allies and refused to aid them in the provincial prohibition referendum of 1923. Perhaps no government could stake its future on a single controversial issue,[16] but the UFA's withdrawal from the debate reflected the impact of powerful anti-prohibition forces. As a result of the 1923 vote, the government made the sale and distribution of liquor a government monopoly, but because the "local option" still permitted a community to ban liquor by vote, the debate over liquor control continued and was revived at the provincial level in 1930-31 following petitions to close "beer rooms."[17] The beer parlours survived, in part because, as one law enforcement officer argued, "if there are no beer rooms every little shanty in the villages will be a speakeasy."[18] Nevertheless, government control did not end the careers of bootleggers because for some people the distribution system implemented in 1924 was so cumbersome and remote as to differ little from prohibition. Any person who lived in an area without a vendor, and who did not want to drink in the beer parlour, had to send "fifty to one hundred miles for beer for his personal use" and had to pay the shipping charges. This was the situation for "people living in areas like Lac La Biche, Athabasca, Provost, Willingdon, Didsbury, Nanton, Vulcan and many other districts" where "the 'moonshine' menace" had become "very serious."[19]

Before 1916, the bar was a place of recreation for many men. Many bars were dirty and smelly, but they were the centre of many men's social life, especially in the small towns, because "there is no town society in the usual acceptance of the term. It is an extraordinary occasion" for a young man to be found "sitting in the parlour of a private home talking to the ladies. He is never asked." Such exclusivity was not so common in farm areas, but in towns the bars necessarily became "the social centre. . .preachers to the contrary." In contrast to poor housing conditions and few if any other recreational options, the bar was "bright and cheery and always on the spot."[20] In coal mining communities, the bar provided the same focus for leisure (often the only one in town) and a place of refuge and escape from the brutalities of working and living conditions.[21] Many early bars were located in hotels, where profits from the bar subsidized the hotel proper. During prohibition, this meant that hotel standards in the province dropped. At the end of prohibition, the bar reappeared as the "beer parlour," again serving the recreational needs of many people. All beer parlours were licensed by the government and all were situated in hotels, a number of which were owned by breweries.[22] Critics argued that the beer parlours increased recreational drinking, which in turn created public drunkenness and social and family problems. They also maintained that social drinking in beer rooms "caters to the treating system" which created drunkards because "one man buys the drinks for the crowd and probably they won't finish until they have all bought."[23]

The repeal of prohibition therefore did not mean that sentiment against drunkenness vanished or that the social problems caused by liquor disappeared. Intoxication in a public place was an offence under The Alberta Liquor Control Act and although statistics on incarceration (as opposed to conviction) under the provincial liquor control statute and the federal Inland Revenue Act (mainly for bootlegging) were officially reported only for the period from 1927 to 1930, in that period between 25 and 40 percent of all prisoners at the Fort Saskatchewan jail were committed under these two statutes. As late as 1954, 48 percent of the inmates at Fort Saskatchewan were serving sentences imposed under the provincial liquor control act, mainly for being drunk in a public place.[24] Such levels of incarceration attest to the continuing ability of the anti-liquor forces to shape the public response to liquor and drinking. James Gray has observed that the post-prohibition regulation of liquor was "based on the theory that what was mainly wrong with boozing was where it was done" and from this "grew the notion that the social evils attending excessive drinking would be overcome if drinking was confined to the home." In keeping with this attitude, liquor regulations to restrict drinking places were drawn up in great detail.[25] In part, however, this conclusion can be challenged: the prohibitionists saw the evil of the bar manifested in home and family deprivation and violence. The regulation of bars aimed not only to define the places for public drinking, but also to prevent their contamination from spreading to the home, family, and society in general by restraining the consumption and behaviour of beer parlour patrons. The hotel in Smith lost its license to sell beer in 1929 because it had allowed labourers from the road crew to become "intoxicated, in many instances. . .[causing absence] from their work for two and three days at a time." Such circumstances proved that the hotel was a "cheap, third rate, roadside saloon" and the government had "no intention of granting anyone a license to run a saloon to the detriment of road construction work which the people of this Province are paying for."[26] The government insisted that all beer parlours be places of quiet, "sober" drinking and in 1924 the supervisor of licenses ordered "observations" of all beer parlours in Edmonton. Most passed inspection and received the accolade, "everything very quiet and orderly." At the Selkirk Hotel beer parlour, "every seat. . .was occupied, as is usual just before closing time. . .There was no evidence of intoxication." The St. James Hotel was the roughest: "one man swore while I was there, but was checked by the waiter for same." This behaviour was not unexpected, however, since the patrons of the St. James were "foreigners" who were likely to be "fairly noisy."[27] All in all, the socializing proved to be very low key indeed, and the beer parlours seem to have had a rather funereal atmosphere.

The decision to go or not to go into a beer parlour was subject to powerful social forces. People concerned with respectability largely boycotted the beer parlours. Yet oddly, "reputable citizens" did not lose respectability by buying liquor illegally; they could preserve their dignity by having recourse to a bootlegger instead of going into a beer parlour.[28] Of course, if they had sufficient money for a membership, they could also drink at private clubs, such as the Ranchmen's Club in Calgary or the Chinook Club in Lethbridge, or at the private golf clubs in the province. Legion members could also drink at the Legion hall. A few others, like the Miner's Club in Lethbridge, also had beer licenses, but the province had little sympathy with working mens' clubs. As Premier Greenfield observed in 1923, if the "workingmen in other towns" organized clubs similar to the Lethbridge Miner's Club, "they might multiply indefinitely and there is the danger."[29] In any event, it was assumed that working men had the beer parlours to themselves; according to a 1934 report, "a certain class of people who would be good spenders . . . will not go into beer parlours." Both tourists and many local people found beer parlours "inconvenient or objectionable." Demands for tourist development were sometimes linked to demands for less stringent control of public places providing liquor so that tourists could drink without having to endure surroundings they disliked.[30]

As Jean Burnet found in her 1946 study, at Oyen the "division between the 'respectable' and the drinking groups in the community" was so important that it cut across local class lines. Although this did not create two "armed camps" in the community, "a considerable number of people look with disapproval upon those who indulge in drinking."[31] The question of women in beer parlours, however, brought the issue of respectability to the fore. Plainly, a woman who drank was not respectable (although she might have been "smart"), but a drunken woman was beyond the pale. The Alberta movie censors believed that films showing women in scenes of drunkenness should be banned or offending scenes eliminated. Nevertheless, women in Alberta were allowed to drink in beer parlours after 1924, although by 1943 some communities required separate rooms for men and women. Mixed drinking continued to be allowed in some places, and Banff and Cochrane supposedly became destinations for men and women from Calgary who wanted to drink in groups. Similarly, St. Albert became "notorious as a rendezvous for drinking parties from Edmonton." According to the Associated Temperance Forces, mixed drinking in these places in 1947 led to "the staging of wild orgies" and, more believably, to a great number of car accidents on the St. Albert Trail and the highway to Cochrane.[32] The implications of mixed drinking were frequent matters for concern. One woman from Mirror complained to Premier Aberhart (who was a teetotaller) that

> I know of one instance where my husband went in for a Beer and sat at a table by his self at once a lady picked up her Beer and moved to my husbands table without his invitation and this is often the same with other men. If she had been in a ladies part this couldent happen and if any husband went into ladies Beer Parlour his wife would have a direct complaint with him.[33]

For many, respectability seems to have been a powerful constraint preventing them from patronizing the beer parlours. Those who visited these establishments met a constraint of a different sort because hours of operation were inconvenient for many. The "rush time" was in the evening, and it was noted in 1934 that farmers, "who work late in the evenings," were unable to get to the beer parlours before closing time or else they arrived "a few minutes before closing time, and consequently are unable to enjoy their glass of beer, or the social contact with their friends, which, in many cases, is just as important as the beer."[34]

During World War II, as in World War I, liquor was subject to wartime controls to channel manufacturing into wartime needs. Liquor rationing began in 1943 and the prospect of future limited supplies led to huge line-ups at liquor stores and extraordinary increases in the prices of bootleg liquor. People who had never purchased liquor in their lives now bought it because they had a ration coupon for liquor, and coupons became the cause of innumerable scams and subterfuges.[35] Although the temperance and prohibition forces had hoped for a continuation of rigid controls after the war, rationing ended in 1946.[36]

The debate over liquor and the attempt to enforce Ontario-style Protestant respectability upon the society had implications well beyond the bar. Brothels also posed moral problems for the dominant culture, but prostitution did not receive the consistent attention of reformers that liquor did. Indeed, prostitution often became an issue specifically because it was associated with liquor.

In 1914, estimates of the number of brothels in Edmonton ranged as high as five hundred, and in 1912 at least one hundred brothels in the town were located in buildings owned by "eminently respectable citizens and corporations." Whatever the exact numbers, prostitutes were common in Alberta towns and cities, but the "periodic outbursts against prostitution" were only "temporary diversions from the great prohibition crusade." The official prudery of the age limited public talk about sex, and liquor touched, and damaged, more lives than did prostitution.[37] Poolrooms and cafés often raised as much public concern as did brothels, and the state regulated and inspected the former to ensure that they were not only clean, but orderly and free from drinking.

Poolrooms were found in almost every town and village in the province, although the 362 poolrooms and bowling alleys licensed in 1914 declined to 208 by 1931.[38] The great majority of these places were small, having five or fewer tables. Most had confectionery counters at the front, many had barber shops as well, and some added a single lane bowling alley along one side of the room. Early in the century, poolrooms had gained a reputation for wickedness that placed them on a par with bars. This seems to have arisen in the reform movements of the turn of the century, when pool and billiards were often played in bars.[39] The connection with liquor seems to have been the basis for concern about poolrooms, which intensified during prohibition because bootleggers worked the poolrooms and poolroom owners were commonly suspected of being (and many were) bootleggers. As well, the poolroom was a male institution that reformers, especially women, disliked as a place of male resistance to their ambitions for social purity. Moreover, the gambling associated with pool was thought to pauperize its victims and, at least in WCTU minds, to encourage its "companion evils" of "cigarette smoking and profanity." Others objected on the principles that gambling was "gain without merit" and "gain through another's loss."[40]

By 1916, the war and prohibition had intensified all of these tensions. Since poolrooms were often a focus for bootlegging, enforcement of prohibition brought with it increased surveillance of pool halls. In 1918, poolrooms were prohibited from selling soft drinks because they could be used to disguise liquor.[41] Poolrooms were useless for promoting the war effort, and as the provincial deputy attorney general observed in 1918, "very little more" of the general criticism of poolrooms would lead the province to ban them. This was "partly due to the fact that at the present every able bodied man is supposed to be at work in some useful occupation," not loitering in a poolroom.[42] But even during the war, the standard critique emphasized gambling. As the Reverend Mr. Brough of Red Deer observed in 1918:

> He had never saw [sic] a pool room run right [sic], and he had seen a good many of them. Most of the customers would not patronize the pool room unless they could gamble. It was like the theatre; if the theatre was confined to clean shows it would go out of business and the moving picture shows were not much better.

The Reverend Mr. Brough's solution was simple and authoritarian: "he believed in the destructive first, and then the constructive. Raze the evil to the ground, and then build something in its place."[43] At the same time, A.W. Coone, general secretary of the Alberta Social Services League, still flush with victory and optimism after the success of the prohibition campaign, labelled poolrooms as "far from helpful" gambling dens and "Blind Pigs." Unless they were cleaned up, "I can clearly see that there will soon be a public demand for their removal."[44]

Hopes for the abolition of poolrooms were premature, and the hysteria about them dropped off after the war. The prohibitionists had bigger battles to fight in their efforts to preserve prohibition. Even so, the government continued to watch poolrooms closely to ensure that they were not the location for gambling or bootlegging, but the suggestion that they be abolished was rarely repeated. In many small villages there was nothing other than the poolroom for amusement in the winter time, when the poolrooms did most of their business.[45] Provincial authorities rejected abolition in favour of regulation because poolrooms were a necessary evil. Although they had great potential for corruption, they nevertheless were the best available and among the few recreational facilities for men in many small towns. They were obviously better than bars, speakeasies and brothels. Observers in Drumheller recommended keeping open the poolroom that catered to miners to keep the men "out of worse" activities.[46] Until the "best citizens" began to show an interest in matters like poolrooms, "other than to talk about such places and wonder why they are so bad," suggested one critic in 1918, the poolrooms would never "improve." Indeed,

> If the day ever comes when our Churches and school rooms are

made attractive, so that men in their spare moments, especially strangers in Town, can come to these places and feel that the atmosphere is congenial, the pool room as of today will go out of business. But until those who are interested in helping men can bring about such a state of affairs I am afraid that all that can be done is to surround the pool room with as many safeguards as possible and do all in our power to make it a place which can be frequented by men and women alike, without any fear of contamination.[47]

The first Pool Room Act in Alberta was passed in 1912 and provided for licensing all poolrooms, controlling hours of operation, and regulating the age and behaviour of patrons. An applicant hoping to open a poolroom was screened to determine moral character and reputation. Applications for a license had to be endorsed by the relevant mayors or reeves and licenses were carefully distributed on the basis of population. If there was too much competition among poolrooms in a town, it was believed that the owner would not be able to make "a reasonable living" and would turn to bootlegging or gambling.[48] The Department of the Attorney General regularly inspected poolrooms and monitored the behaviour of patrons. The authorities could cancel a license if a proprietor allowed drunks into the poolroom or permitted swearing, vulgar language, and the telling of off-colour stories. Children under seventeen were strictly prohibited from entering a poolroom.[49] Before 1912, any age restrictions were imposed by local bylaws; in 1911 a Calgary bylaw prohibited children under sixteen from entering a poolroom unless accompanied by a parent or guardian. Local enforcement was often lax,[50] and this problem was recognized in the 1912 Pool Room Act. In 1918, to make public surveillance easier, every poolroom was required to install a glass partition to separate the pool tables from the confectionery counter and barber shop.[51] If the partition was not in place, children under the age of seventeen could not go to the barber or the confectionery counter since both were technically in the poolroom. Regular inspections led to fines for infractions of the Act or, in extreme or repeat cases, to the suspension of the license. Occasionally, patrons were also fined for swearing and telling off-colour stories in poolrooms.

The prevention of gambling was never far from the minds of those who criticized poolrooms and those who justified their regulation. This was evident not only in the nature of the regulations but also in the definition of acceptable games. Dice were outlawed in 1918[52] and another ruling stipulated that "baseball billiards"

The first pool hall in Big Valley, 1912. (GAI NA-1005-4)

could not be played in Alberta. The largest poolroom equipment supplier in the country, the Brunswick-Balke-Collendar Company, marketed this game and provided the game sheets and rules. It was played on an ordinary pool table but added six balls to the fifteen used for pool. There were twelve sheets for recording the scores, "each sheet having space for 15 players; these sheets are referred to in the game as an inning, and for each inning a player pays the sum of 10 cents to the proprietor." The winner won a prize valued at about five dollars, always consisting of merchandise and never cash. The deputy attorney general found baseball billiards offensive because it was not "in the public interest that games upon billiard tables should be made more alluring than they are by offering substantial prizes." He concluded that the game was a "great deal more objectionable than live pool," and the government would not "permit the playing of live pool where the game is managed and the stakes are handled by the Proprietor."[53]

The regulation of poolrooms was thus founded upon a critique of gambling, liquor, and profanity, all commonly connected to ethnic and class distinctions. These distinctions can be seen in pool-room licensing evidence. In southern Alberta, Chinese proprietors ran some poolrooms. In 1922, the Alberta Billiard Association petitioned the government to refuse further pool hall licenses to Chinese, arguing that they were unable to control noisy and violent patrons because Europeans had no respect for Chinese. Moreover, the rowdiness of Chinese poolrooms would spread to poolrooms everywhere. The province rejected this petition on the grounds that many Chinese "conduct businesses in a very proper manner and are quite capable."[54] Jews, on the other hand, were said not to be "proper" people to run a poolroom, and a Jew would have received a license to run a poolroom only after great difficulties.[55] In other cases, although religion or place of origin were not cause for outright rejection of a license, they were a cause for suspicion. Many poolrooms in southern Alberta were run by American immigrants, who were reportedly not "used to living up to the [Pool Room] Act." American applicants for poolroom licenses were therefore screened and watched especially carefully.[56]

Dalton Pool Hall, Hinton, 1912. (GAI NA-379-3)

Otherwise, licenses were granted to a broad spectrum of people. Almost all proprietors were male; only two women held poolroom licenses in 1918 and they apparently used male managers.[57] In some areas, poolrooms were operated primarily by non-Anglo-

358

Saxons. In east central Alberta, Ukrainians seemed to have had "an informal monopoly on the operation and ownership of billiard halls," which were often the first and only businesses owned by Ukrainians.[58] In 1918, about one-third of the poolrooms in Edmonton were licensed to people with non-Anglo-Saxon surnames, and just over 60 percent of the licenses in 1925 and 1927 were issued to people with identifiably non-Anglo-Saxon surnames. In Cal the proportion was smaller: about 25 percent in each year.[59] In all of these cases, inspectors carefully noted the ethnic origins of the owners and apparently made poolroom operators fully aware that their ethnicity counted in official assessments. Two Russian owners of a Calgary poolroom were perceived to be "very careful, perhaps moreso than an English speaking poolroom man."[60]

The patronage of poolrooms often followed ethnic lines as well, at least in urban areas with more poolrooms. In 1918, one poolroom in Calgary was described as "a place where a Russian can meet his fellow." One was Chinese, another was "Austrian," and still another was West Indian. Some poolrooms catered to particular classes: business and professional men and people of "the better class" patronized certain Calgary poolrooms.[61] Business men patronized one of Hanna's two poolrooms, and railway workers the other.[62] Indians were apparently common patrons, and in 1925 the federal Department of Indian Affairs requested that Indians be prohibited from going into poolrooms where they allegedly obtained liquor.[63] On the whole, poolrooms remained a male preserve during the period under review, although, according to one 1918 report, women played pool and bowled in the evenings at Warneck's poolroom in Barons.[64] Most small town and city poolrooms were, however, not considered respectable for women.

Once again, the notion of respectability was powerful in determining poolroom attendance, especially in small towns where there was usually only one poolroom and everyone in the town knew everyone else. As the deputy attorney general commented to an Edmonton lawyer in 1922, "persons like you and myself, especially in the small towns, go by on the other side and leave the Billiard Room to the more disreputable section of the community." Indeed, he felt that poolroom patronage identified fundamental class divisions because just as the "respectable members of the community" would be uncomfortable in a poolroom, so the poolroom class would be uncomfortable in the haunts of the "respectable" class. Nonetheless, he believed that poolrooms served a useful social function because "I presume that people of that class have to be provided for."[65] Thus, class, respectability, and, inevitably, ethnicity shaped the attitude of the state towards the regulation of poolrooms, and integral to these factors were views on liquor and gambling. At the same time, the agencies that were loudest in their condemnation of the poolroom, notably the churches, often insisted on maintaining a socially exclusive environment that would scarcely welcome everyone regardless of class or ethnic background.

Tearooms, cabarets, cafés, and restaurants provided a different commercial focus for leisure in Alberta. There were no official or formal distinctions among these facilities, although most people would have understood the differences among them. Tearooms served light lunches and high teas and seem to have been patronized largely by women. At cabarets people could dine and dance. Cafés and restaurants presented great variation, and although there was no definition of a restaurant as opposed to a café, the restaurant would often have been considered the top of the line, with better food and a nicer décor. Many restaurants were located in hotels; cafés, usually less formal eating places, were most often located independently from hotels. Both offered regular hours of operation, usually a fixed menu, and facilities where one sat down to eat. Because the distinctions between cafés and restaurants were so impressionistic, the two terms will be used interchangeably in this discussion.

The tearooms and cabarets were the least common. Although tearooms could be found in towns that catered to tourists and in large centres such as Edmonton, Calgary, and Lethbridge, they were not common throughout the province. While patronized by both men and women, the tearoom was largely a women's institution, in some cases a place to see and be seen. In Edmonton about 1907, the Tip Top roof garden tea house served ice cream sodas, tea, and "weeny-teeny cakes and scones." The Cosey Corner had the same type of menu.[66] Common relatives of the tea house were the ice cream bar and the candy shop. These were generally less restrictive in terms of age and gender than the tearooms and would have had a broader social appeal. Ice cream bars and candy shops existed in most towns and cities in the province, and most had counters with stools and perhaps a few tables and chairs.

By the end of World War I, "cabarets," at which one could eat, dance, and listen to music, were becoming popular in Calgary. Even with prohibition, some people nonetheless found these cabarets objectionable. It was the old problem—leisure made people unfit for work, and while dancing was harmless enough, too much was exhausting. The *Calgary Herald* editorialized that cabarets should be regulated,[67] but cabarets endured, although at some point in the early 1920s they came to be known by the more sedate term "supper dance." In 1926, some hotels and restaurants in Calgary were featuring a supper dance on Saturday night and one during midweek. As well, two restaurants in Calgary installed "special phonographs" so that their patrons could "enjoy an hour's dancing after the theatre or during the dinner hour." By 1928 such facilities were "enjoying tremendous popularity" in Calgary, following the trend in other "larger centres in Canada and the United States." Indeed, to meet the demand for such facilities, the Empress Grill in Calgary underwent extensive renovations to install a 1,200 square foot "rubber cushioned oak floor" for dancing, with tables around the floor in "cabaret style."[68] As supper dances became respectable, talk about regulation disappeared.

Of greater importance in terms of number and distribution were cafés and restaurants. Cafés acted as informal gathering spots during afternoons or evenings. Because they were not subject to early closing bylaws, they could be open in the evening. In 1930, the cafés in Cardston were "kept open on any night that a dance is held in town." These dances were "the only amusement that the young folk in this town have during the winter months," and because lunch was not served at the dances, the cafés stayed open so that people could snack and prolong the evening.[69] Because the Lord's Day legislation permitted restaurants to remain open on Sundays, Sunday afternoon outings for some townspeople often included a trip to the café.

All restaurants in the province were provincially licensed and an applicant for a license had to receive the preliminary approval of the local government. A license would not be issued to an individual who had been convicted in the previous twelve months of a charge under the federal opium and drug laws or under the gambling or liquor provisions of The Criminal Code. The conviction of a license holder under any of these provisions also resulted in the cancellation of his or her license. The level of concern over liquor and drugs was reflected in the related provisions of The Restaurant Act, which were far more extensive that those respecting sanitation.[70] Given the significant number of Chinese and non-Anglo-Saxons involved in the restaurant trade in the province, the reference to convictions for liquor and drug infractions was not fortuitous. Common racist and ethnocentric charges held that non-

Anglo-Saxons tended to abuse alcohol and that the Chinese were opium addicts and dealers. Like the campaign against liquor, the campaign against drugs, which began at the turn of the century in Canada, was undertaken on class and racial lines.[71] It appears from a partial survey of the licensing records, however, that no restaurant licenses in Alberta were cancelled during the interwar years because an owner had been convicted or even accused of using opium. In any event, a more typical slur against Chinese café proprietors, especially in small towns, concerned sexual immorality, bootlegging and gambling. In 1923, it was observed that in the "small towns you will find more opposition on the part of the people to license restaurants owing to the foreign people operating them,"[72] and Chinese restaurants were commonly characterized as "dives and places for the creation of immorality and drunkenness." Investigation of such charges very rarely turned up any supporting evidence. An Alberta Provincial Police investigation of such charges in Cardston concluded that, if there was any immorality in Cardston, "it surely does not take place in any of the restaurants." Indeed, it was the "lack of home training. . .where the fault should be found and not in the restaurants."[73]

It is difficult to determine the ethnic origin of restaurant owners from the licensing statistics because restaurant licenses were required not only by restaurants and cafés, but by snack bars, ice cream parlours, pop stands, and even by corner stores selling soft drinks that could be opened and consumed on the premises.[74] Nevertheless, it is clear that by the interwar years the Chinese were significant in the restaurant business in small towns in Alberta. Of the 5 eating spots in Trochu and Three Hills in 1926, 3 were operated by Chinese; and of the 11 in Magrath, Raymond, Stirling, and Spring Coulee, 6 were operated by Chinese or Japanese. In 1931, 11 of the 22 cafeterias, cafés, and tearooms in Lethbridge were owned by Chinese.[75] When overall statistics are considered for the province, however, the proportion of Chinese ownership appears to be considerably smaller. Of a total of 1,600 restaurant licenses granted in Alberta in 1925, slightly fewer than one-quarter were "held by persons whose names suggest they are either Chinese or Japanese."[76] Even when corner stores and similar facilities are accounted for, while the Chinese prove to have been a major force in the restaurant trade in Alberta, they seem to have been far from the monopoly that prairie myth contends.

Many eating spots in towns were associated with hotels, which had to have restaurants in order to have beer parlours, and many were open only at mealtime simply to satisfy the Alberta Liquor Control Board.[77] Many hotel keepers resented the enforced maintenance of a dining room, but as it was observed in 1929, "most people realize that if the dining rooms were closed, the place [sic] would just develop into a drinking place and not a real hotel." Some hotel dining rooms, especially in the larger towns, were "fairly well patronized, especially on Sundays and are being accepted as the place to go if one wants a real meal with good service."[78] The considerable number of commercial travellers who worked the Alberta towns in the interwar years provided eating facilities with a regular trade.[79] In 1939, of the 246 hotels located in places with populations of six hundred or fewer, 162 had dining rooms.[80]

The Public Lunch, Olds, a photograph taken in 1914 or 1915. (GAI NA-1926-1)

By the time of World War II, the restaurant business was changing, and the Alberta Hotel Association argued in 1940 that 95 percent of hotel restaurants operated at a loss because "the whole eating situation" had changed, and "people to-day are not patronizing hotel dining rooms. During the past five years competitive eating places have increased thirty-five percent. At many points there are from three to ten and twelve restaurants, coffee shops and cafes."[81] A 65 percent increase had taken place in the 1930s. In 1930, there were 483 businesses in the "restaurant group" in the census, and by 1941 this had increased to 733, of which 396 were "restaurants, cafeterias, and eating places," 14 were refreshment booths and stands, and 323 were "eating places with other merchandise."[82] Total sales for the whole group stood at about $10.5 million in 1941, $6.4 million of which was generated in Calgary, Lethbridge, Medicine Hat, Edmonton, and Red Deer. Those in small towns naturally generated less money: the four restaurants in Taber, for example, reported total sales of $54,000; the three in Stettler generated $37,000, and the four in Vegreville saw $53,000. Nonetheless, these gross sales were almost double those of 1930.[83]

The dining room of the T. Eaton store in Calgary, 1929. (GAI NA-3992-37)

Before 1922, many cafés had high booths with curtains across the open ends to ensure privacy. In 1922, the government made this illegal and stipulated that "booths must be constructed so that the interior thereof shall be distinctly visible from every part of the main room used by the public for restaurant purposes." This was intended to make cafés more open, like ice cream parlours.[84] It meant that the Queen Restaurant in Castor was in contravention of the law because its booths were 8 feet by 8 feet, were 6 feet high with a 3 foot wide door, and had a 2½ foot wide vertical panel on each side of the doorway. A small dining table and four chairs were squeezed into this space. Although the door was not curtained, the booth provided too much privacy and had to be cut down.[85]

The interior of the Shangrila Cafe, Edmonton, 1945. (PAA BL.876/2)

Redesign of cafés created much expense for owners and a great deal of ill feeling, but the law was enforced and only a few cafés were left with the old system by the end of the 1920s. In mid-1922, one Chinese-run café in Lethbridge continued to have "the booth with the curtains drawn"; much to the displeasure of the Retail Merchants Association of Canada, which complained that Chinese should be forced "to observe the law the same as the native born citizen."[86] In Ponoka where the regulations had not yet been implemented in 1927, the two cafés in town still had high booths, although no curtains. While there was no concern with drinking, the town officials argued to the province that if the booths were "cut down," it would "lessen the obscene language that is reported as going on at times." The reluctance of the province to get involved in this case made it clear that its chief concern was to eliminate drinking and bootlegging and provincial officials merely recommended that the town constable deal with the matter.[87]

The café in the Driard Hotel, Wetaskiwin, 1921. (PAA A.1582)

Eliminating privacy in restaurants was aimed at curtailing other practices as well: before 1914, prostitutes in Calgary had often solicited in restaurants, and it was apparently not unusual for waiters in city restaurants to be pimps.[88] Still, the most important aim of open area restaurants was to prevent gambling, bootlegging, and drinking. Anyone participating in any of these activities under the new arrangements could be seen and, presumably, evicted or reported to the police. The change seems to have worked, for as it was observed in 1930, although men "who may have a bottle in their pocket" would still take "a drink while in the restaurant," it was no longer a major problem.[89]

In the mid-1920s, many small cafés were sufficiently clean to pass inspection, although it appears that the standards of the inspectors were not always consistent. Some cafés were apparently very dirty, poorly designed and poorly run,[90] but far more were reported to be clean and to provide acceptable food.[91] By the early 1930s, the old style of café, with its closed booths, was long forgotten and unlamented. The new style demanded openness and efficiency. The Grill was the first modern café in Edmonton. Seating on stools arranged around a U-shaped counter was augmented with low booths at the back of the café. The kitchen was close to the dining counter to provide fast service and speed was further enhanced by the installation of modern equipment such as high heat grills, gas ovens and a barbecue oven in the front window. It was the apogee of modern efficient design.[92]

The café of the Driard Hotel, Wetaskiwin, after renovations in 1937. (PAA A.1579)

In the early 1900s, a number of cafés and poolrooms installed slot machines in order to produce revenue and to draw customers. Relatively limited before World War I, their number increased dramatically thereafter, but not for long. By 1922, The Billiard Room Act had been amended to prohibit slot machines of any type in poolrooms,[93] and by 1924 a comprehensive ban removed them from cafés, corner stores, and clubs as well. Confectionery stores had the greatest number of slot machines: 85 percent of all slot machines in Edmonton in 1923 were located there. Each store owner paid half of his take to the machine owner, a fifty dollar annual licence fee to the provincial government, and often a licence fee to the local government as well. The slot machines were supplied by various Alberta and Canadian companies. In 1923 the Alberta Vending Machine Company of Edmonton supplied the second largest number of slot machines in the city.[94]

The Lacombe Pool Hall featured a slot machine in 1906. (GAI NA-1583-6)

Many people were concerned about slot machines. The Calgary Trades and Labour Council, the Calgary Board of Trade, reform groups such as the WCTU, and a number of churches opposed them as a form of gambling, particularly because they were commonly found in corner stores. Slot machine players were easy targets with few defenders of any political importance. Playing the slot machine was understood to be a working man's vice, never found in "typical farming communities" in Alberta but in "mining regions, railway terminal towns and cities or other centres where there are industrial payrolls." In 1924, of 541 slot machines licensed in Alberta, 187 were in Calgary, 199 in Edmonton, and 41 in Lethbridge. The next greatest concentrations were found in Drumheller, Taber, Coleman and Edson, each with between 8 and 12 machines.[95]

Slot machines occasioned a number of court challenges in Canada in the early 1920s. Although the courts in other provinces ruled slot machines illegal, the Alberta courts consistently refused to do so. As a consequence, Alberta pressured Ottawa to amend The Criminal Code to ban such machines, which the federal government finally did late in 1924.[96] In the interim, Alberta politicians and department officials publicly railed against slot machines while eagerly, even avariciously, taxing them. The province imposed on each machine a fifty dollar annual license fee that it was extremely careful to collect. This was a massive tax for the time, but the machines were sufficiently profitable to carry it. This license fee was seen as both a "revenue producer" for the province and "at the same time an effective deterrent so far as their use in a hundred smaller communities is concerned."[97]

Three main types of slot machines dominated in Alberta in the early 1920s. The "bona fide" vending machines, "sometimes referred to as Silent Salesmen," sold matches, gum, peanuts, and the like. Initially, the fifty dollar license fee had to be paid on these machines, but they were exempted in 1923. The second type of slot machine, the "so called gum Vending Machine," generated the greatest government objection. Since "the gum in those machines is not fit for chewing. . .no person wants the gum which is left in the machine for months,"[98] the purpose of operating the machine lay in the accompanying prizes. The player deposited five cents, pulled the lever, and received a package of chewing gum. Then,

the machine may register a picture of three bars of gum with Bell Fruit Gum on same which provides 20 trade checks. Again, two or one bars may appear, but there is no reward for this other than the gum. The picture of three plums, two plums and one bar of gum is equivalent to 16 trade checks.

Variations on this pattern produced a lesser number of checks. In all cases, checks could be exchanged for cash or for merchandize such as tobacco and candy.[99] Since these machines always returned something to the player, whether it was a piece of gum, a tune, or whatever, the Alberta courts ruled that this could not be defined as gambling. The third type of slot machine, the "cash machine," received "real money and gives out real money." In this case, the player's return was based purely upon chance; there was no pretense that the player always received something in return. Clearly illegal under The Criminal Code, cash machines were not in widespread use in Alberta. In 1924, they were found only in the Crowsnest Pass and in a few other towns, mostly in southern Alberta, such as Vulcan, Nanton, and Claresholm.[100]

The amendment of The Criminal Code in October 1924 effectively ended the discord over slot machines.[101] The social debate about the bar, the poolroom, and the café was not so easily resolved, however, and many people continued to view these institutions as perversions of proper leisure which caused dissipation and not recreation. And they were easy to attack: their patrons and their owners included many people from outside the dominant culture or from industrial workers. Allegations of sin placed their supporters consistently on the defensive, vulnerable to demands for control and even abolition. Not all were considered to be equally sinful. The bar was obviously the worst, with theoretically the greatest moral and social implications for the society. The sin of the café and the poolroom was more individualized and less socially damaging and could therefore be controlled through state regulation.

All of these institutions showed a remarkable resilience in the face of the power and single-mindedness of their opponents. The defeat of prohibition was largely a defeat of the reform groups grounded in the dominant culture. The failure of prohibition could not be disguised, but it was clear that powerful interest groups, also with a stake in the dominant culture simultaneously depended on the manufacture and consumption of liquor, and these regrouped quickly after World War I. In other terms, the bar, the poolroom, and the café were, in many cases, clearly the only leisure institutions for people excluded by class and ethnicity from many formal leisure institutions. Moreover, and incomprehensible as it may have been for the reformers, many people also liked the ambience, the sociability, and the leisure that they found in these places. To suggest that people went to bars, cafés, and poolrooms merely because they had no other options was to ignore the other side of the issue: people also had genuine preferences based upon cultural and economic forces. The refusal of many in the dominant culture to accept the legitimacy of such leisure, indeed, their definition of it as a social evil, arose from their authoritarian and paternalistic bent. Yet, liquor did present social problems that had to be addressed, and gambling could potentially become a destructive force. The governing reaction was thus sincere, but because it was so paternal and extreme, and because many churches, fraternal clubs, and other leisure institutions in the society were exclusive and not open or attractive to all people regardless of class or ethnicity, imposition of the views of the dominant culture necessarily involved the state.

Conclusion

From the turn of the century until the late 1940s, Alberta, like the rest of the prairies, experienced extraordinary technological change, the accentuated ethnic and religious tensions of two world wars, and a demoralizing series of economic crises. After World War II, Alberta was considerably altered. The urban population surpassed the rural by 1951 and reached three-quarters of the total within twenty-five years. The economic boom that began during the war expanded, especially after the discovery of the Leduc oil fields in 1947, and for the next thirty-five years Alberta experienced steady economic growth, which encompassed a shift in the balance of production from agriculture to petroleum.[1]Leisure patterns, and society in general, changed more slowly than did the economy. While authority in the society continued to be determined largely by ethnic and linguistic criteria,[2] they began in the 1960s and 1970s to exert slightly less influence. In some respects, the dominant English-speaking group became less mean and narrow after the war, but it could afford the charity. Postwar Alberta reflected its culture: not an accommodation among many immigrant traditions, not a mosaic, but the values of the Anglo-Canadian and, increasingly, American world.

In postwar Alberta, the attitude that leisure took its meaning from work began to crumble. While the work ethic retained its charm for most people, the commitment to a leisure that was only meaningful if it contributed education, spiritual growth or recreation for work was breaking down. After World War II, the attitude that leisure was an important measure of the quality of life and a definition of social advancement gained ground; indeed, for some people, leisure became the only important (and often the only conceivable) measure of quality of life.

Government involvement gradually expanded, although its initiatives largely elaborated on its earlier position of giving assistance only to useful and educational leisure activities. As public expectations of the relationship between government and leisure began to change, the government became more active in cultural and leisure affairs. In 1945, in the context of its postwar reconstruction strategy, the provincial government recognized that music, drama, and, significantly, "recreation" were all "seriously handicapped by the lack of co-ordination and of proper direction regarding the development of existing facilities," and adopted the position that only government could provide them.[3] The Alberta Music Board and the Drama Board were established in 1945 and 1948 respectively, and during the same period, a "Cultural Activities" Branch was created to promote libraries, drama, and music. Further, the development of provincial parks, stymied by the Depression, revived and expanded after the war. The involvement of local governments in a more systematic fashion also had implications for senior governments. Few local governments could meet the costs of facility development, and they demanded and increasingly received support from the provincial and federal governments. The Massey Report of 1951 "crystallized" the notion that "the government of Canada had a part to play in fostering culture."[4] The recreation programmes of the 1930s had set precedents for federal participation in leisure activities, a tendency confirmed and extended after World War II.

This acceptance of a government role in leisure development represented in some respects a departure from the past. Before 1945, the history of leisure in Alberta is inseparable from the evolution of cultural and social authority, while the broader state involvement that began after the war at least created a wider focus for the expression of leisure preferences. Alberta after the late nineteenth century broadly developed within the framework of the dominant culture. In retrospect, the process may seem to have been inevitable: the settlers came, they recreated in the new place the worlds they had left behind, and those whose lifestyle did not correspond to the dominant culture were assimilated. But the transplantation of culture was not historically inevitable. The members of the dominant culture, drawing upon their various advantages, shaped the culture to their own standards. Their success was not merely a reflection of numbers and local authority because only their organizations and institutions were represented everywhere in the province. This helped to reinforce their unity and sustain their normative standards as a general measure of upward social mobility. Further, they relied for inspiration on the ethos of Ontario-based English Canadian culture and institutions, which provides support for one popular argument in prairie history—that the transplantation of culture was a part of the working of metropolitan authority on the frontier.

The mechanics of this transplantation went beyond the mere replication of familiar institutions: they presumed the implant of the underlying ideology of the dominant group; an ideology that sometimes transcended class divisions among its members. The members of the dominant culture approached leisure with particular assumptions about social processes, standards and objectives. Leisure was not just activity that filled in spare time. As a touchstone for deeply held beliefs and attitudes, it was an integral part of social life. Part of this process was the definition of standards of acceptable leisure. Such ambitions projected a society that would be North American but British; a society that would function well with order and deference, yet would permit social mobility; a society that would be industrious; and one that would recognize the seriousness of life and the pleasure in simplicity, self improvement, morality, and diligence. Of course, wealth, or at least independence, was also important. In its various manifestations, leisure sometimes supported these ambitions, but at other times it undermined them; just as it offered opportunities, it also provided challenges. The attitudes of the groups of the dominant culture to leisure were not in every respect straightforward or clear-cut, but leisure could never be ignored because it raised significant cultural issues. Of particular significance was the fact that these issues were debated within the framework and the priorities set by the members of the dominant culture.

Never rejected, leisure at one level was thought to be an ennobling manifestation of the human need for companionship. At another level, the sort of leisure that a society enjoyed constituted a measure of its success. In Alberta, this was defined as implanted British-Ontarian ideals, or in the language of the dominant culture, as "civilizing" the new land. Thus, leisure was not merely an end in itself: it was justified by its quality, which was measured by the degree to which it accorded with the virtues of industriousness, diligence, orderliness, private property, and Britishness. In terms of re-creation for work and encouragement of social responsibility and diligence, usefulness was at the core of acceptable leisure.

All of these notions about leisure operated at both formal and informal levels to support a cultural hegemony. Deliberate ranking of leisure initiatives proceeded from underlying psychological and cultural assumptions. The establishment and maintenance of a particular hegemony depended not only upon implanting institutions and rules, but also upon entrenching a world view that encompassed certain implicit assumptions about social organization and proper behaviour. In part, this was a product of will: the assumption of leadership by virtue of ethnic and racial superiority would be made real and ultimately historical from the start. The expression of such a world view often consciously included leisure. The 1896 Dominion Day celebrations at Fort Macleod included a seemingly insignificant polo game, but for some it was a transcendent event. The Indians watching the game, it was reported,

> look like aliens, like visiting strangers. The Englishman doesn't bully the Indian. He simply ignores him, and by pursuing life as nearly as possible like the one he would lead in England, and by appropriating whatever suits his interest or fancy, he makes the Indian understand it is *his* country. He impresses that fact upon him even in his games.[5]

So too would others outside the dominant culture find social authority combined with leisure in the new land.

Such assumptions of superiority operated at conscious and unconscious levels and were neatly integrated with the belief that human behaviour and social organization were deeply influenced by environment, especially although not exclusively during youth. This meant that leisure could not be left to mere play or fun. All physical and psychological circumstances exerted influences for good or evil, an assumption that inevitably created highly interventionist social attitudes. The acceptance of childhood as the time when character was formed, ideally in the home, through instruction, example, precedent, and imitation, posited a distinction between childhood and adulthood. Children needed protection, guidance, and, above all, structures in their lives that would properly mould and form their characters. Their leisure had thus to be directed in a manner that would fit the special needs of the young and reinforce the ideology that underlay home and family life. Although age distinctions had been commonly accepted in labour and education since the nineteenth century,[6] during the twentieth century they also became part of government leisure policy in Alberta. Poolrooms and bars were off-limits to children, and movie attendance was restricted through the classification system.

The views of the dominant culture were thus promoted through formal regulation that expressed social and political authority and through the informal assumptions that guided many of its institutions. The culturally loaded concepts of amateurism and fair play were given authority through institutions such as public schools and regulations such as those governing hunting, and through organizations such as the Boy Scouts, the Alberta Branch, Amateur Athletic Union of Canada, the Young Men's Christian Association and the Young Women's Christian Association. None of these assumptions was static, however, as illustrated by the increasing acceptance of professionals in sport, and changes were often marked by the evolution of definitions of respectability, such as those shown in the debate over liquor. Although most members of the dominant culture defined sobriety, restraint, and seriousness as virtues, which ruled out leisure activities that challenged these qualities, the use of liquor occasioned an intricate range of official responses from outright prohibition to a high level of centralized control. In other cases, definitions of respectability changed more completely: attending movies was somewhat unrespectable at the time of World War I, but entirely acceptable by the time of World War II, perhaps in part because the device of censorship was believed to have established control.

Government authorities were fully committed to shaping provincial society in terms of the assumptions and concerns of the dominant culture and did so through a myriad of devices: censorship of film, regulation of public entertainment, the declaration of holidays, and the control and, for a time, the prohibition of liquor. Of course, government policy must also be understood by what it did not attempt to do. While there was little sustained demand by the members of the dominant culture for state financial subsidy for leisure, when such support was given, it was provided to organizations and institutions that confirmed the emphasis upon useful, especially educational, leisure. Thus, what state support existed was directed to the institutions and needs of the dominant culture. No evidence was located of provincial government support or encouragement for the drama, music, social, and cultural groups in the non-English-speaking population. Informal influence and formal power thus intersected and overlapped to create a mutually reinforcing structure of social authority.

The hegemony of the English-speaking group in Alberta also drew on explicitly articulated concerns like those about the urban environment. The traditional view in Canada that rural life was clean, healthy, and moral, building character and integrity, derived additional impetus in Alberta from the early dominance of the rural population. The economic importance of farming in Alberta and its integration into the mythology of provincial life provided an important justification for the rural life movement.[7] Urban–rural divisions were fuelled by farm politicians who often blamed farmers' problems on urban speculators, middlemen, and businessmen. Yet urban and rural standards of living clearly differed, and the campaign to equalize rural and urban leisure standards to head off antagonisms between farm and city is a measure of the importance accorded to leisure as a social force. Improved leisure opportunities could help to preserve rural life and stop the exodus from the farm of young people looking for urban excitement. The adoption of urban standards of leisure as the norm implicitly recognized that the province's rural tradition was too diffuse to provide a measure for separating the culture of town and country; there were few differences in attitudes or ambitions, mainly differences in ability to realize leisure opportunities. The cultural poverty of farm life was only a disadvantage of place, not of occupation. By the 1930s, however, attention to this issue was diverted by economic crisis and by the assumption that the problem had been resolved through technology; motor vehicles and radio could effectively reduce the disadvantages of rural life.

The same mixture of social and cultural assumptions and conscious ambitions lay behind the way in which work, industriousness, and definitions of economic progress intersected with leisure. Work not only kept people busy and out of trouble, it also provided an honest income and, more immediately, was necessary to develop a new land. The hard work required to clear the land, build houses and accumulate capital reinforced the work ethic typical of the dominant culture (as well as that of many non-English-speaking Albertans). This frontier experience had important implications for leisure, which, in the British and Ontarian inheritance, was already defined in terms of work and usefulness. Leisure was confirmed as a means of reinforcing work as the central fact in people's lives: it was a reward and a means of re-creating people for more work. As well, both rural and urban members of the dominant culture supported the need for regular and punctual work habits. This had been important for the development of mechanized factory production,[8] and while this often had little direct relevance to the particular circumstances of Alberta, its general principles accorded with the acceptance of the work ethic. While the urban pattern of regularized leisure was perhaps not so important for farm people who worked within a seasonal cycle, their increased mobility and interaction with town and city meant that they too adjusted to regularized urban schedules. For urban wage earners and salaried workers at least (for whom time was always money in the absence of paid holidays), this regularization of time was confirmed by elevating public holidays and Sundays to a recurring series of expected breaks in the work week. When regular vacations were added to this structure, relief from work was confirmed as a reward. Ideally, these breaks, especially public holidays, celebrated or confirmed the history, values and institutions of the members of the dominant culture. Similarly, Sabbatarian rules constrained leisure on Sunday and channelled it away from commercial activities into less structured activity.

At the same time, fundamental changes in the technology of transportation and communications had direct and significant impacts on leisure and social authority. Modern private transportation, such as motor vehicles, and modern communications, like radio and film, came to dominate leisure activity for many people. In general terms, those committed to the dominant culture accepted the technological changes as positive developments that would reinforce their desires for Alberta society. For rural people, the radio would brighten and make the farm home more appealing, and private transportation would strengthen family and rural life in a better integrated society. Technological change had become a measure of the quality of life, and as a correspondent in *The UFA* noted in 1933, although it had become fashionable "to be superior about our modern inventions and deplore them," this attitude was misguided.

> As I heard one speaker commenting on the depression and remarking that we were not able to have the cars and the radios and the telephones we formerly had...we were finding we could put on...plays ourselves [but] I thought to myself that probably very few had been put on with-out a goodly number of telephone messages or...a car gathering the members together unless they lived in the city and could resort to the street cars.[9]

Thus, the economic and philosophic premises of the machine age included the belief that the social consequences of the new machines could be controlled and that the changes they stimulated would enrich life within the framework of established social authority. Moreover, the members of the dominant culture did not wish, nor were they able, to reject technological change because for them it confirmed the superiority of the social and economic initiatives of the English-speaking world.

Inevitably, technological transformations took place within the controlling cultural context and were incorporated into it. Fairs continued, even though motor vehicles permitted people to choose which fair they would attend. The fairs, amateur concerts and dances of the 1940s shared fundamental similarities with those of the 1890s. Despite changes in camping and hunting because of the new access to private transportation, each continued over the half-century to reflect earlier attitudes towards nature and the outdoors. In general, new technology gave people new opportunities, but these opportunities were realized within the parameters of the hegemonic culture. By the interwar years, large numbers could participate in leisure activities away from home, and even away from the community, in a way that was possible for only a few before World War I. Significantly, this did not challenge work or the regularization of time, but served to entrench them. The creation of provincial parks illustrated the facility with which modern transportation could be integrated into the implementation of traditional social assumptions. Even where technological change created wholly new leisure activities, they maintained a basic continuity. From the start, touring served family and educational leisure and also reflected traditional attitudes to man's interaction with nature. The new phenomenon of radio for a time drew upon the traditions of the variety show for its programming. Movies initially followed stage traditions, easing the transition to a completely new leisure activity by the time of the talkies.

Continuity and change also characterized the way in which new and changing forms of leisure affected gender roles. That leisure activities of men and women were often distinctive served to reinforce the social and economic differences between men and women. Technological change, especially in transportation, reinforced and even expanded male dominance. Largely operated by men, motor vehicles enhanced male authority, especially as they so quickly became crucial in everyday life. As they enabled men to expand their leisure activities, such as hunting and team sports, they were integrated with the attendant symbols of male authority. For women, the situation was somewhat different. Under pioneer conditions most women enjoyed no leisure.[10] Among urban women at the turn of the century, only those with wealth had leisure because they were freed from the never ending labour of house and home. For these women, some sports, the theatre, community work, teas, and socializing provided leisure outlets. As Alberta society became more settled, leisure increased for most women, but it reflected women's auxiliary position in a male world. The Women's Institutes, church women's clubs, and the women's auxiliaries to fraternal and service clubs confirmed women's places as mothers and housekeepers, expressing a "maternal feminism" never intended, as Carol Bacchi has shown, to challenge patriarchy or assert women's equality.[11] In effect, women continued to be excluded from a great number of leisure activities. Overall, hunting, many team sports, especially contact games, bars, and poolrooms remained out of bounds, at least for respectable women. Increases in leisure opportunities for women took place mainly within the context of family and home, and this was the same for all women, regardless of ethnicity. Expanding opportunities to go camping, fishing, or to the fair still presented women with family activity, and radio was a home centred form of leisure. The new leisure activities helped to perpetuate women's existing role in the society, although film added vigour to the presentation of woman as sexual object. At the same time, some women operated outside the traditional strictures. Women who hunted were legitimized by the tradition of the frontier, and farm women, who performed hard physical labour, disproved the theory that women should be excluded from leisure activities requiring physical strength and stamina.

The non-English-speaking members of Alberta society experienced social change in far greater measure. Their assimilation and control was an important goal for leaders of the dominant culture who brought the full weight of such institutions as the school to bear on the problem. They also saw twentieth century communications technology as an important tool to create a unilingual English society. This objective may even have helped to balance their often negative view of American commercial leisure which, ignoring its other faults, was at least expressed only in English. From the point of view of the colonizing dominant culture, after the indigenous people had been marginalized and isolated, attention turned to the acculturation of non-English-speaking European settlers. The "alien" immigrants subject to this hostility must have viewed the new communications technology with mixed emotions. Radio, movies, sports, and English language books and magazines all served as forces of cultural assimilation. For these peoples, leisure and the technology of the interwar years were part of the pleasures of the new land, yet they also encouraged assimilation, a consequence agreeable to some but not to others.

Simultaneously, the new technology sometimes aided resistance to assimilation. Although culturally distinctive leisure perhaps expressed alienation, it could also constitute resistance. Churches, ethnically defined clubs and associations, non-English language newspapers and magazines (some from the United States) as well as some community organizations and facilities helped to perpetuate and retain cultural patterns by using leisure to create ethnic cohesion and continuity. Such resistance was easiest in areas of bloc settlement or in ethnically concentrated districts in urban areas, but because of improvements in private transportation, even dispersed members of a group could communicate more easily with each other and express cultural unity through leisure. The travelling Polish amateur theatre group of Edmonton allowed a relatively dispersed ethnic group to realize a cultural focus through a shared leisure activity made possible by modern transportation. Nonetheless, many gradually assimilated and adopted the ethos of the dominant culture, although it is unclear if in this process they were more susceptible or eager to absorb American popular culture than were their Anglo-Canadian fellows.

During the interwar years, the very period in which the second generation of prewar non-English-speaking peoples underwent significant assimilation, the dominant culture itself was beginning to be more integrated, sometimes willingly, sometimes with resistance, into the American commercial lifestyle. While it needs to be recognized that Canadian culture was cast in a North American mould, it is nonetheless evident that modern forms of leisure changed the dominant culture by further emphasizing American institutions and popular culture. Although American influence on leisure in Alberta had been great almost from the beginning of settlement through commercial productions, such as travelling stage shows, some sports, fairs, and midways, exposure to them was relatively limited before World War I, especially outside the cities. After the war, however, American influence in Alberta increased through radio and film, which gave it a new authority. In addition, transportation provided greater access to the commercial network. The American commercial presence in Alberta leisure became so widespread between the wars that it can be seen as a substantive social change. There was a significant level of debate in the dominant culture about this development: the UFA, some labour spokesmen, and many leaders of opinion were critical of many aspects of commercial leisure and their commitment to public broadcasting in part arose from this position. Yet in many other respects they were not so critical, and overall there was little sustained quarrel with commercial leisure, even though in this commercial matrix American models had a profound impact and influence.

The standards of leisure in Alberta changed because the expansion of commercialization gave leisure a uniformity and accessibility rarely known before. People began to demand more leisure, which they increasingly defined in the language of American commercial culture. As this process quickened between the wars, standards of leisure derived less and less from the traditions of the dominant culture. The province no longer seemed to matter in cultural terms: gradually in the interwar years, and with growing force after 1945, many came to believe, and many more suspected, that important developments happened elsewhere, especially in the United States. The confidence and sense of importance attached to provincial society before 1914 died between the wars. In part, this may have come from the destructive impact of the war and the disillusion of the Depression, but it also came from new or transformed types of leisure that gave no credence to the traditions of the Canadian frontier but drew on the mythology of the United States. Radio was especially important because it was invasive and persistent in a way that no other commercial leisure activity had been. Yet Canadians seemed to be reassured that national broadcasting was a sufficient antidote to American models of entertainment. Perhaps this was due in part to the fact that radio always had a local dimension because most stations were locally owned and operated. Even when radio was full of American programming, either from Canadian stations or through reception of American stations, its home and family focus mitigated feelings that it was a cultural threat.

Film, and not radio, provoked the most fear for the dominant culture, and authorities fought to sustain the prevailing ideology through censorship. Censorship could not, however, obscure the central irony that the authority of the dominant culture would ultimately become questionable and its traditions anachronistic unless it too absorbed the new styles. Popular American service clubs caused the older fraternal orders to adopt the language of American social service and democracy, and American films and radio programmes confirmed the importance of American style. The result was a significant cultural tension, for while many of the dominant culture in some ways eagerly aped American fashions in leisure, the old rhetoric about a British society continued to hold tremendous sentimental power.

Standards of leisure were thus not only diffused from the dominant culture to common practice, but new and different standards were incorporated into the dominant culture itself. While it championed British heritage and loyalty, it increasingly took its reference from a society it theoretically despised. Robert Stamp has argued that the decline of Imperial celebrations in Ontario during the interwar years was related to the growing Americanization of Canada.[12] Yet, as John Thompson concluded in his study of the interwar years, Canadians, despite the growing and often welcomed American presence in their cultural lives, continued to possess a sense of distinctiveness and superiority in North America, which was reinforced through the images and messages they received about the United States through American films, radio programmes and magazines. "What they saw and heard," Thompson concludes, "provided further evidence to support their longstanding unfavourable interpretation of the United States."[13] Whether a culture defining itself largely in terms of negative stereotypes, which drew heavily on ethnic arrogance, could sustain and creatively regenerate itself remains an open question. Yet it was important, perhaps even symbiotic, that in this process Anglo-Canadian ideals and values, modified in response to modern American technical and commercial forms, spread through the society, simultaneously entrenching and extending traditional patterns of power and authority.

Endnotes

Introduction

1. Stanley Parker, *The Sociology of Leisure* (New York: International Publication Service, 1976), 12. Sebastien de Grazia has explored the problems in defining the terms "leisure" and "recreation." He has argued that recreation was not just free time but was "activity that rests men from work, often by giving them a change (distraction, diversions) and restores (recreates) them for work." In this approach, leisure is defined within the framework of classical thought, as being a state of mind and an attitude towards life and place in society. Thus leisure is an intellectual ideal based upon the importance of rational, disinterested thought (Sebastien de Grazia, *Of Time, Work and Leisure* (New York: The Twentieth Century Fund, 1962), 223-24).

2. Hugh Cunningham, *Leisure in the Industrial Revolution, c. 1780-c. 1880* (London: Croom Helm, 1980), 12.

3. G.H. Lewis, "Between Consciousness and Existence: Popular Culture and the Sociological Imagination," *Journal of Popular Culture* 15 (1982): 81. For an example of this theoretical approach, see also his *Side Saddle on the Golden Calf: Social Structure and Popular Culture in America* (Pacific Palisades: Goodyear, 1972). Lewis also deals with the "merit" of popular culture. For discussions of this issue in historical context, a more suggestive treatment is Peter Bailey, "'A Mingled Mass of Perfectly Legitimate Pleasures': The Victorian Middle Class and the Problem of Leisure," *Victorian Studies* 21 (1977): 7-28.

4. Cunningham, *Leisure in the Industrial Revolution*, 13.

5. In 1901, 18.4 percent of the population was "Indian"; by 1911, it had dropped to 3 percent. In 1901, the single largest non-"British" group in the province was German with 10.7 percent of the population. By 1941, the largest non-Anglo-Saxon group was "Polish/Ukrainian" with 12.4 percent of the population. (Alberta, Bureau of Statistics, *Alberta Statistical Review Annual: 75th Anniversary Edition* (1980),Table 4, 5).

6. Gerald Friesen, "The Prairie West Since 1945: An Historical Survey," in *The Making of the Modern West: Western Canada Since 1945*, ed. A.W. Rasporich (Calgary: University of Calgary Press, 1984), 3.

7. Lewis G. Thomas, *The Liberal Party in Alberta* (Toronto: University of Toronto Press, 1959), 31. See also Lewis G. Thomas, "Prairie Settlement: Western Responses in History and Fiction, Social Structures in a Canadian Hinterland," in *Crossing Frontiers: Papers in American and Canadian Western Literature*, ed. Dick Harrison (Edmonton: University of Alberta Press, 1979), 59-72.

8. Howard Palmer, *Patterns of Prejudice: A History of Nativism in Alberta* (Toronto: McClelland and Stewart Ltd., 1982), 163-64.

9. R. Douglas Francis, " 'Rural Ontario West': Ontarions in Alberta," in *Peoples of Alberta: Portraits in Cultural Diversity*, ed. Howard and Tamara Palmer (Saskatoon: Western Producer Prairie Books, 1985), 123-42.

10. Lewis G. Thomas, "Alberta Perspectives, 1905," *Alberta History* 28 (1980): 3.

11. Palmer, *Patterns of Prejudice*, 13, 23-25.

12. C.B. Macpherson, *Democracy in Alberta: Social Credit and the Party System*, 2nd ed. (Toronto, University of Toronto Press, 1962), 21.

13. John Richards and Larry Pratt, *Prairie Capitalism: Power and Influence in the New West* (Toronto: McClelland and Stewart Ltd., 1979), 150-51.

14. Gerald Friesen, *The Canadian Prairies: A History* (Toronto: University of Toronto Press, 1984), 300. See also W. Peter Ward, "Class and Race in the Social Structure of British Columbia, 1870-1939," in *British Columbia: Historical Readings*, ed. W. Peter Ward and Robert A.J. McDonald (Vancouver: Douglas and McIntyre Ltd., 1981) 581-99.

15. Morris Berman, " 'Hegemony' and the Amateur Tradition in British Science," *Journal of Social History* 8 (1975): 33.

16. Ibid.; Edward Said, *Orientalism* (New York: Vintage Books, 1978), 6-7.

17. E.P. Thompson, *The Making of the English Working Class* (New York: Pantheon Books, 1964), 11.

18. See Carl Berger, *The Sense of Power: Studies in the Ideas of Canadian Imperialism, 1867-1914* (Toronto: University of Toronto

Press, 1970), 147-52. See also the relevant chapters on different ethnic groups in J.S. Woodsworth, *Strangers Within Our Gates* (1909; reprint, Toronto: University of Toronto Press, 1972).

19. The recently popular analytical concept of "social control," in which a ruling group controls society through a system of conscious control, is thus too narrow a concept to be the sole analytical tool for a topic such as leisure. Although social control operated in some aspects in the history of leisure in Alberta, social authority is not merely "propaganda, conscious manipulation and lies"; it is "too complex to be reduced to simplistic, direct socioeconomic interest." (William Muraskin, "The Social Control Theory in American History: A Critique," *Journal of Social History* 9 (1976): 566).

20. Howard and Tamara Palmer, eds. *Peoples of Alberta: Portraits in Cultural Diversity* (Saskatoon: Western Producer Prairie Books, 1985).

21. Orest T. Martynowych, *The Ukrainian Bloc Settlement in East Central Alberta, 1890-1930: A History*, Historic Sites Service Occasional Paper, no. 10 (Edmonton: Alberta Culture, 1985).

22. On persistence of cultural patterns, see the work of John Lehr on Ukrainian folk architecture in Alberta. John Lehr, *Ukrainian Vernacular Architecture in Alberta*, Historic Sites Service Occasional Paper, no. 1 (Edmonton: Alberta Culture, 1976); "The Landscape of Ukrainian Settlement in the Canadian West," *Great Plains Quarterly* 1-2 (1982): 94-105.

23. Bailey, "A Mingled Mass," 7-28.

24. Cunningham, *Leisure in the Industrial Revolution*, 9-10, 194-95.

25. Maria Tippett, "The Writing of English Canadian Cultural History, 1970-1985," *Canadian Historical Review* 67 (1986): 560-61.

1. Infrastructures of Leisure

1. The broadest application of this approach is Fernand Braudel, *The Mediterranean and the Mediterranean World in the Age of Philip II*, vol. 1, trans. Sian Reynolds (New York: Harper and Row Publishers, 1972), 352-53.

2. Alberta, Bureau of Statistics, *Alberta Statistical Review Annual: 75th Anniversary Edition* (1980), Table 4, 5.

3. Howard Palmer, *Patterns of Prejudice: A History of Nativism in Alberta* (Toronto: McClelland and Stewart Ltd., 1982), 26-27.

4. Howard Palmer, "Immigration and Ethnic Settlement, 1880-1920," in *Peoples of Alberta Portraits of Cultural Diversity*, ed. Howard and Tamara Palmer (Saskatoon: Western Producer Prairie Books, 1985), 5, 17-18.

5. Frances Swyripa, "The Ukrainians in Alberta," in *Peoples of Alberta*, 214-19.

6. Ann and David Sunahara, "The Japanese in Alberta," in *Peoples of Alberta*, 399.

7. Alison Prentice, *The School Promoters* (Toronto: McClelland and Stewart Ltd., 1977), 25-44. The pioneer study on imperialism and nationalism in Canada was by Carl Berger, *The Sense of Power: Studies in the Ideas of Canadian Imperialism 1867-1914* (Toronto: University of Toronto Press, 1970).

8. Richard Allen, *The Social Passion: Religion and Social Reform in Canada 1914-1928* (Toronto: University of Toronto Press, 1973), 12.

9. E.A. Corbett, "Mike & Mrs. Mike," 1925, 74-23-40, University of Alberta Archives (hereafter UAA).

10. Minutes, Calgary Council on Child and Family Welfare, November 25, 1931, (hereafter Minutes), M6466, Glenbow-Alberta Institute Archives (hereafter GAI).

11. *Farm and Ranch Review*, April 21, 1913.

12. Minutes, November 25, 1931, M6466, GAI.

13. J.M. MacEachern, "Crime and Punishment," *The Press Bulletin*, May 6, 1932.

14. *Farm and Ranch Review*, January 5, 1928.

15. *Camrose Canadian*, December 10, 1903.

16. *Farm and Ranch Review*, January 5, 1928.

17. Ibid., May 20, 1913.

18. Ibid., June 20, 1913.

19. *The UFA*, May 2, 1932.

20. Ibid., November 1, 1927.

21. Minutes, January 26, 1945, M6466, GAI.

22. Alberta Post-War Reconstruction Committee, *Report of the Subcommittee on Social Welfare* (Edmonton: King's Printer, March 1945), 19.

23. Sunahara, "The Japanese in Alberta," 399.

24. John Herd Thompson, *The Harvests of War* (Toronto: McClelland and Stewart Ltd., 1978), 73-94.

25. Alan F.J. Artibise, "The Urban West: The Evolution of Prairie Towns and Cities to 1930," *Prairie Forum* 4 (1979): 239. See pages 240 and 243 for statistics on urban development in Alberta.

26. Paul Voisey, "The Urbanization of the Canadian Prairies, 1871-1916," *Histoire sociale/Social History* 8 (1975): 94-95.

27. Yves Dubé, J.E. Howes and D.L. McQueen, *Housing and Social Capital* (Ottawa: Royal Commission on Canada's Economic Prospects, 1957), 10.

28. William Bowers, *The Country Life Movement in America, 1900-1920* (Port Washington, N.Y.: Kennikat Press, 1974).

29. Allen, *The Social Passion*, 24.

30. *Edmonton Journal*, April 4, 1919. For a summary of the beliefs of the country life movement on the prairies, see David C. Jones, "'There is Some Power About the Land': The Western Agrarian Press & Country Life Ideology," *Journal of Canadian Studies* 17 (1982): 96-108.

31. *The Press Bulletin*, December 12, 1930.

32. *Farm and Ranch Review*, May 5, 1922.

33. Ibid., November 5, 1920.

34. John Burchard and Albert Bush-Brown, *The Architecture of America* (Boston: Little, Brown and Co., 1961), 117.

35. *The Press Bulletin*, November 23, 1928.

36. *Farm and Ranch Review*, September 1907.

37. *Calgary Herald*, March 26, 1912.

38. Cecil Blackburn, "The Development of Sports in Alberta, 1900-1918," (M.A. thesis, University of Alberta, 1974), 450.

39. Alberta, Department of Railways, *Annual Report, 1927*, Schedule 4.

40. R.F.P. Bowman, *Railways in Southern Alberta* (Lethbridge: Whoop-up Country Chapter, Historical Society of Alberta, 1973), 32-33.

41. See, for example, *Calgary Herald*, June 17, 1922; *Edmonton Journal*, August 6, 1921.

42. *Farm and Ranch Review*, June 1909.

43. For example, special fares for the Camrose fair were available to people as far north as Strathcona (Edmonton); to Red Deer in the west, and to Hardisty in the east (*Camrose Canadian*, September 15, 1910).

44. *The UFA*, June 1, 1933.

45. Ibid., April 1, 1922.

46. *Calgary Herald*, May 10, 1939.

47. *Edmonton Bulletin*, May 6, 1895.

48. Vernon Elliot, *Heavy Trucks in Alberta to 1955*, Reynolds-Alberta Museum Background Paper, no. 13, (Edmonton: Alberta Culture, 1983), 181.

49. Clipping, 1926, Walter Fulmer Collection, M398, GAI.

50. Alberta, Department of Public Works, *Annual Report, 1927-28*, 26; *Annual Report, 1931-32*, 34; *Annual Report, 1937-38*, 30.

51. Elliott, *Heavy Trucks in Alberta*, 185

52. J.G. MacGregor, *A History of Alberta*, 2nd ed. (Edmonton: Hurtig Publishers, 1981), 180.

53. Elise Corbet, *Light Service Vehicles Used in Alberta Prior to 1955*, Reynolds-Alberta Museum Background Paper, no. 14, (Edmonton: Alberta Culture, 1984), 87-89.

54. *Edmonton Journal*, March 1, 1930; MacGregor, *A History of Alberta*, 250.

55. *Census of Canada, 1941*, vol. 1, Table 100, 858. On the automobile in Saskatchewan see: G.T. Bloomfield, "I Can See a Car in That Crop: Motorization in Saskatchewan 1906-1934," *Saskatchewan History* 37 (1984): 5.

56 *Census of Canada, 1921*, vol. 5, Table 23, p. xxxvi; *Census of Canada, 1931*, vol. 8, Table 29, p. lxxiv; Canada, Department of Agriculture, *Changes in Farm Family Living in Three Areas of the Prairie Provinces, from 1942-43 to 1947*, by M.A. MacNaughton and M.E. Andal, with a supplement by M.A. MacNaughton and J.M. Mann, Publication no. 815 (Ottawa, 1949), 33.

57. D. MacGregor, ed., *The Alberta Club Woman's Blue Book* (Calgary: Calgary Canadian Women's Press Club, 1917), 43.

58. *Family Herald and Weekly Star*, June 19, 1940.

59. Ibid., April 7, 1920.

60. *Red Deer Advocate*, February 20, 1920.

61. *The UFA*, June 1, 1925.

62. *Expenditures on Roads, Bridges and Ferries*, August 23, 1921, Premiers' Papers (hereafter PP), File 294A, Provincial Archives of Alberta (hereafter PAA).

63. *Western Municipal News*, February 1923, 38.

64. See correspondence in PP, Files 294A and 295A, PAA.

65. *The UFA*, July 15, 1929.

66. Resolutions, UFA 37th Convention, January 1946, PP, File 1513, PAA.

67. David R. Richeson, "The Telegraph and Community Formation in the North-West Territories," in *The Developing West*, ed. John Foster (Edmonton: University of Alberta Press, 1983), 144-50.

68. Lewis G. Thomas, *The Liberal Party in Alberta* (Toronto: University of Toronto Press, 1959), 51-53.

69. "Brief History and Development of the Alberta Government Telephones," n.d., (ca. 1926), PP, File 399A, and Baxter to Smith, June 21, 1928, PP, File 381A, PAA.

70. *The UFA*, October 2, 1922, and October 1, 1927.

71. John Blackburn, *Land of Promise* (Toronto: Macmillan of Canada, 1970), 43.

72. *Census of Canada, 1931*, vol. 8, Table 1, p. xxviii, and Table 26, p. lxviii.

73. Minister of Telephones to Clark, November 14, 1951, PP, File 1748, PAA.

74. *Farm and Ranch Review*, February 2, 1931. Local governments had been empowered to establish telephone companies in 1906.

75. Ithiel de Sola Pool, *The Social Impact of the Telephone* (Cambridge, Massachusetts: The MIT Press, 1977), 173.

76. For example, see *Farm and Ranch Review*, June 1907.

77. Circular, "Western Canada Air Mail Schedule," Edmonton, Post Office, March 6, 1930, PP, File 254, PAA. While apparently abandoned in 1932, this experiment set the precedent for air mail service (*Claresholm Local Press*, February 26, 1932).

78. Sebastien de Grazia, *Of Time, Work and Leisure* (New York: The Twentieth Century Fund, 1962). For grain farms in Alberta, see Paul Voisey, *Vulcan: The Making of a Prairie Community* (Toronto: University of Toronto Press, 1988), 158.

79. Alberta Regulation Governing Attendance, Conduct and Discipline of Employees, Order-in-Council 1880/20, September 18, 1920; McCormack to Sullivan, July 10, 1922, PP, File 459, PAA.

80. *Civil Service Bulletin*, September 1922.

81. McCormack to Sullivan, July 10, 1922, PP, File 459, PAA.

82. Memorandum of Legislative Programme Presented to Premier...by...Alberta Federation of Labour, December 15, 1947, p. 7.

83. C.A. Dawson and Eva R. Younge, *Pioneering in the Prairie Provinces: The Social Side of the Settlement Process* (Toronto: Macmillan of Canada Limited, 1940), 243.

84. Allen, *The Social Passion*, 13, 21-22.

85. *Farm and Ranch Review*, May 1906.

86. *Calgary Herald*, May 17, 1906.

87. Dawson and Younge, *Pioneering in the Prairie Provinces*, 243.

88. *Calgary Herald*, July 22, 1912.

89. Deputy Attorney General to Greenfield, October 2, 1924, PP, File 73A, PAA.

90. Memorandum, Alberta Provincial Board, The Retail Merchants Association of Canada, n.d., (ca. 1927), PP, File 242, PAA.

91. See correspondence, 1926 and 1929, in PP, File 73B, PAA.

92. McMillen to Pattison, September 19, 1932, Human Resources Research Council, 79.107, File 140, PAA.

93. Webber to Brownlee, July 25, 1930, PP, File 319A, PAA.

94. Wilson to Graham, January 5, 1948, PP, File 1555, PAA.

95. McCormack to Sullivan, July 10, 1922, PP, File 459, PAA.

96. Memorandum of Agreement Between Lethbridge Automotive Dealers Association and Garage Mechanics, Lethbridge, July 1928, PP, File 506A, PAA.

97. Typescript, "Interview with Tom Scott, Pincher Creek," "First Hand Narratives," Alberta Folk Archive, Bruce Peel Special Collections Library, University of Alberta (hereafter BPSC).

98. *Edmonton Bulletin*, July 5, 1884.

99. *Calgary Herald*, July 2, 1907.

100. *Edmonton Journal*, July 3, 1923.

101. Minutes, Committee for Celebration of Diamond Jubilee of Confederation, n.d., (ca. April 1927), PP, File 219, PAA. On Canadian nationalism in the 1920s, see John Herd Thompson with Allen Seager, *Canada 1922-1939: Decades of Discord* (Toronto: McClelland and Stewart Ltd., 1985), 158-61.

102. *The Press Bulletin*, April 15, 1921. For events at Edmonton schools for Victoria Day in 1925, see *Edmonton Journal*, May 23, 1925. On Empire Day (the school holiday preceding May 24 in Ontario) see Robert Stamp, "Empire Day in the Schools of Ontario: The Training of Young Imperialists," *Journal of Canadian Studies* 8 (1973): 33-42.

103. *Edmonton Journal*, May 25, 1929.

104. Letter 165, May 10, 1943, A. Balmer Watt Collection, BPSC.

105. Editorial, *Canadian Architect and Builder* 7 (1894): 110.

106. *Calgary Herald*, September 8, 1904.

107. Ibid., September 7, 1897.

108. Ibid., September 8, 1904.

109. *Edmonton Journal*, August 30, 1930.

110. Ashenhurst to Manning, August 31, 1948, and McKay to Manning, November 19, 1948, PP, File 1599, PAA.

111. "Souvenir of the Queen's Diamond Jubilee Celebrations at Edmonton," Northwest Territories, June 22-23, 1897, Rutherford Pamphlet Collection, BPSC.

112. "Royal Visit, Pictorial Review Commemorating The Alberta Visit of George VI, 1939," Rutherford Pamphlet Collection, BPSC. The photographer was Alfred Blyth.

113. See *Edmonton Bulletin*, April 26, 1894; *Red Deer Advocate*, May 1, 1914; Manning to Maurer, February 19, 1948, PP, File 1599, PAA.

114. Gardiner to Talbot, April 26, 1924, Alberta Agricultural Societies, M2360, File 212, GAI.

115. *Calgary Herald*, July 22, 1910.

116. *Red Deer Advocate*, April 28, 1922.

117. *Edmonton Bulletin*, June 21, 1894; July 1, 1895.

118. Ibid., March 19, 1894.

119. *Farm and Ranch Review*, March 15, 1930.

120. A. Navalkowsky, "Shandro Church," *Alberta History* 30 (1982): 27.

121. Jane McCracken, *Stephan G. Stephansson: The Poet of the Rocky Mountains*, Historic Sites Service Occasional Paper, no. 9, (Edmonton: Alberta Culture, 1982), 114.

122. Orest Martynowych, *The Ukrainian Bloc Settlement in East Central Alberta 1890-1930,*

A History, Historic Sites Service Occasional Paper, no. 10, (Edmonton: Alberta Culture, 1985), 211.

123. *Calgary Herald,* January 8, 1920.

124. Warren Caragata, *Alberta Labour: A Heritage Untold* (Toronto: James Lorimer and Co. Ltd., 1979), 11, 121.

125. Phelan to Manning, January 31, 1947, PP, File 1433, PAA.

126. Jenny Podoluk, *Incomes of Canadians* (Ottawa: Dominion Bureau of Statistics, 1968), 3.

127. *Census of Canada, 1931,* vol. 5, Table 9, 18.

128. *Calgary Herald,* February 28, 1920.

129. Piva calculated a monthly average budget from retail prices published in the *Labour Gazette* (Michael J. Piva, *The Condition of the Working Class in Toronto, 1900-1921* (Ottawa: University of Ottawa Press, 1979), 36-37). The corresponding figures were used to calculate a budget for Calgary and Edmonton. Local factors were accounted for as available in the statistics. The budget includes only basic food items, a six-room house with sanitary facilities, coal, wood and coal oil for lighting and heating. In Edmonton the weekly average expenses were $27.91 and in Calgary $29.18 (*Labour Gazette,* "Retail Prices," June 1920-May 1921). The Department of Labour estimated this represented 60-80 percent of the expenditure of an average family of five. Piva uses the very conservative figure of 80 percent. Using the same formula for Calgary and Edmonton, total expenditures have been estimated by extrapolating these basic expenditures to 100 percent for all other expenses, such as clothing, leisure and medical.

130. *Farm and Ranch Review,* February 2, 1931.

131. "Amusement Taxes," 1927, PP, File 359, PAA.

132. McLennan to Greenfield, March 27, 1923, PP, File 90, PAA.

133. *Census of Canada, 1931,* vol. 11, Table 1, 396-97.

134. *Census of Canada, 1941,* vol. 11, Table 1, 436.

2. The Structure of Everyday Life: Home and Family

1. Alberta, Department of the Attorney General, *Annual Report 1915,* "Dependent and Delinquent Children," 38.

2. *Farm and Ranch Review,* December 1907.

3. G. Pelton, "Some of the Causes and Remedies for Juvenile Delinquency," p. 4, September 30, 1927, Premiers' Papers (hereafter PP), File 235, Provincial Archives of Alberta (hereafter PAA).

4. See, for example, *Farm and Ranch Review,* August 20, 1918.

5. Joanna Matejko, "The Polish Experience in Alberta," in *Peoples of Alberta: Portraits of Cultural Diversity,* ed. Howard and Tamara Palmer (Saskatoon: Western Producer Prairie Books, 1985), 278.

6. Howard Palmer, "Patterns of Immigration and Ethnic Settlement in Alberta: 1880-1920," in *Peoples of Alberta,* 26.

7. During the period under review, the Census reported that Alberta had a highly literate population. Census definitions of literacy, however, have little importance for determining the extent of reading for pleasure. See *Census of Canada, 1911,* vol. 2, Table 28, 462, and *Census of Canada, 1931,* vol. 2, Table 28, 462.

8. "Some Recent Fiction Worth Reading," n.d., (ca. 1920), 74-23-42, University of Alberta Archives (hereafter UAA).

9. *The UFA,* October 15, 1929.

10. "National Crusade for Good Reading," 1939, PP, File 1234, PAA.

11. *Calgary Herald,* June 19, 1902, and August 22, 1903.

12. For Fort Saskatchewan as an example, see Peter Ream, *The Fort on the Saskatchewan* (n.p.: Metropolitan Printing, 1974), 501.

13. For a full list of magazines, see *Edmonton Bulletin,* December 16, 1882.

14. Jane McCracken, *Stephan G. Stephansson: The Poet of the Rocky Mountains,* Historic Sites Service Occasional Paper, no. 9, (Edmonton: Alberta Culture, 1982), 115.

15. Howard and Tamara Palmer, "Estonians in Alberta," in *Peoples of Alberta,* 201; Krystyna Lukasiewicz, "Polish Community in the Crow's Nest Pass," *Alberta History* 36 (1986): 6.

16. Michael Harris, "Public Libraries and the Decline of the Democratic Dogma," *Library Journal* 101 (Nov. 1, 1976): 2225-30; Bruce Curtis, "'Littery Merrit', 'Useful Knowledge' and the Organization of Township Libraries in Canada West, 1840-1860," *Ontario History* 68 (1981): 285-311.

17. *Calgary Herald,* June 19, 1902, and June 17, 1907.

18. *Edmonton Journal,* June 16, 1923.

19. Ibid., April 5, 1924.

20. The relationship between public libraries and ethnicity in Alberta is uncharted. The Reading Camp Association (Frontier College) aimed, in part, to assist in the assimilation of non-English-speaking labourers through its literacy programmes in work camps (M. Robinson, "Reading

Camp Associations in Alberta," *Alberta History* 29 (1981): 36-40).

21. "Some Recent Fiction Worth Reading," 74-23-42, UAA.

22. Ibid.

23. "Report of Southern Trip," 1934, 75-76-37, UAA.

24. Leslie Fiedler, "Canada and the Invention of the Western: A Meditation on the Other Side of the Border," in *Crossing Frontiers: Papers in American and Canadian Western Literature,* ed. Dick Harrison (Edmonton: University of Alberta Press, 1979), 94.

25. "The Library in the Community," n.d., (ca. 1935), 75-76-37, UAA.

26. Ibid.

27. Minister of Economic Affairs to Sorsdahl, June 20, 1949, PP, File 1668, PAA.

28. Memorandum for Premier Manning from the Alberta Library Board, August 27, 1949, PP, File 1668, PAA.

29. Minutes, Alberta Library Association, Annual Meeting, May 28, 1947, 75-76-41, UAA.

30. University of Alberta, *Report of the Department of Extension for the Year Ending March 31,* (hereafter *Extension Annual Report), 1924,* n.p.; Ibid., *1940,* 20.

31. University of Alberta, Department of Extension, *Division of Travelling Libraries Open Shelf Catalogue No. 4,* 1924.

32. *Extension Annual Report, 1931,* 11.

33. Ibid., 1934, 16.

34. Ibid., 1935, 18.

35. Most of the stories were often what can be termed "morality tales" and were largely written to formula. Analysis of them would be a useful glimpse into popular culture.

36. Clipping, *Saturday Night,* 74-23-47, UAA; John Herd Thompson with Allen Seager, *Canada 1922-1939: Decades of Discord* (Toronto: McClelland and Stewart Ltd., 1985), 185-86.

37. "Maclean's: Review of 1925," PP, File 11B, PAA.

38. Thompson with Seager, *Canada 1922-1939,* 183-84; Chipman to Robb, May 16, 1927, PP, File 224A, PAA.

39. "Maclean's: Review of 1925," PP, File 11B, PAA.

40. Ibid.

41. Petersen to Brownlee, May 31, 1926, PP, File 11B, PAA.

42. Donald B. Smith, "A History of French Speaking Albertans," in *Peoples of Alberta,* 96-97 n39.

43. Michael M. Marunchak, *The Ukrainian Canadians: A History* (Winnipeg and Ottawa: Ukrainian Free Academy of Sciences, 1970), 272-76.

44. Howard Palmer, "Patterns of Immigration and Ethnic Settlement in Alberta, 1880-1920," in *Peoples of Alberta,* 17-18; Howard and Tamara Palmer, "Estonians in Alberta," in *Peoples of Alberta,* 201-202; Howard and Tamara Palmer, "The Hungarian Experience in Alberta," in *Peoples of Alberta,* 315.

45. *Farm and Ranch Review,* June 20, 1913.

46. *The UFA,* October 1, 1925.

47. *Farm and Ranch Review,* February 25, 1927.

48. *The UFA,* March 1, 1933.

49. *Farm and Ranch Review,* October 1905.

50. Helmut Kallman, *A History of Music in Canada, 1534-1914* (Toronto: University of Toronto Press, 1960), 162; Howard and Tamara Palmer, "The Romanian Community in Alberta," in *Peoples of Alberta,* 260.

51. *The UFA,* November 15, 1928.

52. Helmut Kallman, Gilles Potvin and Kenneth Winters, eds., *Encyclopedia of Music in Canada* (Toronto: University of Toronto Press, 1981), 783; Canada, Department of Agriculture, *Changes in Farm Family Living in Three Areas of the Prairie Provinces, from 1942-43 to 1947,* by M.A. MacNaughton and M.E. Andal, with a supplement by M.A. MacNaughton and J.M. Mann, Publication no. 815 (Ottawa, 1949), 39-40.

53. Lloyd Rodwell, "The Saskatchewan Association of Music Festivals," *Saskatchewan History* 16 (1983): 2; Kallman, *A History of Music in Canada,* 218.

54. For programmes, see Alberta Registered Music Teachers Association (ARMTA), Calgary Branch, M6365, File 1, Glenbow-Alberta Institute Archives (hereafter GAI). Also, see Edith Hamilton Collection, M6364, Boxes 1-3, GAI. The records of the Edmonton Branch, ARMTA, and the provincial records, ARMTA, may be found in 67.277, 74.107, 78.168, 81.125, PAA.

55. *Calgary Albertan,* October 13, 1928.

56. "Entertainers and Entertainment," 1926, Clipping File, GAI.

57. *Farm and Ranch Review,* December 5, 1917.

58. *Red Deer Advocate,* June 30, 1916.

59. *Farm and Ranch Review,* April 1909.

60. *Extension Annual Report, 1931,* 7.

61. *Farm and Ranch Review,* December 5, 1917.

62. Kallman, *A History of Music in Canada,* 172.

63. *Calgary Herald,* June 16, 1928.

64. *Farm and Ranch Review,* August 20, 1918, and November 5, 1920.

65. "Games," p. 3, 79.19, PAA; L.J. Roy Wilson, "Children, Teachers and Schools in Early Medicine Hat," *Alberta History* 32 (1984): 17.

66. Retail catalogues are a good source for

information about commercially available games.

67. John Blackburn, *Land of Promise* (Toronto: Macmillan of Canada, 1970), 52.
68. *Calgary Herald,* January 18, 1909.
69. Ibid.
70. *The UFA,* November 1, 1933.
71. See Douglas Owram, *The Promise of Eden: The Canadian Expansionist Movement and the Idea of the West 1856-1900* (Toronto: University of Toronto Press, 1980), 23-25, 70-74.
72. *Edmonton Journal,* April 21, 1923.
73. David C. Jones, "'There is Some Power About the Land': The Western Agrarian Press and the Country Life Ideology," *Journal of Canadian Studies* 17 (1982): 99.
74. Greg Thomas and Ian Clarke, "The Garrison Mentality and the Canadian West," *Prairie Forum* 4 (1970): 85.
75. *Calgary Herald,* December 13, 1909; *Edmonton Journal,* April 21, 1923.
76. Annora Brown, *Sketches from Life* (Edmonton: Hurtig Publishers Ltd., 1981), 52.
77. Information from Betty Vladicka, Alberta Tree Nursery, Edmonton, 1987.
78. Richardson to Craig, August 30, 1926, Department of Agriculture Records, 73.307/20/249, PAA.
79. *Prize List, 1938,* Edmonton Horticultural and Vacant Lots Garden Association, PP, File 1235A, PAA; "Steel Briggs Seeds for Western Farms and Gardens," (catalogue) 1929.
80. Brown, *Sketches from Life,* 109-11.
81. *Calgary Herald,* February 3, 1911.
82. Christopher Varley, "Winnipeg West: The Postwar Development of Art in Western Canada," in *The Making of the Modern West: Western Canada Since 1945,* ed. A.W. Rasporich (Calgary: University of Calgary Press, 1984), 226; "The Alberta Society of Artists," n.d., 76.411, PAA; D. Campbell, "Community Art Schools," *MAT* (June 1951): 4; Helen Collinson, "Lars Haukaness, Artist and Instructor," *Alberta History* 32 (1984): 11-20.
83. *The UFA,* May 1, 1929.
84. "The Alberta Home & School News," November 15, 1939, PP, File 711B, PAA.
85. *The UFA,* September 15, 1930.
86. Humphrey Carver, "Home Made Thoughts on Handicrafts," *Royal Architectural Institute of Canada Journal* (April 1940): 54.
87. Scrapbook, 1933, M1670, File 67, GAI; *The UFA,* July 3, 1933.
88. Hoadley to Brownlee, May 19, 1933, PP, File 159A, PAA.
89. *Extension Annual Report, 1935,* 25-26.
90. *The Peace River Record,* January 8, 1932, PP, File 158A, PAA.
91. *Edmonton Bulletin,* December 29, 1888.
92. Blackburn, *Land of Promise,* 194-96.
93. *Edmonton Bulletin,* December 3, 1896.
94. Hugh Dempsey, *Christmas in the West* (Saskatoon: Western Producer Prairie Books, 1982), 121-22; Lukasiewicz, "Polish Community in the Crow's Nest Pass," 6.
95. For menus, see *Farm and Ranch Review,* December 1905; *The UFA,* December 11, 1928.
96. Letter, January 25, 1941, A. Balmer Watt Collection, Bruce Peel Special Collections Library, University of Alberta.
97. *Calgary Herald,* December 6, 1924.
98. *Red Deer Advocate,* December 4, 1908; November 17, 1906. See also Dempsey, *Christmas in the West,* 93, 121.
99. *Calgary Herald,* November 29, 1911.

3. Leisure and the Community

1. *Edmonton Bulletin,* October 4, 1884.
2. Hugh Cunningham, *Leisure and the Industrial Revolution, c. 1780-c. 1880* (London: Croom Helm, 1980), 181.
3. Keith Sandiford, "Cricket and Victorian Society," *Journal of Social History* 15 (1983): 305-6.
4. Carl Betke, "The Social Significance of Sport in the City: Edmonton in the 1920s," in *Cities in the West: Papers of the Western Canadian Urban History Conference,* ed. A.R. McCormack and I. MacPherson, Mercury Series, no. 10 (Ottawa: National Museum of Man, 1975), 220.
5. *Calgary Herald,* November 19, 1903.
6. Ibid., January 8, 1903.
7. Ibid., June 15, 1909; *Red Deer Advocate,* March 10, 1922.
8. Paul Voisey, *Vulcan: The Making of a Prairie Community* (Toronto: University of Toronto Press, 1988), 183-94.
9. C.A. Dawson and Eva R. Younge, *Pioneering in the Prairie Provinces: The Social Side of the Settlement Process* (Toronto: Macmillan of Canada, 1940), 210, 216-18, 225.
10. Howard and Tamara Palmer, "The Religious Ethic and the Spirit of Immigration: The Dutch in Alberta," in *Peoples of Alberta: Portraits of Cultural Diversity,* ed. Howard and Tamara Palmer (Saskatoon: Western Producer Prairie Books, 1985), 144.
11. *Calgary Herald,* October 30, 1902.
12. Information provided by Jane McCracken, Historic Sites Service, Alberta Culture and Multiculturalism, 1987.
13. Jane McCracken, *Stephan G. Stephansson:*

The Poet of the Rocky Mountains, Historic Sites Service Occasional Paper, no. 9 (Edmonton: Alberta Culture, 1982), 113-19.

14. *La Survivance* was edited by Father Bréton (Donald Smith, "A History of French Speaking Albertans," in *Peoples of Alberta,* 96, 102).

15. Joanna Matejko, "The Polish Experience in Alberta," in *Peoples of Alberta,* 278-79, 284-87.

16. Gillis to Brownlee, March 14, 1932, Premiers' Papers (hereafter PP), File 158A, Provincial Archives of Alberta (hereafter PAA).

17. *Edmonton Journal,* May 24, 1924.

18. *Calgary Herald,* March 25, 1946.

19. Frances Swyripa, "The Ukrainians in Alberta," in *Peoples of Alberta,* 236-37.

20. Ol'ha Woychenko, "Community Organizations," in *A Heritage in Transition: Essays in the History of Ukrainians in Canada,* ed. Manoly Lupul (Toronto: McClelland and Stewart Ltd., 1982), 174.

21. D. MacGregor, ed., *The Alberta Club Woman's Blue Book,* (Calgary: Calgary Canadian Women's Press Club, 1917), 61-62.

22. *Farm and Ranch Review,* April 1937.

23. Minutes, Clover Bar United Church Women, 1935-1945, 82.288, PAA. The Minute Book includes financial statements, which are valuable indicators of expenditures and receipts, and therefore of activity.

24. *Farm and Ranch Review,* April 1937.

25. Minute Book, Edmonton Chapter Hadassah, 1914-1937, 76.5, PAA.

26. Dawson and Younge, *Pioneering in the Prairie Provinces,* 215.

27. Clipping, correspondence, April 9, 1925, PP, File 11B, PAA.

28. *Edmonton Bulletin,* March 2, 1896. See also Voisey, *Vulcan,* 184-86.

29. Margaret Prang, " 'The Girl God Would Have Me Be': The Canadian Girls in Training, 1915-1939," *Canadian Historical Review* 66 (1985): 155-56.

30. Circular Materials, 1945, Alberta CGIT Association, M5931, File 135, Glenbow-Alberta Institute Archives (hereafter cited as GAI).

31. "A History of CGIT in Alberta," 1954, M5931, File 1, GAI.

32. "Suggested Money Raising Activities," n.d., (ca. 1934-1938), M5931, File 134, GAI.

33. In 1947 and 1954, CGIT had 3,428 and 3,564 members respectively ("A History of CGIT in Alberta," 1954, M5931, File 1, GAI). The 1946 *Census of the Prairie Provinces* showed the total number of non-farm rural and urban girls, 12-18 years of age, as 26,138 (*Census of the Prairie Provinces, 1946,* vol. 1, Table 15, 496).

34. "A History of CGIT in Alberta," 1954, M5931, File 1, GAI.

35. D. Macleod, "Act Your Age: Boyhood, Adolescence and the Rise of the Boy Scouts of America," *Journal of Social History* 16 (1982): 3-20; Roderick Nash, *Wilderness and the American Mind,* rev. ed. (New Haven: Yale University Press, 1973), 147-48.

36. *Calgary Herald,* April 8, 1912.

37. *Red Deer Advocate,* November 16, 1923.

38. George Altmeyer, "Three Ideas of Nature in Canada, 1893-1914," *Journal of Canadian Studies* 11 (1976): 26.

39. *Red Deer Advocate,* May 12, 1922.

40. Ibid., April 16, 1920.

41. *Calgary Herald,* March 20, 1920.

42. *The UFA,* May 1, 1926. See also Warren Caragata, *Alberta Labour: A Heritage Untold* (Toronto: James Lorimer and Company Ltd., 1979), 55; *Red Deer Advocate,* May 12, 1922.

43. "Grants," PP, File 417, PAA. This was a significant grant at the time; in 1928-29 orphanages in the province received $3,000.

44. "Boy Scouts Association, Statement . . . 1928," PP, File 417, PAA. The total number of scouts and cubs in Canada in 1928 was 45,110.

45. The Boy Scouts Association, Alberta Provincial Council, "Scouting in Alberta," *Annual Report, 1947,* 6.

46. See *Calgary Herald,* March 20, 1920; Malcolmson to Greenfield, October 9, 1923, PP, File 416A, PAA.

47. Malcolmson to Greenfield, October 9, 1923, and Greenfield to Malcolmson, October 23, 1923, PP, File 416A, PAA.

48. Morris to Greenfield, February 5, 1925, PP, File 416A, PAA.

49. Dick to Brownlee, June 25, 1929, PP, File 417, PAA.

50. Minutes, Calgary Council on Child and Family Welfare, September 26, 1941, M6466, GAI.

51. "History of Young Men's Movement in Edmonton," 1908, Edmonton YMCA, Board Minutes Book, 1908-14, 68.210, PAA.

52. *Calgary Herald,* April 30, 1910. On the Calgary Young Men's Club, see *Calgary Herald,* September 27, 1906.

53. Alberta Tuxis Parliament Handbook, p. 5, Torrence Papers, 77.3/1/8, PAA. Circular letter from Pike, November 14, 1925, PP, File 218, PAA; *Calgary Herald,* April 2, 1921.

54. Lapp to Brownlee, April 7, 1927, PP, File 417, PAA.
55. Edmonton YMCA, *Annual Report 1935*.
56. *Calgary Herald*, October 2, 1937.
57. Edmonton YMCA, *Annual Report 1935*.
58. Bayne to Baker, September 14, 1933, PP, File 138B, PAA.
59. *Calgary Herald*, October 2, 1937.
60. Membership Guide, 1938-39, Edmonton Hi-Y Club, Records Re: Youth Groups, 68.195/68, PAA.
61. *Handbook for Laymen*, 77.3/30, PAA; Minutes of Executive Meeting, Young People's Committee, October 23, 1944, 68.195/75, PAA.
62. "A Wholesome Movement," clipping, 1944, 77.3/23, PAA.
63. MacGregor, *The Alberta Club Woman's Blue Book*, 21.
64. *Calgary Herald*, July 3, 1909.
65. Story to Aberhart, March 27, 1939, PP, File 970, PAA. One of the main "problems" they hoped to avert was prostitution. See James Gray, *Red Lights on the Prairies* (Scarborough: New American Library, 1973), 131-32.
66. "Edmonton 'Y,' Calling All Girls," 1937-38, PP, File 1232, PAA.
67. Corbett to Birks, September 25, 1922, 75-112-87, University of Alberta Archives (hereafter UAA).
68. "The History of the [Extension] Movement," 1921, 74.23.14, UAA.
69. *The Press Bulletin*, November 23, 1928.
70. Donald Cameron, *The Impossible Dream* (n.p.: Alcraft and Bulletin Printers, 1977), 80.
71. Alberta Library Association, Annual Meeting, May 26, 1948, 75.76.4, UAA.
72. "Forging a Nation's Metal," n.d., (ca. 1925), 74.23.37, UAA.
73. *Farm and Ranch Review*, November 5, 1920.
74. *The Press Bulletin*, November 23, 1928.
75. Report of the Educational Committee (UFA), n.d., (ca. 1931), PP, File 170A, PAA.
76. Aberhart to Fleischman, March 10, 1938. PP, File 728A, PAA.
77. *The Press Bulletin*, November 20, 1931.
78. "Town Planning in Alberta," Article 5, October 20, 1930, PP, File 247, PAA.
79. Aberhart to Macintyre, March 2, 1936, PP, File 728A, PAA.
80. Wirsch to Aberhart, February 18, 1936, PP, File 728A, PAA.
81. Fleischman to Social Credit Board, February 3, 1938, PP, File 728A, PAA.
82. John Chalmers, *Schools of the Foothills Province* (Toronto: University of Toronto Press for the Alberta Teachers' Association, 1967), 46. On school consolidation in the Vulcan area, see Voisey, *Vulcan*, 180-81.
83. LeRouzic to Aberhart, October 5, 1939, PP, File 728A, PAA.
84. Anderson to McNally, June 25, 1936, PP, File 739, PAA.
85. *Farm and Ranch Review*, November 5, 1920.
86. Orest Martynowych, *The Ukrainian Bloc Settlement in East Central Alberta 1890-1930: A History*, Historic Sites Service Occasional Paper, no. 10 (Edmonton: Alberta Culture, 1985), 230-31.
87. See, for example, Namao UFA Community Hall Minute Book, 1925-1949, 81.177, PAA.
88. Martynowych, *Ukrainian Bloc Settlement*, 321.
89. "History of Rycroft Board of Trade," pp. 86-87, Rycroft Agricultural Society Papers, 82.154/2/5, PAA. For a description of community halls in East Central Alberta see Martynowych, *Ukrainian Bloc Settlement*, 229-30.
90. *Farm and Ranch Review*, April 1937.
91. For example, see Silverwood Community Hall Association Account Book, 1939-1949, 69.152, PAA.
92. Edey to Registrar of Companies, September 24, 1951, Spirit Valley Community Association Papers, 76.517/4, PAA.
93. C.A. Dawson and R.W. Murchie, *The Settlement of the Peace River Country: A Study of a Pioneer Area* (Toronto: Macmillan of Canada, 1934), 225.
94. Kerr to Cameron, August 22, 1940, and Cameron to Kerr, August 26, 1940, 73.24.2, UAA.
95. Peter Ream, *The Fort on the Saskatchewan*, 2nd ed. (n.p.: Metropolitan Printing, 1974), 283-84.
96. *Edmonton Journal*, January 5, 1924.
97. Ibid., January 11, 1925.
98. Ibid., January 5, 1924.
99. *Farm and Ranch Review*, August 20, 1917.
100. For a discussion of the literature on the American playground movement, see S. Hardy and A. Ingham, "Games, Structures and Agency: Historians on the American Play Movement," *Journal of Social History* 17 (1983): 285.
101. See, for example, *Calgary Herald*, August 6, 1909, and July 18, 1910.
102. *Calgary Herald*, May 4, 1917.
103. *Public Health Journal* 4 (1913): 606.
104. *Calgary Herald*, March 15, 1912.
105. Ibid., July 22, 1922.
106. *Edmonton Journal*, June 1, 1929.
107. See *Calgary Herald*, July 22, 1922.
108. Ibid., May 4, 1917.
109. *Public Health Journal* 4 (1913): 609.
110. *Edmonton Journal*, July 5, 1924.

111. *Public Health Journal* 4 (1913): 609. Such qualifications in supervisors were still in demand in 1938 (Minutes, Calgary Council on Child and Family Welfare, March 25, 1938, M6466, GAI).

112. *Calgary Herald*, May 4, 1917; Minutes, September 27, 1940 and September 22, 1939, M6466, GAI.

113. *Edmonton Journal*, July 5, 1924.

114. *Western Municipal News*, May 1922, 144.

115. *Calgary Herald*, September 8, 1910.

116. Ibid., July 18, 1910.

117. *Social Welfare*, November 1931, 25, 28, 33.

118. *Calgary Herald*, May 21, 1932.

119. *The Press Bulletin*, November 20, 1931.

120. James A. Proudfoot, "Some Aspects of the Recreational Geography of the North Saskatchewan River Valley—Edmonton" (M.A. thesis, University of Alberta, 1965), 15-16.

121. *Red Deer Advocate*, October 3, 1924.

122. Ibid., April 18, 1924.

123. Itemized Estimate, Rotary Playground, Pleasant Park, n.d., (ca. 1931), M1700, File 103, GAI.

124. Rotary Club to Foulds, July 19, 1943, and Rotary Club to Mayor, June 23, 1938, and Garnett to Rinman, August 31, 1949, Rotary Club of Calgary Papers, M1700, File 103, GAI.

125. Elsie M. McFarland, *The Development of Public Recreation in Canada* (n.p.: Canada Parks/Recreation Association, 1970), 42.

126. *Edmonton Journal*, July 5, 1924.

127. McFarland, *The Development of Public Recreation*, 42-43.

128. Max Foran, *Calgary: An Illustrated History* (Toronto: James Lorimer and Company Ltd., 1978), 24; *Calgary Herald*, May 2, 1888; South Edmonton IOOF Minute Book, 1893-1929, 84.98, PAA; Ream, *The Fort on the Saskatchewan*, 377.

129. John Herd Thompson with Allen Seager, *Canada 1922-1939: Decades of Discord* (Toronto: McClelland and Stewart Ltd., 1985), 175; "The Rotary Club of Calgary: 50 Golden Years, 1914-1964," H.J. Snell Papers, File 65.7.1-6, Red Deer and District Archives.

130. *Calgary Herald*, May 3, 1924.

131. Patricia Jasen, "The Oddfellows in Early Calgary," *Alberta History* 35 (1987): 9-11.

132. Whether members believed in the ancient pedigrees of their orders is unclear. The Masons' claims to ancient lineage are well known. Some members of the Oddfellows also claimed an ancient line of descent from the Jewish legion of the Emperor Titus. Most Oddfellows seem to have been sceptical of this pedigree and recognized the eighteenth century origins of their Order (*Calgary Herald*, April 24, 1912). The Shriners, the top rank of the Masons, wore oriental costumes and fezzes. During a Shriner Convention in Calgary in 1915, a number of Shriners went out to the Sarcee Camp where recruits were being trained. One soldier reportedly mistook the Shriners for Montenegrins, and when he was told that "them ain't Montenegroes...them's Shriners," the soldier retorted, "Well, who the h--- are they going to fight for?" (*Calgary Herald*, July 10, 1915).

133. *Red Deer Advocate*, February 14, 1908; *Calgary Herald*, December 17, 1903; Jasen, "The Oddfellows in Early Calgary," 11.

134. *Edmonton Bulletin*, September 24, 1894.

135. *Red Deer Advocate*, February 3, 1922.

136. C.A. Dawson and R.W. Murchie, *The Settlement of the Peace River Country: A Study of a Pioneer Area* (Toronto: Macmillan of Canada, 1934), 88.

137. Ibid., 169.

138. *Coronation Souvenir* (Edmonton: May 12, 1937), p. 43, PP, File 1233A, PAA.

139. Canadian Legion of the British Empire Service League, "Tenth Anniversary of the Founding of the Canadian Legion," (Ottawa, 1935), p. 4, PP, File 1233A, PAA.

140. Briefing note, n.d., (ca. 1919), PP, File 165, PAA.

141. Deputy Provincial Secretary to Manning, December 20, 1944, PP, File 970, PAA.

142. Petition by Cochrane Branch, Canadian Red Cross, July 17, 1941, PP, File 861, PAA.

143. Beattie to Greenfield, November 29, 1923, PP, File 97C, PAA.

144. Circular, Canadian Legion, B.E.S.L., October 19, 1936, PP, File 1233A, PAA. A list of licensed veterans' clubs in 1928 can be found in "Club Room Licenses, 1928," PP, File 98C, PAA.

145. S. Bosetti, "The Rural Women's University: Women's Institutes in Alberta from 1909 to 1940" (M.Ed. thesis, University of Alberta, 1983), 3, 52.

146. "A Brief History of the Alberta W.I.," n.d., (ca. 1950), p. 9, Alberta Women's Institute Papers, 76.174, PAA.

147. *Farm and Ranch Review*, April 1937.

148. Kathleen Strange, *With the West in Her Eyes* (Toronto: Macmillan of Canada Ltd., 1945), 113-14.

149. *Farm and Ranch Review*, November 5, 1913.

150. See Baron's Women's Institute Papers, M5762, File 3, GAI.

151. *Farm and Ranch Review*, April 1937.

152. *The UFA*, November 1, 1927.

153. *Farm and Ranch Review*, April 1937.

154. Bosetti, "The Rural Women's University," 44-45, 206-7.
155. "Official Review, 24th Annual Convention, Benevolent Protective Order of Elks, 1936," p. 21, PP, File 1235A, PAA.
156. Ibid.
157. Ibid., 23.
158. *Red Deer Advocate*, June 26, 1925, and December 12, 1924.
159. RCMP Report, Victory Shows, July 31, 1946, Department of the Attorney General Records, 73.344/33/480, PAA. The Carnival was investigated by the RCMP because it featured "games of chance."
160. John Norris, "Functions of Ethnic Organizations," in *Immigration and the Rise of Multiculturalism*, ed. Howard Palmer (Toronto: Copp Clark Publishing, 1975), 166-67.
161. Norma Milton, "The Scots in Alberta," in *Peoples of Alberta*, 121.
162. *Edmonton Bulletin*, April 6, 1896.
163. J. Fainella, "The Development of Italian Organizations in Calgary," *Alberta History* 32 (1984): 22-23.
164. H. Radecki and B. Heydenkorn, *A Member of a Distinguished Family: The Polish Group in Canada* (Toronto: McClelland and Stewart Ltd., 1976), 61-72. On Polish clubs in the Crowsnest Pass, see Krystyna Lukasiewicz, "Polish Community in the Crow's Nest Pass," *Alberta History* 36 (1988): 4.
165. Donald Avery, *Dangerous Foreigners* (Toronto: McClelland and Stewart Ltd., 1979), 62-63.
166. Howard and Tamara Palmer, "Estonians in Alberta," in *Peoples of Alberta*, 201.
167. *Edmonton Journal*, July 14 and August 3, 1936.
168. E. Bettcher to Aberhart, June 7, 1940, and Aberhart to Bettcher, June 12, 1940, PP, File 680A, PAA.
169. Fainella, "The Development of Italian Organizations," 24.
170. "Alberta Youth Congress, 1937, Reports," PP, File 1235A, PAA.
171. McFarland, *The Development of Public Recreation*, 51.
172. Ainlay to Manning, January 22, 1946, PP, File 1508, PAA.
173. McFarland, *The Development of Public Recreation*, 45.
174. Pardee to Manning, January 22, 1944; Manning to Pardee, February 7, 1944, PP, File 1223, PAA.

4. To be a Gentleman: Sports in Alberta

1. Morris Mott, "The British Protestant Pioneers and The Establishment of Manly Sports in Manitoba, 1870-1886," *Journal of Sport History* 7 (1980): 27-30. See also his "One Solution to the Urban Crisis: Manly Sport and Winnipeggers, 1900-1914," *Urban History Review* 12 (1983): 57-70.
2. Crumblehulme to Brownlee, February 13, 1932, Premiers' Papers (hereafter PP), File 571, Provincial Archives of Alberta, (hereafter PAA).
3. *Calgary Herald*, June 16, 1928.
4. Ibid., June 26, 1928.
5. *Farm and Ranch Review*, June 20, 1913. Only the Hutterites among major Alberta groups actually discouraged competitive sports, rejecting such activity on moral grounds.
6. *Public Health Journal* 4 (1913): 608.
7. Minutes, Calgary Council on Child and Family Welfare, October 22, 1931, M6466, Glenbow-Alberta Institute Archives (hereafter GAI).
8. *Calgary Herald*, June 16, 1928; see also July 8, 1907.
9. Ibid., December 4, 1920.
10. See, for example, *Calgary Herald*, September 11, 1915.
11. *Calgary Herald*, November 10, 1928.
12. *Public Health Journal* 4 (1913): 607.
13. *Town Planning and Conservation of Life* 6 (1920): 23.
14. *Public Health Journal* 11 (1920): 119-25.
15. Bowen to Greenfield, April 6, 1923, PP, File 416A, PAA. The Rifle Association received provincial grants from 1906-14.
16. David Bourdon, "Militarism, Sport and Social Control in Alberta, 1900-1920" (M.A. thesis, University of Calgary, 1985), 93-112.
17. See, for example, *Calgary Herald*, January 14, 1911.
18. *Calgary Herald*, August 16, 1911.
19. Quoted in Carl Betke, "The Social Significance of Sport in the City: Edmonton in the 1920s," in *Cities in the West: Papers of the Western Canadian Urban History Conference*, Mercury Series Paper, no. 10, ed. A.R. McCormack and I. MacPherson (Ottawa: National Museum of Man, 1975), 226.
20. M. Hall, "A History of Women's Sport in Canada Prior to World War I" (M.A. thesis, University of Alberta, 1968), 116.
21. H. Lenskyj, "Femininity First. Sport and Physical Education for Ontario Girls,

1890-1930," *Canadian Journal of Sport History* 13 (1982): 12.

22. Ibid., 10.

23. *Farm and Ranch Review,* March 15, 1930.

24. *Calgary Herald,* November 27, 1928.

25. *Farm and Ranch Review,* March 15, 1930.

26. D. MacGregor, ed., *The Alberta Club Woman's Blue Book* (Calgary: Calgary Canadian Women's Press Club, 1917), 23.

27. *Civil Service Bulletin,* October 1935, 10.

28. Wotherspoon to Brownlee, March 20, 1934, PP, File 159C, PAA.

29. "Leisure Hours," Canadian National Parks Association, *Newsletter,* no. 50.

30. Rogers to Aberhart, May 15, 1937, PP, File 746, PAA; Canadian Department of Labour, *Review of the Dominion Provincial Youth Training Programme for the Fiscal Year Ending March 31, 1939* (Ottawa, 1939), 5.

31. "Leisure Hours."

32. Ian Jobling, "Sport in Nineteenth Century Canada: The Effects of Technological Changes on its Development" (Ph.D. diss., University of Alberta, 1970), 354-95; Alan Metcalfe, *Canada Learns to Play* (Toronto: McClelland and Stewart Ltd., 1987), 49-51.

33. Ronald Lappage, "Selected Sports and Canadian Society, 1921-1939" (Ph.D. diss., University of Alberta, 1974), 185.

34. *Edmonton Bulletin,* July 1, 1895.

35. *Camrose Canadian,* June 17, 1909.

36. "Sports Programme, University Week for Farm Young People," 1921, 74-118-1, University of Alberta Archives (hereafter UAA).

37. Carl Betke, "Sports Promotion in the Western Canadian City: The Example of Early Edmonton," *Urban History Review* 12 (1983): 47.

38. Peter Ream, *The Fort on the Saskatchewan,* 2nd ed. (n.p.: Metropolitan Printing, 1974), 387; William M. McLennan, *Sport in Early Calgary* (Calgary: Fort Brisebois Publishing, 1983), 105, 218.

39. Betke, "Sports Promotion," 48.

40. Bourdon, "Militarism, Sport and Social Control," 46-47.

41. Betke, "Sport in the City: Edmonton," 220.

42. McLennan, *Sport in Early Calgary,* 107-8.

43. Dave Leonard, John McIsaac, and Shelagh Jamieson, *A Builder of the Northwest: The Life and Times of Richard Secord, 1860-1935* (Privately printed, 1981), 91.

44. McLennan, *Sport in Early Calgary,* 113. Usually these rinks were converted into roller skating rinks during the summer to produce year-round revenue.

45. *Farm and Ranch Review,* November 2, 1920.

46. *Calgary Herald,* June 14, 1909.

47. Ibid., March 21, 1913.

48. *Edmonton Journal,* May 30, 1931.

49. Ibid., January 11, 1925; Minutes, November 24, 1944, M6466, GAI.

50. *Red Deer Advocate,* September 12, 1924; June 12, 1925.

51. Edmonton YMCA, *Annual Report, 1935.*

52. Nancy and Maxwell Howell, *Sports and Games in Canadian Life* (Toronto: Macmillan of Canada, 1969), 67; Metcalfe, *Canada Learns to Play,* 123-24.

53. *Calgary Herald,* July 8, 1907.

54. Ibid., June 4, 1909.

55. Ibid., July 12, 1919.

56. Howell and Howell, *Sports and Games,* 93, 95, 151. In 1884 it was called the Amateur Athletic Association. It changed its name in 1898 to the Canadian Amateur Athletic Union and changed it again in 1909 to the Amateur Athletic Union of Canada. (See Metcalfe, *Canada Learns to Play,* 102-19).

57. Cecil Blackburn, "The Development of Sports in Alberta, 1900-1918" (M.A. thesis, University of Alberta, 1974), 429.

58. H. Lang to Members, August 25, 1925, Alberta Amateur Athletic Union Papers, M6461, GAI.

59. Blackburn, "The Development of Sports in Alberta," 430.

60. Hall, "A History of Women's Sports," 177-78.

61. Blackburn, "The Development of Sports in Alberta," 432-33.

62. Minutes, n.d., (ca. 1919), M6461, GAI.

63. Minutes, May 17, 1919, M6461, GAI.

64. Crumblehulme to Brownlee, February 13, 1932, and Small to Brownlee, February 3, 1932, PP, File 571, PAA.

65. *Red Deer Advocate,* May 23, 1919.

66. Minutes, November 13, 1920, M6461, GAI.

67. Resolution of Alberta Amateur Athletic Union, September 3, 1928, PP, File 156A, PAA.

68. Lappage, "Sports and Canadian Society," 62.

69. *Edmonton Journal,* May 16, 1931.

70. Gary Zeman, *Alberta on Ice* (Edmonton: Westweb Press, 1985),14.

71. *Camrose Canadian,* July 7, 1910.

72. Betke, "Sports Promotion," 55.

73. Deputy Provincial Secretary to Brownlee, October 27, 1926, PP, File 364, PAA.

74. Bill McNeil and Morris Wolfe, *The Birth of Radio in Canada: Signing On* (Toronto: Doubleday Canada Ltd., 1982), 149.

75. Sebastien de Grazia, *Of Time, Work and Leisure* (New York: The Twentieth Century Fund, 1962), 223-24.

76. *Edmonton Journal,* June 14, 1924.

77. T. Vellathottam, "A History of Lacrosse in Canada Prior to 1914" (M.A. thesis, University of Alberta, 1968), 87.
78. Lappage, "Sports and Canadian Society," 40-43, 64-65.
79. *Edmonton Bulletin,* August 12, 1895.
80. *Edmonton Journal,* June 7, 1983.
81. *Lethbridge Herald,* June 19, 1937.
82. See Howell and Howell, *Sports and Games,* 104.
83. Blackburn, "The Development of Sports in Alberta," 230.
84. *Edmonton Journal,* July 30, 1921.
85. Betke, "Sport and the City: Edmonton," 232 n.28.
86. *Calgary Herald,* June 25, 1910.
87. Minutes, St. Andrews Golf Club, March 3, 1916, M1675 GAI.
88. See *Calgary Herald,* March 31, April 7, April 24, 1923.
89. *Edmonton Journal,* July 30, 1921.
90. Lappage, "Sports and Canadian Society," 56; Circular Letter, May 28, 1937, M6278, File 14, GAI.
91. *Edmonton Journal,* July 30, 1921.
92. Canadian Golf Ball Co. to Robb, December 21, 1926, PP, File 224A, PAA.
93. Barclay to Barclay, September 22, 1928, Barclay Papers, M6126, GAI.
94. Gordie to Matthews, June 11, 1937, Alberta Golf Association Papers, M6278 File 14, and Munro to Broadfoot, August 23, 1945, File 21, GAI.
95. "Early History of Mayfair Golf and Country Club," p.7, Mayfair Golf and Country Club Papers, 82.179, PAA.
96. Circular Letter, March 6, 1924, 74-23-39, UAA.
97. *Edmonton Journal,* April 1, 1922. In this respect, it should be recalled that the percentage of urban people with cars was relatively low in the years before 1940.
98. Blackburn, "The Development of Sports in Alberta," 231.
99. Dickins to Matthews, June 4, 1936, M6278. File 13, GAI.
100. Howell and Howell, *Sports and Games,* 253.
101. Canadian Golf Ball Co. to Robb, December 21, 1926, PP, File 224A, PAA; Circular Letter, May 28, 1937, and Broadfoot to Anderson, April 5, 1939, M6278, File 14, GAI.
102. See correspondence, M6278, Files 11-14, GAI.
103. Alberta Provincial Report, n.d., M6278, File 26, GAI.
104. Letter from Banks, January 5, 1948, M6278, File 28, GAI; Howell and Howell, *Sports and Games,* 256-57.
105. Metcalfe, *Canada Learns to Play,* 85-95.
106. *Edmonton Bulletin,* July 5, 1884.
107. Blackburn, "The Development of Sports in Alberta," 81.
108. "Cardston: Always a Great Sports Town," Newspapers, File 11, Alberta Folk Archive, Bruce Peel Special Collections Library, University of Alberta (hereafter cited as BPSC).
109. Blackburn, "The Development of Sports in Alberta," 93-96.
110. John Herd Thompson with Allen Seager, *Canada 1922-1939: Decades of Discord* (Toronto: McClelland and Stewart Ltd., 1985), 187; Howell and Howell, *Sports and Games,* 284.
111. "Cardston," Alberta Folk Archive, BPSC.
112. Paul Voisey, *Vulcan: The Making of a Prairie Community* (Toronto: University of Toronto Press, 1988), 164; [Drayton Valley High School], "History of Drayton Valley" (n.p.: typescript, [1974]), p.4.
113. Blackburn, "The Development of Sports in Alberta," 97-98.
114. Howell and Howell, *Sports and Games,* 285-86.
115. Blackburn, "The Development of Sports in Alberta," 103.
116. "Cardston," Alberta Folk Archive, BPSC.
117. *Farm and Ranch Review,* November 5, 1920.
118. Webber to Brownlee, July 25, 1930, and Brownlee to Webber, July 28, 1930, PP, File 319A, PAA.
119. Rolf Lund, "Skiing on the Prairies," *Saskatchewan History* 32 (1979): 29-30; Rolf Lund, "Skiing in Canada: The Early Years," *The Beaver,* Outfit 308.3 (1977): 53; Rolf Lund, "A History of Skiing in Canada Prior to 1940" (M.A. thesis, University of Alberta, 1971), 163-65, 187.
120. *Edmonton Journal,* January 20, 1923.
121. Lund, "A History of Skiing in Canada," 177-87.
122. Lappage, "Sports and Canadian Society," 51. In Calgary in 1915 a December chinook created a "sportsman's elysium." The winds melted the snow and allowed golf and baseball to be played, but the temperature remained low enough to permit skating (*Calgary Herald,* December 6, 1915).
123. Betke, "Sport in the City: Edmonton," 225-28; Lappage, "Sports and Canadian Society," 51.
124. See, for example, diaries and personal papers, Allison Collection, M16, GAI.
125. See, for example, *Calgary Herald,* December 20, 1910.
126. McLennan, *Sport in Early Calgary,* 119.
127. *Red Deer Advocate,* September 12, 1924.
128. "Speed Skating Championship, 1953," p. 23, PP, File 1798B, PAA.
129. Zeman, *Alberta on Ice,* 2.

130. Ibid., 9, 106, 164, 261.
131. Blackburn, "The Development of Sports in Alberta," 261-64; James Gray, *A Brand of its Own: The 100 Year History of the Calgary Exhibiton and Stampede* (Saskatoon: Western Producer Prairie Books, 1985), 73.
132. *Edmonton Journal*, January 11, 1925.
133. H. Eckert, "The Development of Organized Recreation and Physical Education in Alberta" (M.A. thesis, University of Alberta, 1953), 52. See also *Edmonton Journal*, January 27, 1923.
134. *Edmonton Journal*, January 27, 1923.
135. Letter, April 20, 1940, A. Balmer Watt Collection, BPSC.
136. Zeman, *Alberta on Ice*, 27-32, 40-44.
137. Lappage, "Sports and Canadian Society," 195.
138. Howell and Howell, *Sports and Games*, 213-15; Thompson with Seager, *Canada 1922-1939*, 188-89.
139. Howell and Howell, *Sports and Games*, 204-5; Blackburn, "The Development of Sports in Alberta," 240. On early hockey rules and playing techniques in western Canada see Morris Mott, "Flawed Games, Splendid Ceremonies: The Hockey Games of the Winnipeg Vics, 1890-1903," *Prairie Forum* 10 (1985): 169-87.
140. Jobling, "Sport in Nineteenth Century Canada," 242, 252.
141. Blackburn, "The Development of Sports in Alberta," 456.
142. Ibid., 186. A curling club was organized in Edmonton in 1888 and in Calgary in 1885.
143. Jean Burnet, *Next-Year Country: A Study of Rural Social Organization in Alberta* (Toronto: University of Toronto Press, 1978), 68.
144. Voisey, *Vulcan*, 165.
145. *Edmonton Bulletin*, November, 9, 1889; Ream, *The Fort on the Saskatchewan*, 391-94; *Edmonton Journal*, December 23, 1922.
146. Blackburn, "The Development of Sports in Alberta," 186.
147. "The Opening of Artificial Ice, Debolt Curling Rink," 1969, Debolt Country and Curling Club Papers, 71.22/17, PAA.
148. Scrapbook, Hill Papers, M522, GAI.
149. Blackburn, "The Development of Sports in Alberta," 188-89; Howell and Howell, *Sports and Games*, 174-75; Voisey, *Vulcan*, 164-65.
150. *Edmonton Bulletin*, January 26, 1893; Howell and Howell, *Sports and Games*, 172.
151. Blackburn, "The Development of Sports in Alberta," 177.
152. Ibid., 179-85.
153. Wilson to Manning, January 12, 1948, PP, File 1798A, PAA.
154. Howell and Howell, *Sports and Games*, 175.
155. *Calgary Herald*, January 17, 1912.
156. Marshall to Aberhart, December 30, 1935, PP, File 1060, PAA.
157. *Red Deer Advocate*, April 7, 1922.
158. Scrapbook, M522, GAI.
159. *Farm and Ranch Review*, April 1948. The Macdonald Brier Tankard was established in 1927.
160. Wilson to Manning, January 12, 1948, PP, File 1798A, PAA.
161. For reviews of the American historical literature on theories about sport see: B. Rader, "Modern Sports: In Search of Interpretations," *Journal of Social History* 13 (1979): 307-21; S. Reiss, "Sport and the American Dream: A Review Essay," *Journal of Social History* 14 (1980): 295-305. Issues of a more abstract theoretical importance are dealt with in Hart Cantelon and Richard Gruneau, *Sport, Culture and the Modern State* (Toronto: University of Toronto Press, 1982); C. Bray, "Sport, Patriarchy and Capitalism: A Socialist Feminist Analysis" (Ph.D. diss. University of Alberta, 1985).
162. Betke, "Sport and the City: Edmonton."

5. A Sense of Sportsmanship: Hunting and Fishing

1. *Calgary Herald*, September 4, 1909. On market hunting in Canada, see Janet Foster, *Working for Wildlife: The Beginning of Preservation in Canada* (Toronto: University of Toronto Press, 1973), 58, 121, 124.
2. Wallace to Mullen, January 6, 1939, Premiers' Papers (hereafter PP), File 663A, Provincial Archives of Alberta (hereafter PAA).
3. Minister of Agriculture to Premier, October 25, 1933, PP. File 15, PAA.
4. Hugh Cunningham, *Leisure in the Industrial Revolution, c. 1780-c. 1880* (London: Croom Helm, 1980), 17-20.
5. *Good Roads*, August 1922, 7.
6. *Calgary Herald*, September 17, 1903.
7. Camrose Board of Trade, *Where Farming Pays*, n.d., (ca. 1912), 16-17.
8. *Edmonton Bulletin*, February 2, 1884. Restrictions on spring hunting of waterfowl began in 1890.
9. *An Ordinance to Amend and Consolidate As Amended ''The Game Ordinance''*, Statutes of the Northwest Territories, no. 8 of 1893, s. 5.
10. *An Act for the Protection of Game*, Revised Statutes of Alberta (hereafter RSA), 1942, c. 70.

11. *An Ordinance to Amend and Consolidate as Amended "The Game Ordinance,"* Statutes of the Northwest Territories, no. 8 of 1893, s. 12.

12. *Edmonton Bulletin,* October 9, 1893.

13. *The UFA,* November 1, 1929.

14. Mullen to Aberhart, July 31, 1939, PP, File 663B, PAA.

15. Dan Gottesman, "Native Hunting and the Migratory Birds Convention Act: Historical, Political and Ideological Perspectives," *Journal of Canadian Studies* 18 (1983): 70, 73.

16. Canada, Commission of Conservation, *Report on the Ninth Annual Meeting* (Ottawa, 1918), 122.

17. *The Press Bulletin,* February 18, 1921.

18. Canada, Department of the Interior, *Migratory Birds Convention Act and Federal Regulations for the Protection of Migratory Birds, 1936.*

19. There is a substantial literature on American conservation. See, for example, Roderick Nash, *Wilderness and the American Mind,* rev. ed. (New Haven: Yale University Press, 1973); Samuel Hays, *Conservation and the Gospel of Efficiency: The Progressive Conservation Movement 1890-1920* (Cambridge, Mass.: Harvard University Press, 1959); Elmo Richardson, *The Politics of Conservation: Crusades and Controversies 1897-1913* (Berkeley: University of California Press, 1962).

20. Gottesman, "Native Hunting," 73; Foster, *Working for Wildlife,* 3. On natural history societies in Alberta, see Margaret Lewis, *To Conserve a Heritage* (Calgary: Alberta Fish and Game Association, 1979), 148-51.

21. Lewis, *To Conserve a Heritage,* 123; *The Game Act,* S.A., 1928 (Office Consolidation).

22. *Red Deer Advocate,* March 19, 1920; *Calgary Herald,* March 8, 1907.

23. Foster, *Working for Wildlife,* 59. In 1881 it was reported that a few bison could be found north of the south Branch of the Saskatchewan River. The mentality that had led to the near extermination of bison was clearly shown: hunters were after even these few miserable remnants of the great herds. (*Edmonton Bulletin,* November 26, 1881.)

24. *Edmonton Bulletin,* August 13, 1894.

25. Canada, Commission of Conservation, *Report of the Ninth Annual Meeting* (Ottawa, 1918), 127-33; Lewis, *To Conserve a Heritage,* 63; *Claresholm Review Advertiser,* May 4, 1917.

26. *Calgary Herald,* March 8, 1907; Alberta, "Report of the Chief Game and Fire Guardian," *Annual Report of the Department of Agriculture for 1908,* 101.

27. *Calgary Herald,* September 4, 1909.

28. *Claresholm Review,* August 10, 1911.

29. Ducks Unlimited (Canada), *Newsflight No. 55,* 1939, 7-8, PP, File 663B, PAA.

30. Walker to Brownlee, October 24, 1932, PP, File 15, PAA.

31. *Calgary Herald,* September 4, 1909.

32. Ibid., March 6, 1902.

33. Briefing note, no title, ca. 1935, PP, File 663, PAA.

34. *The Press Bulletin,* February 18, 1921.

35. *Eaton's Catalogue,* 1898-99, 168.

36. *The Nor'West Farmer,* October 1898.

37. *Red Deer Advocate,* September 3, 1910.

38. *Macleod's Fall & Winter Catalogue,* 1949-50, 11.

39. Inglewood Bird Sanctuary, May 17, 1938, PP, File 891, PAA.

40. Wallace to Aberhart, January 6, 1939, PP, File 663B, PAA.

41. See, for example, Fisher to Aberhart, July 15, 1939, PP, File 663B, PAA.

42. See, for example, *Edmonton Bulletin,* August 9, 1894. A somewhat overstated analysis of the positive connection between conservation and hunting in the United States is John Reiger, *American Sportsmen and the Origins of Conservation* (New York: Winchester Press, 1975).

43. *Calgary Herald,* September 4, 1909.

44. Ibid., March 6, 1902.

45. Gottesman, "Native Hunting," 80-86; Lewis, *To Conserve a Heritage,* 189-91.

46. *Calgary Herald,* September 4, 1909.

47. Ibid., May 14, 1921.

48. *The Game Act,* S.A., 1928 (Office Consolidation).

49. *Edmonton Bulletin,* August 13, 1894.

50. *Calgary Herald,* July 11, 1929; Wyman to Aberhart, November 12, 1935, PP, File 663A, PAA.

51. Circular letter from Hayden, June 26, 1929, PP, File 59, PAA.

52. Lewis, *To Conserve a Heritage,* 6.

53. Ibid., 13-14; *Calgary Herald,* April 20, 1909.

54. Lawton to Brownlee, October 28, 1927, PP, File 59, PAA.

55. "Ducks Unlimited," 1937, PP, File 663A, PAA; Lewis, *To Conserve a Heritage,* 33-39.

56. Resolutions, UFA 37th Convention, January 1946, PP, File 1513, PAA.

57. Walker to Aberhart, September 23, 1940, PP, File 771B, PAA.

58. Clipping, "Bird Sanctuary," (ca. 1937) Sear Collection, A.S243, Glenbow-Alberta Institute Archives.

59. Inglewood Bird Sanctuary, May 17, 1938, PP, File 891, PAA.

60. Gottesman, "Native Hunting," 77.

61. *Calgary Herald,* March 26, 1910.

62. Canadian National Parks Association, *Circular no. 40*, January 3, 1938.
63. Eric Fromm, *The Anatomy of Human Destructiveness* (New York: Holt, Rinehart and Winston, 1973), 136.
64. Ibid., 136-40.
65. *Good Roads*, August 1922, 17.
66. *Farm and Ranch Review*, June 10, 1927.
67. *Edmonton Bulletin*, September 14, 1893.
68. Ibid.
69. *Calgary Herald*, October 28, 1938.
70. *Edmonton Bulletin*, September 4, 1893.
71. *Edmonton Journal*, June 16, 1928.
72. See, for example, Bond to Luke, July 31, 1914, Bond Papers, MS1, File 15, City of Edmonton Archives.
73. Camrose Board of Trade, *Where Farming Pays*, 16.
74. "Cardston Always Good Sports Town," Newspapers, File 11, Alberta Folk Archive, Bruce Peel Special Collections Library, University of Alberta; *Red Deer Advocate*, August 14, 1908.
75. J. McIllree and M.H. White Fraser, "Fishing in Southern Alberta," *Alberta History* 31 (1983): 36-38.
76. *Calgary Herald*, June 3, 1911; Walker to Brownlee, May 25, 1935, PP, File 15, PAA; Walker to Aberhart, September 23, 1940, PP, File 771B, PAA.
77. *Claresholm Review*, May 29, 1913.
78. *Western Motordom*, May 1931.
79. The provincial legislation was *An Act Respecting the Rights of Fishery*, RSA 1931, c. 45. As late as 1932, fishing licenses were not required in order to fish in national parks (*Western Motordom*, May 1931).
80. *Calgary Herald*, June 3, 1911.
81. *Red Deer Advocate*, April 3, 1925.
82. Hayden to Brownlee, July 21, 1930, PP, File 59, PAA.
83. Ibid., Hayden to Brownlee, April 29, 1931.
84. Mullen to Aberhart, July 21, 1939, PP, File 663B, PAA.
85. Director of Publicity to King, September 15, 1943, PP, File 1212, PAA; Alberta, Department of Economic Affairs, *The Alberta Story, An Authentic Report on Alberta's Progress, 1935-1952* (Edmonton: Queen's Printer, 1952), 56.
86. "Sylvan Lake" (pamphlet), n.d., (ca. 1938), n.p., PP, File 931, PAA.
87. Gottesman, "Native Hunting," 85.
88. Marcel Giraud, *The Métis in the Canadian West*, vol. 2, trans. George Woodcock (Edmonton: University of Alberta Press, 1986), 458. *The Migratory Birds Convention Act* was not applied consistently to Indian hunters until 1953.

6. In God's Great Glorious Outdoors

1. See John Walton, *The English Seaside Resort: A Social History 1750-1914* (New York: St. Martin's Press, 1983).
2 George Altmeyer, "Three Ideas of Nature in Canada, 1893-1914," *Journal of Canadian Studies* 11 (1976): 21-34. For the United States, see Roderick Nash, *Wilderness and the American Mind*, rev. ed. (New Haven: Yale University Press, 1973). Douglas Owram argues that Canadian views in the 1850s about the wilderness tended towards the attitude either that it was romantic and a place of adventure and freedom, or that it was a heathen and dangerous place. In the 1860s these attitudes began to shift towards the view that nature was a source of inspiration, beauty and peace. Nevertheless, the economic potential of nature was the important definitional criterion in a concept of "beauty" and the western landscape was therefore beautiful because it had economic potential (Douglas Owram, *Promise of Eden: The Canadian Expansionist Movement and the Idea of the West, 1856-1900* (Toronto: University of Toronto Press, 1980), 16-20; 70-74).
3. *Farm and Ranch Review*, October 5, 1909.
4. J. Benidickson, "Paddling for Pleasure: Recreational Canoeing as a Canadian Way of Life," in *Recreational Land Use*, ed. G. Wall and J. Marsh (Ottawa: Carleton University Press, 1982), 324.
5. *Calgary Herald*, July 6, 1929.
6. *Edmonton Journal*, June 16, 1928.
7. *Calgary Herald*, July 7, 1923.
8. Ibid., July 1, 1911.
9. Ibid., July 7, 1923.
10. *Farm and Ranch Review*, July 20, 1910.
11. *Calgary Herald*, July 1, 1911.
12. Ibid., July 23, 1907. On the connection between Canadian nationalism and ideas about racial characteristics, see Carl Berger, *The Sense of Power* (Toronto: University of Toronto Press, 1970), 130-31.
13. *Farm and Ranch Review*, June 6, 1910.
14. *Calgary Herald*, June 7, 1930.
15. John Blackburn, *Land of Promise* (Toronto: Macmillan of Canada, 1970), 132.
16. Canada, Department of Agriculture, *Changes in Farm Family Living in Three Areas of the Prairie Provinces from 1942-43 to 1947*, by M.A. MacNaughton and M.E. Andal, with a supplement by M.A. MacNaughton and J.M. Mann, Publication no. 815 (Ottawa, 1949), 30.
17. See, for example, *Edmonton Bulletin*, Febru-

ary 7, 1895.

18. See, for example, *The UFA*, September 1, 1928.

19. *Edmonton Bulletin*, December 23, 1895.

20. *Red Deer Advocate*, September 12, 1924.

21. "The Gleam," vol. 5, no.4, Alberta CGIT Association Papers, M5931, Glenbow-Alberta Institute Archives (hereafter cited GAI).

22. Canada, Department of Marine and Fisheries, *Canada, Her Natural Resources, Navigation, Principal Steamlines, and Transcontinental Railways* (Ottawa, 1912), 214.

23. 'Dorothy' to Miss Barclay, August 13, 1926, Barclay Papers, M6126, File 7, GAI.

24. John Mavor, "Auto Trip Across Prairie," *Alberta History* (Spring 1982): 37-38. For a description of a more adventurous trip from Calgary to New York city by auto see *Calgary Herald*, March 8, 1913.

25. Calgary Auto Club to Greenfield, September 10, 1925, Premiers' Papers (hereafter PP), File 216, Provincial Archives of Alberta (hereafter PAA).

26. Williamson to Department of Public Works, December 17, 1937, Department of Transportation, 83.97, File 6, PAA.

27. "Sylvan Lake," (pamphlet), n.d., (ca. 1938), n.p., PP, File 931, PAA.

28. Director of Publicity to King, September 15, 1943, PP, File 1216, PAA.

29. *Western Municipal News*, June 1922, 174.

30. Ibid., April 1923, 113; *Edmonton Journal*, August 1, 1925.

31. *Edmonton Journal*, July 18, 1925.

32. *Good Roads*, September 1929.

33. *Calgary Herald*, May 14, 1921.

34. E.J. Hart, *The Selling of Canada* (Banff: Altitude Publishing Ltd., 1983), 41-44, 55-56.

35. R.C. Scace, "Banff Townsite: An Historical Geographical View of Urban Development in a Canadian National Park," in *Recreational Land Use*, ed. Wall and Marsh, 208-12.

36. *Calgary Herald*, August 15, 1911.

37. *Red Deer Advocate*, July 21, 1916.

38. *Calgary Herald*, April 12, 1911.

39. *Edmonton Journal*, November 1, 1930.

40. "Facts Relating to Proposed Trackway, Calgary to Banff," n.d. (ca. 1930), p. 5-6, PP, File 604, PAA.

41. Duke to Fallow, April 4, 1940, and Unwin to Aberhart, May 2, 1940, PP, File 894, PAA.

42. J.T.H. Connor, "Preservatives of Health: Mineral Water Spas of Nineteenth Century Ontario," *Ontario History* 75 (1983): 148-49; "Let's Develop and Publicize our Spas!" (pamphlet), n.d. (ca. 1947), n.p., PP, File 1374, PAA.

43. *Edmonton Journal*, November 1, 1930.

44. *Calgary Herald*, May 12, 1927.

45. Anderson to Manning, July 5, 1949, PP, File 1769, PAA.

46. *The UFA*, June 1, 1922.

47. D. MacGregor, ed., *The Alberta Club Woman's Blue Book* (Calgary: Calgary Women's Press Club, 1917), 23.

48. Cecil Blackburn, "The Development of Sports in Alberta, 1900-1918" (M.A. thesis, University of Alberta, 1974), 338.

49. Benidickson, "Paddling for Pleasure," 328.

50. *Calgary Herald*, February 1, 1917.

51. *Calgary Herald*, May 14, 1921.

52. B.J.C. McKercher, "The Prince of Wales Hotel, Waterton Lakes National Park, Alberta: Its Significance" (Typescript, Historic Sites Service, Alberta Culture, 1982), p. 6.

53. Jasper Park Lodge, 65.6, PAA, and "Jasper Park, a Quarter of a Century," Jasper Park Lodge 65.10, PAA; *The UFA*, April 15, 1925.

54. Letter no. 89, May 3, 1940, A. Balmer Watt Collection, Bruce Peel Special Collections Library, University of Alberta (hereafter BPSC).

55. Director of Publicity to King, September 15, 1943, PP, File 1216, PAA.

56. *Edmonton Journal*, July 22, 1922; "Submission of the Jasper Park Development Committee...," 1946, PP, File 1418, PAA. Competition between the two parks was often intense; in the 1920s the CPR had fought competition from Jasper because it feared for its interests in Banff (Hart, *The Selling of Canada*, 107).

57. Cecil Burgess, "Provincial Page, Alberta," *Royal Architectural Institute of Canada Journal*, July 1939, 170.

58. *Edmonton Journal*, May 22, 1926.

59. G. Wall and R. Wallis, "Camping for Fun: A Brief History of Camping in North America," in *Recreational Land Use*, ed. Wall and Marsh, 346-47; *Farm and Ranch Review*, July 20, 1910.

60. Wall and Wallis, "Camping for Fun," 342.

61. *Edmonton Journal*, June 16, 1923. Tents mounted on the side of a car were manufactured in Edmonton.

62. For evidence of this equipment in Alberta during the 1920s see the advertisements in various issues of *Good Roads*.

63. *Red Deer Advocate*, July 11, 1924, and July 14, 1916.

64. Annora Brown, *Sketches From Life* (Edmonton: Hurtig Publishers Ltd., 1981), 138.

65. *Edmonton Journal*, June 4, 1921.

66. R.P. Cull, "History of Seba Beach," p. 14, Separate Typescripts File 3, Alberta Folk Archive, BPSC. The legislation was *An Act to Amend The Village Act*, Statutes of Alberta, 1918, c. 47.

67. Burgess, "Provincial Page, Alberta," 170.

68. Mackay to Brownlee, February 18, 1930, PP, File 319A, PAA.
69. Shand to Brownlee, October 25, 1929, PP, File 319A, PAA.
70. *Edmonton Journal,* August 6, 1932.
71. Alberta Parks Committee to Brownlee, July 28, 1930, and Brownlee to Webber, July 28, 1930, PP, File 319A, PAA.
72. *Red Deer Advocate,* June 14, 1907.
73. *Edmonton Journal,* August 6, 1932.
74. "Sylvan Lake," (pamphlet), n.d., (ca. 1938), n.p., PP, File 931, PAA; *Calgary Herald,* June 5, 1926.
75. "Alberta to Provide Parks for People," press release, n.d., (ca. 1929), PP, File 319A, PAA.
76. *Journal of the Town Planning Institute,* August-October 1929, 90, and April 1930, 44.
77. Cantelon to Riddle, July 19, 1943, PP, File 934, PAA; Alberta, Department of Economic Affairs, "The Alberta Story. An Authentic Report on Alberta's Progress, 1935-1952," 54.
78. Director of Publicity to King, September 15, 1943, PP, File 1216, PAA.
79. Alberta Parks Committee to Brownlee, November 7, 1929, PP, File 319A, PAA.
80. For lakes accessible to Edmonton, see *Edmonton Journal,* June 13, 1925.
81. *Camrose Canadian,* September 16, 1909.
82. Brownlee to Seymour, May 31, 1932, PP, File 247, PAA.
83. Aiken to Brownlee, May 20, 1932, PP, File 319A, PAA; Lethbridge Northern Irrigation District...Park Lake Committee, Advisory Committee to Provincial Parks Board, July 2, 1937, M2408, GAI.
84. *Red Deer Advocate,* July 19, 1907.
85. Ibid., August 14, 1908.
86. *Camrose Canadian,* September 16, 1909.
87. Erskine Board of Trade to Brownlee, October 25, 1929, M2408, GAI.
88. Alberta Federation of Labour to Reid, February 16, 1935, PP, File 319A, PAA.
89. *Camrose Canadian,* June 23, 1910.
90. Blackburn, "The Development of Sports in Alberta," 39.
91. Provincial Parks Board to Brownlee, April 27, 1931, PP, File 319A, PAA.
92. *Red Deer Advocate,* June 14, 1907; "Sylvan Lake," (pamphlet), n.d., (ca. 1938), n.p., File 931, PP, PAA.
93. *Calgary Herald,* July 20, 1911.
94. Blackburn, "The Development of Sports in Alberta," 40.
95. *Red Deer Advocate,* July 16, 1916.
96. Ibid., August 8, 1924.
97. History of Stone Family, p. 12, Stone Papers, M6762, GAI.
98. Trowbridge to Brownlee, September 29, 1932, PP, File 359, PAA.
99. Stevens to Trowbridge, April 10, 1933, PP, File 358, PAA.
100. Ibid., Draft Order-in-Council, April 19, 1933.
101. Colpitts to Deputy Provincial Secretary, July 21, 1933, PP, File 366, PAA.
102. Canadian Girl Guides Association, "Landmarks," pp 15, 35, 68.73/105, PAA, *Calgary Herald,* July 18, 1911.
103. MacGregor, *The Alberta Club Woman's Blue Book,* 61.
104. See Camp Tuxis Summary, 1938, Torrance Papers, 77.3/1, File 7, PAA.
105. Margaret Prang " 'The Girl God Would Have Me Be': The Canadian Girls in Training," *Canadian Historical Review* 66 (1985): 160.
106. "A History of CGIT in Alberta" (1954), M5931, File 1, GAI.
107. Report of Girls' Camps, 1945, M5931, File 135, GAI.
108. George Altmeyer, "Three Ideas of Nature," 31-32.
109. *Calgary Herald,* July 27, 1929.
110. Camp Fire Programme and Application Forms, CGIT, 1927, M5931, File 134, GAI.
111. Circular Letter, May 31, 1928, M5931, File 134, GAI.
112. Walker to Aberhart, April 14, 1938, PP, File 1235, PAA.
113. Frost to Aberhart, April 18, 1940, PP, File 934, and CYHA to Manning, June 13, 1945, PP, File 1223, PAA.
114. Records Re: Youth Groups, CYHA, Newsletters, 1944, 68.195, File 96, PAA.
115. Walker to Aberhart, March 29, 1939, and Walker to Aberhart, April 14, 1939, PP, File 1234, PAA.
116. Walker to Aberhart, April 14, 1938, PP, File 1235, PAA.
117. City of Edmonton Town Planning Commission, *Interim Report on a Major Street Plan for the City of Edmonton, Alberta, 1930.*
118. For a perceptive analysis on this issue see Bruce Greenfield, "The Rhetoric of Exploration Narratives," *Dalhousie Review,* (Spring 1985): 56-65.
119. Brown, *Sketches From Life,* 138.
120. Roderick Nash argues that in the United States the attractiveness of nature and wilderness increased as did urbanization and higher standards of material life. (Nash, *Wilderness and the American Mind,* 143).
121. Canadian National Parks Association, *Bulletin,* no. 1 (1924).

402

7. Theatre and Music:
The Performing Arts as Leisure

1. *The UFA*, April 1, 1929.
2. James Sheremeta, "Entertainment and Theatre in Edmonton Before 1914" (M.A. thesis, University of Alberta, 1970), 63.
3. *Edmonton Bulletin*, April 13, and May 18, 1896.
4. Ibid., February 11, 1882.
5. *Red Deer Advocate*, October 3, 1924.
6. Georgina Kravetz, "The Pantages Theatre in Edmonton, Alberta, 1913-1921" (M.A. thesis, University of Alberta, 1983), 5.
7. Brooke Baldwin, "The Cakewalk: A Study in Stereotype and Reality," *Journal of Social History* 15 (1981): 212.
8. Howard and Tamara Palmer, "The Black Experience in Alberta," in *Peoples of Alberta: Portraits of Cultural Diversity*, ed. Howard and Tamara Palmer (Saskatoon: Western Producer Prairie Books, 1985), 384-85.
9. Sherrah to Provincial Secretary, November 14, 1929, Department of Labour Records, 73.347, File 470, Provincial Archives of Alberta (hereafter PAA).
10. L.J. Roy Wilson, "Cultural Life in Medicine Hat, 1883-1905," *Alberta History* 33 (1985): 1.
11. John Orrell, *Lost Empires: The Lost Theatres of Edmonton* (Edmonton: NeWest Press, 1981), 41.
12. Ibid., 73; *Calgary Herald*, March 24, 1924.
13. E. Ross Stuart, *A History of Prairie Theatre: The Development of Theatre in Alberta, Manitoba and Saskatchewan, 1833-1982* (Toronto: Simon and Pierre, 1984) 40, 43-48, 73.
14. Sheremeta, "Theatre in Edmonton Before 1914," 145-49; "Entertainers and Entertainment," Clipping Files, Glenbow-Alberta Institute Archives (hereafter GAI).
15. Orrell, *Lost Empires*, 124-25.
16. Henney to Provincial Secretary, March 2, 1936, 73.347/443, PAA; Michkota to Provincial Secretary, April 5, 1939, 73.347/448, PAA. Michkota's show was headquartered in Lindberg, Alberta.
17. Orrell, *Fallen Empires*, 92.
18. New Empire Theatre, Edmonton, "Grand Opening Program," 1920, Rutherford Pamphlets, Bruce Peel Special Collections Library, University of Alberta (hereafter BPSC).
19. Orrell, *Fallen Empires*, 95.
20. Sheremeta, "Entertainment and Theatre in Edmonton," 102, 108.
21. Stuart, *History of Prairie Theatre*, 65-66.
22. Orrell, *Fallen Empires*, 124-26.
23. Ibid., 128.
24. Sheremeta, "Entertainment and Theatre in Edmonton," 31-34.
25. *Camrose Canadian*, February 18, 1908.
26. Sheremeta, "Entertainment and Theatre in Edmonton," 104.
27. Kent to Deputy Provincial Secretary, April 8, 1932, 73.347/462, PAA.
28. Deputy Provincial Secretary to Reap, July 12, 1932, 73.347/462, PAA.
29. Stuart, *A History of Prairie Theatre*, 69.
30. Gwen Pharis Ringwood, "Some Memories of the Theatre in Alberta," *Stagedoor* (April 1944): 5.
31. *Calgary Albertan*, October 13, 1928, clipping, M97, File 8, GAI.
32. Orrell, *Fallen Empires*, 70-71.
33. *Calgary News Telegram*, March 12, 1912, clipping files, GAI.
34. Orrell, *Fallen Empires*, 73.
35. Stuart, *A History of Prairie Theatre*, 73-75.
36. Kravetz, "The Pantages Theatre in Edmonton," v.
37. Orrell, *Fallen Empires*, 113; Sherman Grand Theatre, Calgary, Program, 1914, BP.S553, GAI; Allen Palace Theatre, Calgary, "Programme," 1922, M2888, GAI. A fine collection of autographs and signed photos of vaudeville and theatre stars who visited Edmonton between 1910 and 1920 is in the Springer Hotel Records, 78.208, PAA.
38. Bernhardt returned to Alberta in 1918 when she played in Calgary, but by then she was beyond her prime and commanded a top price of only $1.00 (J. Hare and R. Hathorn, "Sarah Bernhardt's Visits to Canada: Dates and Repertory," *Theatre History in Canada* 2 (1981): 97, 109-10.
39. New Empire Theatre, "Grand Opening Program," 9.
40. Orrell, *Fallen Empires*, 115.
41. Ibid., 131.
42. *Edmonton Journal*, April 5, 1919.
43. Akitt to Brownlee, October 18, 1929, Premiers' Papers (hereafter PP), File 365, Provincial Archives of Alberta (hereafter PAA).
44. Riley to Brownlee, November 27, 1928, and Brownlee to Riley, October 11, 1929, PP, File 235, PAA. See also Minutes, Calgary Council on Child and Family Welfare, November 22, 1928, M6466, GAI.
45. Stuart, *History of Prairie Theatre*, 65-69.
46. *Edmonton Journal*, April 7, 1928.
47. *Calgary Herald*, May 10, 1924.
48. Shelagh Jamieson, *Chautauqua in Canada* (Calgary: Glenbow-Alberta Institute, 1979), 28.
49. Ibid., 1.
50. *Edmonton Journal*, August 13, 1921.

51. Ibid., August 27, 1921.
52. Jamieson, *Chautauqua in Canada*, 108-10. For the 1928 programme mounted in Edmonton see *Edmonton Journal*, July 7, 1928.
53. Memo for Mr. Reid, February 16, 1928, PP, File 359, PAA.
54. Jamieson, *Chautauqua in Canada*, 108ff.
55. Ibid., 138; *Edmonton Journal*, June 4, 1927.
56. D'Alton to Department, October 28, 1924, Department of the Attorney General's Records, 75.126/2603/129, PAA.
57. Memo for Mr. Reid, February 16, 1928, PP, File 359, PAA.
58. *Farm and Ranch Review*, September 16, 1929.
59. Evans to Reid, February 1, 1928, PP, File 359, PAA. In 1928, 205 chautauquas were set up in Saskatchewan.
60. Jamieson, *Chautauqua in Canada*. 139-40.
61. *Edmonton Bulletin*, January 28, 1895. On early drama in Calgary and Edmonton, see Stuart, *The History of Prairie Theatre*, 37-50.
62. Sheremeta, "Entertainment and Theatre in Edmonton," 43.
63. Stuart, *A History of Prairie Theatre*, 105-7.
64. University of Alberta, *Report of the Department of Extension for the Year Ending March 31, 1936*, 26, (hereafter *Extension Annual Report*).
65. Duggan to Corbett, June 20, 1927, 74-23-40, University of Alberta Archives (hereafter UAA).
66. Minutes, Wauneta Club, 1914, 77-149, UAA.
67. *Calgary Herald*, March 24, 1924.
68. Joanna Matejko, "The Polish Experience in Alberta," in *Peoples of Alberta*, 286; Stuart, *A History of Prairie Theatre*, 87.
69. Haynes to Aberhart, March 6, 1937, PP, File 750, PAA.
70. *The UFA*, June 1, 1933.
71. Stuart, *A History of Prairie Theatre*, 101.
72. For a later Alberta statement on social context and theatre, see J.G.C., "The Artist in the World Today," *Stagedoor* (December 1944): 3-6.
73. Ringwood, "Memories of the Theatre in Alberta," 7; John Herd Thompson with Allen Seager, *Canada 1922-1939: Decades of Discord* (Toronto: McClelland and Stewart Ltd., 1985), 171-72.
74. *Extension Annual Report, 1937*, 27-28; *Extension Annual Report, 1936*, 26.
75. *Extension Annual Report, 1934*, 28.
76. *The Press Bulletin*, March 24, 1921.
77. *Extension Annual Report, 1924, 1929, 1931*, and *1934*.
78. Ibid., *1934*, 22.
79. Ibid., 24.
80. Ibid., *1936*, 31.
81. "Memorandum re Extension Work in Drama," 1946, 74-23-24, UAA.
82. Donald Cameron, "The Banff School of Fine Arts" (Typescript speech, March 15, 1946), 74-23-30, UAA.
83. *The UFA*, June 1, 1933.
84. *Extension Annual Report, 1935*, 29.
85. J. Pollette, "Drama in The Alberta Schools," *The Stagedoor* (January 1944): 3-4.
86. "The Earl Grey Musical and Dramatic Trophy Competitions," [1911], pp. 150, 157, Rutherford Pamphlets, BPSC.
87. Nascelles to Brownlee, October 10, 1932, PP, File 244, PAA.
88. Ringwood, "Some Memories of the Theatre in Alberta," 7.
89. "Brief presented on behalf of The Alberta Drama Board to the Royal Commission on National Development in the Arts, Letters and Sciences," September 15, 1949, p. 6, Beuckert Collection, File 3, BPSC (hereafter Alberta Drama Board Brief).
90. S. Risk, "From the South to the North," *The Stagedoor* (May/June 1945): 10-11.
91. Ibid., 2.
92. Edwards to MacDonald, November 17, 1948, Department of the Provincial Secretary's Records, 71.273/A125, PAA.
93. MacDonald to Moore, November 24, 1948, Department of the Provincial Secretary's Records, 71.273/A125, PAA; "Alberta Drama Board Brief," p. 2.
94. Stuart, *A History of Prairie Theatre*, 103-7.
95. Clipping, 1928, A.B622, File 8, GAI.
96. "Alberta Drama Board Brief," p. 4.
97. Stuart, *A History of Prairie Theatre*, 103-7.
98. O.G. Broderson, "Canadian Dramatists," *The Prairie Call Boy* (May 1944): 4. An even more critical view was that of A.J. Phelps, in "Canadian Drama," *University of Toronto Quarterly* (1939), Beuckert Collection, File 3 (8), BPSC.
99. *Extension Annual Report, 1937*, 30-31.
100. Broderson, "Canadian Dramatists," 5-6.
101. *The Prairie Call Boy* (May 1944): 4-5.
102. E. Park Gowan, "Radio and Canadian Theatre," November 6, 1949, Beuckert Collection, File 3 (1), BPSC.
103. *Extension Annual Report, 1932*, 8.
104. Ibid., *1934*, 9.
105. "A Submission to the Board of Governors, Canadian Broadcasting Corporation, concerning Broadcasting Services in Edmonton, Alberta by Edmonton Broadcasting Company," March 1951, PP, File 1873, PAA.
106. *Annual Report of the CBC for the Fiscal Year Ending March 31, 1949*, 10.
107. *The UFA*, November 1, 1927.
108. R.H. Knight, *Report on District East of*

Vegreville, Alberta: A Guide for Intending Settlers (Typescript, Department of the Interior, 1924), p. 42, 68.321, PAA.

109. Bill McNeil and Morris Wolfe, *The Birth of Radio in Canada: Signing On* (Toronto: Doubleday Canada Ltd., 1982), 146-47.

110. Kathleen Strange, *With the West in Her Eyes* (Toronto: Macmillan of Canada Ltd., 1945), 124.

111. *Red Deer Advocate*, April 21, 1916.

112. Resolutions, UFA, 1931, PP, File 170A, PAA.

113. Grobau to Deputy Provincial Secretary, July 15, 1937, 73.347/1, PAA.

114. *The UFA*, August 15, 1922.

115. Ibid., November 1, 1922, August 15, 1922, and August 15, 1928.

116. *Calgary Herald*, February 22, 1908.

117. Ibid., February 19, 1903.

118. Ibid., April 23, 1927.

119. *Edmonton Bulletin*, February 3, 1896.

120. For dance programmes, see Bishop Collection, M97, File 2, 1921, GAI; Strange, *With the West in Her Eyes*, 124.

121. *Calgary Herald*, October 16, 1926.

122. "The Good Old Dances," Binder 6, Alberta Folk Archive, BPSC.

123. Andriy Nahachewsky, "First Existence Folk Dance Forms Among Ukrainians in Smoky Lake, Alberta and Swan Plain, Saskatchewan" (M.A. thesis, University of Alberta, 1985), 83-178, *passim*.

124. Ibid., 51-53, 193-99; Krystyna Lukasiewicz, "Polish Community in the Crow's Nest Pass," *Alberta History* 36 (1988): 3.

125. Report from Onoway, in *Edmonton Journal*, July 4, 1925.

126. Meredith Dance Orchestra, 78.34, PAA.

127. "History of Rycroft Board of Trade," p. 74, Rycroft Agricultural Society, 82. 154, Book 5, PAA.

128. Trainor Scrapbook, M1244, GAI.

129. Vernon to Crossfields Baseball Club, May 20, 1925, Alberta Agricultural Societies Records, M2360, File 80, GAI.

130. *Red Deer Advocate*, August 15, 1924.

131. Orrell, *Fallen Empires*, 24. On Albani, see Helmut Kallman, *A History of Music in Canada 1534-1914* (Toronto: University of Toronto Press, 1960), 229-31.

132. *Calgary Herald*, October 1, 1910.

133. Ibid., January 28, 1897.

134. *Red Deer Advocate*, October 11, 1907.

135. Sheremeta, "Entertainment and Theatre in Edmonton," 88-90.

136. Programmes in E. Hamilton Collection, M6365, Files 1, 2 and 3, GAI.

137. New Empire Theatre, "Grand Opening Programme," 11.

138. Kallman, *A History of Music in Canada*, 168-71, 201.

139. *Edmonton Bulletin*, November 9, 1893.

140. Helmut Kallman, Gilles Potvin and Kenneth Winters, ed., *Encyclopedia of Music in Canada* (Toronto: University of Toronto Press, 1981), 134.

141. Ibid., 297, 542; *Red Deer Advocate*, March 1, 1918.

142. M6365, File 1, GAI.

143. M6365, File 3, GAI; Kallman, *A History of Music in Canada*, 167, 183-84.

144. Sheremeta, "Entertainment and Theatre in Edmonton," 14; *Calgary Herald*, December 30, 1907.

145. *Red Deer Advocate*, January 22, 1909.

146. *The UFA*, July 2, 1930; Howard Palmer, "Patterns of Immigration and Ethnic Settlement in Alberta: 1920-1985," in *Peoples of Alberta*, 39.

147. Programme, "Great Western Canadian Folksong-Folkdance," March 1930, Rutherford Pamphlets, BPSC.

148. Kallman, Potvin and Winters, eds., *Encyclopedia of Music*, 697.

149. *Edmonton Journal*, September 28, 1929; Rookwood to Manning, May 7, 1949, PP, File 1703, PAA. For the papers of the society see 82.117, PAA, and for various programmes, 1936-1942, see Edmonton Playbills, 68.86, PAA.

150. M97, File 18, GAI. *Calgary Albertan*, October 13, 1928; Kallman, Potvin and Winters, eds., *Encyclopedia of Music*, 134; Clipping, "Symphony Needs to be on More Permanent Basis," n.d., (ca. 1940), Augade Collection, M36, File 10, GAI.

151. Kallman, Potvin and Winters, eds., *Encyclopedia of Music*, 297; *Edmonton Journal*, September 27, 1919, and November 27, 1926.

152. *Calgary Herald*, April 10, 1926.

153. Kallman, *A History of Music in Canada*, 159, 178.

154. Kallman, Potvin and Winters, eds., *Encyclopedia of Music*, 162, 256, 688.

155. *Calgary Herald*, July 14 and 16, 1909.

156. Kallman, Potvin and Winters, eds., *Encyclopedia of Music*, 57.

157. *Camrose Canadian*, September 15, 1910.

158. Alberta Registered Music Teachers Association, M6364, File 2, GAI.

159. *Calgary Herald*, April 10, 1926.

160. *Red Deer Advocate*, May 8, 1925.

161. Letter, August 24, 1940, A. Balmer Watt Collection, BPSC.

162. Donald Cameron, "The Banff School of Fine Arts" (Typescript Speech, March 15, 1946), 74-23-30, UAA.

163. "A Brief Presented on Behalf of the Alberta Music Board to the Royal Commission on

National Development of Arts, Letters and Sciences," September 15, 1949, Alberta Music Board Records, PP, File 1923, PAA.

164. Alberta, Department of the Provincial Secretary, Cultural Activities Branch, *Annual Report, 1947*, typescript, 71.273/A51, PAA.

165. Stuart, *A History of Prairie Theatre*, 62-64.

8. Film and the Appeal of Pure Entertainment

1. *Edmonton Bulletin*, December 22, 1883, and March 23, 1893.
2. Paper read by H. Douglas, "The Motion Picture in Education," (hereafter "The Motion Picture in Education (1922)"), Minutes of the Annual Meeting of the Association of Provincial Censor Boards...September 18, 1922, Premiers' Papers (hereafter PP), File 364, Provincial Archives of Alberta (hereafter PAA).
3. *The UFA*, March 15, 1930.
4. Ibid., April 2, 1928.
5. Peter Morris, *Embattled Shadows: A History of Canadian Cinema, 1895-1939* (Montreal: McGill-Queen's University Press, 1978), 23.
6. *Camrose Canadian*, November 25, 1909; Allen Palace Theatre, Programme, 1922, M2888, Glenbow-Alberta Institute Archives (hereafter GAI).
7. "In the Matter of the Labour Disputes Act, 1926 and of a Dispute Between Capitol and Empress Theatres, Edmonton, and Locals Numbers 360 and 210, IATSE," Transcript of Proceedings, September 25, 1929, pp. 10, 16, 53 (hereafter "Theatre Labour Dispute, 1929"), PP, File 365, PAA.
8. *Calgary Herald*, April 10, 1926.
9. Thurston to Aberhart, August 26, 1935, and Aberhart to Thurston, February 5, 1936, PP, File 927A, PAA.
10. *Edmonton Journal*, July 6, 1929.
11. Secretary Treasurer to Waite, March 9, 1911, City of Edmonton Papers, RGC.25/68, City of Edmonton Archives.
12. *Calgary Herald*, January 2, 1912. Conversion of old stores into cinemas was common. See, for example, Peter Ream, *The Fort on the Saskatchewan*, 2nd ed. (n.p.: Metropolitan Printing, 1974), 429; *Camrose Canadian*, June 16, 1910.
13. *Edmonton Journal*, April 5, 1919.
14. Ibid.; Elise Corbet, "The Palace Theatre, Calgary" (Typescript, Historic Sites Service, Alberta Culture, 1982) 2-4.
15. Hugh Dempsey, ed., *The Best of Bob Edwards* (Edmonton: Hurtig Publishers Ltd., 1975), 249.
16. Alberta, Department of the Provincial Secretary, *Annual Report, 1922*, "Theatres and Amusement Tax Branch," 61. In 1919 and 1924 alone, about 650 and 1030 films respectively passed through censorship in Alberta. The names of most films passing through censorship in Alberta are in 73.347/40, Provincial Archives of Alberta (hereafter PAA).
17. *Edmonton Journal*, May 25, 1929.
18. Ibid., July 6, 1929 (2 separate articles).
19. Eric Hounsom, "Designing the Canadian Moving Picture Theatre," *Royal Architectural Institute of Canada Journal* (February 1938): 29-30.
20. Canada, Dominion Bureau of Statistics, *Motion Picture Statistics 1934*, (1935), 4-6; Alberta, Department of the Provincial Secretary, *Annual Report, 1941-42* (Typescript), 4, PAA.
21. Interview with Fred Levitt, 1978, 78.141/3, PAA. The first drive-ins in North America opened in the United States in the mid-1930s. The Calgary drive-in was called the Chinook, the Edmonton one, the Starlight.
22. *Motion Picture Statistics 1934*, 2-6. Each moviegoer paid an amusement tax, but the statistics on amusement taxes are too general to be used in estimating attendance at movies.
23. "Theatre Labour Dispute, 1929," pp. 8-12, 71.
24. Alberta, Department of the Provincial Secretary, "Theatres and Amusement Tax Branch," *Annual Report, 1922*, 61; Sharp to Hoadley, March 19, 1927, Brunker to Brownlee, n.d., (ca. December, 1930), Brunker to Aberhart, January 13, 1941, and Whaley to Manning, February 1, 1949, PP, Files 365, 359, 861 and 1545, respectively, PAA.
25. *Calgary Herald*, October 26, 1910; *Red Deer Advocate*, August 4, 1916.
26. Minutes, Calgary Council on Child and Family Welfare, January 22, 1925, M6466, Box 1, GAI.
27. Alberta Theatre Owners to Brownlee, October 29, 1930, PP, File 366, PAA.
28. *Calgary Herald*, April 23, 1927.
29. *Motion Picture Statistics 1934*, 2.
30. Trowbridge to Brownlee, December 30, 1933, PP, File 359, PAA.
31. *Calgary Herald*, August 29, 1931, and March 4, 1933.
32. Trowbridge to Brownlee, October 19, 1928, PP, File 365, PAA.
33. *Edmonton Journal*, July 6, 1929.

34. "Theatre Labour Dispute, 1929," pp. 11-12.
35. *Edmonton Journal*, April 19, 1930.
36. *Census of Canada, 1931*, vol. 11, Table 3, 404.
37. "Theatre Labour Dispute, 1929," p. 10.
38. *Canadian Encyclopedia* (Edmonton: Hurtig Publishers Ltd., 1985), 629-30; Corbet, "The Palace Theatre, Calgary," 6; John Herd Thompson with Allen Seager, *Canada 1922-1939: Decades of Discord* (Toronto: McClelland and Stewart Ltd., 1985), 177-78.
39. Trowbridge to Brownlee, October 19, 1928, PP, File 365, PAA.
40. "Theatre Labour Dispute, 1929," p. 10.
41. Thurston to Aberhart, August 26, 1935, PP, File 927A, PAA.
42. *Edmonton Journal*, April 13, 1929.
43. Alberta Theatre Owners to Brownlee, October 29, 1930, PP, File 366, PAA.
44. Pearson to Trowbridge, January 19, 1933, 73.347/37, PAA. In 1933, there were over thirty-two makes of sound equipment on the market, but 50 percent of Canadian theatres used Northern Electric equipment. In 1935, Northern Electric and RCA Sound Equipment Ltd. amalgamated to form Dominion Sound Ltd. (Lewis to Pearson, April 4, 1933, and Pike to Deputy Provincial Treasurer, October 28, 1935, 73.347/37, PAA.)
45. Letter to Brownlee, November 25, 1933, PP, File 362, PAA.
46. Pearson to Brownlee, March 3, 1930, PP, File 366, PAA.
47. *Motion Picture Statistics 1934*, 3.
48. Trowbridge to Brownlee, October 27, 1926, PP, File 364, PAA.
49. Pearson to L'Ami, March 14, 1935, 73.347/37, PAA.
50. "The Motion Picture in Education (1922)." In the 1930s, the Department of Health usually included the film *Mickey Mouse* in its programme for the children. These film presentations were, however, a major social event for everyone in the community, not just for the children (C.A. Dawson and Eva Younge, *Pioneering in the Prairie Provinces: The Social Side of the Settlement Process* (Toronto: Macmillan of Canada, 1940), 66).
51. "The Motion Picture in Education (1922)."
52. University of Alberta, *Catalogue of Sixteen Millimeter Motion Picture Films, Silent and Sound and Terms of Service* (Edmonton: 1939), 2-3.
53. *Farm and Ranch Review*, January 1944, 8, 17.
54. *Red Deer Advocate*, July 15, 1921.
55. Alberta, Department of the Provincial Secretary, *Annual Report, 1932-33*, 10, and *1937*, 2 (Typescripts).
56. [Drayton Valley High School], "The History of Drayton Valley" (Typescript, [1974]), 4.
57. Smitten to Brownlee, May 7, 1932, PP, File 502, PAA.
58. Pearson to Cooper, March 2, 1936, 73.347/28, PAA.
59. Alberta, Department of the Provincial Secretary, *Annual Report, 1941-42* (Typescript), 4.
60. "Agricultural Society—The Social Centre," and "History of Rycroft Board of Trade," 82.154, PAA.
61. Pearson to Cooper, March 2, 1936, 73.347/28, PAA.
62. *Calgary Herald*, January 12, 1910; *Red Deer Advocate*, September 3, 1910.
63. These films were run at probably no more than sixty feet per minute (*Edmonton Journal*, July 6, 1929).
64. *Red Deer Advocate*, February 22, 1918.
65. *Calgary Herald*, September 3, 1918.
66. *Red Deer Advocate*, August 4, 1916.
67. *Calgary Herald*, November 6, 1918.
68. *Red Deer Advocate*, July 19,1921, February 3, 1923, May 8, 1925; *Calgary Herald*, July 10, 1915; *Claresholm Review Advertiser*, January 21, 1915.
69. *International Encyclopedia of Film* (London: Michael Joseph, 1972), 51-53; D. Shipman, *The Great Movie Stars: The Golden Years* (London: Angus & Robertson, 1979), 9.
70. "Theatre Labour Dispute, 1929," 11.
71. "Moving Picture Censorship in Alberta," (ca. 1933), 73.347/37, PAA.
72. Pearson to Cooper, January 25, 1933, 73.347/37, PAA.
73. Clipping, 1929, PP, File 365, PAA.
74. *Edmonton Journal*, April 6, 1929.
75. Pearson to Wyngate, August 18, 1935, 73.347/37, PAA.
76. *Edmonton Journal*, September 29, 1928; Pierre Berton, *Hollywood's Canada: The Americanization of our National Image* (Toronto: McClelland and Stewart Ltd., 1975), 32.
77. *Reflections: Lethbridge Then and Now* (Lethbridge: Historical Society of Alberta, 1980); *International Encyclopedia of Film*, 51-53.
78. Pearson to Cooper, July 22, 1935, 73.347/28, PAA.
79. Arthur Knight, *The Liveliest Art: A Panoramic History of the Movies* (New York: Macmillan, 1978), 141.
80. *Calgary Herald*, August 29, 1931; E. Ross Stuart, *The History of Prairie Theatre: The Development of Theatre in Alberta, Manitoba and Saskatchewan 1933-1982* (Toronto: Simon and Pierre, 1984), 69-70.
81. *International Encyclopedia of Film*, 51-53.

82. *Calgary Herald*, October 26, 1910, and January 2, 1912.

83. Ibid., December 8, 1911.

84. Censorship in Alberta, n.d. (ca. 1933), 73.347/37, PAA. Howard Douglas was a Methodist who had come west from Ontario about 1882. (David C. Jones, "The Reflective Value of Movies and Censorship on Interwar Prairie Society," *Prairie Forum* 10 (1985): 387).

85. Briefing Note, n.d., (ca. 1920), PP, File 634. PAA.

86. Gerald Pelton, "Some Causes and Remedies for Juvenile Delinquency," September 30, 1927, p. 3, PP, File 235, PAA.

87. *Calgary Herald*, October 28, 1911; *Farm and Ranch Review*, May 20, 1913.

88. *Calgary Herald*, January 2, 1912; "The Motion Picture in Education (1922)."

89. Minutes, Annual Meeting of the Association of Provincial Censor Boards... September 18, 1922, PP, File 364, PAA.

90. Douglas Bocking, "The Saskatchewan Board of Film Censors, 1910-1935," *Saskatchewan History* 24 (1971): 59-60.

91. Alberta, Department of the Provincial Secretary, "Theatres and Amusements Tax Branch", *Annual Report, 1922*, 61.

92. Reply to Communication from the Calgary Board of Trade Re: Censorship, n.d., (June 1932), PP, File 366, PAA. See also "Standards of the Association of Moving Picture owners," n.d., (ca. 1926), PP, File 364, PAA.

93. Censorship in Alberta, n.d., (ca. 1933), 73.347/37, PAA.

94. Reply to Communication from the Calgary Board of Trade Re: Censorship, n.d., (June 1932), PP, File 366, PAA.

95. Censorship in Alberta, n.d., (ca. 1933), and Pearson to Cooper, January 25, 1933, 73.347/37, PAA.

96. Statistics are scattered, but patterns of censorship can be reconstructed from Comparative Statements Regarding Pictures Censored (1922), PP, File 364, PAA; and Annual Statements, Alberta Censor, 1928-1944, 73.347/39, PAA.

97. Reply to Communication from the Calgary Board of Trade Re: Censorship, n.d., (June 1932), PP, File 366, PAA; *Calgary Herald*, April 8, 1937.

98. Terry Chapman, "Film Censorship in Lethbridge, 1918-1920," *Alberta History* 33 (1985): 4.

99. Reply to Communication from the Calgary Board of Trade Re: Censorship, n.d., (ca. June 1932), PP, File 366, PAA.

100. Calgary Board of Trade, Extract from Members' Letter Re: Law and Order, June 2, 1932, and Reply to Communication from the Calgary Board of Trade Re: Censorship, n.d., (June 1932), PP, File 366, PAA.

101. Pearson to Cooper, July 22, 1935, 73.347/28, PAA.

102. Vangro to Pearson, October 31, 1934, 73.347/37, PAA.

103. Hardy to Pearson, September 22, 1937, and Wood to Pearson, October 27, 1937, 73.347/37, PAA.

104. Cooper to Blankstein, December 14, 1934, 73.347/28, PAA.

105. Minutes, Annual Meeting of the Association of Provincial Censor Boards... September 18, 1922, and Films Censored and Passed, 1921-1922, PP, File 364, PAA.

106. Minutes, Annual Meeting of the Association of Provincial Censor Boards... September 18, 1922, PP, File 364, PAA; Seelheim to Pearson, September 9, 1936, and October 27, 1936, and Wurdels to Pearson, December 18, 1937, 73.347/37, PAA.

107. Brownlee to Greenfield, December 5, 1924, PP, File 364, PAA.

108. "Motion Picture Censorship and Control in Alberta," n.d., PP, File 1923; Darling to Deputy Attorney General, January 28, 1947, and Byrne to Arthurs, December 30, 1946, 71.170/1, PAA.

109. *Edmonton Journal*, February 20, 1946; Roberts to Lieutenant Governor in Council, February 27, 1946, "Film Censorship," March 11, 1946, and Fernyhough to Hooke, March 15, 1946, PP, Files 1368, 1371 and 1370, respectively, PAA.

110. Hooke [?] to Maclean, January 3, 1947 and Hooke to Fleming, February 8, 1947, PP, File 1371, PAA.

111. Pearson to Brownlee, February 23, 1932, and Pearson to Brownlee, January 31, 1934, PP, Files 366 and 190, respectively, PAA.

112. Pearson to Brownlee, March 3, 1930, PP, File 366, PAA. See also *Canadian Encyclopedia*, 630.

113. Pearson to Wingate, December 30, 1932, 73.347/37, PAA.

114. *Calgary Herald*, August 28, 1920; Gibsone to Greenfield, October 31, 1925, PP, File 364, PAA.

115. Douglas to Brownlee, November 12, 1925, PP, File 364, PAA.

116. Pearson to L'Ami, March 14, 1935, 73.347/37, PAA.

117. Douglas to Brownlee, March 3, 1935, PP, File 366, PAA.

118. Berton, *Hollywood's Canada*, 30-121.

119. S. Kula, "Steam Movies, Railroads and Moving Images," in *The CPR West: The Iron Road, and the Making of a Nation*, ed. Hugh

Dempsey (Vancouver: Douglas and McIntyre Ltd., 1984), 254.

120. Pearson to Brownlee, March 3, 1930, PP, File 366, PAA.
121. Alberta, Department of Provincial Secretary, "Theatres and Amusement Tax Branch," *Annual Report, 1922*, 63.
122. *Calgary Herald*, August 25, 1917.
123. *Canadian Encyclopedia*, 629-30. Curwood was an American who was hired by the Canadian government to write propaganda novels about Canada (Berton, *Hollywood's Canada*, 27).
124. *Edmonton Journal*, May 15, 1920, and February 21, 1920.
125. Ibid., March 25, 1922.
126. Ibid., July 22, 1922, December 2, 1922, and March 17, 1923.
127. Kula, "Steam Movies, Railroads and Moving Images," 254-55. On the movie industry in Alberta, see M1117, GAI.
128. *Canadian Encyclopedia*, 629-30, and Berton, *Hollywood's Canada*, 169-70.
129. *Edmonton Journal*, February 15, 1919 (article and advertisement).
130. Morris, *Embattled Shadows*, 194.
131. During the 1920s the British government imposed a quota system in British cinemas to encourage the showing and making of British films. Since the regulation was for "British Empire" films, United States producers immediately set up branch plants in Canada to make (American) films for the British market (Morris, *Embattled Shadows*, 179-81).
132. Cooper to Brownlee, June 2, 1926, PP, File 364, PAA.
133. Pearson to Brownlee, March 3, 1930, PP, File 366, PAA.
134. See, for example, Brownlee to Parlby, February 2, 1929, PP, File 365, PAA.
135. *Calgary Herald*, March 20, 1913.
136. *Edmonton Journal*, April 5, 1919.
137. Petition by Calgary Council on Child Welfare, January 13, 1927, PP, File 365, PAA.
138. Douglas to Trowbridge, February 9, 1927, PP, File 365, PAA.
139. Memorandum for Branch Managers, December 20, 1927, PP, File 365, PAA.
140. Minutes, October 25, 1928, M6466, Box 1, GAI.
141. Circular Letter, May 15, 1935, PP, File 862, PAA.
142. Fleming to Arthurs, March 21, 1949, 71.170/1, PAA.
143. Pearson to Boylen, June 30, 1934, 73.347/37, PAA.
144. Rothwell to Pearson, February 18, 1935, and Pearson to Rothwell, February 20, 1935, 73.347/37, PAA.
145. Taylor to Pearson, November 4, 1933, 73.347/37, PAA.
146. *Calgary Herald*, April 8, 1937.
147. Minutes, September 22, 1927, M6466, Box 1, GAI.
148. Minutes, January 22, 1925, and Minutes, March 27, 1936, M6466, Box 1, GAI.
149. Pearson to Whitton, October 17, 1934, 73.347/37, PAA.
150. "The Movies," *Civil Service Bulletin* (November 1930): 8-9.
151. *Family Herald and Weekly Star*, June 19, 1940.
152. Northrop Frye, *The Great Code* (Toronto: Academic Press Canada, 1982), 6-7.

9. On the Edge of History: Radio

1. Albert Shea, *Broadcasting the Canadian Way* (Montreal, Harvest House, 1963), 101.
2. *The Press Bulletin*, December 26, 1930.
3. *Farm and Ranch Review*, August 10, 1925.
4. Ibid., Advertisement, September 25, 1924.
5. "Radio Licenses" file, Alberta Department of Trade and Commerce, Bureau of Vital Statistics Records, 74.462, Provincial Archives of Alberta (hereafter PAA). Not everyone licensed their radios. In 1922, many people ignored the licensing requirement, although it seems that the licensing rules were soon enforced (*Edmonton Journal*, May 27, 1922).
6. *Census of Canada, 1931*, Table 21, 672-73, and Table 34, 696-97. Forty-two percent of radios were found in census divisions 4, 6, 8, and 11, which included the areas around Calgary and Edmonton. This area contained 34 percent of the farm population.
7. *Census of Canada, 1941*, Table 85, 847.
8. Bill McNeil and Morris Wolfe, *The Birth of Radio in Canada: Signing On* (Toronto: Doubleday Canada Ltd., 1982), 155.
9. John Blackburn, *Land of Promise* (Toronto: Macmillan of Canada, 1970), 150-51; Carl Buchanan, "A Winter's Day on the Homestead," *The Beaver*, Outfit 307:3 (1976): 9.
10. McNeil and Wolfe, *The Birth of Radio in Canada*, 145.
11. *Edmonton Journal*, May 13, 1922.
12. See *Farm and Ranch Review*, March 25, 1924.
13. Blackburn, *Land of Promise*, 151.
14. Stonecrop to Aberhart, November 21, 1935, Premiers' Papers (hereafter PP), File 1156A, Provincial Archives of Alberta (hereafter PAA); Blackburn, *Land of Promise*, 150-51.
15. *Macleod's Catalogue, Spring and Summer,*

1927, 42, and *1930,* 38; Taylor and Pearson Ltd. to Newland, November 21, 1938, PP, File 711A, PAA.

16. Shea, *Broadcasting the Canadian Way,* 101; A.F. Toogood, *Broadcasting in Canada: Aspects of Regulation and Control* (Ottawa: The Canadian Association of Broadcasters, 1969), 13, 40, 57.

17. Taylor and Pearson Ltd. to Newland, November 21, 1938, PP, File 711A, PAA.

18. Newland to Aberhart, March 13, 1939, PP, File 711B, PAA.

19. Clash to Aberhart, June 10, 1940 (table), PP, File 914A, PAA.

20. Gaunt to Manning, February 25, 1939, PP, File 921B, PAA.

21. Clash to Aberhart, June 10, 1940, PP, File 914A, PAA.

22. Gaunt to Manning, February 25, 1939, PP, File 921B, PAA.

23. See, for example, *Farm and Ranch Review,* November 1, 1929. The use of jargon in the 1920s and early 1930s was typical in advertisements for radios. By the 1940s, the jargon was gone, replaced with straightforward language, a change that indicates the increasingly matter-of-fact way in which radio was now viewed by the public.

24. *The Press Bulletin,* December 26, 1930.

25. McNeil and Wolfe, *The Birth of Radio in Canada,* 146.

26. *Red Deer Advocate,* October 20, 1922.

27. McNeil and Wolfe, *The Birth of Radio in Canada,* 146.

28. Interview with George Brown, 1978, 78.141/24, PAA.

29. T.J. Allard, *Straight Up: Private Broadcasting in Canada, 1918-58* (Ottawa: Canadian Communications Foundation, 1979), 25; Records re CJCA, 1948-49, PP, File 1873, PAA; McNeil and Wolfe, *The Birth of Radio in Canada,* 145.

30. Records re: CJCA, 1948-49, PP, Files 1872 and 1873, PAA.

31. E. Austin Weir, *The Struggle for National Broadcasting in Canada* (Toronto: McClelland and Stewart Ltd., 1965), 89.

32. "A Submission to the Board of Governors, Canadian Broadcasting Corporation concerning Broadcast Services in Edmonton, Alberta," by Edmonton Broadcasting Company, March 1951, PP, File 1873, PAA. CQAC was established on May 2, 1922 in Calgary. It changed its call letters to CHQC a week later, and then later the same year again changed its letters to CFAC.

33. Weir, *The Struggle for National Broadcasting,* 25. The issue of direct and indirect advertising provoked great debate in the 1920s in Canada. Indirect advertising, such as the sponsorship of a programme identified by an advertiser's name but not involving advertisement of a particular product or prices, was permissable. In 1923, direct advertising, that is, selling a particular product or giving prices, was permitted only before 6 p.m. It was forbidden completely in 1925 but by 1929 it was being carried by many stations in defiance of the law (Frank Peers, *The Politics of Canadian Broadcasting, 1920-1951* (Toronto: University of Toronto Press, 1969), 280).

34. *Calgary Herald,* January 14, 1931.

35. McNeil and Wolfe, *The Birth of Radio in Canada,* 145.

36. A.E. Ottewell, "CKUA on the Air," *New Trail* 3 (1945): 158.

37. *The Press Bulletin,* September 27, 1935.

38. Weir, *The Struggle for National Broadcasting,* 89; Peers, *The Politics of Canadian Broadcasting,* 350.

39. "Rate Charts...CFCN," 1939, PP, File 1157, PAA. A few months after CFCN obtained its increase to 10,000 watts, a Toronto station obtained the same power (Peers, *The Politics of Canadian Broadcasting,* 79).

40. Meeting of the Radio Board, December 5, 1940, 74-23-17, University of Alberta Archives (hereafter UAA).

41. *Calgary Herald,* January 14, 1931; Grant to Director of Radio, March 18, 1931, Love Papers, M693, File 7, Glenbow-Alberta Institute Archives (hereafter GAI).

42. Toogood, *Broadcasting in Canada,* 30.

43. *Calgary Herald,* January 14, 1931.

44. Grant to Aberhart, July 3, 1936, PP, File 1156A, PAA.

45. *Report of the Canadian Broadcasting Corporation for the Period November 2, 1936 to March 31, 1937* (hereafter *CBC Annual Report*), 9.

46. Meeting of the Radio Board, December 15, 1940, 74-23-17, UAA.

47. Typescript on Havana Treaty, December, 1940, 74-23-20, UAA; Toogood, *Broadcasting in Canada,* 56.

48. McNeil and Wolfe, *The Birth of Radio in Canada,* 183.

49. Toogood, *Broadcasting in Canada,* 13.

50. McNeil and Wolfe, *The Birth of Radio in Canada,* 145, 183. The CNR paid rent for the phantom license, which was often an important part of the income of many struggling western stations (Weir, *Struggle for National Broadcasting,* 226).

51. Peers, *The Politics of Canadian Broadcasting,* 24.

52. *Farm and Ranch Review,* February 25, 1925.

53. Peers, *The Politics of Canadian Broadcasting,*

25; McNeil and Wolfe, *The Birth of Radio in Canada,* 186.

54. "Minutes of Meeting of Committee for Celebration of Diamond Jubilee of Confederation," n.d., (ca. April 1927), PP, File 219, PAA.

55. Peers, *The Politics of Canadian Broadcasting,* 20, 75-77; John Herd Thompson with Allen Seager, *Canada 1922-1939: Decades of Discord* (Toronto: McClelland and Stewart Ltd., 1985), 182.

56. *Calgary Herald,* January 14, 1931; *Canadian Encyclopedia,* 2nd ed. (Edmonton: Hurtig Publishers Ltd., 1988), 2064.

57. Toogood, *Broadcasting in Canada,* 13, 40, 57.

58. Canadian Radio Broadcasting Commission, *Report of the Commissioners for the Year Ending March 31, 1935* (hereafter *CRBC Annual Report*), 7.

59. *CBC Annual Report, 1936-37,* 8.

60. Circular Letter, CRBC, February 1, 1933, M693, File 10, GAI.

61. *CRBC Annual Report, 1935-36,* 7.

62. *CBC Annual Report, 1936-37,* 9.

63. A statement of this criticism is the "Brief of the Canadian Association of Broadcasters to the Royal Commission on National Development in the Arts, Letters and Sciences," Ottawa, April 12, 1950 (hereafter "Brief, CAB, 1950").

64. *CBC Annual Report, 1937-38,* 6.

65. Peers, *The Politics of Canadian Broadcasting,* 241-42. The system became further complicated in 1944 with the creation of two national CBC networks: The Trans-Canada Network and the Dominion Network. The Trans-Canada Network broadcast all day, the Dominion Network only in the evenings. This was designed to give Canadians alternatives in programmes (Shea, *Broadcasting the Canadian Way,* 108).

66. *CBC Annual Report, 1938-39,* 12; Cameron to Parlee, October 13, 1942, 74-23-5, UAA.

67. Weir, *The Struggle for National Broadcasting,* 246; "Brief CAB, 1950."

68. McNeil and Wolfe, *The Birth of Radio in Canada,* 146; Allard, *Straight Up,* 57.

69. Baxter to Smith, January 11, 1927, PP, File 401, PAA; A.E. Ottewell, "CKUA on the Air," 157.

70. *Edmonton Journal,* October 3, 1931.

71. Weir, *The Struggle for National Broadcasting,* 24.

72. See, for example, broadcast schedules in *Edmonton Journal,* February 24, 1923, and April 21, 1923.

73. Weir, *The Struggle for National Broadcasting,* 98-99.

74. *Calgary Herald,* March 29, 1929.

75. *Edmonton Journal,* June 7, 1930.

76. "CKUA Programme, 1939-40," Bulletin of the Department of Extension, University of Alberta.

77. McNeil and Wolfe, *The Birth of Radio in Canada,* 149, 155.

78. Ingrey to Aberhart, October 26, 1937, PP, File 1156A, PAA.

79. CFCN Radio Station, "Fact Sheet," M2258, GAI.

80. *CBC Annual Report, 1939-40,* 7, 13.

81. Ibid., *1938-39,* 5.

82. Macdonald to Bowlen, n.d., (1947), Bowlen Collection, M118, File 76, GAI.

83. Allard, *Straight Up,* 27; "Coronation Souvenir," 1937, PP, File 1233A, PAA.

84. *Edmonton Journal,* October 23, 1926.

85. Submission to Board of Governors' Meeting held May 17-19, 1948 inclusive, re: "Cancellation of License in the name of the Edmonton Broadcasting Company," PP, File 1873, PAA.

86. Programme Schedule, CFAC, May 1, 1923, Brown Collection, M5659, GAI.

87. *CBC Annual Report, 1939-40,* 10; Longman to MacMillan, July 21, 1943, Department of Agriculture Records, 73.307/18/229. PAA.

88. *The UFA,* January 16, 1928.

89. Ibid., April 16, 1928.

90. Ibid., August 15, 1927.

91. Wigmore to Aberhart, September 26, 1939, PP, File 1157, PAA.

92. See, for example, McGuire to Aberhart, November 1, 1937, PP, File 1156A, PAA. Social Credit broadcasts were made more controversial in regulatory terms since there was so much religion mixed with the politics. Religious broadcasting had been a contentious issue in Canadian broadcasting in the late 1920s (Peers, *The Politics of Canadian Broadcasting,* 31-32).

93. *CBC Annual Report, 1936-37,* 15; McGuire to Aberhart, March 5, 1941, and "Canadian Broadcasting Corporation Revised Edition of CBC's Policy with respect to Political and Controversial Broadcasting," 1944, PP, Files 1157 and 1163, respectively, PAA.

94. Davidson to Aberhart, March 8, 1937, PP, File 1156A, PAA.

95. University of Alberta, *Annual Report of the Department of Extension for the Year Ending March 31, 1934,* 9.

96. A.E. Ottewell, "CKUA on the Air," 160; "Programme Principles for CKUA," June 24, 1943, 73-24-2, UAA.

97. *Farm and Ranch Review,* April 1938.

98. McNeil and Wolfe, *The Birth of Radio in Canada,* 147; *Edmonton Journal,* May 6, 1922.

99. Interview with G.R.A. Rice, 1978, 78.65/16,

PAA. CJCA bought record turntables from either the Strand or the Capitol Theatres in Edmonton in 1929 and used them for broadcasting recordings.

100. CFCN to CRBC, April 22, 1933, M693, File 10, GAI.

101. Interview with George Brown, 1978, 78.141/24, PAA.

102. *The Press Bulletin,* September 27, 1935.

103. Cameron to Kerr, October 1, 1940, 74-23-2, UAA.

104. *CBC Monthly Guide,* no. 3, December 1944.

105. Peers, *The Politics of Canadian Broadcasting,* 216, 229; McNeil and Wolfe, *The Birth of Radio in Canada,* 15, 212.

106. *CBC Annual Report, 1939-40,* 7. "The Happy Gang" ran until 1959.

107. *Farm and Ranch Review,* April 1938.

108. *CBC Annual Report, 1939-40,* 10; McNeil and Wolfe, *The Birth of Radio in Canada,* 265-69.

109. See Chapter 7, 231-32.

110. Sise to Manning, October 2, 1945, PP, File 1157, PAA.

111. McNeil and Wolfe, *The Birth of Radio in Canada,* 149.

112. *CBC Annual Report, 1939-40,* 12.

113. Allard, *Straight Up,* 55-56.

114. *CBC Monthly Guide,* no. 3, December 1944.

115. Priestly to Aberhart, August 7, 1940,PP, File 751A, and Priestly to Wallace, October 4, 1933, PP, File 170A, PAA.

116. Stopp to University of Alberta, September 11, 1927, File 401, and "A Christian" to Aberhart, February 22, 1938, PP, File 750, PAA.

117. Peers, *The Politics of Canadian Broadcasting,* 241-42.

118. "Report and Recommendations to Dr. Kerr Regarding Future Policy with Respect to Radio Station CKUA," November 28, 1939, 74-23-19, UAA.

119. Cameron to Parlee, October 13, 1942, 74-23-5, UAA.

120. "Radio Broadcasting in Canada. A Brief Presented by the Association of Canadian Advertisers to the Parliamentary Committee on Radio—1936," p. 11, PP, File 1193, PAA; McNeil and Wolfe, *The Birth of Radio in Canada,* 265-69.

121. Rice to Manning, September 30, 1948, PP, File 1872, PAA.

122. Sebastien de Grazia, *Of Time, Work and Leisure* (New York: The Twentieth Century Fund, 1962), 242-43.

123. *Farm and Ranch Review,* November 1, 1929.

124. Stonecrop to Aberhart, November 1935, PP, File 1156A, PAA. Another issue connected to the history of radio in Alberta relates to the assumption that Aberhart's

victory in 1935 was due in part to radio, which had given his ideas wide exposure. It should be observed, however, that in rural Alberta—the main area of Social Credit support—radios were not widespread in the early 1930s. Although there was a substantial increase in radio ownership in Alberta in 1934-35, a correlation between constituency votes and the number of radios in such constituencies would be useful.

125. *Family Herald and Weekly Star,* June 19, 1946.

126. *CBC Annual Report, 1939-40,* 11.

127. McNeil and Wolfe, *The Birth of Radio in Canada,* 274.

128. "Broadcast Talks, Hints to CBC Microphone Speakers," n.d., (ca. 1947), PP, File 1447, PAA.

129. Grant to Steel, April 29, 1933, M693, File 10, GAI.

130. "Submission to Board of Governors of CBC in Opposition to the Application for a French Language Station in Alberta," n.d., (ca. 1947), PP, File 1492, PAA. An excellent example of the anti-French rhetoric that was common in this connection can be found in Casson to Chase, September 21, 1947, M118, File 76, GAI.

131. Quoted in Donald Smith, "A History of French Speaking Albertans," in *Peoples of Alberta: Portraits of Cultural Diversity,* ed. Howard and Tamara Palmer (Saskatoon: Western Producer Prairie Books, 1985), 102.

132. Thurston to Aberhart, January 30, 1936, PP, File 927A, PAA.

133. "Brief Presented on behalf of the Alberta Music Board to the Royal Commission on National Development in the Arts, Letters and Sciences," vol. 50, n.p., PP, File 1923, PAA.

134. *The UFA,* March 11, 1926; *Red Deer Advocate,* April 4, 1924.

135. In 1940, for example, there were 1,469 car radio sets sold in both Alberta and Saskatchewan. In the previous seven years, the total number of car radios sold in the two provinces was 6,372 (*Radio Trade Builder* 19 (1942): 20-21).

136. The way the *Edmonton Journal* reported in the early 1920s about CJCA is a good illustration of this reaction by newspapers. This is not to say that newspapers were only cynically promoting their own interests; they seem to have genuinely seen their radio stations as heralds of a new age and as proof of progress and growth.

137. Quoted in Ithiel de Sola Pool, ed., *The Social Impact of the Telephone* (Cambridge:

MIT press, 1977), 123.

10. Agriculture Fairs and Rodeos

1. David C. Jones, *Midways, Judges and Smooth Tongued Fakirs* (Saskatoon: Western Producer Prairie Books, 1983), 6.
2. Grant MacEwan, *Agriculture on Parade* (Toronto: Thomas Nelson and Sons (Canada) Ltd., 1950), 3-8; Marijke Kerkhoven, "A Cross Section of Life: Agricultural Fairs in Alberta and Saskatchewan, 1879-1915," *Alberta Museum's Review* (Fall, 1986), 10-11.
3. Distribution of Grants to Agricultural Societies in NWT, 1905, and Deputy Commissioner to Williams, January 24, 1901, Alberta Agricultural Societies, M2360, File 2, Glenbow-Alberta Institute Archives (hereafter GAI).
4. Department of Agriculture, Calgary Exhibition, Government Grants, n.d., 73.307, File 249, Provincial Archives of Alberta (hereafter PAA); *Farm and Ranch Review,* December 5, 1910.
5. Hoadley to Weir, June 8, 1932, 73.307/244, PAA.
6. Canada, "Appendix to the Report of the Minister of Agriculture, Experimental Farms, for the Year Ending March 31, 1916," *Sessional Papers,* 1917, p. 1474.
7. *Red Deer Advocate,* August 22, 1913.
8. Report, Innisfail Agricultural Society, 1906, M2360, File 1, GAI.
9. *Edmonton Bulletin,* October 28, 1882.
10. Edmonton Exhibition Association Ltd., *Report of the President and Manager, Financial Statements, 1914* (Edmonton, 1914), 6, (hereafter Edmonton Exhibition Association, *Report for 1914.*)
11. Secretary Treasurer to A. Diller, June 26, 1908, 9 (27) File Q, City of Red Deer Papers, Red Deer and District Archives.
12. List of Licences, Edmonton, 1921, MS 209, File 432, City of Edmonton Papers, City of Edmonton Archives.
13. *Camrose Canadian,* January 6, 1910. The rivalry between the Calgary and Edmonton Exhibitions was heightened by the fact that Calgary received a higher grant for its fair than did Edmonton.
14. *Farm and Ranch Review,* December 5, 1910.
15. Ibid.
16. Ibid., July 1909; James Gray, *A Brand of its Own: The 100 Year History of the Calgary Exhibition and Stampede* (Saskatoon: Western Producer Prairie Books, 1985),

23-24, 110. Richardson retired in 1940.
17. Statistics are scattered and often contradictory. These figures are compiled from fair dates published in Alberta newspapers and from records in 73.307/244 (1922-1928), PAA; 73.307/245 (1938-1942), PAA; and a letter from Chant to Aberhart, May 20, 1936, Premiers' Papers (hereafter PP), File 1050A, Provincial Archives of Alberta (hereafter PAA).
18. Jones, *Midways, Judges and Smooth Tongued Fakirs,* 126.
19. Dunning to Department of Agriculture, November 22, 1922, and June 6, 1923, M2360, File 282, GAI.
20. Gardner to Huxley, March 23, 1927, M2360, File 211, GAI.
21. *Farm and Ranch Review,* June 1908 and June 1909; *Red Deer Advocate,* July 18, 1919.
22. Hoadley to Wilson, December 21, 1931, 73.307/244, PAA; Letter 70, July 28, 1938, A. Balmer Watt Collection, Bruce Peel Special Collections Library, University of Alberta (hereafter cited as BPSC).
23. *Agricultural Alberta* 1(1), 1920; *Red Deer Advocate,* July 1, 1922.
24. Chant to Aberhart, May 20, 1936, PP, File 1050A, PAA; Carlyle to Craig, November 12, 1931, 73.307/244, PAA.
25. Hoadley to Buckle, December 10, 1930, 73.307/244, PAA.
26. Minutes, 27th Convention, Alberta Agricultural Fairs Association, Edmonton, December 28, 1935, M2360, File 355, GAI.
27. Chant to Aberhart, May 20, 1936, PP, File 1050A, PAA.
28. Sundal to Department of Agriculture, April 20, 1937, M2360, File 10, GAI, and Minutes, 27th Convention, Alberta Agricultural Fairs Association, M2360, File 10, GAI.
29. Tony Cashman, *Edmonton Exhibition: The First Hundred Years* (Edmonton: Edmonton Exhibition Association, 1979), 69, 84-85, 114-15; Gray, *A Brand of its Own,* 55-58.
30. Report, Innisfail Agricultural Society, 1906, M2360, File 1, GAI.
31. Gillespie to Hoadley, September 11, 1934, 73.307/247, PAA.
32. *Farm and Ranch Review,* October 20, 1910; Alberta Fairs, 1931-1939, 73.307/245, PAA. The population of Edmonton proper in 1911 was almost 25,000; Calgary almost 44,000. In 1931, Edmonton proper had a population of about 79,000 and Calgary about 84,000. In 1941, the population of Edmonton proper was about 94,000 and Calgary proper was about 89,000.
33. *Farm and Ranch Review,* June 20, 1918; Putnam to Longman, September 30, 1942,

413

73.307/245, PAA; Letter 118, July 21, 1941, A. Balmer Watt Collection, BPSC.

34. Letter 118, July 21, 1941, A. Balmer Watt Collection, BPSC; Edmonton Exhibition Association Ltd., *Annual Report, 1946*, 19.

35. *Farm and Ranch Review*, October 20, 1910.

36. David C. Jones, "From Babies to Buttonholes: Women's Work at Agricultural Fairs," *Alberta History* 29 (1981): 27-30.

37. *Farm and Ranch Review*, June 1909 and June 1908.

38. *Edmonton Bulletin*, October 11, 1894.

39. *Farm and Ranch Review*, June 1908.

40. Yule to Manning, April 16, 1948, PP, File 1878, PAA.

41. *Red Deer Advocate*, July 25, 1924.

42. Ibid.; *Farm and Ranch Review*, June 1908.

43. Ibid., July 1908.

44. *Calgary Herald*, March 31, 1909, and June 25, 1909.

45. *Edmonton Journal*, July 11, 1925.

46. Grout to Aberhart, July 14, 1938, PP, File 1275, PAA.

47. *Farm and Ranch Review*, June 1909.

48. Jones, *Midways, Judges and Smooth Tongued Fakirs*, 52.

49. Moyer Amusement Company, Circular Letter, 1927-28, M2360, File 22, GAI.

50. See, for example, *Edmonton Journal*, July 9, 1921.

51. Minutes, Meeting in Moose Jaw, March 7, 1930, M2360, File 13, GAI.

52. Jones, *Midways, Judges and Smooth Tongued Fakirs*, 56-57.

53. *Farm and Ranch Review*, September 5, 1910.

54. *Red Deer Advocate*, January 13, 1922.

55. See, for example, Department of Manpower, RCMP Report, Canmore, August 11, 1938, 73.347/484/33, PAA.

56. *Red Deer Advocate*, July 26, 1918.

57. *Farm and Ranch Review*, June 1909.

58. *Red Deer Advocate*, July 19, 1918; Cashman, *Edmonton Exhibition*, 98-102.

59. *Red Deer Advocate*, July 18, 1919.

60. *Edmonton Journal*, July 9, 1921.

61. *Farm and Ranch Review*, October 1908.

62. Edmonton Exhibition Association, *Report for 1915*, 6.

63. *Red Deer Advocate*, July 14, 1916.

64. Minutes, Meeting in Moose Jaw, March 7, 1930, M2360, File 13, GAI.

65. *Edmonton Journal*, August 27, 1921.

66. *Red Deer Advocate*, July 25, 1924.

67. See, for example, Ibid., August 22, 1913.

68. Espedal to Carlyle, November 19, 1929, M2360, File 14, GAI.

69. Edmonton Exhibition Association, *Report for 1914*, 5.

70. Edmonton Exhibition Association, *Report for 1915*, 6; *Red Deer Advocate*, July 14, 1916;

Family Herald and Weekly Star, July 31, 1946.

71. Kerkhoven, "A Cross Section of Life," 11-12.

72. Keith Regular, "On Public Display," *Alberta History* 34 (1986): 1-9; Gray, *A Brand of its Own*, 80-81.

73. *Red Deer Advocate*, July 25, 1924.

74. G. Potter, "History of Rycroft Board of Trade" (typescript), 91, 82.154/2/5, PAA.

75. "The Edmonton Exhibition," *Twenty Third Annual Meeting of the Canadian Association of Exhibitions, November 24 and 25, 1949* (pamphlet), (Toronto, 1949) (hereafter "Edmonton Exhibition, 1949").

76. Scott to Secretary, Crossfields Agricultural Society, May 20, 1924, M2360, File 80, GAI.

77. "Edmonton Exhibition, 1949."

78. *Red Deer Advocate*, July 12, 1918.

79. *Camrose Canadian*, September 15, 1910.

80. *Farm and Ranch Review*, June 1945.

81. *Edmonton Bulletin*, August 2, 1894.

82. Ibid., July 7, 1883.

83. Ibid., March 7, 1881.

84. On turf associations and racing in Calgary and southern Alberta, see William McLennan, *Sport in Early Calgary* (Calgary: Fort Brisebois Publishing, 1983}, 294-337.

85. Minutes, Claresholm Turf Association, 75.270, PAA.

86. *Camrose Canadian*, July 7, 1910; *The UFA*, September 1, 1928; *Farm and Ranch Review*, June 1908 and June 1909.

87. *Farm and Ranch Review*, February 1908.

88. *Red Deer Advocate*, July 13, 1917.

89. Edmonton Exhibition Association, *Report for 1914*, 4.

90. *Calgary Herald*, May 9, 1910.

91. *Red Deer Advocate*, June 26, 1908; MacEwan, *Agriculture on Parade*, 73; Cashman, *Edmonton Exhibition*, 91; Gray, *A Brand of its Own*, 33-34.

92. "Spring Meetings," 1929, 31ff, Prairie Thoroughbred Breeders and Racing Association, 67.32, PAA.

93. In 1905 the Calgary WCTU addressed the Calgary City Council on gambling and vice. Betting on horses was not mentioned; the only gambling dealt with was slot machines. Indeed, they placed more emphasis on prohibiting smoking than gambling (*Calgary Herald*, June 15, 1905). As another example, around 1910, a bill was introduced in the House of Commons to outlaw betting on horses, but it was withdrawn because of strong opposition. Nevertheless, this became a focus for cleaning up racing instead of abolishing it, and provided an indirect boost to the pari-mutuel system (*Calgary Herald*, May 9, 1910). One last example will suffice: in

1921 the UFA resolved that pari-mutuel betting was an evil, but the resolution had no effect on government policy (Jones, *Midways, Judges and Smooth Tongued Fakirs,* 62).

94. Alberta, Department of the Provincial Secretary, *Annual Report for Year Ending December 31, 1927,* 4; Christie to Brownlee, August 18, 1933, PP, File 368, PAA.

95. Craig to Chant, January 1, 1937, and Trowbridge to Longman, October 17, 1944, 73.307/248, PAA. From 1935 until 1951 the tax collected totalled almost $1 million. This amount was split evenly between the associations and the province (Speers to Manning, July 16, 1951, Statistical table, PP, File 1703, PAA).

96. Speers to Manning, July 16, 1951, PP, File 1703, PAA.

97. *Family Herald and Weekly Star,* July 31, 1946.

98. Richardson to Brownlee, March 7, 1932, PP, File 368, and Wilson to Manning, January 6, 1947, PP, File 1272, PAA.

99. Richardson to Brownlee, June 9, 1932, PP, File 368, PAA.

100. *The UFA,* May 1, 1926.

101. Speers to Manning, July 16, 1951, PP, File 1703, PAA.

102. C. Eamer and T. Jones, *The Canadian Rodeo Book* (Saskatoon: Western Producer Prairie Books, 1982), 6.

103. *Edmonton Bulletin,* February 2, 1884.

104. Eamer and Jones, *The Canadian Rodeo Book,* 10; *Red Deer Advocate,* July 4, 1913.

105. Eamer and Jones, *The Canadian Rodeo Book,* 7.

106. *Edmonton Bulletin,* August 2, 1894.

107. *Camrose Canadian,* July 7, 1910.

108. S. Jamieson, "The Millarville Races," Separate Typescripts File 3, Alberta Folk Archive, BPSC.

109. "Memories of a Cowboy's Wife," E. Grandeur Collection, 72.27, PAA.

110. *Red Deer Advocate,* March 19, 1920. A "rodeo" was held at Neutral Hills in 1919 and was advertised in Edmonton. It was a combined sports day, wild west show, rodeo, and carnival. Rodeo events were outnumbered by other events (*Edmonton Journal,* June 28, 1919).

111. *Farm and Ranch Review,* April 1947; Minute Book, DeBolt Stampede Committee, 1937-1949, 71.22/1, PAA.

112. Vincent Varga, "Gentlemen Ranchers—High Class Cowboys," *Journal of the West* 23 (1984): 54-55; "The Calgary Stampede," *Twenty Third Annual Meeting of the Canadian Association of Exhibitions, November 24 and 25, 1949* (pamphlet) (Toronto, 1949) (hereafter "Calgary Stampede, 1949").

113. Guy Weadick, "Origin of the Calgary Stampede," *Alberta Historical Review* 14 (1966): 21.

114. Clem Gardner, "My Impression as a Contestant in the Calgary Stampede of 1912" (not paginated), vol. 6, First Hand Narratives, Alberta Folk Archive, BPSC (hereafter Gardner, "Stampede of 1912").

115. Eamer and Jones, *The Canadian Rodeo Book,* 12.

116. Gardner, "Stampede of 1912"; Gray, *A Brand of its Own,* 37.

117. Gardner, "Stampede of 1912."

118. Richardson to Brownlee, October 26, 1927, PP, File 417, PAA.

119. Varga, "Gentlemen Ranchers," 55.

120. "Calgary Stampede, 1949."

121. Ibid.; Gray, *A Brand of its Own,* 147.

122. *Farm and Ranch Review,* June 25, 1927, and June 1945. Slim Moorehouse was from Vulcan and his feats at events like the Stampede were seen by Vulcan boosters as good advertising for the town (Paul Voisey, *Vulcan: The Making of a Prairie Community* (Toronto: University of Toronto Press, 1988), 61).

123. *Farm and Ranch Review,* June 1945.

124. Gray, *A Brand of its Own,* 76-80, 92-93.

125. Richardson to Brownlee, October 26, 1927, PP, File 417, PAA.

126. *Edmonton Bulletin,* October 13, 1883.

127. Jones, *Midways, Judges and Smooth Tongued Fakirs,* 124-26; MacEwan, *Agriculture on Parade,* 195-200.

11. Hanging Around: Bars, Poolrooms, and Cafes

1. Stan Horrall, "'A Policeman's Lot is Not a Happy One': The Mounted Police and Prohibition in the North-West Territories, 1874-1891," *Historic and Scientific Society of Manitoba Transactions,* Series 2, 30 (1973-74): 7-16.

2. James Gray, *Booze* (Scarborough: New American Library, 1974), 19-34.

3. *Fort Macleod Gazette,* August 25, 1892. See also Paul Voisey, *Vulcan: The Making of a Prairie Community* (Toronto: University of Toronto Press, 1988), 163.

4. Gerald Hallowell, *Prohibition in Ontario* (Ottawa: Love Printing Services Ltd. for the Ontario Historical Society, 1972), 6-7, 13-23, 159-62.

5. Robert Craig Brown and Ramsay Cook, *Canada, 1896-1921: A Nation Transformed* (Toronto: McClelland & Stewart Ltd., 1976), 24.

6. Nancy Sheehan, "Temperance, the WCTU and Education in Alberta 1905-1930" (Ph.D. diss., University of Alberta, 1980), 141.

7. John H. Thompson, *The Harvests of War* (Toronto: McClelland and Stewart Ltd., 1978), 97-103. The best summary of the national debate during the interwar years is John Thompson with Allen Seager, *Canada 1922-1939: Decades of Discord* (Toronto: McClelland and Stewart Ltd., 1985), 63-69.

8. Hugh Dempsey, ed., *The Best of Bob Edwards* (Edmonton: Hurtig Publishers Ltd., 1975), 247.

9. Kerkham to Deputy Attorney General, April 4, 1924, Department of Attorney General Records, 75.126/2839B, Provincial Archives of Alberta (hereafter PAA); Gray, *Booze*, 81-82.

10. Thompson, *Harvests of War*, 104-5; Hallowell, *Prohibition in Ontario*, 7.

11. Minutes, Meeting with Brewers, 1923, and Smith to Greenfield, August 15, 1921, Premiers' Papers (hereafter PP), Files 97C and 97A respectively, Provincial Archives of Alberta (hereafter PAA); *The UFA*, February 1, 1930.

12. Barton to Greenfield, June 7, 1922, PP, File 97A, PAA.

13. Keay to Boyle, March 4, 1919, 75.126/69, PAA.

14. Dempsey, *Bob Edwards*, 21-22. For Bob Edwards as a social reformer, see Max Foran, "Bob Edwards and Social Reform," *Alberta History* 21 (1973): 13-17.

15. Gray, *Booze*, 75-76.

16. Richard Allen, *The Social Passion: Religion and Social Reform in Canada, 1914-1928* (Toronto: University of Toronto Press, 1973), 276-77.

17. *Farm and Ranch Review*, September 1, 1930. The UFA convention in 1930 resolved that there should be a provincial referendum on closing the beer parlours (*The UFA*, February 1, 1930).

18. Traunweiser to Brownlee, October 1, 1932, PP, File 99B, PAA.

19. Dinning to Brownlee, January 19, 1934, PP, File 99B, PAA.

20. Dempsey, *Bob Edwards*, 116-17; Gray, *Booze*, 70, 86.

21. S. Babaian, comp., *The Coal Mining Industry in the Crow's Nest Pass* (Edmonton: Historic Sites Service, Alberta Culture, 1985), 80-81; A.A. den Otter, "Social Life in a Coal Mining Community: The Coal Branch," *Alberta Historical Review* 17 (1969): 7.

22. Cross to Manning, February 26, 1946, PP, File 1433, PAA.

23. "The Searchlight," September 1930, PP, File 99A, PAA; Minutes, Meeting with Brewers, 1923, PP, File 97C, PAA.

24. Report on Fort Saskatchewan Jail, in Alberta, Department of Public Works, *Annual Report, 1927-28—1929-30*; Survey of Imprisonment for Intoxication, Fort Saskatchewan Jail, 1954, 70.427/982, PAA. For partial list of arrests for drunkenness and liquor related offences, see Gray, *Booze*, 210-11.

25. Gray, *Booze*, 197-98.

26. Alberta Liquor Control Board (hereafter ALCB) to Vallie, November 29, 1929, PP, File 99A, PAA.

27. Forster to Dinning, September 30, 1924, PP, File 97D, PAA.

28. Dinning to Brownlee, January 19, 1934, PP, File 99B, PAA.

29. Minutes, Meeting with Brewers, 1923, PP, File 97C, PAA.

30. Morton to Brownlee, March 3, 1934 and Alberta Hotel Association to Aberhart, October 25, 1935, PP, File 99B, PAA.

31. Jean Burnet, *Next Year Country* (Toronto: University of Toronto Press, 1951), 70-71.

32. Associated Temperance Forces of Alberta to Manning, February 13, 1947, PP, File 1429, PAA.

33. Coomes to Aberhart, April 8, 1943, PP, File 963, PAA.

34. Alberta Hotel Association to Brownlee, January 3, 1934, PP, File 99D, PAA. Before 1916, bars were open until 10:30 P.M. on weekdays and until 7:00 P.M. Saturdays. In 1934 they were open 7:00 A.M. to 10:00 P.M. weekdays and 7:00 A.M. to 9:00 P.M. Saturdays. By 1946 they were open Monday to Saturday 10:00 A.M. to 10:00 P.M. except between 12:30 Noon and 1:30 P.M. and 5:30 P.M. to 7:30 P.M. (*Calgary Herald*, August 25, 1910; ALCB to Brownlee, January 19, 1934, PP, File 99B, and Popil to Gerhart, August 26, 1946, PP, File 1429, PAA).

35. Watt to Colebaugh, February 6, March 1, and March 15, 1943, Bruce Peel Special Collections Library, University of Alberta.

36. Resolutions, Stettler Presbyterian Meeting, October 22, 1946, PP, File 1431, and Synopsis, Cabinet Meeting re: ALCB, April 25, 1946, PP, File 1429, PAA.

37. James Gray, *Red Lights on the Prairies* (Scarborough: New American Library, 1973), 29-38, 144, 217.

38. Statement re: Pool Room and Bowling Alley Licenses, August 31, 1914, 70.414/86, PAA; *Census of Canada, 1931*, Table 9, 412-14.

416

39. William McLennan, *Sport in Early Calgary* (Calgary: Fort Brisebois Publishing, 1983), 367.
40. *Calgary Herald,* June 15, 1905. This social evil was not confined to gambling; the exploitation of workers was equally an antisocial act for "whether the shuffle is a bunch of cards or a mass of suffering humanity, the distinction is not a difference" (*Calgary Herald,* April 26, 1906).
41. Deputy Attorney General to Miller, May 2, 1918, 75.126/67a, PAA.
42. Browning to Garrison, May 7, 1918, 75.126/67a, PAA.
43. *Red Deer Advocate,* June 28, 1918.
44. Coone to Browning, October 17, 1918, 75.126/68, PAA.
45. Browning to Marks, February 3, 1922, File 732, and Miller to Browning, May 1, 1918, 75.126, File 67a, PAA.
46. Report of Pool Room Inspector, 1918, 75.126/68, PAA.
47. Browning to Lockhart, July 5, 1918, 75.126/68, PAA.
48. Brownlee to Smith, October 23, 1923, 75.126/75b, PAA.
49. *The Pool Room Act,* Statutes of Alberta (hereafter S.A.) 1915 (Consolidation).
50. *Calgary Herald,* February 3, 1911.
51. Browning to Leffingwell, May 14, 1918, 75.126/68, PAA.
52. Deputy Attorney General to Downey, October 24, 1918, 75.126/68, PAA.
53. Report, "E" Division, Alberta Provincial Police (hereafter APP), July 3, 1926, and Smith to Brunswick-Balke-Collendar Company, July 19, 1926, 75.126/76, PAA.
54. Gardner to Downey, October 2, 1922, and Downey to Gardner, October 3, 1922, 75.126/74, PAA.
55. APP Report, November 19, 1923, 75.126/74, PAA.
56. Piper to APP, March 20, 1918, 75.126/67b, PAA.
57. Pool Rooms, 1918-1919, 75.126/69, PAA.
58. Orest Martynowych, *The Ukrainian Bloc Settlement in East Central Alberta 1890-1930: A History,* Historic Sites Service Occasional Paper, no. 10 (Edmonton: Alberta Culture, 1985), 284.
59. Report of Pool Room Inspector, 1918, File 68, List of Billiard Rooms, 1925, File 75a, and List of Licenses, 1927, File 76, 75.126, PAA. In Edmonton, two poolrooms were owned by companies.
60. Report of Pool Room Inspector, 1918, 75.126/67b, PAA.
61. Ibid.
62. Report of Pool Room Inspector, 1918, 75.126/68, PAA.
63. McLean to Smith, April 9, 1925, 75.126/75b, PAA.
64. Report of Pool Room Inspector, 1918, 75.126/67a, PAA.
65. Browning to Marks, February 3, 1922, 75.126/732, PAA.
66. Clippings, 1907-9, 85-42-3, University of Alberta Archives.
67. *Calgary Herald,* January 5, 1917.
68. Ibid., October 16, 1926, and September 1, 1928.
69. APP Report, March 14, 1930, 75.126/2850, PAA.
70. *The Restaurant Act,* Statutes of Alberta, 1922, c. 228.
71. Terry Chapman, "Drug Use in Western Canada," *Alberta History* 24 (1976): 26; Emily Murphy, *The Black Candle* (1922; reprint, Toronto: Coles Publishing Co., 1973).
72. Minutes, Meeting with Brewers, 1923, PP, File 97C, PAA.
73. Correspondence re Restaurants in Cardston, 1930, 75.126/2850, PAA.
74. Deputy Attorney General to Bishop, September 22, 1922, 75.126/2838b, PAA.
75. Restaurant Licence Inspection, APP, "C" Division, October 4, 1926, and "D" Division, September 18, 1926, File 2842, and Lethbridge APP Report, Restaurants, 1931, File 2853, 75.126, PAA.
76. Assistant Deputy Attorney General to Pelton, September 18, 1925, 75.126/2840a, PAA.
77. Memorandum to Board of Industrial Relations, January 29, 1940, PP, File 928A, PAA.
78. ALCB to Brownlee, July 6, 1929, PP, File 98B, PAA.
79. Dinning to Brownlee, February 25, 1925, 75.126/2840b, PAA.
80. Memorandum to Board of Industrial Relations, January 29, 1940, PP, File 928A, PAA.
81. Memorandum to Board of Industrial Relations, January 29, 1940, PP, File 928A, PAA.
82. *Census of Canada, 1941,* vol. 10, Table 2, 12, and Table 9, 416.
83. *Census of Canada, 1941,* vol. 10, Table 8, 252-54, and Table 13, 418.
84. Boyton to Deputy Attorney General, June 8, 1922, and Deputy Attorney General to Boyton, June 10, 1922, 75.126/2838b, PAA. See also *Calgary Herald,* July 15, 1922.
85. Boyton to Deputy Attorney General, June 8, 1922, and Deputy Attorney General to Boyton, June 10, 1922, 75.126/2838b, PAA.
86. Kellas to Brownlee, June 24, 1922, 75.126/2838b, PAA.

87. Ferguson to Assistant Deputy Attorney General, September 7, 1927, 75.126/2843a, PAA.

88. Judy Bedford, "Prostitution in Calgary 1905-1914," *Alberta History* 29 (1981): 7; Gray, *Red Lights on the Prairies,* 132.

89. APP Report, March 14, 1930, 75.126/2850, PAA. No public restaurants in Alberta were licensed to sell liquor before 1945.

90. See, for example, the descriptions of the café in Minburn in ALCB to Brownlee, February 25, 1925, 75.126/2840b, PAA.

91. See APP Trochu Detachment, Report, 1926, and Magrath Detachment, Report, 1926, 75.126/2842, PAA.

92. *Edmonton Journal,* April 18, 1931.

93. Shute to Browning, February 6, 1922, 75.126/732, PAA.

94. McLennan to Greenfield, March 27, 1923, and Carol to Greenfield, March 27, 1923, PP, File 90, PAA.

95. Bishop to Brownlee, January 10, 1924, 75.126/2476b, PAA, and *Slot Machines Tax Act,* 1924. The machines included in these statistics were slot machines only and did not include vending machines. The 1923 statistics on slot machines show a much higher number of machines operating in the province because in that year they also included vending machines.

96. Attorney General to Hanna, February 11, 1924, 75.126/2476b, PAA.

97. Bishop to Brownlee, January 10, 1924, 75.126/2476b, PAA.

98. Report, "A" Division, APP, June 21, 1924, 75.126/2476b, PAA.

99. Report, "D" Division, APP, June 24, 1924, 75.126/2476b, PAA.

100. Assistant Deputy Attorney General to Bryan, September 13, 1923, File 2475, and Bishop to Brownlee, January 10, 1924, File 2476b, 75.126, PAA.

101. In the 1930s, Alberta, unlike Saskatchewan, refused to permit the operation of pin-ball machines because it defined them as slot machines (Attorney General to Pen, October 5, 1937, PP, File 681A, PAA).

Conclusion

1. In 1935, 53.9 percent of the total value of production in the province was agricultural while almost 11 percent was in mining. In 1975, 11.4 percent of total value of production was in agriculture and almost 52 percent in mining (Alberta, Bureau of Statistics, *Alberta Statistical Review, 1980,* Table 26, 15).

2. John Porter, *The Vertical Mosaic* (Toronto: University of Toronto Press, 1965), 83-90.

3. Hooke to Manning, September 25, 1945, Premiers' Papers, File 819, Provincial Archives of Alberta.

4. Bernard Ostry, *The Cultural Connection* (Toronto: McClelland and Stewart Ltd., 1978), 77.

5. Theodora Reeves, "To Canada With Love, Part Three," *Alberta History* 34 (1980): 10. Italics in original.

6. Philippe Ariès has argued that the idea of childhood as a distinctive phase of life arose in the seventeenth century. The idea was firmly in place in Europe by the eighteenth century, and expanded unevenly in the nineteenth century (Philippe Ariès, *Centuries of Childhood: A Social History of Family Life,* trans. Robert Baldick (New York: Vintage Books, 1962), 128-33). On twentieth century English Canada, see Neil Sutherland, *Children in English Canadian Society: Framing the Twentieth Century Consensus* (Toronto: University of Toronto Press, 1976). The history of childhood can often be approached through the history of education. See, for example, Alison Prentice, *The School Promoters* (Toronto: McClelland and Stewart Ltd., 1977).

7. David C. Jones, "'There is Some Power About the Land'—The Western Agrarian Press and Country Life Ideology," *Journal of Canadian Studies* 17 (1982): 96-108.

8. Hugh Cunningham, *Leisure in the Industrial Revolution c. 1780-c. 1880* (London: Croom Helm, 1980), 45-46, 58-63.

9. *The UFA,* June 1, 1933.

10. Eliane Silverman, *The Last Best West: Women on the Alberta Frontier, 1880-1930* (Montreal: Eden Press, 1984), 141-51.

11. Carol Lee Bacchi, *Liberation Deferred? The Ideas of the English Canadian Suffragists 1877-1918* (Toronto: University of Toronto Press, 1983), 146-49.

12. Robert Stamp, "Empire Day in the Schools of Ontario: The Training of Young Imperialists," *Journal of Canadian Studies* 8 (1973): 41.

13. John Herd Thompson with Allen Seager, *Canada 1922-1939: Decades of Discord* (Toronto: McClelland and Stewart Ltd., 1985), 191.

Index

Boy Scouts, 81-84, 119, 208, 377
Boyle, J. R., 273
Bow Island, 244
Boxing, 136, 137, 302
Bragg Creek, 210
Bréton, Father, 306, 392 n14
Brewster Transport Company, 16, 195
British Columbia, province of, 101, 197, 264, 290, 348
British influence on Alberta leisure, 5, 7, 55, 58, 60, 74, 110, 125, 131, 142, 152, 155-56, 160-61, 168, 189, 218, 222, 226, 272-73, 311; settlers, xviii-xix, 3-4, 5, 13, 33, 115, 240, 385 n5
Britishness, 5, 9-10, 12, 28, 30, 48-49, 125, 131, 136, 138, 142, 184, 262, 267, 272, 334, 375, 383-84
Broadcasting. *See* Radio
Brothels, 353-54, 355
Brown, Annora, 60, 212
Brownlee, J.E., 130, 204, 222
Buffalo Lake, 182, 202
Bugnet, George, 60
Burt, A. L., 12
Buses. *See* Transportation
Business, 10-11, 18, 30, 32-33, 38-39, 104, 108, 116, 182, 192, 198, 222, 312-13, 364

C

Cabarets, 360-61
Cadomin, 24
Cafés, 24, 38, 345, 348, 360-67, 370
Calgary, xvii, 10, 14-16, 21, 29-30, 35-37, 38, 52, 76, 132, 198, 218, 237-38, 244, 356, 413 n32; clubs/organizations, 26, 29-30, 47, 60, 62, 77, 85-87, 103-10, 113, 130, 132, 133, 142, 143, 145, 146, 147, 152, 153, 154, 176, 182, 192, 196, 225, 226, 230, 238-41, 243, 266-67, 273, 314, 320, 330, 352, 368; facilities, 50, 61, 77, 85, 100-102, 103, 110, 130, 131, 134-35, 142-44, 154, 193, 217, 219, 230, 252-53, 256, 315, 316, 352, 360, 369
Calgary Council on Child and Family Welfare, 6, 85, 221, 273, 274, 275
Calgary Local Council of Women, 221, 275
Calgary Stampede, 158, 314, 318, 332, 334-40
Camping, 80, 83, 86, 193, 198-201, 205, 208-10, 315, 380, 401 n62
Camrose, 60, 149, 166, 181, 204, 218, 226, 243, 298, 329
Canada Day, 25-28, 146, 376
Canadian Broadcasting Corporation. *See* Radio
Canadian Club, 26
Canadian Council on Child Welfare, 273
Canadian Girls in Training, 73, 80-81, 84-85, 88, 209-10
Canadian Legion. *See* Veterans' Clubs
Canadian National Parks Association, 212
Canadian Pacific Railway, xvii, 14-16, 194, 196-97, 217, 239, 240, 270, 272, 293, 401 n56
Canadian Radio Broadcasting Corporation. *See* Radio
Canmore, 225,226
Card games, 58, 79, 96
Cardston, 146, 147, 181, 361, 362
Carnegie Foundation, 50, 63, 227, 231
Carson, H., 290

Hunting, 165-180, 184-85, 196, 376, 380, 381, 399 n23

I

Icelandic settlers, 4, 34, 48, 53, 77
Immigrants, assimilation of, xvii, xxi-xxiii, 4-5, 9-10, 27-28, 34, 40, 68, 76-78, 84, 96-97, 100, 114-17, 125, 131, 236, 305-6, 347, 376, 381-82, 389 n20
Imperial Order Daughters of the Empire, 50, 102, 243, 266, 293
Independent Order of Foresters, 104
Innisfail, 266, 316
Irish settlers, 33
Italian settlers, 116, 117

J

Japanese settlers, 4, 9, 362
Jasper, 150, 196, 197-98, 401 n56
Jewish settlers, 79, 225, 358

K

Kasota Beach. *See* Lake Wabamum
Kinsmen Club, 104
Kiwanis Club, 84, 103, 240
Knights of Columbus, 77
Knights of Pythias, 50, 105, 107

L

La Due, Flores, 222, 334
Labour Day, 25, 29-30
Labour organizations, 22, 29-30, 84, 206, 288, 368, 382
Lac La Biche, 350
Lacombe, 201, 322, 326
Lacrosse, 141
Lake Louise, 198
Lake Wabamum, 15, 201, 207, 209
Leisure: and class, xix-xxi, 9, 29-30, 104-5, 126, 142-43, 158, 160-61, 180, 225, 244, 352, 357-58, 359, 368-69, 370; cost and affordability, 15-16, 20, 21-22, 34-38, 51, 54, 55-56, 65, 66, 93-94, 96, 101, 105, 134, 143-44, 154, 165, 166, 171-72, 183, 191, 196, 198-200, 206-7, 208, 210, 217, 218, 221, 240, 244, 245, 254, 284-85, 315, 324, 328, 378-79, 389 n129; dangers of, 8-9, 43-45, 73, 234, 262-64, 273, 323, 345, 347, 354-55, 361, 370-71; defined, xvi, xxiv, 3, 7-9, 22, 39-40, 375, 385 n1; and gender, 25, 44, 58, 62, 88, 100-101, 104-5, 120, 125-26, 129, 137, 148, 153, 154, 158-59, 178-79, 180, 184, 189, 209, 349, 350, 354, 358, 359, 360, 380-81; need for, 7-9, 11-13, 22-23, 29, 32-33, 39-40, 43-44, 45, 74-75, 86-87, 99-101, 126-28, 130-31, 189-90, 211, 225-26, 233, 281, 293, 373-74, 375; and relationship to work, xvi, 3, 7-9, 21-22, 24-25, 29, 32-33, 39-40, 131, 149, 189-90, 211-12, 347, 373, 378-79; seasonality of, 18-20, 28-29, 57, 60, 89, 129, 140-41, 149-50, 154, 180, 184, 189-90, 196-97, 201,233-34, 299, 355, 397 n122; and technological change, xxiii, 13-14, 39, 55-56, 62, 68-69, 118-19, 131, 139-40, 153-54, 171-72, 178, 180, 191-92, 198-200, 212, 226, 231-32, 246, 249-51, 277-78, 281, 307-8, 314-15, 325, 341, 379-84; time available for, xvi, 3, 21-25, 131, 149, 198, 378-79, 380-81

211-12, 380, 400 n2
New Norway, 329, 333
New Year's Day, 25, 157
Newspapers and Magazines, 11, 20, 21, 33, 51-53, 139-40, 160, 260, 288, 293, 296, 297, 381, 390 n35, 412 n136
Norwegian settlers, 4, 65-66, 79
Nose Creek, 93

O

Oddfellows Club, 104, 105, 106, 108, 394 n132
Okotoks, 274
Ontario, influence on Alberta leisure, xviii, 3, 13, 23-24, 39-40, 48-49, 53, 60, 142, 145-46, 160-61, 263, 346-47, 374, 375
Opera. *See* Music
Orange Order. *See* Loyal Orange Lodge
Orchestras, 6, 113, 203, 208, 223, 236-37, 240-41, 242-43, 299-300, 307, 318, 326-27
Orpheum theatres, 217, 220
Ottewell, A.E., 13, 89, 92, 295
Oyen, 352

P

Painting, 60-61
Palmer, J., 288
Pantages theatres, 217, 219-20
Page, Percy, 150
Parades, 26, 29, 30, 106, 318, 320, 338
Pari-Mutuel Betting, 331-32, 414 n93
Park Lake, 204
Parks: Federal, 15, 16, 101, 142, 149-50, 177, 193-98, 201, 207, 340, 352-53, 401 n56; Provincial, 203-4, 211-12, 374, 380 *(see also by location)*; Urban, 94, 101-3, 120, 134-35 *(see also* playgrounds)
Peace River, 193, 314
Peace River District, 88-89, 96, 108, 204, 219, 332
Pearson, Robert, 265, 266
Pelton, G., 44, 263
Phonographs, 54, 55-56, 200, 234, 282, 289, 299, 319, 361
Physical Exercise, 9, 40, 74-75, 118, 126-28, 129-30, 190, 234
Pigeon Lake, 201
Pincher Creek, 349
Playgrounds, 92, 94, 98-103, 118, 120, 394 n111
Polish settlers, 48, 66, 77, 116, 119, 225, 382, 385 n5
Polo, 141, 329, 376
Ponoka, 240, 365
Poolrooms, 10, 38, 345, 348, 354-60, 367, 370-71, 376, 381
Postal system, 10, 21
Prohibition. *See* Bars; Liquor
Prostitution, 353-54, 355, 366
Provost, 350

R

Races: Foot, 25, 78, 96, 141, 326, 329; Horse, 25, 78, 96, 131-32, 316, 318, 329-32,

414 n93

Radio, xxiii, 11, 28, 65, 139-40, 160, 224, 231-32, 242, 281-308, 378, 379, 382, 383, 409 n6, 410 n23, 410 n50, 411 n99, 412 n135;Canadian Broadcasting Corporation, 231-32, 294-95, 296-97, 299, 300, 301, 302, 303, 305, 306-7; Canadian Radio Broadcasting Corporation, 293-94, 300, 306-7; networks, 289-90, 291-95, 306-7, 411 n65; personalities and programmes, 140, 282, 292, 295-302, 306-7; regulation, xxiii, 281-82, 288, 289, 290-91, 294, 298, 409 n5, 410 n33, 411 n92

Radio stations: CBK (Watrous), 295; CBX (Lacombe), 295; CFAC (Calgary), 242, 288, 292, 294, 296, 297, 302, 410 n32; CFCN (Calgary), 242, 288, 289, 290, 296, 297, 300; CFGP (Grande Prairie), 290; CFRN (Edmonton), 288, 294, 301; CJCA (Edmonton), 232, 282, 288, 289, 292, 294, 295, 296, 297, 298, 299, 301, 302, 305, 412 n136; CJCJ (Calgary), 232, 282, 288, 294, 296; CJOC (Lethbridge), 288, 294, 300; CKLC (Red Deer), 288, 292; CKUA (Edmonton), 89, 90, 231-32, 288, 289, 290, 296, 297, 298-99, 300, 302, 303, 304; CKXL (Calgary), 288

Railways. *See* Canadian Pacific Railway; Transportation

Raymond, 150, 312, 332, 362

Reading, 45-53, 77-78, 389 n7, 389 n20, 390 n35

Rebekahs Club, 104

Red Deer, 15, 50, 83, 102, 107, 135, 158, 192, 193, 202, 204, 207, 216, 226, 239-40, 243, 254, 257, 259, 287, 288, 292, 312, 316, 317, 319, 322, 323, 326, 328, 331, 355, 364

Redcliff, 16

Religion. *See* Churches

Remembrance Day, 33

Resorts, 15, 26, 30, 101, 149, 182, 189, 191-92, 194, 197, 201-4, 206, 207, 208, 212, 327, 360. *See also by name of resort*

Restaurants. *See* Cafés

Rice, G. R. A., 282, 288, 292, 303

Richardson, E. L., 314, 413 n16

Ringwood, Gwen P., 219, 231

Roads. *See* Transportation

Robertson, John, 217

Rochon Sands. *See* Buffalo Lake

Rocky Mountain House, 192

Rodeos, 23, 96, 311, 312, 314, 318, 332-41, 415 n110

Roselea, 349

Rotary Club, 102-3, 104, 216, 225

Rural life and leisure, xix, 10-14, 20, 21, 24, 30, 36-38, 44, 50, 52, 53, 55, 58, 66, 81, 84, 89, 91-97, 99, 108, 110, 111-13, 120, 129-30, 134, 145, 147, 149, 154, 155, 160, 165, 177, 185, 191, 202, 208, 215, 218-19, 223-24, 227, 233, 236, 245, 249, 253-54, 257-58, 269, 281, 282, 297-98, 299, 304, 311, 313-16, 318, 321, 323, 334, 341, 350, 352, 353, 355, 359-60, 368-69, 373, 377-79, 382, 407 n50

Rycroft, 95, 236, 258

Ryley, 224

S

Sabbatarianism, 22-25, 142, 149, 167, 208, 361, 379

Saint Albert, 353

Saskatchewan, province of, 17, 132, 140, 193, 219, 224, 238, 264,290, 295, 321, 331, 341, 418 n101

School of Fine Arts at Banff, 89-90, 227, 244

Schools, xxi-xxii, 9, 34, 91-94, 120, 127, 128, 131, 135, 147, 150, 228, 234, 244, 255

Scottish settlers. *See* British settlers

Seba Beach. *See* Lake Wabamum